AMERICAN VISTAS

1877 to the Present

American Vistas

1877 to the Present

Third Edition

Edited by
LEONARD DINNERSTEIN
UNIVERSITY OF ARIZONA

and

KENNETH T. JACKSON
COLUMBIA UNIVERSITY

New York
OXFORD UNIVERSITY PRESS
1979

Library of Congress Cataloging in Publication Data

Dinnerstein, Leonard, comp.
  American vistas.

  Includes bibliographical references.
  CONTENTS: [1] 1607-1877.—[2] 1877 to the present.
  1. United States—History—Addresses, essays, lectures.
I. Jackson, Kenneth T., joint author. II. Title.
E178.6.D53   1979   973   78-17423
ISBN 0-19-502468-0 (Vol. I)
ISBN 0-19-502469-9 (Vol. II)

Printed in the United States of America

For
Irene and Ben Rosenberg
and
Kenneth Gordon Jackson

PREFACE TO THE THIRD EDITION

Once again we are gratified that reader enthusiasm for *American Vistas* dictated the publication of a new edition. As in the earlier volumes, we have endeavored to put together a group of significant historical essays that combine modern interpretations with eminently readable prose. We have also been guided by the principle of including articles that expand upon, or take off from, rather than merely repeating, points covered in most textbooks.

As in the past, the nature of our times has to some extent influenced our selection. Because instructors seem to be giving more attention to social history in their courses, we have enhanced our coverage of minorities, women, families, immigration, and population movements. At the same time we recognize that political and diplomatic topics are still an integral part of the introductory survey and have not slighted those areas.

When we prepared our second edition, students seemed particularly concerned with contemporary affairs. Our section in volume two of the second edition, therefore, reflected that attitude. Subsequent surveys, however, suggested that most history courses deal more with the past than the present and several individuals indicated that it would be more helpful for both instructors and students if we toned down the "relevance." As a result we have expanded earlier sections in the text to coincide with the teaching realities.

For the third edition we have been particularly fortunate in having a large number of serious critics who provided us with candid analyses of our previous selections. Their comments were so valuable that some essays which *we* had intended to drop were kept while others which *we* had liked were eliminated. Among those who provided cogent criticisms were Louis L. Athey, B. A. Barbato, S. Becker, William N. Bisehoff, Ronald G. Brown,

Charles Bryan, James Burran, Hoyt Canady, Loren B. Chan, Thomas V. DiBacco, Alan Edwards, W. J. Fraser, Jr., J. B. Freund, Lloyd J. Graybar, Gary J. Hunter, Helen F. James, Daniel P. Jordan, Albert S. Karr, Donald S. Lamka, Robert E. Levinson, Melvin E. Levison, Monroe H. Little, Donald MacKendrick, William E. Mahan, Jonathan Morse, Ronald A. Mulder, John Muldowny, J. W. Needle, Carol O'Connor, Robert Rodey, Robert D. Schulzinger, Jordan Schwarz, Donna J. Spindel, Roger Tate, William H. Woodward, Jr., and Eugene R. Wutke.

The secretaries in the University of Arizona History Department have greatly facilitated our work. Marilyn Bradian produced the manuscript with efficiency and dispatch; Dawn Polter and Dorothy Donnelly graciously provided a wide variety of other services. Joseph Coghlan of Oxford University Press made some astute observations concerning our selection of articles. As in the past, both editors would be grateful for individual comments and suggestions from readers. We also hope that articles included in this edition are as useful for classes as those that were selected for our earlier volumes.

L. D.

K. T. J.

August 1978

CONTENTS

I INDUSTRIAL DEMOCRACY, 1877–1920

II MATURE NATION, 1920–1979

I. INDUSTRIAL DEMOCRACY
1877–1920

I

The Enduring Custer Legend

ROBERT M. UTLEY

• Long before Frederick Jackson Turner gave his famous 1893 address on "The Significance of the Frontier in American History," the idea of the West was important to Americans. In a vast, almost unexplored and unknown land, the men who first faced the wilderness and the savages were obvious candidates for national hero-worship. Oral legends circulated about a Tennessee backwoodsman named Davy Crockett even before he was dead; when he fell at the Alamo in 1836, his place in folklore was assured. Kit Carson, Wild Bill Hickok, and Buffalo Bill were among other superhuman heroes who shaped a national ideology of self-reliance, energy, and optimism.

Of course the image of the West did not conform to reality; the average frontiersman did not kill wild animals with his bare hands, and the streets of Dodge City did not regularly run with the blood of high noon shootouts. Contrary to the popular Hollywood stereotype, the Plains Indians were not incompetent strategists who rode around in circles until white marksmen could shoot them off their mounts. And at no time in the nineteenth century did the West account for as much as ten percent of the national population.

Yet the images and the legends live on. One of the most famous incidents in American history is the Battle of the Little Bighorn, where Colonel George Armstrong Custer and his entire force of 264 men were annihilated by 2,500 Sioux warriors led by Chiefs Rain-in-the-Face, Crazy Horse, and Sitting Bull. Custer was not a great field commander, and his "Last Stand" was of little historical importance. It did not tip the balance of power, and it did not represent a military turning point. Although the victory greatly heartened the Indians, it did not win them their cause. But the story of the Montana confrontation caught the country's imagination as soon as it hit the newspapers in 1876; to this day the facts continue to *be debated and researched by scholars and popular writers. With a century of study having been done on a relatively unimportant battle that lasted but a single day, one might think that some sort of consensus has been reached. But as the following article by Robert M. Utley demonstrates, many questions remain unresolved.*

In 1876 the United States celebrated its Centennial. The birthday party was held in Philadelphia, where a century earlier delegates from the colonies had cut the imperial ties with Great Britain. Here, in an exposition replete with elaborate displays of industrial might and cultural progress, Americans proudly congratulated themselves on a century of achievement. On the night of July 4, almost two months after President Ulysses S. Grant had formally opened the Centennial Exposition, fireworks burst over flag-draped Independence Hall, illuminating throngs of celebrants noisily rejoicing in the nation's 100th birthday.

Two days later, amid continuing festivities, exposition visitors read in the morning newspapers an electrifying dispatch from the Western frontier: "Advices have been received from both Bozeman and Stillwater, in Montana, of a battle on the 25th ult. [June] between General Custer's force and about 5,000 Indians, near the Little Big Horn River, in which Custer and fifteen officers and all the men of five companies of soldiers, about 300 in number, were killed."

To a public that remembered George Armstrong Custer as the "boy general" of the Civil War and now saw him as the very embodiment of the Indian-fighting army, such a calamity seemed preposterous. On July 7 reporters at the exposition sought out General Philip H. Sheridan, who ridiculed the report. Then they interviewed General William T. Sherman, who branded it as lacking official confirmation. As he spoke, however, an aide handed him a telegram: "Dispatches from

From *American History Illustrated,* June 1976. Reproduced through the courtesy of The National Historical Society publishers of *American History Illustrated,* P.O. Box 1831, Harrisburg PA 17105. Published 10 times a year.

General Terry . . . confirm the newspaper reports of a fight on the
25th of June, on the Little Horn, and of Gen. Custer's death."

It was true enough. Custer and his regiment, the 7th Cavalry, about
600 strong, had come upon an Indian village that may have numbered
10,000 Sioux and Cheyennes, with perhaps 3,000 fighting men. He
had divided his command and attacked. Major Marcus A. Reno and
three companies had been repulsed and had joined with Captain
Frederick W. Benteen and three more, together with the supply train
and still another company, in hilltop positions. From here, for two
days, they had held out against besieging warriors. When help finally
arrived, causing the Indians to withdraw, scouts had found the bodies
of Custer and the men of five companies, some 225 troopers, scattered
along a ridge four miles down the river from Reno's hill. No man of
that contingent had survived.

And so in the Centennial summer a national tragedy saddened the
celebration of a century of stirring history. It was a tragedy full of
drama, horror, mystery, controversy, and compelling human interest,
one destined to obsess students and public alike for generations to
come. Now, in the summer of 1976, the celebration of the Bicenten-
nial of the birth of the republic is a reminder too of the centennial of
the Battle of the Little Bighorn. It is an anniversary to be noted,
though possibly not celebrated, and an occasion for pondering how
this bloody encounter between Indian and soldier on the remote
frontier could have attained so prominent and enduring a place in the
history and folklore of America.

For endured it has. In the century since that hot June, Sunday
printing presses have poured forth a steady stream of books, pamphlets,
and magazine and newspaper articles about Custer's Last Stand. Poets
from Longfellow to anonymous hacks have found the subject irresistible. Painters and illustrators have turned out graphic representa-
tions varying from giant canvases in oil to crude drawings on gum
wrappers and bottle caps. Generations of children and parents have sat
in front of motion pictures and television screens watching hordes of
Sious warriors once again swarm over the little band of cavalrymen
and deal the mortal blow to Yellow Hair. Today there is a nationwide
organization, complete with newsletter and "Research Review," devoted solely to the study of the Custer Battle. It is called the Little

Bighorn Associates. Custer emerges as the symbol of a nation's guilt, as even bumper stickers proclaim that "Custer died for your sins."

The story of the Little Bighorn has endured, in part because of Custer himself: a dashing, flamboyant, gold braid-bedecked cavalier who inspired love or hatred in acquaintances but never indifference; major general at 25, captain then lieutenant colonel in the Regular Army at 26, court-martialed and disgraced at 28, lionized for a brilliant Indian victory at 29, controversial explorer, hunter, plainsman, sportsman, publicist of the West, author, Indian fighter, crusader against political corruption, personification of the U.S. Cavalry, ideal husband— and dead on the Little Bighorn at 36. Surely this brief career, climaxed so dramatically and amid such mystery, contains enough elements to hold the attention of a hero-worshipping public and feed eternally the fires of controversy.

The Little Bighorn has endured also because people, quite as much today as a century ago, find cavalrymen and Indians a source of compelling fascination. The man on horseback has always ridden in the vanguard of our folk heroes, and in our image of the West the blue-shirted trooper and painted warrior have never been far behind the cowboy. And when these stereotypes are particularized, it is usually to Custer's 7th Cavalry and the Sioux Indians of Sitting Bull and Crazy Horse.

And the Little Bighorn has endured because the disaster to Custer's command, like the annihilation of the Texans at the Alamo, left no survivor to tell the story. The rescue column found the unclad, unmutilated body of Custer, pierced by two bullets, lying amid the scattered bodies of his men and the carcasses of their horses. The details of the fighting could only be guessed. Even the men of Major Reno's battalions who had fought for two days only four miles distant could not say. They had seen nothing.

For a century the full truth of what happened on that Montana ridge has eluded the assiduous quest of countless students. They have studied the documents and the battlefield itself, interviewed soldiers and Indians who were there, and endlessly speculated and argued over events and personalities. Today we know a good deal about what happened and why. But many fundamental questions remain unanswered, and into the void has fallen such an accumulation of myth and legend that a perpetually fascinated public has little chance to distinguish truth from fiction.

The nation's press gave birth to much of the mythology that was to burden the history of the Custer Battle. Although the first reports were garbled, a long and surprisingly accurate account reached the New York *Herald* from Dakota on July 6. Clement M. Lounsberry of the *Bismarck Tribune* began dictating to a telegraph operator at midnight on July 5, soon after the steamer *Far West* with its cargo of wounded docked at the Bismarck landing. All night they labored over the telegraph key. The dispatch ran to 50,000 words and cost the *Herald* $3,000 in telegraph tolls, but the paper boasted the most comprehensive and factual account.

Even so, the *Herald* no less than its competitors in New York and everywhere else promptly began to embroider and sensationalize. In the florid prose so dear to the Victorian temperament, correspondents penned vivid accounts drawn from fertile imaginations rather than from Lounsberry's dispatch. Said the *Herald* on July 13:

> In that mad charge up the narrow ravine, with the rocks above raining down lead upon the fated three hundred, with fire spouting from every bush ahead, with the wild, swarming horsemen circling along the heights like shrieking vultures waiting for the moment to sweep down and finish the bloody tale, every form, from private to general, rises to heroic size, and the scene fixes itself indelibly upon the mind. "The Seventh fought like tigers," says the dispatch; yea, they died as grandly as Homer's demigods. In the supreme moment of carnage, as death's relentless sweep gathered in the entire command, all distinctions of name and rank were blended, but the family that "died at the head of their column" [i.e. Custer, two brothers, a nephew, and a brother-in-law] will lead the throng when history recalls their deed. . . . Success was beyond their grasp, so they died—to a man.

To press accounts such as this the popular writers of the day turned for source material. Custer's first biographer, Frederick Whittaker, relied almost wholly on newspapers for his reconstruction of the Little Bighorn. His *Life of Custer*, a thick, turgid tome published in December 1876, powerfully influenced a whole generation of pulp writers as well as a host of publicists posing as serious historians. Book after book during the 1880s and 1890s either drew directly from the newspaper columns or, more often, simply paraphrased or even directly copied Whittaker. And almost as regularly, writers of the twentieth century found their "facts" in the same place.

Most of the well-known tales of the Little Bighorn originated and were embedded in "history" in this way. The story of Rain-in-the-Face, a prominent Sioux warrior with a grudge against both General Custer and his brother, Captain Tom Custer, furnishes an illuminating example.

A press account of July 12, 1876 declared that "Rain-in-the-Face cut the heart from Gen. Custer's body, put it on a pole and held a grand war dance about it." Whittaker went a step further and identified Rain-in-the-Face as the slayer of Yellow Hair: "The Indian made a hand-to-hand charge in which Custer fought like a tiger with his saber when his last shot was gone." He "killed or wounded three Indians with his saber and . . . as he ran the last man through, Rain-in-the-Face kept his oath and shot Custer." (As a matter of fact, no one in the 7th carried a saber.)

Later writers built on this theme. Wrote one: "Then Rain-in-the-Face . . . gathered his most trusty followers for a hand-to-hand charge. Custer fought like a tiger. With blood streaming from half a dozen gaping wounds, he killed or disabled three of the enemy with his saber, and when his last support was gone, as he lunged desperately at his nearest enemy, Rain-in-the-Face kept his oath and shot the heroic commander dead."

"Hardly had his brave heart ceased to beat," declared another creator of penny dreadfuls, "when the savage whom he would have hanged for the murder of two helpless old men bent over him, intent upon securing some ghastly trophy of vengeance." Still another left nothing to imagination: "The painted, blood-begrimed demon approached the body of our beloved General, were scarce the noble spirit had flown, and with fiendish glee *cut the heart from his body*."

And Henry Wadsworth Longfellow assured that generations of school children would thrill to the horror of the scene:

But the foeman fled in the night
And Rain-in-the-Face, in his flight,

> Uplifted high in the air
> As a ghastly trophy, bore
> The brave heart, that beat no more
> Of the White Chief with the yellow hair.

In other versions, it was Tom Custer who incurred the wrath of Rain-in-the-Face. At Coney Island in 1894, where he was on exhibition, the once-proud warrior "confessed"—or so it was claimed by two journalists who had primed him with firewater and recorded his words for posterity:

> The long sword's blood and brains splashed in my face. It felt hot, and blood ran in my mouth. I could taste it. I was mad. . . . I saw Little Hair [Tom Custer]. I remembered my vow. I was crazy; I feared nothing. . . . I don't know how many I killed trying to get at him. He knew me. I laughed at him. I saw his mouth move, but there was so much noise I couldn't hear his voice. He was afraid. When I got near enough I shot him with my revolver. My gun [rifle] was gone, I don't know where. I leaped from my pony and cut out his heart and bit a piece out of it and spit it in his face.

A decade later, however, sober and talking to a more sympathetic recorder, Rain-in-the-Face related another story:

> Many lies have been told of me. Some say that I killed the chief, and others say that I cut the heart out of his brother, Tom Custer, because he caused me to be imprisoned. Why in that fight the excitement was so great that we scarcely recognized our nearest friends. Everything was done like lightning. After the battle we young men were chasing horses all over the prairie; and if any mutilating was done, it was by the old men.

This statement rings true. It is consistent with what other Indians have told of those last moments on Custer Hill. It is consistent, too, with the fact that Custer's body was not mutilated. Nor was Tom's heart removed, although he had been badly cut up. But truth rarely overtakes falsehood, and still today Rain-in-the-Face is often credited with the deeds so vividly described by the first newspapermen and the popular writers who relied upon them.

Scores of tales, equally fanciful, have come down to us from the same sources. The first of the "only survivor" stories, that of the Crow Indian scout Curley, appeared in the press dispatches of 1876, was embraced by Whittaker, and from the *Life of Custer* found its way into popular literature. Beginning with Curley, "only survivors" proliferated steadily over the years. The number on record today must exceed the entire number of troopers who died with Custer. None, however, has proved his case, and the only incontestable survivor remains Comanche, the horse that bore Captain Myles W. Keogh. Discovered near death by burial details, Comanche recovered to live for fifteen years as a venerated symbol of the regiment's ordeal on the Little Bighorn.

In two other ways as well the press stimulated interest and controversy that helped to implant the Little Bighorn in public awareness. For one, it made the battle a political issue. For another, it served as a forum in which army officers debated the question of who should be blamed for the disaster.

In the bitter election year of 1876 Democrats saw hope of capturing the White House from an administration riddled with corruption and wracked by scandal. Custer had naively lent himself to Democratic purposes by testifying to fraud on the Indian frontier, and President Grant, personally affronted, had removed him from command, although he later relented. (Some recent students have seen Custer as anxious to win a great Indian victory in hopes of gaining the Democratic presidential nomination, but this thesis is scarcely credible.) Custer's death provided antiadministration papers with ample ammunition, and they fired it wildly.

CUSTER AND HIS ENTIRE COMMAND SWEPT OUT OF EXISTENCE BY THE WARDS OF THE NATION AND SPECIAL PETS OF EASTERN ORATORS

headlined a Western journal. "The five massacred companies of Custer attest the inhumanity and imbecility of the republican administration," added the New Orleans *Picayune*. The Custer disaster, agreed the Indianapolis *Sentinel*, could be laid squarely to Grant's "timid, vacillating, indecisive" policy, "with its concomitant curses of swindling agents and corrupt rings."

"Who Slew Custer?" asked the New York *Herald*, a leading opposition paper. "The celebrated peace policy of General Grant," it answered, "which feeds, clothes and takes care of their noncombatant force while the men are killing our troops—that is what killed Custer. . . . That nest of thieves, the Indian Bureau, with its thieving agents and favorites as Indian traders, and its mock humanity and pretence of piety—that is what killed Custer."

Few editors defended either the President or the Indian, although the old abolitionist Wendell Phillips was moved to ask in the Boston *Transcript:* "What kind of a war is it, where if we kill the enemy it is death; if he kills us it is a massacre?" For the remaining months until the election, politically motivated journalists repeatedly described the Little Bighorn as the fruit of the President's Indian policy.

In seeking out and printing the judgments of prominent military authorities, the press also added fuel to the controversy over who was to blame. Not surprisingly, President Grant set the tone: "I regard Custer's Massacre as a sacrifice of troops, brought on by Custer himself, that was wholly unnecessary—wholly unnecessary." Generals Sherman and Sheridan followed with similar pronouncements, although each was to modify his indictment later. Others, too, joined in the attack on Custer, most prominently General Samuel D. Sturgis, whose son had died on the Little Bighorn. Custer, declared Sturgis to a reporter for the St. Louis *Globe-Democrat*, "was a brave man, but also a very selfish man. He was insanely ambitious of glory." He was "tyrannical and had no regard for the soldiers under him." And on the Little Bighorn he "made his attack recklessly, earlier by thirty-six hours than he should have done, and with men tired out from forced marches."

Custer had his defenders, too, and their equally emphatic opinions were likewise aired in the newspapers. Curiously, former Confederate generals were among the most vociferous. One, John McCausland, said he would have done just what Custer did. "The only way to fight with cavalry is with a dash—to charge. I don't blame him." Another, Thomas B. Rosser, Custer's West Point classmate and opponent in the Shenandoah Valley campaigns of 1864, absolved his old friend of the charge of recklessness and laid the blame entirely on Major Reno, who "took to the hills, and abandoned Custer and his gallent comrades to their fate."

Ever present in the background of this dispute was the shadow of Elizabeth Custer. The tragic figure in black, widowed at 34, prompted silence in many who might have spoken in criticism. Furthermore, she shaped on her own the public's memory—and thus posterity's conception—of her dead husband. She worked closely with Frederick Whittaker and insured that the image projected by Custer's first biography coincided with her own. She wrote three books herself—*Boots and Saddles* (1885), *Following the Guidon* (1890), and *Tenting on the Plains* (1893). All were intimate portrayals of a saintly husband and an idyllic marriage, and they made their legions of readers see him as she saw him. "Libby" devoted the rest of her long life to protecting and defending the memory of her "Autie." And if there was in fact a "conspiracy of silence" to withhold public attacks on Custer until she died, it was a futile conspiracy for she outlived all the conspirators. She died on April 6, 1933, two days short of her ninety-first birthday and almost fifty-seven years after that July day when the *Far West* tied up at Fort Lincoln with its shattering tidings from the Little Bighorn.

As the narrative of Rain-in-the-Face suggests, the Indians themselves added tremendously to the mythology of the Custer Battle. The rush to get their side of the story began as soon as the first of Custer's slayers surrendered at the Indian agencies in the autumn of 1876. Since then, Indian participants have contributed scores of eyewitness accounts to the voluminous literature on the Little Bighorn.

For the most part the Indian testimony was marked more by confusion than by clarity. Interrogators asked the wrong questions, or asked the right questions in the wrong way. Too often they then embroidered the answers or fabricated them altogether. Interpreters failed to translate accurately either questions or answers or sometimes simply made them up themselves. And the Indians had a variety of reasons for not wishing to divulge the full truth, not least of which was the fear of reprisal. Finally, cultural differences interposed enormous obstacles to true communication. What to an Indian was a perfectly clear story could to the white man be wholly incomprehensible. It has been observed that the only sure way to get the Indian side of the story was to interview one Indian.

Typical of the fantasies that characterize so much Indian testimony are two accounts that Sitting Bull gave during his exile in Canada. In one, he moved the women and children out of the village and posted his warriors on the surrounding hills. As Custer's cavalry approached, the chief sent out several young men under a white flag to make peace.

But as expected, Custer killed them and charged headlong into the decoy village. The Sioux then burst from concealment and killed all the soldiers.

The second story is almost a parable, seemingly designed to draw a moral rather than convey facts. Custer sent repeated messages to Sitting Bull demanding a showdown on the battlefield while Sitting Bull just as repeatedly protested his peaceful disposition. At length, in despair of reasoning with his tormentor, the Sioux leader prepared for battle. In the clash with Reno he wiped out all but five men and an interpreter, who shouted that Custer was with the other unit of soldiers. Sparing these survivors, the Sioux then turned on Custer. A great thunder storm enveloped the field of action, evidencing divine favor. Thus aided by the Great Spirit, the warriors easily annihilated Custer's command. Again sparing five soldiers and an interpreter, Sitting Bull withdrew his men.

Despite an abundance of such fancy, Indian evidence cannot be lightly dismissed. For the careful student, the eyewitness accounts of Sioux and Cheyenne participants are potentially the most valuable of all sources. But they are valuable only when painstakingly studied in relation to one another, the official reports and personal reminiscences of Reno's men, and the battlefield terrain itself. Above all, they are valuable only to the student who clearly understands the strengths and weaknesses of this kind of evidence. Very few such students have appeared. More common is the feature writer who has discovered "the true story of Custer's Last Stand" by reading the single account of an Indian who was, or who purported to have been, there.

The controversy among army officers over who was to blame for the Custer disaster did not end when the newspapers turned to more timely topics. Whenever opportunity presented, they continued to voice their opinions, often in outspoken terms.

The high point of this "great debate" occurred in the 1890s. By this time it had resolved itself largely into the question of whether Custer had disobeyed the orders of his immediate superior, General Alfred H. Terry, in attacking the Sioux village when and how he did. These orders, couched in permissive language, had been argued over for years and, depending upon one's interpretation, could be read to support either side of the debate. But the clergyman who delivered

General Terry's funeral oration in 1890, Reverend Theodore Munger, failed to note this fact when he declared unequivocally that "Custer's fatal movement was in direct violation of both verbal and written orders," and that General Terry had deliberately obscured this disobedience.

The response from Custer's friends was not long delayed. The January 1892 issue of *Century Magazine* contained a richly detailed and objective account of the Custer Battle by Captain Edward S. Godfrey, a veteran of the fight on Reno Hill. Less temperate were appended "remarks" by retired General James B. Fry. Fry was a sort of self-constituted authority on all matters military, or as one of his contemporaries put it, "there has been nothing since the birth of Christ that old Fry does not think he knows all about it." Fry vigorously exonerated Custer of the charge of disobedience and justified all that he had done. Moreover, Fry had learned the source of Reverend Munger's "indictment of one dead soldier at the Christian burial of another." He was Colonel Robert P. Hughes, General Terry's brother-in-law and his aide-de-camp in the 1876 campaign. Fry challenged Hughes to produce the orders Custer had disobeyed.

Hughes rose to the challenge. He wrote a long, dull article marshaling the official documents in a carefully reasoned indictment of Custer. *Century* rejected it as too long. Three years passed. In 1895 a noted historian, E. Benjamin Andrews, wrote a serialized history of the United States for *Scribner's Magazine*. For his account of the Custer Battle he relied mainly on Captain Godfrey's article. But he added, in language as unqualified as Reverend Munger's: "Some of General Terry's friends charged Custer with transgressing his orders in fighting as he did. This has now been disproved." Angry, Hughes at once published his rejected article in the *Journal of the Military Service Institution of the United States*. This was a professional journal of limited circulation, but Hughes's counterattack on Fry further fired the controversy in military circles.

In the same year (1896) that Hughes's article appeared, no less a personage than the commanding general of the army, Nelson A. Miles, entered the fray with the publication of his memoirs. An Indian fighter of lustrous reputation himself, General Miles staunchly defended Custer and ascribed his defeat and death to the timidity of Major Reno. Moreover, Custer did not disobey Terry's orders, and Miles had an affidavit to prove it. It contained the statement of a witness to the last conversation between Terry and Custer before the 7th Cavalry left the Yellowstone River on its fatal march to the Little Bighorn. Terry allegedly advised Custer to use his own judgment and do what he thought best if he struck the Indian trail. Such a document, of course, sanctioning any course of action Custer wished to pursue, would have been vital evidence, but Miles failed to name its author.

Army officers and historians alike tried in vain to gain access to General Miles's affidavit or at least to learn the name of the affiant. But the Olympian Miles turned all aside with an icy silence. In 1911, however, in still another book of reminiscences, he gave a partial reply to the doubters by identifying the affiant as General Custer's servant.

Not until 1923 was the mystery solved. While working on the book subsequently published as *The Story of the Little Big Horn*, Colonel W. A. Graham called in General Miles, now long retired and quite ancient, at his home in Washington, D.C. and asked to see the affidavit. "I think Mrs. Custer has it," was his only response. Graham then prevailed on the old veteran of the Little Bighorn, General Godfrey, to ask Mrs. Custer to look for it. Thus was it finally produced. The affiant turned out to be one Mary Adams, the black cook whom Mrs. Custer calls Maria in her books. Godfrey and two other surviving officers of Reno's command pronounced the affidavit worthless, for Maria had not even accompanied the expedition from Fort Lincoln. Further search by Colonel Graham led to the notary before whom the affidavit was sworn. He recalled that Maria had been brought before him by an infantry officer who later served under Miles and from whom he had doubtless obtained the document.

And so today the question remains without definitive answer. Yes, he disobeyed orders, declares one school with compelling certitude. No, answers the other, he did not.

Within the army the "great debate" began to wane in the 1920s as the old soldiers of 1876 one after another passed on. But already the historian and a new generation of popular writers had taken over the debate and pumped new life into it. Colonel Graham, E. A. Brininstool, Fred Dustin, Frederick F. Van de Water, Charles E. DeLand, Frazier Hunt, W. J. Ghent, Charles Kuhlman, and others intensely studied the evidence and the terrain and argued their conflicting interpretations and conclusions even more vehemently than the old soldiers. In time these men, too, passed on and others took their place—Edgar Stewart, Mari Sandoz, Jay Monaghan, D. A. Kinsley, David H. Miller, John M. Carroll. And there is no reason to doubt that generations unborn will continue the tradition of study and debate.

Newspapermen, army officers, Indians, popular writers, historians, dramatists, poets, artists, TV and movie producers—all have contributed mightily to the Custer legend. In the span of a century they have amassed a truly extraordinary body of literature and graphics. More words, it has been repeatedly asserted, have been written about this minor frontier clash than about any other engagement in American history save Gettysburg—although it is doubtful that anyone has ever actually counted the words. Still the presses roll and the cameras turn, still the public buys, still the controversy rages, and still there is no consensus of what happened or why on that bleak Montana hilltop in the Centennial summer.

2

The "Black Codes"

JERRELL H. SHOFNER

• *The surrender terms offered by General Ulysses S. Grant to Robert E. Lee's proud but dwindling Army of Northern Virginia were among the most generous in history, especially in view of the suffering, anguish, and emotion which accompanied the Civil War. At Appomattox Court House, the commander of the Union Army was both magnanimous and sensitive. All that was required was that Confederate soldiers put down their arms and go home in peace.*

But the battlefield result did not immediately make clear what the political future would be for those southern whites who had led their states out of the Union. According to tradition, and to a considerable segment of northern sentiment, such men were traitors to the United States. Southern voters understandably took a different view and promptly returned many leaders of the secessionist movement to Washington as members of Congress. Simultaneously, other fire-brands of the old Confederacy gained dominance over the various state legislatures and promptly began to limit the social, political, and economic rights of the former slaves.

The result was a series of racist and repressive laws known to history as the "black codes." They were intended both to guarantee the subservience of the entire black population and to assure the continued division of southern society along strict racial lines. Although they varied from state to state in severity, the black codes generally prevented Negroes from bearing arms or from working at occupations other than farming and domestic service.

As Jerrell H. Shofner makes clear in the following article, these initial inhibitions proved to be only the first set of a long series of measures designed to preserve the "southern way of life." The black codes were followed by the "Jim Crow" laws between 1890 and 1910. These new restrictions, which legalized segregation in public facilities and which in-

troduced such concepts as the literary test, the "grandfather clause," the white primary, and the poll tax, made it almost impossible for blacks to rise above the lowest rung of the economic ladder, or indeed even to protest effectively. Thus a rigidly enforced segregation system came to dominate all aspects of southern life. Even after two decades of militant civil rights activity, this legacy has just begun to be erased.

In October 1956, Dr. Deborah Coggins, health officer for Madison, Jefferson, and Taylor counties, sat down to lunch in Madison, Florida, with a public health nurse to discuss a matter of mutual official concern. Because of their busy schedules the lunch hour was the only mutually available time for the meeting. But since the doctor was white and the nurse black, the business luncheon led to the dismissal of the doctor by indignant commissioners of the three counties. Her "breach of social tradition" had been so serious, according to the commissioners, that it rendered her unfit to continue in the office to which she had been appointed about six months earlier. While Governor LeRoy Collins disagreed, and incensed citizens of South Florida condemned the commissioners, most white North Floridians nodded approval. As they saw it, Dr. Coggins had violated one of the strictest taboos of her community when "she ate with the darkies." As a native of Tampa married to a descendant of an old Madison County family, she should have known better.

Social intercourse between whites and blacks was forbidden by both law and custom in Florida in the 1950s. And it had been that way as long as most people then living could remember. The one brief period following the Civil War when things had been different had merely proved that segregation was the best way for all concerned. This belief was reinforced by all the myths and folk tales, social institutions, and statute laws with which Floridians of the 1950s were acquainted.

Those few years following the Civil War had been crucial ones for white Floridians, most of whom had sympathized with and supported the Confederate war effort. Defeated, disorganized, and bankrupt in

From *Florida Historical Quarterly*, January 1977.

1865, they had taken heart when President Andrew Johnson announced his plans for reconstructing the nation. Guaranteeing former Confederates retention of all their property except slaves, he appointed William Marvin as provisional governor to oversee the formation of a new government. To gain readmission to the Union, Florida had only to repudiate slavery, secession, and debts incurred in support of the Confederacy, and recognize all laws enacted by Congress while the state was out of the Union. Marvin repeatedly told white audiences that if they would change the laws to provide civil rights to the newly freed blacks that he believed they would not be required to implement Negro suffrage. Retrospectively this implied promise seems to have been an unfortunate one. Radical congressmen had been contending with Abraham Lincoln and later Andrew Johnson for control of Reconstruction policy. What white Floridians regarded as major concessions to former slaves was far less than Radical congressmen believed necessary. The latter watched with growing concern as the southern state governments created by President Johnson enacted their "black codes" which distinguished between black and white citizens. And the final decision on Johnson's Reconstruction program rested with Congress.

The delegates to the 1865 constitutional convention and the members of the 1865–1866 legislature who enacted the Florida black code had spent their lives as members of the dominant white class in a society whose labor system was based on racial chattel slavery. They brought to their law-making sessions all their past experiences gained from a lifetime acquaintance with a comprehensive ideological and legal framework for racial slavery. They believed that blacks were so mentally inferior and incompetent to order their own affairs that subjection to the superior white race was their natural condition. Whites benefited from the labor of blacks, and they were in turn obligated to provide guidance and welfare for their workers. Now that slavery was abolished these men met to comply with Andrew Johnson's requirements, while, at the same time, trying to salvage as much as possible of that system under which whites with their paternalistic responsibilities to blacks, and Negroes with their natural limitations, had lived peacefully.

Florida had a comprehensive slave code regulating almost every activity touching the lives of blacks. Because "free Negroes" had constituted an anomaly in a society where racial slavery was so central, there was also an extensive set of laws regulating their affairs. It was understandable that the lawmakers of 1865–1866 should draw on their past experiences and on the codes regulating slaves and free blacks. But in doing so they invited criticism from suspicious Radicals in Congress who believed that the president had erred in his lenient requirements.

A three-member committee was named by the constitutional convention of 1865 to recommend to the first legislature, scheduled to meet the following year, changes in the old laws necessary to make them conform to the postwar situation. The committee's report did nothing to assuage congressional suspicions. It urged the legislature to preserve, insofar as possible, the beneficial features of that "benign, but much abused and greatly misunderstood institution of slavery." It strenuously asserted the legislature's power to discriminate. Such power had always been executed by all the states of the Union, including those of New England. Slavery had been abolished, but nothing had been done to the status of the "free negro." Certainly, therefore, "Freedmen" could not possibly occupy a higher position in the scale of rights than had the "free negro" before the war.

Provisional Governor William Marvin, who had been appointed by President Johnson in 1865, warned that Congress was likely to intervene unless the state legislature accepted the concept of Negro freedom and extended to freedmen equal protection of the law. Despite this warning, the legislature followed the committee's recommendations. It enacted laws dealing with crime and punishment, vagrancy, apprenticeship, marriages, taxation, labor contracts, and the judicial system which were collectively referred to as the black code. The code clearly established a separate class of citizenship for blacks, making them inferior to whites.

A long list of crimes was enumerated and penalties assigned. The death penalty was imposed for inciting insurrection, raping a white female, or administering poison. Burglary was punishable by death, a fine not exceeding $1,000, or a public whipping and the pillory. Malicious trespass, buying or selling cotton without evidence of ownership, defacement of public or private property, and other crimes of similar nature were punishable by fines, imprisonment, or whipping and the pillory. Whipping or the pillory was also the prescribed punishment for injuring someone else's livestock, hunting with a gun on another's property, or unauthorized use of a horse whether in the employ of the owner or not. According to an antebellum statute continued in force by the 1865–1866 legislature, Negroes were specifically denied the right to carry firearms, bowie knives, dirks, or swords without a license from the probate judge. The punishment was forfeiture of the weapon and a whipping, the pillory, or both. This provision reflected some concern among white Floridians at the time about a rumored Negro insurrection, which had no substantive basis.

"An act to punish Vagrants and Vagabonds" made all persons subject to arrest who could not demonstrate that they were gainfully employed. Aimed at preventing congregation of freedmen in the towns, this law was especially alarming to Radical congressmen. A convicted vagrant could post bond as a guarantee of good behavior for the following year, but if no bond was posted, he could be punished by the pillory, whipping, prison, or by being sold for his labor up to one year to pay his fine and costs. "An act in relation to Apprentices" allowed the courts to apprentice the children of vagrants or paupers to persons who could supervise their activities, provide for them, and teach them a trade. It applied to both races, but in the aftermath of emancipation most of the children affected were black. This was only a slight extension of an antebellum law requiring that all free blacks over twelve years of age have a duly registered white guardian.

For the first time, a statute defined a Negro as any person with one-eighth Negro blood. Although that standard still left much to interpretation, some such ruling was necessary to the enforcement of several acts intended to separate the races. Both blacks and whites were enjoined from attending the meetings of the other race. They were also required to ride only in railroad cars designated for their respective races. Marriages between Negro men and white women were prohibited. White violators of the enactment could be fined $1,000, jailed for three months, or both. In addition to the fine, Negroes could be made to stand in the pillory for one hour, receive thirty-nine lashes, or both.

One of the most controversial enactments was "An act to establish and enforce the Marriage Relation between Persons of Color." Negro couples were given nine months to decide whether they wished to continue living together. After that time they had either to separate or be legally married. This method of correcting a problem arising from slavery and its abolition caused so much criticism in the northern press that the legislature in November 1866 simply passed a law declaring all freedmen living as man and wife to be legally married.

Even the revenue laws seemed discriminatory. There was a provision for a five-mill property tax on real property and a capitation tax of three dollars on every male between twenty-one and fifty-five. The Negroes often did not learn of the tax in time or did not have the money to pay it. If they were delinquent they could be arrested and sold for their labor for a period long enough to liquidate the obligations incurred. Several cases of tax-delinquent blacks being sold for a year's labor soon caught the attention of the northern press. Such an exorbitant punishment for failure to pay a three dollar tax seemed to some congressmen to be a substitute for the bonded servitude which had just been abolished.

Although the legislators followed closely a system already established by the military commanders, their "ACT in relation to Contracts of Persons of Color" also distinguished between the races. Contracts were to be in writing and witnessed by two white persons. If Negroes broke their agreements, they could be punished as common vagrants by being whipped, put in the pillory, imprisoned, or sold for up to one year's labor. They could also be found in violation of their contract for "willful disobedience," "wanton impudence," "disrespect" to the employer, failure to perform assigned work, or "abandonment of the premises." If the employer broke the contract, the laborer could seek redress in the courts. Although the state attorney general ruled the law unconstitutional, the next legislature rewrote it so as to apply to both races in occupations limited almost entirely to Negroes.

An early crop lien law was intended to keep tenants on the land. A landlord was empowered to seek a writ placing a lien against growing crops on rented land if the rent was not paid within ten days of the due date. If a tenant did not pay out at the end of the year, the lien could be extended to the next year and he could be legally held on the land. Attracting little attention as part of the black code at the time, this statute, with subsequent additions, contributed largely to an agricultural system which kept many tenants in economic bondage for years after the Civil War.

Central features of the black codes were "AN ACT to extend to all the inhabitants of the State the benefits of the Courts of Justice and the processes thereof" and another "prescribing additional penalties for the commission of offenses against the State, and for other purposes." The convention-appointed committee in its recommendations to the legislature had bemoaned the loss of that highly efficient institution which had existed on the plantations for punishing those "minor offenses to which Negroes are addicted." Since those offenses were now under the jurisdiction of the judiciary, the committee declared that circuit courts would be unable to handle the increased volume of litigation. It accordingly proposed that criminal courts be established in each county and the legislative assembly complied. These courts were soon handling cases, but the heritage of slavery days was too much for them. The legislators had permitted Negroes the right to testify only in cases involving blacks, and juries were made up of white men only. These whites had lived in a society where Negro slaves had had no standing in the courts, and they were now unwilling to accept the word of blacks. The courts were abject failures as legal remedies for freedmen accused of crimes or seeking redress of wrongs committed by whites.

The law "prescribing additional penalties" was a response to the special committee's recommendation that "whenever a crime be punishable by fine and imprisonment we add an alternative of the pillory for an hour or whipping up to thirty-nine lashes or both at the discretion of the jury." This discrimination was "founded upon the soundest principles of State policy, growing out of the difference that exists in social and political status of the two races. To degrade a white man by physical punishment is to make a bad member of society and a dangerous political agent. To fine and imprison a colored man . . . is to punish the State instead of the individual."

The Floridians who enacted the "black code" were surprised and angered by the national reaction they caused. Thomas W. Osborn, assistant commissioner of the Freedmen's Bureau in Florida, intervened to prevent the administration of corporal punishment. Radicals in Congress pointed to the discriminatory legislation to show that Negroes could not expect equal treatment as long as the antebellum Florida leaders remained in power. With similar legislation in other former Confederate states, the Florida black code helped the Radicals convince their moderate colleagues that President Johnson's Reconstruction plan had failed to furnish necessary protection to newly-freed persons. In a mammoth executive-legislative struggle which lasted through most of 1866, Congress overturned the Johnson governments in the South and implemented Congressional Reconstruction in 1867–1868.

Based on Negro suffrage—which Provisional Governor Marvin had said would not happen—and military supervision, the congressional plan seemed to Floridians to be a broken bargain. In late 1866 Governor Walker complained that the state had complied with President Johnson's Reconstruction requirements, but that Floridians were still being denied their rights. The subsequent implementation of Negro suffrage, enactment of the 1868 constitution, and the election victory of the newly-founded Florida Republican party were considered by local whites as unwelcome and unwise invasions of the rights of the state.

These developments also embittered them toward their former slaves. When Negro suffrage was first announced, the planters assumed that they could control the freedman's vote. At assemblages throughout the black belt counties former owners competed with "carpetbaggers" for the allegiance of the new voters. When the blacks quite understandably ignored their former masters in favor of the new Republican leaders, the native whites lost most of their paternalistic sentiment toward the freedmen. They determined to resist Negro suffrage and Republican hegemony by every means they could muster.

Landowners and storekeepers applied economic pressures on black voters. Politicians resorted to ingenious political tactics. Conservatives in the legislature blocked action whenever possible by dilatory parliamentary maneuvers. But by far the most visible, and in the long run the costliest, method was violence. With black legislators sitting in the Capitol, black marshals advertising their tax-delinquent property for sale in the county seats, and white Republicans wielding power dependent on black voting majorities, white Floridians believed that destruction of Republican power was a goal which justified any successful means. According to one sympathetic historian who lived in post-Reconstruction Pensacola, "in this contest for a very necessary supremacy many a foul crime was committed by white against black." According to their reasoning, Republican politicians in Washington had overpowered reasonable, well-meaning President Johnson and had implemented, over his vigorous vetoes and in violation of agreements already made with southern leaders, and contrary to sound constitutional theory, a policy of Negro suffrage. Although it was not the fault of the blacks, this policy had subjected an educated, property-owning class to the mismanagement and corruption of ignorant Negroes and their carpetbagger leaders. This wrong had to be corrected regardless of the methods necessary. But in permitting the use of violence for this purpose, the white leaders unleashed a force which was almost impossible to stop.

As soon as the military commander turned over control of the state to Republican Governor Harrison Reed in July 1868 and withdrew his troops to garrison duty, violence began increasing. At first night-riding bands of hooded horsemen attempted to frighten rural Negroes into submission. But partially because many blacks showed more courage than expected and partially because it was easy to commit excesses against helpless people while shrouded in the anonymity of darkness and disguise, the scare tactics soon degenerated into merciless beatings and murder. Threats were delivered and when they went unheeded, recipients were ambushed. Dozens of white Republicans and Negroes were assassinated throughout the Florida black belt from Jackson County on the Apalachicola River to Columbia County on the Suwannee and southward to Gainesville. In Jackson County alone between 1868 and 1871, more than 150 persons were killed.

Congress responded with corrective legislation. A national elections law empowered the United States government to place supervisors at every polling place in Florida and the other southern states. Military guards were also to be deployed during elections to potentially dangerous locations. Two enforcement acts authorized President Grant to declare martial law and employ soldiers where disorder was beyond the ability of state governments to control. Before the 1872 election the worst of the violence had subsided in Florida, as much from the belief among native whites that it had achieved its purpose as from the presence of United States military forces. This episode nurtured the growth of two important aspects of the evolving myth of the Lost Cause: the idea that helpless white Southerners were being mercilessly suppressed by the military power of a hostile central government, and that they were driven to the use of violence to correct an even greater wrong—dominance of the state by an ignorant Negro electorate.

After years of delay due to opposition from Conservative-Democrats and some of the white Republicans, the legislature of 1873 enacted a civil rights law calling for equal accommodations in public places, although it *permitted*, without requiring, integrated schools. Within months of its enactment it was essentially nullified by a Leon County jurist. When several Negroes complained that they had been denied access to a skating rink in Tallahassee, the judge ruled that private owners or commercial establishments had the right to refuse service to anyone they chose. Although it remained on the books for a time, the 1873 civil rights law was a dead letter. Because its principles were opposed by a majority of white Floridians, it did nothing to change social conduct.

During the four years following President Grant's reelection in 1872 the Reconstruction process continued with diminishing velocity. Most southern states were recaptured by native white Conservative-Democratic parties despite the efforts of the Grant administration. A national depression, repeated scandals in the administration, and other matters caused northern interest in the South to wane. As the 1876 presidential election approached, many Northerners were anxious for a settlement of "the southern question." The stage was set for the final episode in the growth of the myth of the Lost Cause. When the campaign of Samuel J. Tilden and Rutherford B. Hayes for president ended in an uncertain election, the nation was subjected to nearly four months of anxiety. Hayes was ultimately inaugurated after tacitly agreeing to withdraw United States soldiers from the South. This resolution of the disputed election became known as the "compromise of 1877." When he withdrew the troops, all remaining Republican administrations in the South collapsed, and Conservative-Democratic regimes took over in their places. The men who headed those new governments came to be called "Redeemers" who had ousted the carpetbaggers and restored "home rule" in the southern states.

Left to their own devices, white and black Republicans were unable to maintain themselves. During the next few years the southern Republican parties became permanent minorities and eventually almost disappeared. The United States Supreme Court's 1883 decision in the *Civil Rights Cases* was regarded as national acceptance of the failure of Reconstruction and restoration of white supremacy in the South. In that decision the court limited the civil rights guarantees of the fourteenth amendment so that they applied only against official discrimination. Thus, while it was unconstitutional for a state to pass a law discriminating on grounds of race, it was legal for private owners of hotels, restaurants, and theaters to refuse service to blacks.

Cautiously at first, but with increasing confidence, white Floridians began rewriting their laws with a view to establishing a society similar to that envisioned in the black codes of 1865–1866. The 1868 constitution was regarded as a carpetbagger document, imposed on the state by outsiders supported by a black electorate and military force. The demand for its replacement swelled in the early 1880s. Attended by a minority of Republicans, only seven of whom were Negroes, an 1885 convention wrote a constitution which prepared the way for disfranchisement of blacks and dissolution of the Republican Party. It authorized a poll tax as a condition for voting and required that all officeholders post bonds before assuming office. The latter was intended to make it difficult for blacks to qualify for office if they were able to win in the northern counties where there were overwhelming majorities of blacks. But the poll tax provision was most important. The 1889 poll tax law required that potential voters pay their tax for two years immediately prior to elections. If the county records did not show the tax paid, then the would-be voter was required to produce receipts to prove that he was eligible to vote. An accompanying statute required separate ballot boxes for each office. These made it necessary that the voter be able to read the names on the boxes in order to place his ballots in the correct places and have them counted. The result was dramatic. Statewide Republican candidates received more than 26,000 votes in 1888; in 1892 they received fewer than 5,000.

The legal changes were accompanied by incessant racist rhetoric from public officials and the state press. School histories taught young children that the "Redeemers" had saved the state from the excesses of "Radical Reconstruction." When white Floridians divided on policy matters, Conservative-Democratic politicians reminded the voters that whites must stand together or risk a return to "Negro rule."

This tactic prevented the sundering of the paramount white man's party, but it also increased the gap between the races. Violence had declined after 1872, but it had never ceased. As the possibility of federal intervention diminished in the 1880s and the doctrine of white supremacy became more firmly entrenched, violence as a means of repressing blacks increased. The brutal Savage-James lynching at Madison in 1882 went without serious investigation. Another in Jefferson

County in 1888 resulted in the arrest of five white men, but all of them were acquitted by all-white juries. Two especially repugnant lynchings in the mid-1890s led Governor William D. Bloxham to deplore the practice in his 1897 inaugural address, but he offered no remedy. The praise of white supremacy and persistent reminders of its alternatives from prominent men perpetuated a climate of tolerance for violence by whites against blacks.

Floridians were reinforced in their views by similar developments in other southern states. Worse yet, racial developments in the South coincided with a growing racial theory throughout the United States. Relying on Joseph Gobineau and other European racist writers, social theorists in the United States were preaching the idea of Anglo-Saxon superiority and the corresponding inferiority of blacks to a receptive audience. At the same time the United States acquired the Philippine Islands, and a little later Theodore Roosevelt added his "corollary" to the Monroe Doctrine. Our decision to uplift our "little brown brothers" in the Philippines and "protect" our Latin American neighbors from European interference by intervening in their internal affairs added powerful impetus to the growing racial theories in our country.

By the turn of the century the Lost Cause myth was virtually beyond question in the South and was gaining adherents elsewhere. It placed little emphasis on the demise of slavery and the failure of secession. Rather it focused on the unsuccessful efforts at postwar Reconstruction. President Johnson had been willing to permit Southerners to reform their society along lines that allowed for the innate inferiority of blacks. But a misguided Radical-controlled Congress had taken direction of Reconstruction away from him. These crusading Northerners had attempted to change natural conditions by legislative fiat, causing immense difficulties for all involved in an experiment which was doomed by nature to failure. Finally seeing the errors of their ways, they had withdrawn from the struggle, leaving Southerners to solve their own racial problems. This was a powerful and satisfying rationale for a caste system which ultimately degraded Negroes to the point where they had absolutely no defense against the worst excesses of the most lawless elements of white society.

Beginning in 1889 a series of Jim Crow laws were passed which gave legal sanction to the segregation which already existed by custom. These laws went far beyond the earlier black codes in separating the races, but they did little more than legalize existing conditions. Racial segregation in Florida was more extensive in 1900 than it had been in 1865.

An 1895 statute prohibited anyone from conducting a school in which whites and Negroes attended either the same classes, separate classes in the same building, or classes taught by the same teachers. Fines and jail sentences were provided for violators. Others soon followed. In 1903 intermarriage was forbidden between white persons and Negroes, including anyone with at least one-eighth Negro blood. Either or both parties to such a marriage could be punished by up to ten years imprisonment or $1,000 fine. A 1905 enactment required separation of the races on street cars and required companies operating them to provide separate facilities. Failure of the company to do so was punishable by a $50 fine with each day constituting a separate offense. Passengers violating the statute were subject to fines of $25 or up to thirty days in jail. Negro nurses travelling with white children or sick persons were exempt. Since slavery days there had been almost unlimited contact between the races where the blacks were in a servant capacity, and this continued. Segregation was a class rather than a physical matter.

In 1905 constables, sheriffs, and others handling prisoners were forbidden to fasten white male or female prisoners to colored prisoners, subject to fines up to $100 or sentences up to six months. The same legislature required terminal and railroad companies to provide separate waiting rooms and ticket windows for whites and Negroes. The penalty for failure was a fine up to $5,000. A 1909 statute required "equal" and "separate" railroad cars or divisions of cars.

These legal reinforcements of existing practices had great significance. Law and custom had been in harmony during antebellum slavery days. The 1865–1866 black code reflected the social experiences of those who enacted them. Then it was overturned by national legislation which ran counter to the beliefs of the dominant groups of Florida society. Because they disagreed with the Reconstruction legislation and the circumstances of its enactment, native white Floridians not only overturned the laws but also developed a rationale—the Lost Cause myth and its corollary of the necessity for white supremacy—which justified and reinforced their actions following the celebrated 1876 election dispute. The Jim Crow laws were the final necessary step. By the early twentieth century white Floridians were living in a society whose customs, ideology, and law code were once more in harmony.

The first third of the twentieth century was the nadir of race relations in Florida and the nation. Although segregation seemed to be permanently entrenched, whites did not let the matter rest. Politicians always referred to it in their campaigns. Newspapers carried editorials dealing with racism and news stories casting obloquy and odium on Negroes. Creative writers dealt with the subject in the same way. There was a widespread movement to solve the race problem by sending the blacks to Africa. A strong advocate of the idea was Frank Clark, an influential Florida congressman who once declared that "Mr. Lincoln said that this nation could not exist 'half slave and half free.' I think it is equally true that this nation can not exist *half white* and *half black*." Likewise, progressive Florida Governor Napoleon B. Broward went so far as to propose mass removal of Negroes from the United States in his 1907 message to the legislature.

Without political rights, economic strength, or legal status, blacks had no defense. Their best hope was to keep away from whites unless they were fortunate enough to identify with someone who would assist them in legal and economic matters. Usually tied to the land by perpetual indebtedness and dependent on the good will of a white man for whatever security they had, blacks in the early twentieth century occupied a social position not significantly different from that of the antebellum "free Negro" who had been obliged by law to have a white guardian. But this unofficial paternalism was not available to all, and it was inadequate to prevent physical abuse on those occasions when blacks came into contact with unruly whites. Insults and petty violence could sometimes be borne in silence. But at other times it was impossible to avoid trouble. With no legal or social restraints, white ruffians and sometimes ordinary citizens angered by some incident assaulted blacks without fear of reprisal.

In 1911 Mark Norris and Jerry Guster of Wadesboro, Leon County, were arrested on a charge of stealing and resisting arrest. B. B. Smith, a sawmill owner who had been deputized especially to arrest them, had struck Norris with a pistol while doing so. In the justice of the peace court in Miccosukee, the two Negroes were acquitted. When they went to Smith's home to talk about the matter, a gun fight ensued, and Smith was killed. A group of blacks gathered to defend the two men against an anticipated mob, but they quietly surrendered when two deputies arrived to arrest them. Ultimately, ten Negroes were arrested, six of whom were charged with murder. A crowd gathered in Tallahassee, and talk of lynching increased. Six of the men were smuggled out of Tallahassee and taken to Lake City for safekeeping. A few evenings later several men drove to Lake City and got the blacks out of jail on a forged release order, took them to the edge of town, and riddled all six with bullets for more than a half hour. No one in Lake City went to investigate the shooting until the assassins were driving away, thus there were no witnesses to the crime. Governor Albert Gilchrist offered a $250 reward for information about the lynching, but a cursory investigation was shortly abandoned without success.

There was almost no provocation for an incident at Monticello in 1913. Sheriff's deputies went into Log Town, a black section, at about eleven o'clock one Saturday evening just "scouting around." Seeing a group of blacks walking down the road, the deputies called on them to stop to be searched. The Negroes ran. The deputies fired and three blacks were wounded; one of them permanently paralyzed by a shot in the back. No weapons were found on any of them. Walking down the road on a Saturday night seemed to be sufficient cause for a presumption of guilt only in the case of blacks.

When J. A. McClellan shot and killed Charlie Perry, a black, in 1918, the coroner's jury found the shooting to have been in self-defense. It was true that an argument between them had been started by Perry. But the reason for the altercation was that McClellan and others had broken into Perry's house and had searched it without either a warrant or the owner's permission. During the 1920 general election, July Perry of Ocoee, Orange County, caused a disturbance when he tried to vote without having paid his poll tax. He even threatened election officials, but it is inconceivable that the aftermath would have been the same had he been white. Whites followed Perry home and ordered him out of his house. He fired on them. When the altercation was over three days later, the entire Negro section of Ocoee had been burned and four innocent people consumed in the fire. The grisly episode ended only after a mutilated July Perry was finally put to death by the mob which had tired of torturing him. Three years later at Rosewood, near Cedar Key, a white mob charged into the black community searching for an alleged rapist, burned six houses and a church, and killed five blacks. This time the blacks fought back and two whites also died.

The lynching of Claude Neal in Jackson County in 1934 was so shocking that it stimulated a renewed effort in Congress to enact anti-lynching legislation. Neal was accused of murdering a white girl with whom it was charged he had had an illicit relationship. Transferred from jail to jail in West Florida and in southern Alabama he was finally overtaken by a mob in the latter state and brought back to Marianna. He was tortured and mutilated, dragged behind a car, and finally displayed on the streets before crowds, including school children, who attacked the then lifeless body. The corpse was hanged on the courthouse square. On the following day mobs threatened blacks on the streets of Marianna, and order was not restored until the militia was called in. The NAACP published a report of the incident which aroused considerable ire across the nation, but nothing was done. The attorney general ruled that the recently enacted federal law against kidnapping across state lines did not apply because a monetary ransom had not been the purpose of the mob. And as always there was no remedy under state law.

Violence was only the extreme and most visible surface of a racially segregated society. Many whites who deplored violence still obeyed the infinite daily reinforcements of their segregated system: separate dining facilities, theaters, restrooms, waiting rooms, railroad cars, and drinking fountains, as well as the customary racial divisions of labor. While blacks and whites often worked at comparable jobs at the lower end of the economic spectrum, nearly all the professional and white collar jobs were limited to whites and the most menial tasks were overwhelmingly filled by blacks. Even where employment of blacks and whites was comparable, compensation was disproportionate. For example, black school teachers in the 1930s in one north Florida county earned from $37.50 to $40 per month, slightly less than half the salaries of their white counterparts. At that time Confederate veterans were drawing pensions of $37.50 per month. Even the New Deal programs of the national government, designed to relieve the poverty of the 1930s, were affected by racism. Relief administration in Jacksonville established a formula which gave forty-five percent of the available funds to Negroes and fifty-five percent to whites, while black relief families outnumbered white by three to one. Florida Negroes were often denied access to the work-relief programs of the Civilian Conservation Corps and the National Youth Administration on the grounds that they were unqualified to meet admission standards.

By the time Claude Neal was lynched in 1934 forces outside the state were already undercutting the racial status quo. Negro migration into northern cities had created potential black political power. Breaking traditional ties with the Republican party, large numbers of urban blacks voted for Franklin D. Roosevelt in 1936, beginning an alliance with the national Democratic party which still exists. The NAACP had gained considerable attention by its publicity of lynching statistics and its lobbying for an antilynch law. It won its first school desegregation case at the graduate level in 1937. In World War II blacks made significant gains in the armed services and in defense jobs at home. Further migrations out of the South occurred. The Truman administration called for fair employment practices and the 1948 Democratic platform endorsed the idea. The military services were integrated in 1949.

Despite all these changes, the 1954 United States Supreme Court decision in *Brown* v. *Board of Education of Topeka* and its 1955 directive to integrate the public schools with "all deliberate speed" fell like a bombshell on Florida and the other southern states. The Florida attorney general sent to the court the results of a study by social scientists showing that attempts to integrate the state's schools would cause violence. On the basis of the report he asked for a stay of execution of the decision. Some public officials said the court decision was too soon; others said it was an invasion of state rights and a usurpation of legislative power by the courts. State Senator John Rawls of Marianna introduced a resolution in the legislature which emphasized that the constitution of Florida added "legal force to the time honored custom and native inclination of the people of Florida, both negro and white, to maintain . . . a segregated public school system . . . integration . . . in the public schools . . . would tend to encourage the . . . unnatural, . . . abhorrent, execrable, and revolting practice of miscegenation."

White Floridians girded themselves to resist. With a full range of laws requiring segregation and the widespread belief in state rights, theirs was a formidable defensive arsenal. Because the segregation laws conformed so closely to the social values of white Floridians, they emphasized the primacy of state legislation and branded the United States Supreme Court an usurper. Opponents of integration eventually destroyed much of the creditability of the national court system by emphasizing the clash of state law with the court. It was at this point that the Jim Crow laws were crucial. Instead of having to face the basic question of how a state could distinguish between its citizens by law, segregationists were able to attack the integrity of the agency which raised the question. It was much more satisfying to defend the right of the state against invasions of the national court than to defend the Jim Crow system on its dubious merits.

Governor LeRoy Collins's unwillingness to defy the court was a setback, but he promised to use all lawful efforts to maintain segregation while at the same time calling on Floridians to obey the law of the land. The legislature went beyond the governor's position, passed a resolution calling on him to interpose the authority of the state to protect Florida citizens from any effort of the national government to enforce the Brown decision, and enacted legislation providing for the closing of the schools if the national government used force to integrate them. Representative Mallory Horne of Leon County led an effort to restrict the authority of the court, and many Floridians prepared to *defend the law by resisting* the Brown decision.

The moderation of Governor Collins made an immense difference in Florida. Despite the attorney general's warnings of incipient violence, and amidst reports of disruptions in other states, Florida passed through this "Second Reconstruction" with markedly little actual violence. Although there was almost no progress toward school integration for years after the Brown decision, the civil rights movement broadened to other areas and accelerated. White Floridians retreated slowly, resisting each attack on their social system by referring to the state laws. Gradually the national court system negated those laws. With constant pressure from the courts, and belatedly from Congress and the president, the legal framework of segregation crumbled.

But the initiative came almost entirely from outside the state. Some Floridians, exasperated at the national government's interference, argued that they had been gradually working out solutions for the racial problem before the Brown decision. Some social scientists argue that as a rural, agricultural society becomes urban and industrialized, racial segregation breaks down because it cannot function in such a society. However that may be, there was little change in the racial caste system in Florida until the nation once more became interested in it. The hideous lynchings of the early twentieth century ceased when Congress started seriously considering antilynching legislation. Education funds went to Negro schools in larger quantity as the NAACP began winning its desegregation cases. New congressional legislation on civil rights, public accommodations, and voting spearheaded changes in these areas.

With assistance from the national courts and marshals, blacks moved from the back of the buses, sat down at public lunch counters, came down out of the theater balconies, attended previously all-white schools at least in small numbers, and moved into the mainstream of Florida society in countless ways which had been denied them by both law and custom in the past. It was still a piecemeal movement, and social approval of segregation was still strong among whites, but the Jim Crow legal system had been nullified by the late 1960s.

Florida society still retains some of its traditional segregation. Negroes still live mostly in the less desirable sections of towns. Many white families have taken their children from the public schools and sent them to "Christian" schools which cropped up rapidly after 1968. But there is a significant difference. Supported by custom *and the law* only a few years ago, segregation and its correlative of white supremacy and black inferiority were taken for granted by most political and other opinion leaders. Some applauded it as beneficial and even necessary for the South. Gubernatorial candidate Bill Hendricks campaigned throughout Florida in the 1950s as the Ku Klux Klan candidate. White supremacists rested confidently and comfortably with their views, knowing that they were supported by the laws of the state.

That has changed. Few Floridians now speak publicly against basic civil rights for blacks. Racial jokes have moved from most drawing rooms into the restrooms. Denial of the legal sanction for segregation has reversed the burden of public approval. It is no longer popular to advocate segregation, at least directly. Those who believe in it are on the defensive. In the 1974 election, Jeff Latham, a candidate for statewide office ruined his creditability and his chances for election when he admitted appealing for support from a racist organization.

It is difficult to change the values of society by law—or in the jargon of the capitol hallways "You can't legislate morality"—but it is possible to take away the legal basis for repugnant practices. Jim Crow legislation had provided an immense reinforcement of a segregated society and the rationale for it. Its repeal was difficult because it complemented the values of the most powerful groups of Florida society. But once that legislation was nullified, segregationists found themselves on the opposite side of the law. Interposition was a last-ditch effort to justify the system in terms of state sovereignty along lines enunciated by John C. Calhoun more than a century earlier and negated by the Civil War. The state rights defense was gradually discredited in the 1960s by repeated revelations of southern law enforcement officials using the color of law to commit criminal acts in defense of segregation.

Finally forced to the basic question of how to justify segregation on its merits in terms of mid-twentieth century America and without the support of Jim Crow laws—much as their ancestors had had to deal with the problem of converting slaves to freedmen in 1865–1866— white Floridians have exerted remarkable effort to overcome their segregationist views. They have come far from the time when violence was justified on the ground of the necessity for white supremacy. Many people who still prefer a segregated society restrain themselves from open advocacy of it. And most important of all, most Floridians are willing to accept recent changes, albeit sometimes reluctantly, because they are reinforced by the law.

Racial divisions of American society persist and have become a national problem, but they are no longer being dealt with at the level to which they had descended in the early twentieth century. Americans have probably gone as far toward an integrated society as legal changes will take them. Difficulties encountered with the Supreme Court's "busing" decisions reveal the limits on law as a positive force. Legal provisions cannot diverge too far from custom and belief without disruption. But the disparity is not as great in 1977 as in 1867–1868 when the black code was replaced by laws calling for equality. With time— history—and tolerance, custom and the law will once more coincide as they did for white Floridians before 1860.

3

A Compulsory Heaven at Pullman

RAY GINGER

• Although the concept of the company town was not introduced in Pullman, Illinois, first the yellow-bricked planned community for sleeping car workers on the fringes of Chicago attracted national and international attention in the 1880s. Industrial giant George M. Pullman viewed with paternal pride the comfortable homes, the parks, the library, the band, the church, and the shopping center and confidently expected that his controlled environment would improve the performance of his workers, and at the same time yield a 6 percent return on the company's capital investment.

When the company reduced wages but not rents, the brainchild became rebellious toward its Puritanical father, however, and in 1894 this pleasant model town touched off the most famous strike in American history. It tied up the nation's rail system and pitted crusading labor leader Eugene V. Debs against the proud George Pullman and Illinois Governor John Peter Altgeld against the President of the United States.

The town of Pullman is memorable for another reason, however. That the experiment was conducted in a relatively isolated environment well outside the boundaries of a booming metropolis was not accidental. George Pullman realized that his factories needed to be located reasonably near the rail network of a great city. But he also believed that saloons, prostitutes, bright lights, and crowded residential districts were not conducive to industrial efficiency or moral strength, and like many people in our own time, he felt that the best answer to urban problems was to escape them. Pullman failed, but generations of suburbanites have followed his panacea and fully planned communities are now operative in Reston, Virginia, and Columbia, Maryland, to name only the most recent examples. Do these communities offer a

viable alternative to the problems of modern life? Was the
fate of Pullman, Illinois, merely an isolated case of the failure of one man's attempts to be a benevolent dictator or
does it indicate the inevitable outcome of all utopias?

In so far as philanthropists . . . are cut off from the great moral
life springing from our common experiences, so long as they are
"good to people" rather than "with them," they are bound to
accomplish a large amount of harm.

                                                                    JANE ADDAMS

I

George Mortimer Pullman was one of the great industrialists of the
age, not just one of the most successful, but also one of the most creative. Inventor, strategist, executive, he was the perfect businessman.
More than that, he recognized that the lives of his employees did not
end when they left the shop at night. He had a vision of a richer existence for his labor force, and out of it he built the first model town
in industrial America. It was a showplace. Visitors come from all over
the world to admire it. Here was the solution to the labor question.
But as the years passed, George Pullman's vision proved to be both
more complicated and simpler than it had seemed at first. And in
May, 1894, his heaven exploded.

Pullman was born in 1831 in a small town in upstate New York,
one of the ten children of a general mechanic. He quit school early
to be a cabinetmaker, then became a street contractor. His work took
him to Chicago, where he quickly found a chance to show his resource-
fulness. In 1858 the Tremont House, a downtown hotel, seemed to be
settling into a bottomless pit of mud. Although the structure was four
stories tall and made of brick, Pullman vowed that he could raise it
without breaking a single pane of glass or awakening a single guest.
He put 5,000 jackscrews in the basement and assembled twelve hun-

dred men. At a signal, each man gave a half-turn to his four jackscrews. Inch by inch the building was plucked out of the morass.

Pullman began to tinker around at building a sleeping car for the Chicago & Alton Railroad. But when it was finished, the railroads were loath to adopt it; so he wandered out to the newly opened mining fields in Colorado and ran a store. By 1863 he was back to Chicago and working in earnest on his invention. His basic design, the key to which was the hinged upper berth, was just like the modern Pullman. But he decorated the car lavishly: other sleeping cars were built for about $5,000; Pullman spent $20,000 on his. In order to accommodate the berths properly, he made the car a foot wider and 2½ feet higher than ordinary railroad cars. Any railroad that wanted to use Pullmans would have to alter its bridges and its station platforms. Pullman didn't care; he was going to build his car right. He focused on one thing: maximum comfort for the passenger.

And he won out. By 1867 orders were pouring in. On every hand railroads were altering stations, bridges, culverts. The Pullman Palace Car Company was incorporated in Illinois, and gradually plants were built from New York to California. Pullman made other inventions: the restaurant car, the dining car, the chair car. He made railroad cars on contract for the railroads themselves. But his sleeping cars he would not sell. His company operated the cars itself; the railroads simply hauled them around the country. Pullman paid his stockholders a straight 8 percent dividend each year, and the rest of the profits he kept in the firm as surplus. Shares in the Pullman Company rose to twice their par value.

More manufacturing facilities were needed. And George Pullman had his vision. Other companies were frequently beset by labor troubles. Strikes occurred at crucial times and crippled production. Men got drunk and stayed home to recover. Workers strayed off to other jobs as soon as they had acquired the skill you needed. But if you gave them a really decent place to live, you could get a better class of workmen, labor turnover could be reduced, unrest would turn into contentment. Above all, if you owned the entire town, you could insulate your employees from corrupting influences. The environment could be kept as controlled and sterile as an incubator, a church, or a prison.

Some of the Pullman directors objected to using corporate funds for such a purpose. Their business, they said, was manufacturing and operating railroad cars, not real estate. But George Pullman overrode them. A perfect site for the new shops was the prairie twelve miles south of the business district of Chicago. Here was the railroad hub of the United States, accessible to more major railroads than any other spot in the country. But it was a relatively isolated spot, far from the residential areas of the working class. The only way to get a labor force was to build the housing.

But George Pullman never thought of the town solely in terms of its indirect benefits to the company. He also thought about its direct commercial value. Every dollar invested in the town was expected to yield a 6 percent return.

In 1880 the Pullman Company quietly bought a solid tract of four thousand acres, nearly seven square miles, on the west shore of Lake Calumet. It was in the town of Hyde Park, a sprawling congeries of settled areas and huge vacant stretches which adjoined Chicago. The town of Pullman was erected on three hundred acres, surrounded by an empty *cordon sanitaire*. The little community was a beautiful place, especially when compared to the filthy industrial giant just to its north. One tenth of the area of Pullman was taken by its parks. A miniature lake was created for boating and swimming. An island in the lake was used for many types of athletics.

Every street in town was paved with macadam. The sidewalks were paved too, usually with wood, and were lined with shade trees. The front lawn of every house in town was landscaped by the company. The buildings were nearly all yellow brick, made in Pullman itself of clay dredged from the bottom of Lake Calumet. By 1885 the town had fourteen hundred dwelling units. Most of them had five rooms, and they were built as row-houses. The company kept them in good repair. There were occasional complaints in cases where two families had to use a single toilet, but in Chicago few tenements had any indoor plumbing at all. In other respects, too, health conditions in Pullman were excellent. Sanitation was outstanding, the company even furnishing garbage receptacles and emptying them daily.

Pullman had a higher tax assessment for school purposes than any other area in Hyde Park. The term lasted for two hundred days, which was incredibly generous for that time. Schooling was free through the eighth grade, the only condition being that all students had to be vaccinated for smallpox. Another pioneering feature was the kindergarten for children between the ages of four and six. An evening school taught such commercial subjects as bookkeeping and stenography.

The cultural life of the town was quite varied. Besides the extensive athletic program, there was a theater with one thousand seats, where the foremost actors and musicians of the time performed during the 1880s. The library, luxurious with its Wilton carpets and plush chairs, was opened in 1883 with an initial gift of five thousand volumes from George Pullman. The eighty-piece Military Band, good enough one year to win the statewide competition, was composed entirely of men who worked for the company. During the summer it gave free weekly concerts.

This industrial Arcadia grew year by year. It hit its peak in 1893, just before the depression struck, when the population of the town was 12,600. At that time, employment in the Pullman shops was 5,500, with many of the workers living in surrounding towns. The town grew in value too. The land had cost $800,000 in 1880. Twelve years later, George Pullman estimated that it was worth $5 million. He had reason to congratulate himself.

But he had his problems with the town. The most serious was that it never earned the return that he had expected from it. For years it paid only about 4.5 percent. In 1892 and 1893 the return further declined to 3.82 percent.

Even to get that much, Pullman had to fight a continuing war against the town of Hyde Park about his tax rates. He took no interest in civic affairs outside his own town, but his business brought him into politics anyway. In order to keep foreign competition away, he was a high-tariff man, and that prompted him to contribute heavily to the national Republican party. And his desires to keep his taxes down and to be left alone to run his town as he saw fit—together they carried him deep into local politics.

Foremen at the Pullman shops openly solicited votes for the company-approved candidates in elections. Workers were discharged because they persisted in running for public office contrary to the orders of their superiors. When John P. Hopkins, a prosperous storekeeper in Pullman, organized voters for Grover Cleveland in 1888, his landlord made life so difficult for him that he had to move his store to nearby Kensington. The Pullman Company maneuvered and manipulated and coerced for years to prevent Hyde Park from becoming part

of Chicago, but in 1889 it lost that fight, and thereafter George Pullman had to go into Chicago politics to keep his taxes low.

He was an irascible, pompous man who could never see any viewpoint but his own. He thought that liquor was bad, so he banned it
from the town. He thought that prostitution was bad, so he banned that
too. He kept his eye on everything. He had informers in every lodge,
in every social group; sometimes it seemed that he had them in every
parlor on Saturday night. He wanted to know everything that happened. The town was his, and he would run it his way. He believed in
thrift, and hard work and sobriety. He believed in individual responsibility and the other Puritan virtues.

But many of his workers came from other traditions. As early as
1884 more than half of the residents were foreign-born. Eight years
later, 72 percent were, including 23 percent Scandinavian, 12 percent
British, the same proportion of Germans, 10 percent Dutch, 5 percent
Irish. Many of them could see no harm in a pint of beer. Many of
them wanted to worship in their own faith.

George Pullman had his ideas about that too. There was one church
building in town. Pullman owned it, just as he owned everything else.
He was a Universalist who didn't care about doctrinal niceties, but the
church was nonsectarian. It was part of the business; it too had to pay
its way. The rent set on it by Pullman was so high that no congregation in town could afford to pay it. The Presbyterians tried it for a few
years and went bankrupt. The resultant bitterness was summed up by
one Presbyterian minister: "I preached once in the Pullman church,
but by the help of God I will never preach there again. The word
monopoly seems to be written in black letters over the pulpit and the
pews." George Pullman didn't care.

From the very beginning, Pullman's high-handed ways aroused opposition. Prior to 1882 the shops had been expanded more rapidly than
the housing facilities. Many employees were still living in Chicago,
and they had to pay a round-trip fare of 20 cents a day on the Illinois
Central to get back and forth to work. The company paid this fare.
Then it announced that it would pay only half. A thousand men struck.
The strike was broken; the ringleaders fired.

In March, 1884, a group of 150 men in the freight-car department
struck against a wage cut. That strike was broken too. Then the company learned a new technique. In October, 1885, it instituted a wage

cut of 10 percent. But the reduction was introduced first in one depart-ment, then in another; the workers were never unified against it. So a strike did not come until the following spring, when an estimated fourteen hundred workers at Pullman were members of the Knights of Labor. They joined in the general movement for an eight-hour day that was sweeping through Chicago, and to the general demand they added their own—a 10 percent pay increase, to recoup what they had lost. The company refused; the workers struck; within ten days the shops were reopened under guard.

George Pullman wanted no truck with trade unions—and for the next eight years there was no effort at organization in his plant. Small strikes occurred in 1888 and 1891, but they were hardly serious enough to be annoying. In 1893 the company could announce smugly: "Dur-ing the eleven years the town has been in existence, the Pullman work-ingman has developed into a distinctive type—distinct in appearance, in dress, in fact, in all the external indications of self-respect. . . ." A typical group of Pullman employees, said the statement, was "40 per-cent better in evidence of thrift and refinement and in all the outward indications of a wholesome way of life" than any comparable group in America.

The "outward indications"—Pullman could usually control those. But he could not legislate against the bitterness within. As one man protested: "We are born in a Pullman house, fed from the Pullman shop, taught in the Pullman school, catechized in the Pullman church, and when we die we shall be buried in the Pullman cemetery and go to the Pullman hell."

A year after the Company had congratulated itself, the inward bit-terness of its employees burst forth in action, and the "distinctive type" of workingman proved that, if goaded hard enough, he could be an unruly ingrate like anybody else.

II

The financial policies of the Pullman Palace Car Company through-out its history had been so sound that the firm was in excellent position to meet the depression in 1893; usual dividends could have been main-tained for years out of the undivided surplus that had been accumu-lated. But businessmen care about current income as well as about liquidity, and the gross receipts of the Pullman Company fell drastically in 1893. Income from operating its sleeping and dining cars held up well, but much of the firm's manufacturing activity consisted in filling orders from other firms for various types of railroad cars. These outside orders now dried up almost entirely; no railroad adds new equipment when much of what it has is idle.

George Pullman was not a man to stand quietly with his hands in his pockets while his money seeped away. He responded vigorously with a program of lay-offs, reduced hours, wage cuts. In July, 1893, the shops at Pullman employed 5,500 men; the following May, only 3,300. Wage rates were slashed an average of 25 percent, but the pay cuts were far from uniform: machinists in the street-car department claimed that their wages had been reduced more than 70 percent. At a time when painters in Chicago—those lucky enough to be employed—were getting 35 cents an hour, the painters at Pullman were paid 23 cents an hour.

These policies were superbly effective, as the company's accountants had reason to know:

Year ending July 31	Wages	Dividends
1893	$7,223,719	$2,520,000
1894	4,471,701	2,880,000

The outlay for wages had been reduced 38 percent in a single year; but dividends were actually increased. And the company had an undistributed surplus for the year 1893–1894 of $2,320,000!

During all this time, rental charges for housing in Pullman were not reduced. Renting houses was one thing; employing workmen was another; the two had no connection. And so long as the capital invested in the housing remained the same, why should rents be reduced? In regard to this, a Federal commission later concluded: "If we exclude the aesthetic and sanitary features at Pullman, the rents there are from 20 to 25 percent higher than rents in Chicago or surrounding towns for similar accommodations. The aesthetic features are admired by visitors, but have little money value to employees, especially when they lack bread."

As early as December, 1893, the Pullman Company felt constrained to issue a statement denying that extreme distress existed among the residents of Pullman. So the winter dragged on, and the workers and their families suffered. Since George Pullman had always managed the town arbitrarily, its institutions of local government were anemic. The town had no mechanisms for public relief, which was contrary to the owner's ideas of individual self-help. But the typical worker was hesitant to move away even after he had been laid off by the shops. House rents in Pullman were higher than elsewhere, but unemployment was everywhere, and the workers believed that residents of Pullman would be the first to be rehired. So destitution became unbearable; yet there was nothing to do except bear it. In some homes the children lacked the shoes and coats needed to go to school in the severe Illinois winter; in others they were kept in bed all day because there was no coal in the house.

And then came a voice of hope. A dim hope—yes, but still it was something. The previous spring, June, 1893, just as the depression was beginning, fifty railroad workers had met in Chicago to form the American Railway Union. Prior to that time the only trade unions on the railroads had been the various Brotherhoods, a separate one for each of the main occupations in railroading. The Brotherhoods of skilled workers, such as the Engineers, were the strongest and best organized, and they tended always to sneer at their fellow workers in the less skilled crafts—the switchmen, the brakemen, even the locomotive firemen—and they hardly recognized the existence of the men who worked on the railroads but had nothing to do with operating trains, such as the section hands.

The utter lack of cooperation, verging often on civil war, among the various Brotherhoods made it impossible for the unskilled crafts to bargain effectively with the railroads, and even the Engineers achieved many of their gains by ruthlessly sacrificing the interests of other crafts. Beginning about 1885, a movement developed in each of the Brotherhoods that aimed at bringing about joint action among them. Finally in 1889 the Supreme Council of the United Orders of Railway Employes was formed, consisting of the officers of several of the Brotherhoods. The organization for a time seemed to be working well, and it appeared that the other Brotherhoods would join and even that ultimately they might all merge into one big Brotherhood of railroad workers—one industrial union rather than many craft unions. But within less than two years, one of the member Brotherhoods conspired with the Chicago & Northwestern Railroad to destroy another of the member Brotherhoods. The Supreme Council collapsed.

The episode caused some of the more radical officials in the Brotherhoods to despair of their conservative fellows, who seemed determined to seek their own selfish ends and to block any moves toward unification of the different organizations. Chief among these dissidents was Eugene Victor Debs, secretary-treasurer of the Brotherhood of Locomotive Firemen since 1880 and editor of its magazine. When Debs took these jobs, the order was small and moribund, with sixty inactive lodges and a substantial debt. Twelve years later it was out of debt, had twenty thousand members, and was solidly established. Much of this progress was due to Debs personally: to his zeal, his dedication, his relentless drive, above all to his concern for the welfare of the poor.

Thirty-eight years old in 1893, he was a man of awesome vigor. His life was one perpetual organizing trip. Every day, day after day, he could travel two or three hundred miles, give a half-dozen speeches, and have energy left for a good deal of sociable drinking. His stamina welled outward from a tall, austere frame and a copious spirit. Debs was a visionary. He pictured a land from which poverty, whether of the body or of the heart, had disappeared, a land where violence was not even a bad memory, an America where everybody treated his fellows generously of his own will, because he could do no other, an America where everybody smiled and everybody sang.

But he knew that no man can smile with another's face or sing in a foreign language. Debs was no George Pullman, carrying a prefabricated Utopia around in his vest pocket. He spoke of the evils of this world and of the possibility of a better one. About the evils he was explicit: poverty, arbitrary power, treating men solely in terms of their cash value, one man imposing his will on another. But he never spelled out the details of the better life he was always talking about. He exhorted men to love one another; beyond that, they would have to find their own way. Men cannot be driven at all; and they cannot be led down a narrow and fenced road to a waiting corral. The job of leadership is to point a general direction and to awaken in men the hope that they can move in that direction. Debs could do this. When he talked, men came to life, and they moved. He was an agitator. To agitate, all that he needed was to feel sure himself of the general direction that men should go.

In 1892 he was sure. He was fed up with the internecine warfare of the Brotherhoods, which saw each of them cut the throat of the others for some selfish and short-term gain. He was gagging on the smug arrogance of the Brotherhood of Locomotive Engineers. He wanted to see an organization that would really protect the railroaders, all of them, against the tyranny and exploitation of the corporations. But when he declined to stand for reelection as secretary-treasurer of the Firemen in 1892, his plans were very general: "It has been my life's desire to unify railroad employees and to eliminate the aristocracy of labor, which unfortunately exists, and organize them so all will be on an equality." The following spring Debs was one of the founders of the American Railway Union, and became its president.

The ARU started its first local lodge on August 17, 1893. Thereafter a flash flood of members threatened to drown Debs and the two other full-time organizers. Within twenty days, thirty-four lodges had been chartered. Members were joining at the rate of two hundred to four hundred men a day. Entire lodges of Railway Carmen and Switchmen changed their affiliation to the ARU. Conductors, firemen, even engineers, joined the new industrial union. But most of the applicants were previously unorganized men in the less skilled crafts who had been excluded from the Brotherhoods. These were the engine wipers, the section hands, the most exploited and worst paid men on the railroads, who had formerly been left to suffer in isolation. Now they rushed toward the organization that had opened its ranks to them, rushed so eagerly that the ARU had eighty-seven local lodges by mid-November: for three months, a new lodge every day. The surge continued over the winter, and in the spring of 1894 it was vastly accelerated when the ARU won the first strike that any union had ever won against a major railroad.

James J. Hill's Great Northern Railroad stretched westward from Minneapolis clear to the Pacific. When its employees went on strike in April, direction of the walk-out quickly passed into the hands of Debs and his colleagues. After the entire line had been closed down nearly a fortnight, the St. Paul Chamber of Commerce demanded that

Hill and the union should submit the dispute to arbitration. They did so. The award gave the strikers 97½ percent of their demands, an aggregate wage increase of $1,752,000 a year.

Although this victory was won in the Twin Cities, it was widely publicized in Chicago, where the ARU centered in many ways. Its national headquarters were there. Most of its local lodges were on roads running from Chicago westward. And it was there that Debs gave a fervent speech at the Columbian Exposition. It was in the autumn of 1893, before the dreadful winter at Pullman, and Debs did not mention George Pullman by name, but his speech contained an unqualified attack on Pullman's type of paternalism:

> The time is coming, fortunately, when we are hearing less of that old paternal Pharisaism: "What can we do for labor?" It is the old, old query repeated all along the centuries, heard wherever a master wielded a whip above the bowed forms of the slaves . . . We hear it yet, occasionally, along lines of transportation, in mines and shops, but our ears are regaled by a more manly query, . . . which is, "What can labor do for itself?" The answer is not difficult. Labor can organize, it can unify, it can consolidate its forces. This done, it can demand and command.

And in the spring of 1894, at the time of the victory over the Great Northern, the workers in the Pullman shops began to take Debs's advice. They were eligible for membership in the ARU because the Pullman Company operated a few miles of railroad leading to its shops, and, man by man, they joined. Their money was gone, and their patience with it. One blacksmith, when he worked six hours and was paid 45 cents, said that if he had to starve, he saw no reason why he should wear out his clothes at Pullman's anvil at the same time.

The workers went to the vice-president of the company and presented their demands. The official promised to investigate. The grievance committee held a meeting. Even though the top officials of the ARU urged delay, the committee voted a strike. Of the 3,300 workers in the factory, more than 90 percent walked out together on May 11. The company promptly laid off the others. Three days later, Eugene Debs was in Pullman. He had advised against the strike. But after walking through the town, hearing the stories, seeing the paychecks, he realized that it had been an act of desperation. Even the local leader of the strike said that they did not expect to win. They just didn't know what else to do.

The strike dragged along until June 12, when the first national convention of the American Railway Union met in Chicago. In one year, the organization had enrolled 150,000 members. The total membership of all the Brotherhoods was 90,000. But success had not gone to Debs's head. He knew that the union was loosely organized, that it was largely uncoordinated, that it had little money, that it was scanted for experienced leaders, especially in the farflung local lodges. The ARU had won its battle against the Great Northern; Debs was not sure it could win another against an equally powerful corporation.

A committee from Pullman appeared before the convention and made a plea: "We struck because we were without hope. We joined the American Railway Union because it gave us a glimmer of hope. . . . We will make you proud of us, brothers, if you will give us the hand we need. Help us make our country better and more wholesome." A seamstress at Pullman, thin and tired, came to tell how, when her father died, she had been forced to repay $60 back rent that he owed the company.

The sentimental delegates were swept by indignation. One suggested that the convention declare a boycott of Pullman cars. Debs, who was presiding, refused to entertain the motion. Using every recourse available to a chairman to thwart actions that he disapproves, Debs suggested a committee from the convention to confer with the Pullman Company. Twelve men, including six strikers, were chosen to go to the company and propose arbitration of the wage dispute.

The committee returned next day to the convention, to report that the Pullman Company had refused to confer with any members of the ARU. Again a boycott was proposed. Again Debs blocked it. A second committee, consisting solely of strikers, was sent to the company with a request for arbitration. The company said that there was "nothing to arbitrate." After voting relief funds for the strikers at Pullman, the convention set up another committee to recommend a plan of action. When the recommendation came on June 22, it was direct: Unless the Pullman Company agreed, not to a settlement, but merely to begin negotiations within four days, the American Railway Union should refuse to handle Pullman cars. Again Debs urged caution. But the delegates, in no humor for pussyfooting, adopted the committee's report.

Then the committee was sent back to Pullman for a final effort. The firm would concede nothing. Nothing. Its position was that wages and working conditions should be determined by management, with no interference by labor. So the ARU convention unanimously voted the boycott. Debs, his hand forced, devised the tactic: switchmen in the ARU would refuse to switch any Pullman cars onto trains. If the switchmen were discharged or disciplined for this refusal, all ARU members on the line would cease work at once.

III

The boycott began at noon on June 26. At once the union was opposed by the railroads, which took an active hand in the conflict. Here was their chance to cut the ARU down to size. Unified by the General Managers Association, the twenty-four railroads running out of Chicago—with a combined capital of $818 million, with 221,000 employees—declared that their contracts with Pullman were sacred and that they would operate no trains without Pullman cars.

Deadlock. By June 29, twenty railroads were tied up. An estimated 125,000 men had quit work. Agents of the General Managers were busy in Eastern cities hiring unemployed railroaders as strikebreakers. Leaders of the Railroad Brotherhoods were denouncing the ARU. Eugene Debs was sending telegrams all over the Great Plains advising his members to use no violence and to stop no trains forcibly; they should simply refuse to handle Pullmans. But the Illinois Central claimed that its property at Cairo, Illinois, was in danger, so Governor Altgeld, with the permission of the local authorities, sent three companies of the state militia there. A crowd stopped a train at Hammond, Indiana, and forced the crew to detach two Pullmans. Two other trains were temporarily stopped by mobs in Chicago. But there were no major riots. No mail had accumulated in Chicago. As late as July 5, total strike damages to railroad property were less than $6,000.

But the facts were being misrepresented. The Federal district attorney in Chicago wired Washington on June 29 that conditions there were so bad that special deputies were needed. The newspapers were hysterical, with headlines like "Mob Is In Control" and "Law Is Trampled On." The real cause of concern was stated by the Chicago *Herald*: "If the strike should be successful the owners of the railroad property . . . would have to surrender its future control to the class of labor agitators and strike conspirators who have formed the Debs Railway Union." It became common for the press to refer to "Dictator Debs."

Then the Federal government took a hand. On June 30 the General Managers telegraphed Richard B. Olney, Attorney General of the United States, urging him to appoint Edwin Walker as special Federal attorney to handle the strike situation. Walker had been since 1870, and was, at the time of the strike, attorney for a railroad that belonged to the General Managers. But Olney didn't even pause to consult the Federal district attorney on the spot before making the appointment.

Olney, a man as tyrannical as George Pullman, also sent Walker some pointed advice: that the best way to cope with conditions was "by a force which is overwhelming and prevents any attempt at resistance." Olney believed that a national railroad strike was illegal by definition, and that the local and state officials in Illinois could not be trusted to handle matters. In his judgment, the strikers were impeding interstate commerce and the movement of the United States mails. On either score President Cleveland could have used the Federal army to remove the obstructions. But Olney doubted that Cleveland would act except to enforce the order of a Federal court. So the thing to do was to get such an order.

On July 2 in Chicago, Edwin Walker and the Federal district attorney drafted an application for an injunction against the strike leaders. They were aided in its revision, before court opened, by Judges Peter Grosscup and William A. Woods. Satisfied at last, the two judges ascended their impartial bench and granted the application. The breadth of their order was breathtaking: the strike leaders were enjoined from any deed to encourage the boycott. They could not send telegrams about it, or talk about it, or write about it.

If the ARU leaders obeyed the injunction, the boycott would collapse; central coordination was essential. But if they did not obey it, all strikers would be in active opposition to the Federal government, and the leaders might well go to jail for contempt of court. Debs and his colleagues decided to ignore the writ. Debs declared bitterly, "The crime of the American Railway Union was the practical exhibition of sympathy for the Pullman employees." Sympathy was Christian, but practical sympathy was dangerous.

The Attorney General's plan worked out well. If the injunction was sweeping, enforcement of it was more so. An ARU official later testified: "Men have been arrested in Chicago because they refused to turn switches when told to; they were arrested when they refused to get on an engine and fire an engine." So by interpretation, the injunction forbade action by an individual as well as by the group, and required action in addition to forbidding it.

Olney hit a snag when he first proposed sending Federal troops to Chicago: the Secretary of War and the Army Chief of Staff both opposed it. But on July 3 he received a telegram saying that no agency but the army could protect the mails. There was no proof of the statement, but the telegram was signed by Judge Grosscup, Edwin Walker, and the Federal district attorney in Chicago. Now Grover Cleveland was ready to move. On the morning of Independence Day, by his orders, the entire command from Fort Sheridan turned out for active duty in Chicago.

The ARU was incensed. So was Governor Altgeld. The Constitution gives the President power to send the army into a state "on Application of the Legislature, or of the Executive (when the Legislature cannot be convened)" in order to protect the state "against domestic Violence." Altgeld protested to the President that neither he nor the legislature had asked for help. Three regiments of state militia in Chicago could be mustered into active service, but "nobody in Cook county, whether official or private citizen," had asked for their help. The local and state authorities were adequate to what little violence had occurred. "At present some of our railroads are paralyzed," Altgeld told the President, "not by reason of obstruction, but because they cannot get men to operate their trains. . . . The newspaper accounts have in many cases been pure fabrications, and in others wild exaggerations." Lastly, Altgeld protested that "local self-government is a fundamental principle of our Constitution. Each community shall govern itself so long as it can and is ready and able to enforce the law."

The President's reply was brief. He wired back that the postal authorities had asked for the removal of obstructions to the mails, that Judge Grosscup had asked for help in enforcing the injunction, and that there was "competent proof that conspiracies existed against commerce between the states." Any of these conditions, Cleveland contended, was ample to give him power to order Federal troops into Illinois.

Altgeld reasserted his position forcibly and at length. The President closed the discussion curtly: "While I am still persuaded that I have neither transcended my authority nor duty in the emergency that confronts us, it seems to me that in this hour of danger and public distress, discussion may well give way to active efforts on the part of all in authority to restore obedience to law and to protect life and property."

Although Governor Altgeld had to yield to the power of the army, similar protests were made by the governors of four other states. And the dispute between state and Federal officials served to underscore an issue that was not merely constitutional; it was political and ethical also. Even assuming that the President had properly enforced the law as it existed at the time, his action seemed grossly partisan. The full thrust of Federal power was exerted to break the boycott, while nothing was done—nothing was said—to incline George Pullman or the railroads toward a peaceful settlement. Eugene Debs spoke for a sizable group when he telegraphed the President that a "deep-seated conviction is fast becoming prevalent that this Government is soon to be declared a military despotism." This issue of public policy could be resolved only at the ballot boxes and in the convention halls, and in 1896 John Peter Altgeld was to get his revenge against Grover Cleveland.

But for the time the army ruled—along with five thousand special Federal deputy marshals. Since these temporary jobs were unattractive to most men, they were filled by petty criminals, labor spies, riff-raff generally. Local officials told of special deputies who fired without reason into crowds, wantonly killed bystanders, stole property from railroad cars, cut fire hoses while cars burned. The result was chaos.

On July 5, the day after the army reached Chicago, violence there was more serious than before. The next day it reached its peak; railroad tracks were blocked, dozens of railroad cars were burned—a crime for which nobody was ever indicted. Total damage in the one day was $340,000, although on no other day was it more than $4,000. If the army and special deputies were meant to keep the peace, their immediate effect was just the opposite.

Eugene Debs, continuing his efforts to prevent violence, again told the strikers: "Our men have the right to quit, but their right ends there. Other men have the right to take their places, whatever the opinion of the propriety of so doing may be. Keep away from railroad yards, or right of way, or other places where large crowds congregate. A safe plan is to remain away entirely from places where there is any likelihood of an outbreak." Debs repeatedly argued that the rioting was being done by hooligans, not by strikers. During the entire boycott, not a single ARU number in Chicago was killed or wounded by the law-enforcement authorities.

The outbreak of violence was distressing; the propaganda about it was chilling. In Chicago, headlines read:

Unparalleled Scenes of Riot, Terror and Pillage
Anarchy is Rampant
THIRSTY FOR BLOOD
Frenzied Mob Still Bent on Death and Destruction
Violence on Every Hand

Newspapers and ministers charged that Debs was a dipsomaniac. A Brooklyn cleric declared: "The soldiers must use their guns. They must shoot to kill." One of the most prominent religious leaders in the country revived the themes of a year earlier by calling Governor Altgeld the "crowned hero and worshiped deity of the Anarchists of the Northwest."

On July 10, with the boycott obviously on its last legs, a Federal grand jury in Chicago delivered another blow by indicting Debs and three of his colleagues for conspiracy to obstruct a mail train on the Rock Island Railroad. Arrested at once, the four men were released on bail within a few hours, but their freedom made little practical difference. The next day trains were moving even in California, where the boycott had been most effective. The mayors of Chicago and Detroit made a futile call on the vice-president of the Pullman Company to again request arbitration. They found him unyielding. "The issue at question, which was simply that of reopening the shops at Pullman, and carrying them on at a ruinous loss, was not a proper subject for arbitration," he was reported to have said.

The boycott dragged along another week, while at Pullman the leader of the original strikers announced that they were being starved into submission. Then, on July 17, Debs and his associates were again arrested, this time for violating the July 2 injunction. They refused to post bail and were imprisoned. Twenty-four hours later a notice was put up on the gates of the Pullman shops: "These gates will be opened as soon as the number of operatives is sufficient to make a working force in all departments." It was the end.

Of the men now hired at Pullman, one of every four had not worked there before the strike. Every applicant was forced to sign a pledge that he would not join any union. A thousand former employees were left destitute. Governor Altgeld appealed to the Pullman Company to help them. He got no reply. Altgeld then called upon the public for a relief fund. Even the Chicago *Tribune* cooperated in raising it.

In January, 1895, the ARU leaders were brought to trial on the conspiracy charges. For nearly a month their lawyers, Clarence Darrow and S. S. Gregory, used the proceedings as a forum to indict the prosecution. Eugene Debs, seeming very much a benign and immaculate businessman, testified at length about his career on the railroads. Leaders of the General Managers were called to the stand, where they could "not remember" what had happened at their meetings. Then a juror became ill. After four days Judge Grosscup discharged the jury and continued the case until May. It was never reopened.

But Debs went to jail anyway, for six months, for having violated the injunction. The case went all the way to the United States Supreme Court, where the union leaders were represented by Darrow, Gregory, and the aging Lyman Trumbull. The Court decision virtually ignored the Sherman Act, on which the injunction had been based.

Instead the Court unanimously ruled that the equity powers of Federal courts could be used to prevent interference with the mails and with interstate commerce. An injunction, regardless of the validity of its provisions, must be obeyed. Violation could be punished by a jail sentence. And it was.

IV

The end of the boycott did not end the shouting and pondering about what it had meant. President Samuel Gompers of the American Federation of Labor, in sending Debs a contribution to his legal defense, said the money was intended "as a protest against the exercise of class justice, and as a further protest against the violation of rights guaranteed by the Constitution and the Declaration of Independence." In opposition to this was the New York *Tribune,* which charged that Debs was a self-seeking dictator and warned the working people against "surrendering their liberty and prosperity into the hands of a single individual."

A Federal investigating commission appointed by President Cleveland, after hearing testimony from railroad officials, strikers, union leaders, public servants, denounced Pullman's refusal to arbitrate the dispute. The report urged compulsory arbitration as insurance against future strikes on the railroads. Ultimate responsibility for the Pullman boycott, said the commission, "rests with the people themselves and with the government for not adequately controlling monopolies and corporations, and for failing to reasonably protect the rights of labor and redress its wrongs."

Four years later another governmental body, the supreme court of Illinois, passed judgment on one element in the situation that had led to the Pullman strike. Holding that the corporation had no right under its charter to construct the town of Pullman, the court ordered the Pullman Company to dispose of all property not required for its manufacturing activities. Company towns such as this, said the court, were "opposed to good public policy and incompatible with the theory and spirit of our institutions."

The poet Eugene Field, a Chicago newspaperman during the strike, was concerned with the characters of the men involved: "If ye be ill, or poor, or starving, or oppressed, or in grief, your chances for sympathy and for succor from E. V. Debs are 100 where your chances with G. M. Pullman would be the little end of nothing whittled down."

But it was left for Jane Addams, in a speech before the Chicago Woman's Club, to give the most searching interpretation of "the shocking experiences of that summer, the barbaric instinct to kill, roused on both sides, the sharp division into class lines with the resultant distrust and bitterness." All this, she declared, could be endured only if it resulted in some "great ethical lesson."

Like Eugene Field, she was impressed by "the manifestation of moral power" in the efforts of the American Railway Union to aid the strikers at Pullman, men who had done nothing to help the union but were helped by it. Here was evidence that the workingmen were beginning to act on new watchwords: "brotherhood, sacrifice, the subordination of individual and trade interests to the good of the working class." Nor was George Pullman open to indiscriminate condemnation. His standard for treatment of his employees, "exceptionally liberal in many of its aspects," had been close to the ideal of "the best of the present employers." Pullman had manifested that ideal more fully than the others. "He alone gave his men so model a town, such perfect surroundings." His policies, in fact, had seemed to many businessmen a case of intemperate sympathy for the lower classes.

But Pullman had been utterly blind to the "touch of nobility" in the ARU sympathetic boycott. He could recognize nothing as virtuous except the individualism that he had learned in his youth, the ruthless self-reliance that had brought him to the top of the heap. And ironically, he had actually succeeded in teaching part of that morality to his employees at Pullman, so that throughout the strike they were "self-controlled and destroyed no property."

Pullman's failure, then, was the failure of an ideal. The magnitude of his indulgence was watched by the magnitude of the disaster it engendered. He was—and here Jane Addams took her title—"A Modern Lear." King Lear too was lavish in his gifts. Only he had kingdoms to give, and he gave them. But he demanded from everybody the acknowledgment that all gifts flowed from him. He insisted on his right to do things for people, and denied them the right to do things for themselves. He demanded the right for his will to impose itself on others.

Similarly George Pullman, insisting on his right to be a benefactor, had grown away from "the power of attaining a simple human relationship with his employees, that of frank equality with them." Pullman had ceased to be a part of "the great moral life springing from our common experiences," and by setting himself above the common run of men he had done an immense amount of harm. He had failed to sense "that the social passion of the age is directed toward the emancipation of the wage-worker; that a great accumulation of moral force is overmastering men and making for this emancipation as in another time it made for the emancipation of the slave; that nothing will satisfy the aroused conscience of men short of the complete participation of the working classes in the spiritual, intellectual and material inheritance of the human race."

But in this noble effort the workingmen must not become selfish or vindictive. The story of King Lear holds a lesson for them, too. At the beginning of the play Cordelia seeks her salvation alone. She demands her right to be herself, but her vision is not broad enough to include her father. By the time her conscience has reached out to enfold the blinded Lear, "the cruelty and wrath" had become "objective and tragic." Only then, on their way to prison and probable death, do Lear and Cordelia find salvation together. The Pullman strike should be a warning that "the emancipation of the working people will have to be inclusive of the employer from the first or it will encounter many failures, cruelties and reactions."

Jane Addams called on all would-be philanthropists to remember "the old definition of greatness: that it consists in the possession of the largest share of the common human qualities and experiences, not in the acquirements of peculiarities and excessive virtues." The greatest of all Americans was the man who had gathered to himself "the largest amount of American experience": Abraham Lincoln. Seeking to draw out the vital center of Lincoln's life, Jane Addams concluded:

> The man who insists upon consent, who moves with the people, is bound to consult the feasible right as well as the absolute right. He is often obliged to attain only Mr. Lincoln's "best possible," and often have the sickening sense of compromising with his best convictions. He has to move along with

those whom he rules toward a goal that neither he nor they see very clearly until they come to it. He has to discover what people really want, and then "provide the channels in which the growing moral force of their lives shall flow." What he does attain, however, is not the result of his individual striving, as a solitary mountain climber beyond the sight of the valley multitude, but it is underpinned and upheld by the sentiments and aspirations of many others. Progress has been slower perpendicularly, but incomparably greater because lateral.

4

The East European Jewish Migration

LEONARD DINNERSTEIN

• Jews have been in the United States since 1654. By 1790 they numbered perhaps 1,200 and sixty years later about 15,000. Spread thinly throughout the land they had little difficulty finding a place for themselves in the greater society and were accepted as individuals or in small groups. During the middle of the nineteenth century Jews from the German states of Europe entered the United States along with Protestant and Catholic Germans and they, too, were absorbed easily. By the 1880s, however, East European Jews started coming in the hundreds of thousands. A changing industrial society, Pan-Slavism, and continual pogroms proved too difficult a combination to combat, especially while opportunities existed in the United States.

The colonial Jews—mostly Sephardim from the Iberian Peninsula and Brazil—settled mainly in the port cities of Newport, New York, Philadelphia, Charleston, and Savannah and engaged in shopkeeping and mercantile activities. Many chose to assimilate into the dominant community, married gentiles, and raised their children as Christians. The Jews who were a part of the mid-nineteenth-century influx also gravitated toward cities but they did not remain exclusively in the East. Many a Jew put a pack on his back, traveled in different sections of the country, and finally settled down in places as different as Greenville, Mississippi; Boise, Idaho; Columbus, New Mexico; Cleveland; Atlanta; Dallas; and Los Angeles. Other Jews, however, went directly to New York, Cincinnati, Chicago, Philadelphia, and Detroit, and immediately set down roots. As a result, the families of the mid-nineteenth-century Jewish migration were spread throughout the United States. They, too, engaged in the traditional commercial activities usually associated with Jews, but they also had children who were trained for the professions. The German Jews achieved a level of prosperity well above those of other ethnic groups. In 1890, when the majority of American Jews were still of Sephardic or German extraction, the Hebrew community was considerably more prosperous than the national average. Two thirds of all Jewish families in the United States had at least one servant, while over ninety percent of the American population failed to earn enough money to maintain a family in moderate circumstances. But the massive influx of Eastern European Jews, most of them poor, was already operating to lower the aggregate wealth of American Jewry to the point where this ethnic minority became collectively an underprivileged group.

The new migrants differed in several ways from their predecessors. They came in the hundreds of thousands and could not disappear into the American population with relatively little notice. They were also more Orthodox in religion, bizarre in dress, and determined to settle in Jewish enclaves and perpetuate Orthodox customs. They also tended to concentrate in a few localities. More than seventy percent remained in New York City and the surrounding area. They threatened the security of the Americanized Jews who had already moved into the middle class and who feared, correctly, that the newcomers might stimulate waves of overt anti-Semitism in the United States which would victimize all of the Jews.

Most knew how to read and write Hebrew or Yiddish, and the men had some urban and vocational skills. But the opportunities originally available to them were as unskilled or semiskilled laborers, and for years they were plagued with poverty and occupied cheap tenements on New York's Lower East Side.

The story of their experiences, and ultimate accomplishments, is discussed in the following selection.

INTRODUCTION

Jewish migration to the United States in the nineteenth and twentieth
centuries may be divided into three groups: the German, the East
European, and the Central European. During the first period of heavy
Jewish immigration to the United States, mainly during the pre-Civil
War years but roughly from the 1840s through the 1870s, about
50,000 Jews arrived from the German states. They engaged almost exclusively in trade and commerce, many starting off as peddlers and
some moving up quickly into banking and department stores. The
second and most important wave, from the 1870s through 1924, came
primarily from Eastern Europe. Responding to the economic uprooting of society and the frequent pogroms of the late nineteenth and
early twentieth centuries, more than 2,000,000 Jews left Russia, Galicia,
Rumania, and Hungary for the great trek to the United States. These
people included artisans, skilled workers, small merchants, and shopkeepers. They and their descendants have made the greatest impact of
all the Jews in the United States and are the subject of this essay. The
third group, from Central Europe, numbering about 365,000, came to
America between 1925 and 1953, with approximately 132,000 in the
years between 1948 and 1953. Some of these people emigrated for
economic reasons, but the overwhelming majority were victims of
Hitler's rise to power in Germany. In the 1930s Nazi persecutions and
brutalities forced many German Jews to leave the country, and after
the Second World War some concentration camp victims and the displaced refugees were granted opportunities to resettle in the United
States. This third group quickly moved into the Jewish mainstream in
the United States. They made major impacts in the American scientific
and intellectual communities.

Before the Second World War these Jewish groups were quite different and easily identifiable: by income, education, jobs, residence,
and organized associations. In the past twenty-five years, however, the
differences have diminished considerably because of a vast leap in both
educational and income levels of American-born Jews. It would be

quite difficult, if not impossible, today to distinguish among the descendants of the previous generations of Jewish immigrants. In terms of life style, occupation, and income the overwhelming majority of Jewish families are in the middle and upper middle class and their breadwinners occupy professional, technical, and managerial positions.

CAUSES FOR EMIGRATION

The Jews left Eastern Europe for much the same reason that most other peoples left their states—grinding poverty at home made them yearn for a decent life elsewhere. In Russia 94 percent of the Jews lived in the "pale of settlement," a huge belt of land in Western and Southwestern Russia and the Ukraine stretching from the Baltic to the Black Sea. Jews could live outside of this area only by special permission. Within the pale their population increased from 1,000,000 in 1800 to 4,000,000 in 1880 and this expansion constricted the possibilities of economic opportunities. In Rumania they were regarded as aliens, while in Galicia Jews suffered from economic boycotts and other manifestations of hostility.

During the 1870s the industrial revolution began to make a significant impact in Russia. That impact was greatest within the pale, where industrialization took place most rapidly. The Russian government, which had earlier set numerous restrictions on Jews, feared their influence, especially after industrialization began. Jews actively engaged in trade and commerce, which attracted many of the gentiles once they were forced off the land. Competition for positions in a tight economy heightened Christian-Jewish tensions. Industrialization also stimulated the movements of Jews and gentiles from rural to urban areas to seek employment. The city of Lodz, which had eleven Jews in 1797, counted 98,677 one hundred years later and 166,628 in 1910. Warsaw's Jewish population leaped from 3,521 in 1781, to 219,141 in 1891. Industrial expansion also led to a major flight of people to the west. Many Jews went to Germany, France, and England in Europe, and to Argentina, Canada, South Africa, and Palestine. More than 90 percent of the Jewish migrants, however, wound up in the United States.

Other factors also propelled the Jewish exodus. As in the case of emigrants from other nations, flight was impelled by specific items like the unsuccessful Polish uprising of 1863, the Lithuanian famine of 1867–69, the Polish cholera epidemic of 1869, and by the predisposition of young people to try their fortunes in a new world, and the developing political ideologies of Zionism and socialism which made traditional modes of thought and behavior too confining. Many Jews were outspoken socialists. They envisioned a new democratic social order with a more equitable distribution of the nation's wealth and resources. Anti-Semitism, which rose in intensity as Pan-Slavism gripped the Eastern Europeans, however, provided a unique reason for the Jewish migration. Jews were not Slavs and therefore stood as an impediment toward nationalistic unity. The assassination of Tsar Alexander II of Russia in 1881 by a group of socialists spawned a wave of pogroms against the Jews which continued intermittently until the First World War. Major pogroms occurred in 1881, 1882, 1903, and 1906, and hundreds of others have been recorded. These pogroms, often inspired by government officials, resulted in wanton and brutal assaults upon Jews and their property. Russia also codified and curtailed Jewish rights after Tsar Alexander's assassination. The May Laws of 1882 restricted the numbers of Jews that might attend Russian universities and the kinds of occupations Jews might pursue. They could not rent or own land outside of the towns and cities nor could they keep their shops open on the Christian sabbath or on Christian holidays.

American letters and money sent by earlier immigrants, along with the advertisements from railroad and steamship lines anxious to transport emigrants, further stimulated migration from Eastern Europe to the New World. Promising economic conditions in the United States, combined with increased persecutions and deprivations in Russia, Galicia, and Rumania, expanded the exodus to the West, as revealed in the following figures:

1870s: 40,000
1880s: 200,000+
1890s: 300,000 |
1900-14: 1,500,000+

PATTERNS OF SETTLEMENT

Over 90 percent of the more than 2,000,000 Jews who left Eastern Europe between 1870 and 1924 went to the United States. Unlike many other immigrant groups, the Jews mostly traveled with their families. During the years 1899 to 1910, females made up 43.4 percent of the total number of Jewish immigrants and children 24.7 percent, the highest figure for any arriving peoples. During the same period males constituted 95.1 percent of the Greek immigrants and 78.6 percent of the southern Italians. Only the Irish had a larger percentage of females than the Jews (52.1 percent), but it is believed that many of them came alone to work as domestics. Statistical estimates indicate that 71.6 percent of the Jews came from the Russian empire, including Latvia, Lithuania, and Poland; 17.6 percent from Galicia in the Polish area of the Austro-Hungarian empire; and 4.3 percent from Rumania.

Most of these people landed, and remained, in New York City. In 1870 the city's Jewish population had been estimated at 80,000; in 1915 almost 1,400,000 Jews lived there. The newcomers found friends, relatives, jobs, and educational opportunities in New York City, and, in any case, few had the money to travel elsewhere. Moreover, the Orthodox knew that they could find *kosher* butchers which would allow them to maintain Jewish dietary laws, and jobs where they would not have to work on the sabbath. To be sure, those who landed in Boston, Philadelphia, or Baltimore, or even those who made their way to Chicago and other cities, found small Jewish communities in which they could settle. Chicago, in fact, had 200,000 Jews by 1912. But the major center, by far, for East European Jews was New York.

Most of the immigrants who chose to live in New York City settled originally in a small section of Manhattan Island known as the Lower East Side. The boundaries of this ghetto lay roughly within the blocks bordered by Fourteenth Street, Third Avenue and the Bowery, Canal Street, and the East River. The heart of the district, the tenth ward, housed 523.6 people per acre at the beginning of the twentieth century. In the 1890s Jacob Riis, an enterprising reporter, observed that "nowhere in the world are so many people crowded together on a square mile" as in the Jewish quarter. Within the Lower East Side numerous subdivisions could be identified as streets housing primarily Russian, Galician, Rumanian, or Hungarian Jews. The area contained 75 percent of New York City's Jews in 1892, 50 percent in 1903, and 23 percent in 1916.

The tenements where the Jews lived can best be described as dark, dank, and unhealthful. One magazine described the dwellings in 1888 as great prison-like structures of brick, with narrow doors and windows, cramped passages and steep rickety stairs. They are built through from one street to the other with a somewhat narrower building connecting them. . . . The narrow courtyard . . . in the middle is a damp foul-smelling place, supposed to do duty as an airshaft; had the foul fiend designed these great barracks they could not have been more villainously arranged to avoid any chance of ventilation. . . . In case of fire they would be perfect death-traps, for it would be impossible for the occupants of the crowded rooms to escape by the narrow stairways, and the flimsy fire-escapes which the owners of the tenements were compelled to put up a few years ago are so laden with broken furniture, bales and boxes that they would be worse than useless. In the hot summer months . . . these fire-escape balconies are used as sleeping-rooms by the poor wretches who are fortunate enough to have windows opening upon them. The drainage is horrible, and even the Croton as it flows from the tap in the noisome courtyard, seemed to be contaminated by its surroundings and have a fetid smell.

Two families on each tenement floor shared a toilet. In the summer months the heat and stench in these places were unbearable and the stagnant air outside provided little relief.

The first Jewish immigrants, despite their toil, earned barely enough to subsist on. As a result it was not uncommon to find parents, children, other relatives, and some boarders in a two-, three-, or four-room apartment. The boarder may have paid three dollars a month for his room and free coffee, but that came to 30 percent of the family's ten-dollars-a-month rent. Looking back, the prices of four cents for a quart of milk, two cents for a loaf of bread, and twelve cents for a pound of kosher meat may look ridiculously cheap, but when one reckons this on an average weekly income of less than eight dollars, the picture is quite different.

Fortunately for the Jews, their earnings increased sufficiently after a few years in this country so that they did not have to rot in the slums for an interminable period. "It was judged to be a ten-year trek," Moses Rischin tells us, from Hester Street, on the Lower East Side, to Lexington Avenue, in the more fashionable uptown area. The tenements, of course, did not disappear, but their inhabitants continually changed.

Most of the immigrant Jews from Eastern Europe resided first on the Lower East Side and the Hebrew population in that area of the city peaked at more than half a million in 1910; by the 1920s fewer than ten percent of New York's Jews still lived there. The completion of the subways in the early part of the century opened up vast tracts for settlement in upper Manhattan, Brooklyn, and the Bronx (other boroughs of New York City), and the Jewish working class, anxious and able to take up residence in better neighborhoods, moved away.

Jewish immigrants in Boston, Chicago, and other large cities had initial experiences similar to those who remained in New York. In most other places where Jews went, the tenement areas were smaller or nonexistent, the neighborhoods less congested, and the opportunities to live in more healthful surroundings considerably better. East European Jews who went south or west had experiences considerably different from their brethren who went to the urban areas of the Northeast and Chicago, but they constituted fewer than five percent of the entire migration.

Over the years the children and grandchildren of the newcomers moved out of these cities to surrounding suburban areas or flourishing new communities where economic opportunities beckoned. Most of the subsequent growth in the American Jewish population took place in the states closest to New York: Pennsylvania, New Jersey, and Connecticut, with two major and a few minor exceptions. After World War II job opportunities and a pleasant year-round climate drew hundreds of thousands of Jews to California, especially the Los Angeles area, and many older people first visited and then retired in Miami Beach, Florida. The growth of the Jewish population in California and Florida is primarily a phenomenon of the past thirty years.

LABOR AND BUSINESS

East European Jewish immigrants differed from most of the other foreign-born arrivals in the late nineteenth and early twentieth centuries in that 95 percent of them came from urban rather than rural areas. Their urban origins resulted in the development of skills and talents which would aid them greatly in the United States. An 1898 survey of the Russian pale of settlement found that Jews owned one third of all the factories in the area and that Jewish workers concentrated in the clothing (254,384), metal-working (43,499), wood-working (42,-

525), building (39,019), textile (34,612), and tobacco (7,856) industries. The skills they acquired there were also in demand when they reached the United States.

An American survey of the occupations of immigrants entering the United States between 1899 and 1910 listed 67.1 percent of the Jewish workers as skilled compared with a general figure of 20.2 percent for all newcomers. In his study, *The Promised City*, Moses Rischin indicates that

> Jews ranked first in 26 out of 47 trades tabulated by the Immigration Commission, comprising an absolute majority in 8. They constituted 80 per cent of the hat and cap makers, 75 per cent of the furriers, 68 per cent of the watchmakers and milliners and 55 per cent of the cigarmakers and tinsmiths. They totaled 30 to 50 per cent of the immigrants classified as tanners, turners, undergarment makers, jewelers, painters, glaziers, dressmakers, photographers, saddle-makers, locksmiths, butchers, and metal workers in other than iron and steel. They ranked first among immigrant printers, bakers, carpenters, cigar-packers, blacksmiths, and building trades workmen.

In the United States the Jewish immigrants found jobs in distilleries or printing, tobacco, and building trades, while significant numbers of others started out as butchers, grocers, newspaper dealers, or candy store operators.

The majority of the Jewish immigrants, however, found work in the needle trades, which were—because of the increasingly efficient methods of mass production and the existence of a mass market—undergoing rapid expansion. The arrival of the East Europeans with their particular talents coincided with this vast growth. By the end of the nineteenth century Jews had just about displaced the Germans and Irish from the industry. In New York City the development of the clothing industry transformed the economy. In 1880 major clothing manufacturers numbered only 1,081, or 10 percent of the city's factories, and employed 64,669 people, or 28 percent of the city's work force. By 1910 the borough of Manhattan (which before the consolidation of the five boroughs in 1898 had been New York City) had 11,172 clothing establishments, which constituted 47 percent of the city's factories. The industry employed 214,428 people, slightly more than 46 percent of Manhattan's workers. In 1890, 60 percent of the employed immigrant Jews worked in the garment industry and on the eve of the First World War more than half of all Jewish workers, and two thirds of Jewish wage earners, were still to be found in the industry. The Jewish influence was so great that the manufacturing of wearing apparel in the United States came to be regarded as a Jewish endeavor. Hebrews not only labored in the garment factories; they also worked their way up to supervisory positions and the bolder ones opened their own establishments. Before the Second World War it was estimated that Jews controlled 95 percent of the women's dress industry, 85 percent of the manufacturing of men's clothing, and 75 percent of the fur industry.

Initially, the owners were German Jews who at first looked down on their East European coreligionists and exploited their labor. Many of the early twentieth-century factories were nothing more than reconverted lofts and tenements or else small areas of workers' apartments. Many garments were actually finished in home sweatshops. Workdays lasting from 4:00 a.m. to 10:00 p.m. in these hovels were not uncommon, and wages averaged $6.00 to $10.00 a week for men and $3.00 to $5.00 for women. (Children also worked on these garments and in other industrial areas as well. Naturally, they earned lower wages than adults.) Because of the seasonal nature of the work, few had a steady yearly income. The annual wage of the average garment worker came to $376.23 in 1900, $1,222 in 1921, and $873.85 in 1930.

Low wages, appalling working conditions, and the insecurity of workers' positions prompted many to think about union organization. Among the Jewish immigrants were many socialists and members of the Russian Jewish Bund who had tried to improve social conditions in Europe. Many of these men also provided the backbone for unionization in the garment trades in the United States. The International Ladies' Garment Workers Union was founded in 1900 but not until the major strikes of clothing workers in 1909 and 1910 were significant victories won and the union firmly established. In Chicago 40,000 garment workers struck in 1910 and in New York 20,000 waist and dressmakers went out from November 1909 through February 1910. In July 1910 as many as 60,000 cloakmakers struck. The strikes attracted wide attention in the press, among social workers, and throughout the Jewish community. The workers won a victory when in July 1910 a "Protocols of Peace" set up a Board of Arbitration, a Board of Grievances, and a Board of Sanitary Control. Four years later the cloak-makers formed the core of the new Amalgamated Clothing Workers of America, a union which had its origins in Chicago with a less effective group, the United Garment Workers of America.

The International Ladies' Garment Workers and the Amalgamated were the two major Jewish unions in the United States. Because of the socialist heritage of so many of its participants, the two unions were concerned not only with improving labor conditions but with a vast program for improving the living conditions of all of its members. The unions were responsible for ending sweatshops, raising wages, and improving working conditions. They also pioneered in the development of a large number of auxiliary services for members. They built housing developments, established educational programs, maintained health centers, provided pensions, set up vacation resorts, developed a system of unemployment insurance benefits long before the state and federal governments assumed this responsibility, and opened banks giving services at significantly lower cost than other financial institutions. The Jewish unions, in sum, initiated social reforms which other labor organizations adopted. Aside from the ILGWU and the Amalgamated, the only other powerful labor union made up primarily of Jewish workers and leaders was the United Federation of Teachers (now the American Federation of Teachers) which galvanized New York City's schoolteachers in the 1960s and propelled its president Albert Shanker, to the forefront of labor leadership in America.

EDUCATION AND SOCIAL MOBILITY

Despite the benefits obtained by and from the labor unions, Jews had no desire to remain in the working class. Their ambition to "get ahead" knew no bounds and as soon as possible they, and/or their children, strove to move up to more lucrative and prestigious occupa tions. As early as 1900, American-born sons of Russian Jews constituted six times as many lawyers and seven times as many accountants as were to be found in their parents' generation but only one third the number of garment workers. As the years passed, this tendency became even more pronounced. Jewish workers also tried to become manufacturers. Many of those who started out as peddlers eventually moved into small retail outlets and some of the latter then expanded into larger emporiums. It was the rare community, in fact, that did not have some Jewish storekeepers. Random samplings in different decades through the 1940s showed anywhere from 31 to 63 percent of the Jews engaged in trade. In one study of the South the author noted, "It is said, 'If there is a Jewish holiday, you cannot buy a pair of socks in this whole country,' a remark which illustrates how complete the control of the retail dry-goods trade by Jews is supposed to be."

The entertainment industry also provided an avenue of advancement for some immigrant Jews. In 1905 it was estimated that half of the actors, popular songwriters, and song publishers in New York City were Jewish. Within a few years Jews also pioneered in the motion picture industry.

The Jews made great economic and social advances because educational and business opportunities were available to the more enterprising and because the masses of East European Jewish immigrants considered it necessary to "Americanize" their children and have them learn the language and customs of the new country as quickly as possible. From their beginnings in this country, the East European Jews also showed a passion for education and professional advancement unique in American history. Members of other immigrant groups, before or since, have not been as zealous in their quest for knowledge. The newcomers themselves were forced to do manual work, but whenever possible they encouraged their children to remain in school, attain an education, and move up in the world. As Samuel Gompers, leader of the American Federation of Labor, observed, "The Jews were fairly ravenous for education and eager for personal development. . . . All industrial work was merely a steppingstone to professional and managerial positions." Jewish parents wanted their children in high-status positions where they could operate on their own and not be subject to the bigotry of employers. Jewish boys strove to become doctors, lawyers, dentists, accountants, and teachers. They also opened pharmacies and other retail businesses. In these occupations Jewish parents felt their children would be both prosperous and independent at the same time. In 1903 it was estimated that Jews comprised about half of New York City's 5,000 to 6,000 physicians and thirty-four years later 65.7 percent of the city's lawyers and judges, 55.7 percent of its physicians, and 64 percent of its dentists. In the 1960s Jews still made up a majority of these professions in New York City.

Statistics of Jewish occupational categories for other cities are similar. By the 1930s only one third of all Jewish workers were still engaged in manual jobs while two thirds were in white-collar positions. The figures for non-Jews were just the reverse: two thirds in manual occupations, one third in white-collar jobs. Jews also moved into professional positions at a much faster rate and in much higher percentages than non-Jews. In the 1930s eighteen out of every 1,000 Jews in San Francisco were lawyers and judges, while sixteen were physicians. For every 1,000 gentiles the figures were five and five, respectively. Similarly, in Pittsburgh fourteen of every 1,000 Jews were lawyers and judges, thirteen were physicians, while the corresponding figures for non-Jews were five and four, respectively.

The tendency for Jews to seek and obtain the highest status positions in American society has not diminished in recent decades. In 1955, some 55 percent of all gainfully employed Jews, compared with 23 percent of non-Jews, had professional, technical, managerial, executive, or proprietary positions while in 1967, 51 percent of the Jews, compared to 23 percent of the Catholics and 21 percent of the Protestants in the United States were classified as professionals. Among younger Jewish adults the figures for professional occupations were even higher. With higher status occupations came higher incomes. In 1967 the Gallup Poll found that 69 percent of the Jews had incomes over $7,000 a year but only 47 percent of the Catholics and 38 percent of the Protestants claimed earnings of that level or higher. By 1971, 60 percent of the Jewish families where the head of the household was between thirty and fifty-nine years old had annual incomes exceeding $16,000.

But money alone does not tell the whole story. Since the end of World War II not only has there been an almost complete disappearance of Jewish young men in blue-collar jobs, but Jews in increasingly larger numbers have shunned retail businesses frequently owned by their fathers—to seek careers and greater personal satisfaction as journalists, writers, scientists, architects, engineers, and academics, as well as the traditional favorites of the Jewish immigrants: lawyers and physicians. Discouraged earlier by family preferences and gentile bigotry from seeking careers where they would have to be employed by others, the enormous expansion of opportunities in the 1950s and '60s made previously unheralded vocations or fields formerly difficult to enter more attractive and more accessible.

CULTURAL AND RELIGIOUS LIFE

The East European Jews, despite their poverty, arrived in this country with certain advantages. They had a strong commitment to a religion which rigidly dictated much of their daily behavior and gave their lives a structure and continuity which helped them to overcome problems of displacement in a new society. Moreover, unlike other immigrants to the United States who may have been poor at home but who otherwise "belonged," the Jews had been minorities wherever they had dwelled in Europe. As a result they had acquired a knowledge of how to move deftly among the dominant groups who, at best, tolerated them or, at worst, despised them. They had learned how to survive under a variety of hostile conditions and this experience served them well in the United States where they also had to struggle with adversity. Another important advantage that the Jews had brought with them can best be described as a middle-class view of life. They were ambitious, self-disciplined, and intellectually curious. A number of them had been socialists and participants in the revolutionary movement in Russia and Poland. Most had lived in small towns and villages and were attuned to what might now be considered the urban style of life.

The culture that the Jews brought with them to the United States survived in New York City. In recent decades attempts have been made to transplant it, as well, to Miami Beach and Los Angeles. In Boston, Chicago, and other cities where the Jews initially dwelled, they composed too small a percentage of the population to make much impact on the community. They may have had their own food stores and shared an affinity for literature, music, art, and religious observances, and perhaps even were more socialistically inclined than their neighbors, but in time their tastes and views blended with the dominant values of their respective communities, and today outside of the strongholds of the remnants of East European Jewish orthodoxy in New York, Chicago, Cleveland, Pittsburgh, Los Angeles, and Mi-

ami Beach, about the only thing left to distinguish Jews from everyone else in the United States is the Reform Temple.

In New York City, however, an East European Jewish culture flow-
ered for decades and still lends a distinctive tone to the life in this
vast metropolis. Cafés abounded where Jews would sit around and
shmooze (talk) for hours over cups of coffee or glasses of hot tea. "For
immigrant Jews," one chronicler reminds us, "talk was the breath of
life itself." Discussions during these get-togethers ranged over a wide
spectrum of topics and no one ever felt the necessity to refrain from
participation because of a limited knowledge of the topic under consideration. The cafés gave the Jewish East Side a flavor—"a Yiddish
Bohemia, poor and picturesque"—and their patrons included the most
intellectual and articulate Jewish actors, poets, playwrights, journalists,
and politicians of the day.

Jews also relaxed in the theater. The coming of the East European
Jews not only spawned a Yiddish theatre in the ghetto but also stimulated vaudeville and the Broadway stage. They also pioneered in the
radio industry and virtually founded the motion picture industry.

Jews throughout the United States have been known for their patronage of the arts and their interest in literary endeavors. Between
1885 and 1914, for example, over 150 Yiddish daily, weekly, monthly,
quarterly, and festival journals and yearbooks appeared in New York
City, including the daily *Forward* which is still published today. Cultural centers were established wherever sufficient numbers of Jews
congregated. Typically, the Cleveland Jewish Center had a gym, a
roof garden, a library, classes in Hebrew language and literature, a
scouting program, art classes, political forums, sewing and baking
clubs, etc.

Owners of art galleries and concert halls (about one third of whom
in New York City are Jewish) know that the larger a community's
Jewish population the more likely it will be that their showings and
musicales will be rewarded with large audiences. Jews are also heavily
represented in every aspect of radio and television production. They
purchase more books and attend more poetry readings than non-Jews
and have also been among the major book publishers in New York
City.

For the recent arrivals, however, the single most important cultural institution was the synagogue. Unlike the German Jews who came before them and worshiped, for the most part, in Reform temples barely distinguishable from Unitarian churches, the overwhelming proportion of the East Europeans maintained a devout orthodoxy during their first years in the United States. The numbers of synagogues proliferated in geometric proportion. In 1870 there were 189 Jewish congregations in the United States, the majority peopled by German Jews. By 1906 there were 1,769 and twenty years after that 3,118. In New York City alone the number of synagogues increased from 300 at the turn of the century to 1,200 in 1942. Usually these places of worship were no more than converted store fronts or private homes which came into being because one group of men had an argument with another group and then stormed out to find someplace else to pray. Since the end of World War II Americanized Jews have tended to worship in distinguished and substantial edifices but, aside from New York, Miami, and the four or five other cities in the country with large Jewish populations, it would be rare to find a community with even half a dozen Jewish temples or synagogues.

In the Jewish ghettos early in the twentieth century, shops closed on the Sabbath and the men and women, separated by curtains, prayed in the neighborhood synagogues. On the most holy days of the Jewish year, generally in September, 95 percent of the East European Jewish families went to the synagogue. As the Jewish immigrants and their children assimilated and Americanized, this percentage dwindled considerably. Although no statistics on high holy day attendance are available, it would be a safe guess to say that today the figure is at best 50 percent. All we can assert with accuracy, however, is that "all surveys of religious commitment, belief, and practice in the United States indicate that Jews are much less involved in religious activities than Protestants, who are in turn less active than Catholics." Nevertheless, it is still true today that the New York City public schools are closed for the major Jewish holidays because Jews constitute a majority of the teachers and their absence would create severe administrative headaches. Furthermore, on the Jewish holidays many of the city's businesses are closed, restaurants in commercial areas are nearly empty, and the mass transportation system has no more than half, if that many, of its usual patrons.

GERMAN VS. EAST EUROPEAN JEWS

The East European Jews who arrived in the United States in the late nineteenth and early twentieth centuries encountered an unreceptive American Jewry. The American Jews, descended mostly from the German migrations of the middle of the nineteenth century, had achieved a secure middle-class position in the United States. They were doctors, lawyers, bankers, manufacturers, and merchants. They had established or developed some of the leading department stores in the country like Macy's and Sears Roebuck. In addition, they had made every effort to appear indistinguishable from the more prosperous gentile Americans.

The coming of the East European Jews threatened the security of the German Jews. One of them wrote, in 1893, that the experience of the United Jewish Charities in Rochester, New York, "teaches that organized immigration from Russia, Rumania, and other semibarbarous countries is a mistake and has proved a failure. It is no relief to the Jews of Russia, Poland, etc., and it jeopardizes the well being of American Jews." The Americanized Jews felt little kinship with the newcomers and also feared that their presence would constitute a burden on society and stimulate an outburst of anti-Semitism. When the *Hebrew Standard* declared, on June 15, 1894, that "the thoroughly acclimated American Jew . . . is closer to the Christian sentiment around him than to the Judaism of these miserable darkened Hebrews," it probably expressed the dominant sentiment of American Jewry at the time.

Despite their antipathy, the Americanized Jews realized that the gentiles in the United States lumped all Jews together and that the behavior of the Orthodox would reflect on everyone. As Louis D. Brandeis later phrased it,

> a single though inconspicuous instance of dishonorable conduct on the part of a Jew in any trade or profession has far-reaching evil effects extending to the many innocent members of the race. Large as this country is, no Jew can behave badly without injuring each of us in the end. . . . Since the act of each becomes thus the concern of all, we are perforce our brothers' keepers.

One should not minimize, however, the fact that the American Jews also had a paternalistic sympathy for their East European brethren and therefore, since they could not contain the stampede from Russia, Galicia, and Rumania, they set about, after an initial display of coldness, to improve the "moral, mental and physical conditions" of the immigrants.

Once they decided to facilitate assimilation by assisting the newcomers, the American Jews spared no efforts and "few human needs were overlooked." Of all immigrant groups none proved so generous to "their own kind" as did the Jews. Money and organizational talent combined to provide hospitals, orphan asylums, recreational facilities, and homes for unwed mothers as well as for the deaf, the blind, the old, and the crippled. Educational institutions were also established and the "zeal to Americanize underlay all educational endeavor." Part of this Americanizing process also resulted in the building up of the Jewish Theological Seminary in New York City to train Conservative rabbis. The American Jewish establishment could not tolerate orthodoxy but recognized that the East European immigrants would not come around to Reform Judaism. Conservatism provided an acceptable compromise since it preached American values while retaining the most important orthodox traditions.

Another of the projects resulted in an attempt to disperse the immigrants throughout the United States. The Americanized Jews did not want the newcomers to congregate in one massive ghetto. Between 1901 and 1917 the Industrial Removal Office dispatched 72,482 East European Jews to 1,670 communities in forty-eight states. Nevertheless, many of those transplanted eventually returned to New York. In fact, of the 1,334, 627 Jews who did arrive in New York City between 1881 and 1911, 73.5 percent remained there.

The most important and lasting agency set up by the Americanized Jews to help—and lead—their brethren was the American Jewish Committee. Ostensibly formed as a result of the outrageous pogroms in Russia between 1903 and 1905 and dedicated to protecting the civil rights of Jews wherever they were threatened, the American Jewish Committee came into being in 1906 primarily because the established Jewish community in the United States wanted "to assert some control over existing Jewish institutions and mass movements." As Louis

Marshall, one of the American Jewish Committee's leading members and its president from 1912 to 1929, put it in 1908, the purpose of those who formed the organization was "to devise a simple and efficient instrument which might deal quickly, and at the same time deliberately, and with an understanding based on experience, with the problems that might present themselves from time to time."

The American Jewish Committee, composed of wealthy Jews, exercised great influence politically "through private contacts with men in power." Since Jacob Schiff, Cyrus Adler, Louis Marshall, Felix Warburg, Oscar Strauss, Julius Rosenwald, Mayer Sulzberger, and others of their stature dealt regularly with the most prominent Americans of their generation, the Committee "on the whole, acted effectively in the interests of American Jewry." The American Jewish Committee, as one scholar has pointed out, "offered American Jewry a vigorous, disciplined and highly paternalistic leadership as well as a program of Americanization," but its members looked down upon the East Europeans and expected them to follow its leadership. This did not occur. Perhaps if the Committee had been more democratically organized it might have served as a bridge to the newcomers and won them over. But as one of the group said, "let us get away from the idea that the American Jewish Committee must be representative and that its members must be chosen in some way by the vote of the Jews in this country. No great moral movement has been undertaken and carried through except in just such a manner in which we are doing our work."

The enormous assistance provided by the Americanized Jews to the immigrants was accepted with reservations. The established Jews showed disdain for the East Europeans and their culture and the recipients of their largesse felt like beggars and poor relations. The charity may have been given out of a sense of obligation but it did not come with warmth and kindness. And the leadership provided by the American Jewish Committee definitely smacked of elitism which the immigrants would not tolerate. As soon as the East Europeans could provide their own network of charitable and welfare organizations they did so. It would be a long time before they would look upon their "benefactors" without a jaundiced eye.

ANTI-SEMITISM

The German and East European Jews in the United States recognized the vast gulf that separated them socially, economically, and culturally but gentiles did not. The coming of the new Jews intensified latent anti-Semitic feelings among gentile Americans and, as the German Jews had originally feared, this hostility erupted in public. The German Jews felt the sting first. In 1877 a prominent Jewish banker was barred as a guest from a resort hotel that had previously accepted his patronage. As the nineteenth century came to a close, German Jews also found themselves excluded from private schools, prominent social clubs, and other resorts. In 1890 the editors of *The American Hebrew* sent around a questionnaire to prominent Americans inquiring why gentiles were so hostile to Jews and one university president responded that "All intelligent Christians deplore the fact that the historical evidences for Christianity have so little weight with your people."

The East European Jews were not affected at first by social anti-Semitism but in the early years of the twentieth century the bigotry became acute. In rapid succession crude slurs, journalistic reports, and supposedly learned commentaries lambasted the Jews. A letter to the editor of the *New York Herald* complained that "these United States are becoming rapidly so Jew ridden . . . ," while a faculty member at Teacher's College in New York wrote to a colleague and asked him to "please do me the favor of not coming to the banquet tomorrow night, as I have invited a friend who does not like Jews." A magazine writer asked of the Russian Jew, "is he assimilable? Has he in himself the stuff of which Americans are made?" University of Wisconsin sociologist E. A. Ross claimed that "the lower class of Hebrews of eastern Europe reach here moral cripples, their souls warped and dwarfed by iron circumstance . . . many of them have developed a monstrous and repulsive love of gain." Finally, University of Berlin Professor Werner Sombart's prediction "that in another hundred years the United States will be peopled chiefly by Slavs, negroes and Jews," was prominently featured in one of the leading American periodicals of the day.

In view of these prejudices it is no wonder that outside of the garment district and other Jewish-owned establishments Jews had little chance for obtaining decent jobs. Many help-wanted advertisements specified "Christian only," and real estate agents preferred gentile clients. To combat this discrimination one of the older American Jewish fraternal organizations, B'nai B'rith, which had been founded in 1843, established its Anti-Defamation League in 1913. The League over the years has proved quite successful in combating anti-Semitism.

Despite the efforts of the Anti-Defamation League, schools and employers continued discriminating against Jews. Quotas in higher education began in the 1920s and became more rigid during the depression years of the 1930s. As late as 1945 the president of Dartmouth College defended regulations which kept Jewish students out of his school, but he was probably the last outspoken advocate of an already waning policy. Beginning with World War II more opportunities opened to practically all skilled white people and the growth of the economy, the passage of state laws forbidding discrimination in employment and entry into universities, and a generally more tolerant spirit in the land led to widened economic and occupational opportunities for Jews. Law firms, scientific organizations, universities, and businesses needing the very best talent available hired goodly numbers of Jews who were among their few qualified applicants.

Bigotry did not disappear completely. The executive suites of America's largest corporations contain relatively few Jews and one still reads of prominent Jews being denied admission to country clubs. On December 14, 1973, *The Wall Street Journal* ran a story on Irving Shapiro, the new chairman and chief executive of Du Pont and Company, the world's largest chemical concern. Well into the article the author noted that being a lawyer, a Jew, and a Democrat were not helpful to Mr. Shapiro in his rise to prominence within the firm (although his talents, of course, overrode these "handicaps") and then tellingly, "Mr. Shapiro's official biography is noticeably lacking in the kind of club affiliations that adorn those of his colleagues."

LEGISLATION AND POLITICS

There were never any specific laws in the United States regarding East European Jews, but their arrival contributed to the movement for immigration restriction. The major American laws keeping out aliens passed Congress in 1921 and 1924 and these set quotas for groups based on a percentage of their population in the United States in 1910 and 1890, respectively. Such laws were designed to drastically curtail southern and eastern European migration to this country. The Jews, being the second largest immigrant group in the early twentieth century, were obviously one of the major targets of this legislation. As early as 1906 an Italian American had been told by a member of President Theodore Roosevelt's immigration commission that the "movement toward restriction in all of its phases is directed against Jewish immigration. . . ." The Irish, the English, and the Germans who constituted the majority of nineteenth-century immigrants to the United States received the largest quotas. No religious test was allowed by this legislation. Consequently, Jews born in Germany were counted under the German quota and Jews born in England came in under the English quota even though their parents might have come from Russia or Rumania. Subsequent legislation affecting the East European Jews came in 1948 and 1950 when some of the persons displaced by the German policies of the 1930s and the Second World War were allowed to come into the United States under special provisions. Current immigration regulations in the United States make no statement about religion and have done away with quotas based on national origins. Present legislation gives preference to immigrants with close relatives in the United States and to those who have occupational skills in demand in this country.

Jews in the United States have never been legally restrained from pursuing any social or economic interests that struck their fancy. Many states originally restricted voting rights to adult males who believed in the divinity of Jesus Christ, but these were abolished in all but a few states by the beginning of the nineteenth century.

The East Europeans, like other whites, voted after becoming citizens (which took only five years after entering the United States), but they registered and voted in much higher proportion to their numbers than did members of other ethnic groups. They took stands on political issues of concern to them and supported candidates for office who appeared to be in harmony with their own views. A number of Jews have been elected to high political office, such as governor of a state or United States senator, but before the Second World War almost all of these people were of German background. In the past score of years, however, Jews of East European background have achieved simi-

lar prominence. The best known of these are United States Senators
Jacob Javits of New York and Abraham Ribicoff of Connecticut, and
Governors Milton J. Schapp and Marvin Mandel of Pennsylvania and
Maryland, respectively. Numerous Jews who were born, or whose parents were born, in Russia, Rumania, and Poland have been elected to
the United States House of Representatives and the various state
legislatures.

Although Jews have supported Republicans, Democrats, and socialists, since the New Deal era the vast majority have been loyal Democrats both with their votes and their financial contributions. In fact,
their contributions are so lavish and their votes so important that policies affecting American Jews—and especially Israel—have to be taken
into account by the leading Democratic politicos. So devoted to the
Democrats are the Jews that in Richard Nixon's overwhelming re-
election victory in 1972 they were the only white ethnic group in the
nation that gave a majority of its votes to the Democratic nominee
for President, George S. McGovern, although not by the overwhelming support usually accorded Democratic candidates. A few Jews, notably Max Fisher of Detroit, also lubricated Republican coffers. As a
result, an anti-Israel policy simply would not be politically acceptable
to most of the elected officials in Washington.

SUMMARY AND CONCLUSION

The East European Jews have accomplished great things for themselves in the United States. Most of them arrived on the brink of poverty around the turn of the century and their descendants have risen
to comfortable and secure middle-class positions in American society.
They can live where they like, work almost any place where they have
the necessary skills, and worship—or not—in any manner that pleases
them. This almost total freedom has resulted in a good deal of interfaith marriage and a slackening of religious and ethnic ties. During
the past decade one out of every three Jewish marriages has been with
a non-Jew.

Overt anti-Semitism, with the exception of the controversy between
blacks and Jews arising out of the 1967 and 1968 schoolteachers'
strikes in New York City, has subsided considerably during the past
few decades, and recent laws have forbidden discrimination on the

basis of race, creed, or national origins in employment and housing. These laws are not always observed, but they do indicate that the state and federal governments are putting up formal barriers against wanton bigotry. Ironically, diminished discrimination loosens the ties that bind ethnic minorities. The educational system, especially at the college and university levels, inculcates a national culture and a national way of thinking and it is the rare individual who, after being subject to such exposure, can be completely comfortable again in a strictly ethnic setting. With each succeeding generation of educated Jews, therefore, the ties to the traditional culture are weakened. Most American Jews today are products of the American education system and work and live in areas with people of varying ethnic backgrounds. Only some of the Jewish immigrants and their children can still be found in ghettos. And with each passing year their numbers fade.

Also on the wane is Orthodox Jewry. The attachment to the traditional faith was strong among the immigrants and their children but later generations found it a burden. Only a tiny fraction of American Jews keep the Sabbath and only a few more observe the dietary restrictions. Outside of New York, Los Angeles, Chicago, and Miami Beach, the Conservative and Reform branches of Judaism hold sway in temple memberships while the way-of-life practiced by practically all American Jews is in the Reform tradition. Thus attendance at religious services is sparse except at the beginning of the Jewish New Year and the Day of Atonement, and a middle-class life style, almost totally devoid of ethnic flavor, is vigorously pursued.

In the early 1960s one American rabbi said, "Today there is little that marks the Jew as a Jew except Jewish self-consciousness and association with fellow Jews." It is difficult to assess the strength and significance of this self-consciousness. If one "feels" Jewish and seeks out other Jews for companionship, the ties are still there. Jewish identity has also been reinforced by the emergence and travails of the State of Israel. It is impossible, of course, to predict for how many generations such sentiments will sustain American Jewry.

As the Jews become Americanized, strains and dissimilarities between the German and Russian elements have disappeared. When Hitler began persecuting Jews in Germany, and especially in the past score of years, when differences in income and life styles have narrowed considerably, there have been few if any clashes between Jews of German and East European ancestry in the United States. In fact, one might say that with each succeeding generation there is less and less difference among all American Jews regardless of their grandfathers' native lands. Class, geographical location, education, occupation, and income would be more appropriate categories for demarcation than German-Russian or Orthodox-Reform background. The only exception to this generalization would be the American Council for Judaism, whose members are primarily of German-Jewish ancestry. It is supported by only a fraction of 1 percent of the American Jews and it differs considerably from other Jewish organizations in its regard of Israel as just another foreign country with which American Jews should have no special relationships.

Still another aspect of the migration and its subsequent impact in the United States is the fantastic influence that East European Jews have had on the academic, intellectual, medical, political, and cultural life in the country, especially since the end of the Second World War. Whereas in the 1930s it was rare to find Jews, let alone those of East European descent, on the faculties of American colleges, in more recent times Jews whose parents or grandparents came from Russia, Poland, and Rumania adorn the most prestigious American universities. It would be difficult to name them all, but even a cursory cataloging would include sociologists Daniel Bell, Nathan Glazer, and Seymour Martin Lipset of Harvard University (all, by the way, graduates of New York City's City College in the 1930s); Harvard historian Oscar Handlin; and Yale Law School Dean, Abraham Goldstein. Also on the Harvard faculty is the Russian-born Nobel Prize winner, Simon Kuznets. Herbert Stein, one of President Nixon's chief economic advisers; former United States Supreme Court Justice and Ambassador to the United Nations, Arthur Goldberg; the discoverer of the vaccine to prevent polio, Jonas E. Salk; film-maker Stanley Kubrick; musician Leonard Bernstein; violinist Yehudi Menuhin; playwrights Arthur Miller and Neil Simon; and artist Ben Shahn are only a few of the others of East European Jewish descent who have made their mark in the United States. In fact, the East European Jews and their descendants have made a much greater impact, and in a wider range of activities, than people from any of the other contemporary group of immigrants.

And yet, despite their absorption into American society, it is still true, as Jacob Neusner wrote in 1973, that "to be a Jew in America is to be in some measure different, alien, a minority." The dominant culture in the United States is still intolerant of differences among groups of people and of non-Christians loyal to a foreign state or a different faith. This, of course, presents great difficulties to the various ethnic minorities in the United States. On the one hand "cultural pluralism" is celebrated in song and spirit from every official podium while deviation is regarded as a sign of subversion and inferiority. This schizophrenic conflict affects all American minorities and to be a non-WASP is to be somehow marginal and alien. For most Jews who are prosperous, employed, and ensconced in comfortable homes, these feelings are rarely discussed, but the fierce American-Jewish devotion to the State of Israel suggests that even in the United States Jews do not feel absolutely secure. Somehow they feel that loyalty to a Jewish state is necessary. Whether it is because of an attachment to the heritage and traditions of Jewry or because of a sense of being part of the same group, or even because they fear that someday they or their descendants might have to flee the United States and take refuge in Israel is impossible to say. But we do know that the sense of identification with Israel is strong and this, in a very specific way, differentiates Jews from other Americans.

5

Here Come the Wobblies!

BERNARD A. WEISBERGER

• Throughout the nineteenth century organized labor in the
United States never embraced a majority of the industrial
working people. In 1901, only one out of every fourteen non-
agricultural workers belonged to any union, about half the
proportion in Great Britain. The pattern of organizing only
specialized craftsmen resulted partly from the exclusionary
policy of the American Federation of Labor and partly from
public antipathy for the aspirations and organizations of the
unskilled working class. The Knights of Labor championed
industrial unionism in the 1870s and attempted to unite
the nation into one big cooperative enterprise. But it dwindled in effectiveness after the public's false association of it
with the Haymarket Riot and anarchism in 1886.

An even more spectacular effort to broaden the base of
organized labor was the formation in Chicago, in 1905, of the
Industrial Workers of the World. Led by "Big Bill" Haywood of the Western Federation of Miners, the "Wobblies"
wanted to abolish the wage system. They hoped to gain
their objectives by violent abolition of the state and the formation of a nation-wide industrial syndicate governed by the
workers themselves. The "Wobblies" were strongest among
unskilled migratory workers in the West, but they had a
hand in a number of strikes in the East. During World
War I the "Wobblies" suffered from the patriotic fervor of
the government and several vigilante groups, and they waned
as a force in the labor movement. Bernard A. Weisberger's
essay catches the tragedy and the persecution of the International Workers of the World as they sought to protect the
welfare of the American worker.

On a hot June day in 1905 William D. Haywood, a thirty-six-year-old miner, homesteader, horsebreaker, surveyor, union organizer, and Socialist, out of Salt Lake City, stood up before a large crowd in a Chicago auditorium. He gazed down at the audience with his one good eye and, taking up a loose board from the platform, impatiently banged for silence.

"Fellow workers," he shouted, "this is the continental congress of the working class. We are here to confederate the workers of this country into a working-class movement that shall have for its purpose the emancipation of the working class from the slave bondage of capitalism."

Thus, in manifesto, the working-class crusade known as Industrial Workers of the World came to birth. It grew amid storms of dissent, lived always in the blast furnace of conflict, and was battered into helplessness over forty years ago. It is still alive, but as a "church of old men" in one author's words, old men still muttering "No" to the status quo. The *Industrial Worker*, the official newspaper of the "One Big Union," still appears, still carries as its masthead motto "An injury to one is an injury to all," still valiantly runs on its editorial page the uncompromising preamble to the constitution adopted at that Chicago convention in 1905:

> The working class and the employing class have nothing in common. There can be no peace so long as hunger and want are found among millions of working people and the few, who make up the employing class, have all the good things of life. . . .
> It is the historic mission of the working class to do away with capitalism. The army of production must be organized, not only for the everyday struggle with capitalists, but also to carry on production when capitalism shall have been overthrown. By organizing industrially we are forming the structure of the new society within the shell of the old.

But the old society is still here, thriving more vigorously than ever; the workers have late-model cars, and the struggle of the I.W.W.'s young radicals to burst its bonds is history now—good history, full of poets and tramps, bloodshed and cruelty, and roads not taken by American labor. The history not merely of an organization but of an impulse that stirred men from the lower depths of the economy—vagrants, lumberjacks, harvest hands, immigrant millworkers—and set them to marching in step with Greenwich Village literary radicals to the tune of gospel hymns and innocent ballads fitted with new, class-conscious verses.

But it was not all ballads and broadsides. The I.W.W. was radical in the word's truest sense. When it denied that the working and employing classes had anything in common, it meant precisely what it said. The I.W.W. put no faith in the promises of bourgeois politicians or in the fairness of bourgeois courts. It made no contracts with employers, and it spurned other unions—like those enrolled in the American Federation of Labor—that did. It was composed of hard, hard-working men, little known to respectability. As a result, it badly frightened millions of middle-class Americans, and it meant to.

Yet it must be understood that the I.W.W. did not grow in a vacuum. It arose out of an industrial situation for which the adjective "grim" is pallid. In the America that moved to productive maturity between 1880 and 1920, there was little room or time to care about the worker at the base of it all. It was an America in which children of ten to fourteen could and did work sixty-hour weeks in mine and factory; in which safety and sanitation regulations for those in dangerous trades were virtually unknown—and in which industrial accidents took a horrible toll each year; in which wages were set by "the market place" and some grown men with families worked ten to twelve hours for a dollar and stayed alive only by cramming their families into sickening tenements or company-town shacks; in which such things as pensions or paid holidays were unknown; lastly, it was an America in which those who did protest were often locked out, replaced by scabs, and prevented from picketing by injunction and by naked force. At Homestead, Pullman, Coeur d'Alene, Cripple Creek, Ludlow, and other places where strikers clashed with troops or police between 1892 and 1914, the record of labor's frustrations was marked with bloody palm prints. And at the bottom of the scale was the vast army of migrant workers who beat their way by rail from job to job—not only unskilled, unprotected, and underpaid but unnoticed and unremembered.

Out of such a situation grew the I.W.W. It gained much not only from the horror of its surroundings, but from the spirit of an infant century when the emancipation of almost everyone—women, workers, artists, children—from the dragons of the past seemed to be a live possibility, and "new" was a catchword on every tongue.

The opening years of the organization's life were not promising. Its founding fathers were numerous and diverse—discontented trade unionists, Socialists like Eugene V. Debs and the whiskered, professorial Daniel De Leon, and veterans of almost every other left-wing crusade of the preceding twenty years. There was among them all, a recent I.W.W. historian has written, "such a warfare as can be found only between competing radicals." They were, however, united in objecting to the craft-union principles of A.F.L. chieftain Samuel Gompers, whom Haywood described as "a squat specimen of humanity" with "small snapping eyes, a hard cruel mouth," and "a personality vain, conceited, petulant and vindictive."

Gompers' plan of organizing only skilled craftsmen and negotiating contracts aimed only at securing a better life from day to day struck the I.W.W.'s founders not only as a damper upon whatever militancy the labor movement might generate to challenge capitalism, but also as a betrayal of the unskilled laborers, who would be left to shift for themselves. The new leaders therefore created a "single industrial union," as far removed from craft divisions as possible.

All industrial labor was to be divided into thirteen great, centrally administered divisions—building, manufacturing, mining, transportation, public service, etc. Within each of these would be subgroups. But each such group would take in all employees contributing to that industry's product or service. On the steam railroads, as an instance, clerks, telegraphers, and trackwalkers would share power and glory with engineers, brakemen, and conductors. A grievance of one lowly set of workers in a single shop could bring on a strike that would paralyze a whole industry. And some day, on signal from the One Big Union, all workers in all industries would throw the "Off" switch, and the wage system would come tumbling down.

Much of the scheme came from the brain and pen of a priest, Father Thomas Hagerty, who while serving mining parishes in the Rockies had come to believe in Marx as well as Christ. He had the scheme of industrial unionism all worked out in a wheel-shaped chart, with the rim divided into the major industries and the hub labelled "General Administration." Gompers looked at a copy of it in a magazine and snarled: "Father Hagerty's Wheel of Fortune!" He did not expect it to spin very long.

Nor, during the I.W.W.'s first three years of existence, did it seem likely to. Factional quarrels wracked national headquarters and the

Western Federation of Miners, the biggest single block in the entire I.W.W. structure, pulled out. By spring of 1908 the organization, whose paper strength was perhaps 5,000 but whose actual roster was probably much thinner, was broke and apparently heading toward the graveyard that seems to await all clique-ridden American radical bodies.

But the death notices were premature. The headquarters brawls were among and between trade unionists and Socialists, and the I.W.W.'s future was, as it turned out, linked to neither group. It belonged to a rank-and-file membership that was already formulating surprise tactics and showing plenty of vigor. In Schenectady, New York, for example, I.W.W.-led strikers in a General Electric plant protested the firing of three draftsmen by staying at their machines for sixty-five hours, a use of the sit-down strike thirty years before it was introduced by the auto workers as a radical measure during the Great Depression. In Goldfield, Nevada, the I.W.W. under thirty-one-year-old Vincent St. John organized the town's hotel and restaurant workers into a unit with the local silver and gold miners. This unlikely combination of hash-slingers and miners, an extreme example of industrial unionism, forced the town's employers to boost wage scales, temporarily at least, to levels of five dollars per eight-hour day for skilled underground workers, down to three dollars and board for eight hours of dishwashing by the lowly "pearl divers." It seemed to be clear proof that "revolutionary industrial unionism" could work. The fiery St. John was even able to close down the mines one January day in 1907 for a protest parade—on behalf of Haywood, Charles Moyer, and George Pettibone, three officers of the miners' union who had been arrested (they were later acquitted) in the bomb-killing of former Governor Frank Steunenberg of Idaho. St. John's parade brought three thousand unionists into the small-town streets "all wearing tiny red flags."

The real turning point came at the organization's fourth convention, in 1908. The believers in "direct action at the point of production" forced a change in the I.W.W.'s holy writ, the preamble. It had originally contained the sentence: "A struggle must go on until all the toilers come together *on the political, as well as the industrial field,* and take and hold that which they produce" (italics added). Now this "political clause" was scuttled, over the violent protests of Socialist De Leon, who helplessly denounced the change as an exaltation of "physical force." The shock troops of the direct-action group were twenty lumber workers known as the Overalls Brigade. Gathered in Portland by an organizer named Jack Walsh, they had bummed their way to Chicago in boxcars, raising grubstakes along the way at street meetings in which they sang, harangued, peddled pamphlets, and passed the hat. One of their favorite tunes, with which they regaled the convention, was "Hallelujah, I'm A Bum," set to the old hymn tune "Revive Us Again":

> O, why don't you work
> Like other men do?
> How in hell can I work
> When there's no work to do?
>
> Hallelujah, I'm a bum,
> Hallelujah, bum again,
> Hallelujah, give us a handout—
> To revive us again.

Sourly, De Leon dubbed Walsh's men The Bummery, but the day was theirs. The veteran Socialist leader retreated and organized a splinter I.W.W., which dwindled away in seven years.

It was the I.W.W.'s second split in a short history, but its most important. It gave the organization over to soapbox singers and bums, brothers in idealism who were poor in all things save "long experience in the struggle with the employer." They were to break from past labor practices and give the I.W.W. its true inwardness and dynamism; to fit it with its unique costume and role in history.

They gave it, first, a musical voice. Walsh's crusaders sang because when they sought the workers' attention on street corners they were challenged by those competing sidewalk hot-gospellers, the Salvation Army. By 1909, the press of the organization's newspaper, the *Industrial Worker*, was able to put out the first edition of *Songs of the Workers to Fan the Flames of Discontent*. More succinctly known as the "Little Red Songbook," it has gone through over thirty subsequent editions—all scarlet-covered and fitted to the size of an overalls pocket. The songbook and the preamble were to the I.W.W. membership what the hymnbook and the *Discipline of the Methodist Church* had been to frontier preachers—the sum and touchstone of faith, the pearl of revelation, the coal of fire touching their lips with eloquence. Most of the songs were the work of men like Richard Brazier, an English-born construction worker who joined up in Spokane in 1908; or Ralph Chaplin, a struggling young Chicago commercial artist who wanted to chant "hymns of hope and hatred" at the shrine of rebellion; or Joe Hill, born Joel Haaglund in Sweden, who wrote not parodies alone but also original compositions, which Chaplin described as "coarse as home-spun and as fine as silk"; or bards known simply as T-Bone Slim or Dublin Dan. The I.W.W. members soared on those songs, enjoying them as much for their mockery as anything.

To the patriotic cadences of "The Battle Hymn of the Republic" they sang "Solidarity forever, for the Union makes us strong" (a version which Ralph Chaplin had given them and which the entire labor movement took over without credit). To the sentimental notes that enfolded Darling Nelly Gray they sang of "the Commonwealth of Toil that is to be," and to the strains that had taken pretty Red Wing through ribald adventures in every barroom in the country, they roared that "the earth of right belongs to toilers, and not to spoilers of liberty." They raided the hymnbook of Moody-and-Sankey revivalism for "Hold the fort for we are coming, union men be strong," and for "There is power, there is power, in a working band" (instead of "in the blood of the Lamb"). They laughed in sharps and flats at Casey Jones, of the craft-proud Brotherhood of Railway Engineers, as a union scab who "kept his junk pile running" and "got a wooden medal for being good and faithful on the S.P. line." They sang in the hobo jungles, on the picket line, and in the jailhouse, and it was their singing especially that separated them from the A.F.L. by an abyss of spirit.

The "new" I.W.W. soon had a nickname, as derisive and defiant as its songs: the Wobblies. It is not certain how the name was born, though a popular legend declares that a Chinese restaurant owner in the Northwest was persuaded to grubstake I.W.W. members drifting through his town. His identification test was a simple question, "Are you I.W.W.?" but it emerged in Cantonese-flavored English as "Ah loo eye wobble wobble?" Whatever its origin, the name was a badge of pride.

The I.W.W.'s new leadership provided halls in the towns where a wandering Wobbly could find a warm stove, a pot of coffee, a corner in which to spread a blanket for the night, and literature: the *Industrial Worker* and *Solidarity*, leaflets by St. John or Haywood, and books like Jack London's *The Iron Heel*, Edward Bellamy's *Looking Backward*, Laurence Gronlund's *Co-operative Commonwealth*. All of them furnished material for arguments with the unorganized, and also such stuff as dreams were made on.

In 1909 the I.W.W. attracted national attention through the first of its spectacular clashes with civic authority. In Spokane a campaign was launched urging loggers to boycott the "job sharks," employment agents who hired men for work in lumber and construction camps deep in the woods, charging them a fee for the "service." Many a lumberjack who "bought a job" in this way was swindled—sent to a nonexistent camp or quickly fired by a foreman in cahoots with the shark to provide fast turnover and larger shared profits. At street meetings, the Wobblies preached direct hiring by the lumber companies. Spokane's thirty-one agencies retaliated by getting the city council to ban such meetings. The *Industrial Worker* promptly declared November 2, 1909, Free Speech Day and urged every man in the vicinity to "fill the jails of Spokane."

From hundreds of miles around, Wobblies poured in by boxcar, mounted soapboxes, and were immediately wrestled into patrol wagons. In a matter of weeks, the jail and a quickly converted schoolhouse were overflowing with five or six hundred prisoners. They came into court bloody from beatings; they were put to hard labor on bread and water, jammed into cells like sardines, and in the name of sanitation hosed with ice water and returned to unheated confinement. Three died of pneumonia. Among the prisoners was a dark-haired Irish girl from New York, Elizabeth Gurley Flynn. Eighteen years old and pregnant, she complicated her arrest by chaining herself to a lamp post. "Gurley," a proletarian Joan of Arc, was lodged with a woman cellmate who kept receiving mysterious calls to the front office. It turned out that she was a prostitute, serving customers provided by the sheriff "for good and valuable consideration." This fact was trumpeted by the I.W.W. as soon as Gurley figured it out.

Fresh trainloads of Wobblies poured relentlessly into town, while those already in jail kept the night alive with selections from the Little Red Songbook roared at full volume, staged hunger strikes, refused to touch their hammers on the rock pile, and generally discomfited their captors. In March of 1910 the taxpayers of Spokane threw in the towel,

released the prisoners, and restored the right of free speech to the
I.W.W. Other free-speech fights in the next few years carried the
Wobbly message throughout the Far West and helped in organizing
new locals among the militant.

Two years after the end of the Spokane campaign, the I.W.W. made
headlines in the East. In the textile-manufacturing town of Lawrence,
Massachusetts, on January 11, 1912, more than 20,000 workers struck
against a wage cut that took thirty cents—the price of three loaves of
bread—out of pay envelopes averaging only six to eight dollars for a
fifty-four-hour week. It was an unskilled work force that hit the bitter-
cold streets, and a polyglot one, too. Some twenty-five nationalities,
speaking forty-five languages or dialects, were represented, including
French Canadians, Belgians, Poles, Italians, Syrians, Lithuanians,
Greeks, Russians, and Turks.

There was only a small I.W.W. local in Lawrence, but the tactics
of One Big Union under the slogan "An injury to one is an injury to
all" had never been more appropriate. I.W.W. pamphlets and newspapers in several languages had already appeared. Now the leadership
deployed its best veterans in the field—Haywood, William Trautmann,
Elizabeth Gurley Flynn—and in addition a big, jovial-looking Italian
organizer of steelworkers, Joe Ettor, whose usual costume was a black
shirt and a red tie.

For over two months, something akin to social revolution went on
in Lawrence. A strike committee of fifty-six members, representing all
nationalities, filled days and nights with meetings and parades. Haywood stood out like a giant. He hurdled the linguistic barrier by
speeches partly in sign language (waving fingers to show the weakness
of separate craft unions; balled-up fist to demonstrate solidarity), visited workers' homes, and won the women's hearts by joshing the children or smacking his lips over shashlik or spaghetti. He also shrewdly
exploited the publicity that bathed Lawrence, which was near the nation's journalistic capitals. Demonstrations were called with an eye
not only to working-class morale but to public opinion. It was an education for many Americans to read about "ignorant, foreign" mill girls
carrying signs that said: "We Want Bread And Roses, Too."

The employers played into Haywood's hands. National Guardsmen
were called out. Police arrested more than three hundred workers and,

in a climax of stupidity, clubbed a group of mothers and children preparing to leave town by railroad for foster homes. In defiance of the evidence, Ettor and Arturo Giovannitti, another Italian organizer, were arrested as accessories in the shooting of a woman striker. Authorities held them for seven months before a trial. When it came, it not only let the two men go free but gave Giovannitti a chance to spellbind jury and reporters with an oration on behalf of "this mighty army of the working class of the world, which . . . is striving towards the destined goal, which is the emancipation of human kind, which is the establishment of love and brotherhood and justice for every man and every woman in this earth."

Long before that speech, in March of 1912, the bosses had given up and agreed to the strikers' terms. It was the I.W.W.'s finest hour up to then. Flushed with success, the One Big Union next answered the call of silk workers at Paterson, New Jersey, to lead them in a strike that began in February, 1913. The pattern of Lawrence seemed at first to be repeating. There were nearly fifteen hundred arrests, and in addition police and private detectives killed two workers by random gunfire. One of these, Valentino Modesto, was given a funeral at which twenty thousand workers filed by to drop red carnations on the coffin. But after five months even relief funds and singing rallies could not prevail over hunger. The strike was broken.

Not, however, before it produced a unique project and a strange alliance. One of the reporters who came to Paterson on an April day was John Reed—talented, charming, Harvard '10—who was enjoying life to the hilt in the Bohemian surroundings of Greenwich Village, then in its heyday. When Reed stopped to talk to a striker, a Paterson policeman on the lookout for "agitators" hustled him off to jail. There he stayed for four days, sharing smokes and food with the strikers and amiably teaching them college fight songs and French ballads in return for instruction in the arts of survival in prison. On his release he became an enthusiastic supporter of the embattled workers and brought such friends as Mabel Dodge, Hutchins Hapgood, Walter Lippmann, Lincoln Steffens, and others to hear Haywood and other Wobbly leaders speak.

Between the individualistic rebelliousness of the young artists and writers escaping their bourgeois backgrounds and the hard-shelled but dream-drenched radicalism of the I.W.W. leaders, there was instinctive connection. Reed conceived the idea of a giant fund-raising pageant to present the strikers' case. On June 7, thousands of silk workers came into New York by special train and ferry and marched to Madison Square Garden. There they watched hundreds of fellow strikers re-enact the walkout, the shooting of Modesto, his funeral, and the mass meetings that followed. Staged by Reed's Harvard friend Robert Edmund Jones against a backdrop created by the artist John Sloan, the pageant was described by *Outlook* as having "a directness, an intensity, and a power seldom seen on the professional stage." Since it ran for only one night, it failed to earn any money beyond expenses, despite a full house. Yet as a moment of convergence in the currents of radicalism vitalizing American life and letters in the last days of prewar innocence, it has a historic place of its own.

The Lawrence and Paterson affairs were only forays, however. The I.W.W. ran strikes and kept footholds in the East—the dockworkers of Philadelphia were firmly organized in the I.W.W.-affiliated Marine Transport Workers Union, for example—but it lacked staying power in the settled industrial areas. As it moved into its peak years, the future of the One Big Union was in the West, where its message and tactics were suited to the style of migrant workers, and to the violent tempo of what Elizabeth Flynn recalled as "a wild and rugged country where both nature and greed snuffed out human life."

Here, in the mountains and forests, were men who needed protection even more than the unskilled rubber, textile, steel, and clothing workers receiving I.W.W. attention—men like the "timber beasts," who worked in the freezing woods from dawn to dusk and then "retired" to vermin-ridden bunkhouses, without washing facilities, where they were stacked in double tiers like their own logs. The companies did not even furnish bedding, and a lumberjack between jobs was recognizable by his roll of blankets—his "bundle," "bindle," or "balloon" —slung on his back. The bindle stiff who "played the woods," however, was only one member of an army of migrant workers, as many as a half million strong, who as the cycle of each year turned followed the harvests, the construction jobs, the logging operations, and the opening of new mines. Sometimes they got a spell of sea life in the forecastle of a merchant ship; often they wintered in the flophouses of

Chicago or San Francisco; and not infrequently they spent the out-of-season months in jail on charges of vagrancy. The public mind blurred them together, and made no distinction among hoboes, bums, and tramps, assuming them all to be thieves, drunkards, and pan-handlers. But the true migrant was none of these. He was a "working stiff," emphasis on the first word, and thus ripe for the tidings of class war.

The I.W.W. reached him where he lived: in the hobo "jungles" out-side the rail junction points, where he boiled stew in empty tin cans, slept on the ground come wind, come weather, and waited to hop a freight bound in any direction where jobs were rumored to be. The Wobblies sent in full-time organizers, dressed in the same caps and windbreakers, but with pockets full of red membership cards, dues books and stamps, subscription blanks, song sheets, pamphlets. These job delegates signed up their men around the campfires or in the box-cars ("side-door Pullmans" the migrants called them), mailed the money to headquarters, and then followed their recruits to the woods, or to the tents in the open fields where the harvest stiffs unrolled *their* bindles after twelve hours of work in hundred-degree heat without water, shade, or toilets. But there were some whom the organizers could not reach, and the I.W.W. sent them messages in the form of "stickerettes." These "silent agitators" were illustrated slogans on label-sized pieces of gummed paper, many of them drawn by Ralph Chaplin. They sold for as little as a dollar a thousand, and Chaplin believed that in a few weeks a good "Wob" on the road could plaster them on "every son-of-a-bitch of a boxcar, watertank, pick handle and pitchfork" within a radius of hundreds of miles.

The stickers were simple and caught the eye. "What Time Is It? Time to Organize!" shouted a clock. "Solidarity Takes the Whole Works" explained a Bunyan-sized workingman with an armload of trains and factories. The three stars of the One Big Union (Organiza-tion, Education, Emancipation) winked bright red over a black and yellow earth. A "scissorbill"—a workingman without class loyalty—knelt on bony knees and snuffled to the sky, "Now I get me up to work, I pray the Lord I may not shirk." But the most fateful stickers to appear between 1915 and 1917, as the nation moved toward war, were those that urged: "SLOW DOWN. The hours are long, the pay is small, so take your time and buck 'em all"; and those on which appeared two portentous symbols: the wooden shoe of sabotage, and the black cat, which, as everybody knew, meant trouble.

A tough problem for the I.W.W. was how to achieve "direct action" in the migrant workers' spread-eagle world. A factory or a mine could be struck. But how could the I.W.W.'s farmhands' union, the Agricultural Workers' Organization, "strike" a thousand square miles of wheatfield divided among hundreds of farmer-employers? How could the Forest and Lumber Workers' Industrial Union tie up a logging operation spread among dozens of camps separated by lonely miles?

The answer was, as the Wobblies put it, "to bring the strike to the job," or, more bluntly, sabotage. To the average American, sabotage conjured up nightmares of violence to property: barns blazing in the night, crowbars twisting the steel and wire guts out of a machine. The word itself suggested a European tradition of radical workers' dropping their *sabots*, or wooden shoes, into the works. But the I.W.W. leaders insisted that they had something less destructive in mind—merely the slowdown, the "conscientious withdrawal of efficiency," or, in working-stiff terms, "poor pay, poor work." To "put on the wooden shoe," or to "turn loose the black kitty" or "sab-cat," meant only to misplace and misfile order slips, to "forget" to oil motors, to "accidentally" let furnaces go out. Or simply to dawdle on the job and let fruit rot on the ground or let threshing or logging machinery with steam up stand idle while farmers and foremen fumed.

I.W.W. headquarters was vague about where the limits to direct action lay. Nor did it help matters when it printed dim, oracular pronouncements like Bill Haywood's "Sabotage means to push back, pull out or break off the fangs of Capitalism." Such phrases were enough to frighten not only the capitalists, but the Socialists, who in their 1912 convention denied the red sacraments to any who advocated "crime, sabotage or other methods of violence as a weapon of the working class to aid in its emancipation." (The next year, the Socialists fired Haywood from the party's executive board, completing the divorce between the Wobblies and politics.) Still the I.W.W. leaders in the field pushed ahead with their tactics. The Agricultural Workers, to strengthen the threat of mass quittings by harvest hands, organized a "thousand-mile picket line" of tough Wobblies who worked their way through freight trains in the farm belt, signing up new members and unceremoniously dumping off any "scissorbills" or "wicks" who refused a red card. The Lumber Workers forced the camp owners to furnish clean bedding by encouraging thousands of lumberjacks to celebrate May Day, 1918, by soaking their bindles with kerosene and making huge bonfires of them.

Potentially such tactics were loaded with danger, but from 1913 to 1919 they worked. Ralph Chaplin estimated that in early spring of 1917, when the A.W.O. was signing up members at the rate of 5,000 a month, the going wage in the grain belt had jumped from two dollars for a twelve-to-sixteen-hour day to five dollars for a ten-hour day. Two years later northwestern loggers were averaging twenty-five to fifty dollars a month plus board. These facts meant more to the average reader of *Solidarity* and the *Industrial Worker* than I.W.W. theories about the overthrow of capitalism. If he thought about the shape of society after the final general strike, it was only in the vague way of a church deacon who knew there was a celestial crown reserved for him, but did not trouble his mind about it from day to day. Yet the very success of the organization anywhere stirred not only the anger of its enemies but the fears of unsophisticated Americans who were ready to believe that the Wobblies were already putting the torch to the foundations of government and justice. With war hysteria actively feeding the fires of public hostility, the I.W.W. became the victim of new and spectacular persecutions.

Perhaps it was inevitable that the blood of martyrs would splash the pages of the I.W.W.'s book of chronicles. The mine owners, lumber-camp operators, and ranchers whom the Wobblies fought were themselves hard, resourceful men who had mastered a demanding environment. They knew a challenge when they saw one, and the West, in 1915, was not too far past Indian, stagecoach, and vigilante days. Sheriffs and their deputies were ready to use any method to rid their communities of "agitators"—especially those described in the press as "America's cancer sore." The Los Angeles *Times*, for example, said that

> A vast number of I.W.W.'s are non-producers. I.W.W. stands for I won't work, and I want whisky. . . . The average Wobbly, it must be remembered, is a sort of half wild animal. He lives on the road, cooks his food in rusty tin cans . . . and sleeps in

"jungles," barns, outhouses, freight cars . . . They are all in all
a lot of homeless men wandering about the country without fixed
destination or purpose, other than destruction.

"When a Wobbly comes to town," one sheriff told a visitor, "I just
knock him over the head with a night stick and throw him in the river.
When he comes up he beats it out of town." Lawmen furnished similar
treatment to any hobo or "undesirable" stranger, particularly if he
showed a tendency to complain about local working conditions or if,
after April 6, 1917, he did not glow with the proper enthusiasm for the
war to end wars. Hundreds of suspected and genuine Wobblies were
jailed, beaten, shot, and tortured between 1914 and 1919, but some
names and episodes earned, by excess of horror or myth-creating power,
a special framing among dark memories.

There was the case of Joe Hill. He was the most prolific of the
Wobbly bards; the dozens of numbers he composed while drifting from
job to job after his emigration from Sweden to America (where his
name transformed itself from Haaglund into Hillstrom and then into
plain Hill) had done much to make the I.W.W. a singing movement.
His songs had, a recent Wobbly folklorist has written, "tough, humorous, skeptical words which raked American morality over the
coals." They were known and sung wherever Wobblies fought cops
and bosses.

In January, 1914, Salt Lake City police arrested Hill on the charge
of murdering a grocer and his son in a holdup. Circumstantial evidence
was strongly against him, but Hill went through trial and conviction
stoutly insisting that he had been framed. Though a popular ballad
written many years afterward intones, "The copper bosses killed you,
Joe," Hill was not definitely linked to any strike activity in Utah, and
had been in the I.W.W. for only four years. But his songs had made
him a hero to the entire radical labor movement, and he had a sure
sense of drama. Through months of appeals and protest demonstrations he played—or lived—the role of Pilate's victim magnificently.
On November 18, 1915, the day before a five-man firing squad shot
him dead, he sent to Bill Haywood, in Chicago, a classic telegram:
"Goodbye, Bill. I die like a true blue rebel. Don't waste any time
mourning. Organize!" Thirty thousand people wept at his funeral. At
his own request, his ashes were put in small envelopes and distributed
to be scattered, the following May Day, in every state of the Union.

And there was the "Everett massacre." On October 30, 1916, forty-one Wobblies had travelled from Seattle to Everett, Washington, some forty miles away, to speak on behalf of striking sawmill workers. Vigilantes under Sheriff Donald McRae arrested them, took them to the edge of town, and forced them to run the gantlet between rows of deputies armed with clubs, pick handles, and bats. Next morning the grass was stiff with dried blood. Five days later, two steamer loads of I.W.W. members sailed up Puget Sound from Seattle for a meeting of protest. As they approached the Everett docks singing "Hold the Fort for We Are Coming," the sheriff and his men were waiting. They opened up with a hail of gunfire, and five Wobblies were killed, thirty-one wounded; in the confused firing, two vigilantes were also killed. Seventy-four Wobblies were arrested and tried for these two deaths but were acquitted. No one was tried for killing the I.W.W. men.

The following summer Frank Little, a member of the I.W.W. executive board, died violently in Butte, Montana. Little was a dark-haired man, with only one good eye and a crooked grin. He was part Indian, and liked to josh friends like Elizabeth Gurley Flynn and Bill Haywood by saying: "I am a real Red. The rest of you are immigrants." In June, with his leg in a cast from a recent auto accident, he left Chicago headquarters for Butte to take command of the copper miners' strike, denounced by the mine owners as a pro-German uprising. On the night of August 1, 1917, six armed and masked men broke into his hotel room and dragged him at a rope's end behind an automobile to a railroad trestle, from which he was hanged, cast and all. No arrests were made by Butte police.

As a final gruesome example, there was what happened in Centralia, Washington, on Armistice Day, 1919. An American Legion parade halted before the town's I.W.W. hall, long denounced as a center of seditious efforts to stir lumberjacks to wartime strikes and already once raided and wrecked by townsmen. Now, again, a group of men broke from the line of march and swarmed toward the building. The Wobblies inside were waiting. Simultaneous shots from several directions shattered the air; three legionnaires fell dead. The marchers broke in, seized five men, and pursued a sixth. He was Wesley Everest, a young logger and war veteran. He killed another legionnaire before they captured him and dragged him, with his teeth knocked out, to jail. That night a mob broke in and took Everest to a bridge over the Chehalis

River. There he allegedly was castrated with a razor and then hanged from the bridge in the glare of automobile headlights.

The hand of history struck the I.W.W. its hardest blow, however, in September of 1917. The United States government moved to cripple the One Big Union, not because it was a threat to capitalism (the government insisted, without convincing the Wobblies) but because it was impeding the prosecution of the war. Whereas Samuel Gompers had moved skillfully to entrench the A.F.L. deeper in the hearts of the middle class by pledging it fully to Wilson's crusade, the I.W.W. remained hostile. In its eyes, the only war that meant anything to a working stiff was that foretold in the preamble, between the millions who toiled and the few who had the good things of life. Wobblies had seen too many strikes broken by troops to warm to the sight of uniforms. "Don't be a soldier," said one popular stickerette, "be a man."

The General Executive Board knew the dangers of that position once war was declared. The members hedged on expressing any formal attitude toward America's entry, and when the draft was enacted, the board advised them to register as "I.W.W. opposed to war" and thereafter to consult their own consciences. (Wesley Everest had been one of many Wobblies who chose uniformed service.) But the militant I.W.W. campaigns were frank challenges to the official drive for production. Five months after the declaration of war, federal agents, under emergency legislation, suddenly descended on I.W.W. offices all over the country. They confiscated tons of books, newspapers, letters, and pamphlets—as well as wall decorations, mimeograph machines, and spittoons—as evidence, then returned to remove Wobbly officials handcuffed in pairs.

The biggest trial of Wobblies on various counts of obstructing the war effort took place in federal district court in Chicago in the summer of 1918. Relentlessly the prosecutors drew around one hundred defendants a net of rumors and accusations charging them with conspiring to burn crops, drive spikes in logs, derail trains, dynamite factories. Judge Kenesaw Mountain Landis (later to be famous as professional baseball's "czar") presided in shirt-sleeved informality over the hot courtroom as, day after day, government attorneys read into the record every savory piece of I.W.W. prose or verse from which such phrases as "direct action" and "class war" could be speared and held up for horrified scrutiny. The jury took less than an hour to consider thousands of pages of evidence and hundreds of separate alleged offenses, and returned against all but a handful of the defendants a predictable wartime verdict of "guilty" on all counts. The white-thatched Judge Landis handed out sentences running as high as twenty years, as if he were in magistrate's court consigning the morning quota of drunks to thirty days each.

The 1918 federal trials (which were followed by similar episodes in a number of states that hastily enacted laws against "criminal syndicalism") were a downward turning point for the I.W.W. In theory, the One Big Union was wholly responsive to its rank and file, and invulnerable to the destruction of its bureaucracy.[1] But democratic enthusiasm could not override the fact that the veteran officers and keenest minds of the I.W.W. were behind bars, and their replacements were almost totally absorbed in legal maneuvers to get them out. A pathetic Wobbly fund-raising poster compressed the truth into a single line under a picture of a face behind bars: "We are in here for you; you are out there for us." In 1920 there might still have been fifty thousand on the I.W.W. rolls, but they were riding a rudderless craft.

Other troubles beset the One Big Union. The Communist party rose on the scene and sucked into its orbit some respected veterans, including Elizabeth Gurley Flynn (though she had left the I.W.W. in 1916) and William D. Haywood himself. Released from Leavenworth while his case was on appeal, Big Bill jumped bail and early in 1921 fled to the Soviet Union. Forgivably and understandably, perhaps, his courage had at last been shaken. He was fifty-one years old, seriously ill, and certain that he would die—with profit to no cause—if he had to spend any more time in jail. He was briefly publicized in Russia as a refugee from capitalism. He married a Russian woman, and for a time held a job as one of the managers of an industrial colony in the Kuznetsk Basin. But soon there was silence, and rumors of disillusionment. In May of 1928 he died. Half his ashes were sent to Chicago for burial. The other half lie under the Kremlin wall—like those of his old friend of Paterson days, John Reed. By and large, however, Bolshevik

---

1. The fact was that it made valorous efforts to keep its officialdom humble. As general secretary-treasurer, Bill Haywood received thirty-five dollars a week— just twice what a field organizer took home.

politicians had as little appeal for old-time Wobblies as any other kind. (Yet in 1948 the leadership of what was left of the organization refused to sign Taft-Hartley non-Communist affidavits. No contract, and no deals with bourgeois governments. Principle was principle still.)

More cracks crisscrossed the surface of solidarity. Some of the more successful I.W.W. unions experienced a yearning for larger initiation fees, and for just a taste of the financial stability of the A.F.L. internationals—the stability which had never been a Wobbly strong point. They quarrelled with the General Executive Board. A few locals chafed under what they thought was too much centralization. And finally, in 1924, there was an open split and a secession of part of the organization, taking precious funds and property with it. The last great schism, in 1908, had freed the I.W.W. for vigorous growth. Now it was sixteen years later, and time and chance were playing cruel games.

Middle age was overtaking the young lions, dulling their teeth—especially those who, one by one, accepted individual offers of clemency and emerged from prison, blinking, to find a changed world. The harvest stiff no longer took the side-door Pullman. He was a "gas tramp" now, or a "flivver hobo," riding his battered Model T to the job, and beyond the reach of the thousand-mile picket line. The logger, too, was apt to be a "home-guard," living with his family and driving through the dawn hours to where the saws whined and the big ones toppled. The children of the sweated immigrants of Paterson and Lawrence were clutching their high school diplomas, forgetting their working-class background, becoming salesmen and stenographers. Even the worker who stayed in the mill or the mine was sometimes lulled into passivity by the squealing crystal set or the weekly dream-feast of the picture-show. The ferment in the unskilled labor pool was hissing out. A new society *was* being built; but Ford and the installment plan had more to do with it than the visionaries who had hotly conceived and lustily adopted the I.W.W. preamble of 1905.

There was some fight left in the old outfit. It could run a free-speech fight in San Pedro in 1923, a coal strike in Colorado in 1927–28. But it was dwindling and aging. When the Depression came, labor's dynamism was reawakened by hardship. The C.I.O. was created, and fought its battles under the pennons of "industrial unionism," the heart of the Wobbly plan for organizing the army of production. The C.I.O. used singing picket lines, too, and sit-down strikes—techniques pioneered by such men as Haywood and Vincent St. John when labor's new leaders were in knickers. The old-timers who had known Big Bill and The Saint could only look on from the sidelines as the younger generation took over. Moreover, the success of organizing drives in the thirties, and the programs of the New Deal, vastly improved the lot of millions of working people. The agony that had nourished the I.W.W.'s revolutionary temper was now abating. Ironically, the very success of labor in uplifting itself through collective bargaining and politics drove one more nail into the I.W.W.'s coffin.

But "coffin" is perhaps the wrong word. Like Joe Hill, the I.W.W. never died. In its offices scattered across the country, old-timers still sit and smoke under pictures of Frank Little and Wesley Everest, or leaf through copies of the *Industrial Worker* like the great readers they always were. They do not give up; they expect that history will knock some sense into the workers soon, and that then the cry of "One Union, One Label, One Enemy" will rise again from thousands of throats. But meanwhile, their offices are, in the words of a recent observer, haunted halls, "full of memories and empty of men."

By contrast, the steel and glass office buildings of the bigtime A.F.L.-C.I.O. unions are alive with the ring of telephones, the hum of presses, the clatter of typewriters, and the clicking of secretaries' heels hurrying through the doors behind which sit organized labor's well-dressed statisticians, economists, lawyers, accountants, editors, co-ordinators, and educators. They have given much to their workers, these unions— good wages, decent hours, vacations, benefits, pensions, insurance. But they may be incapable of duplicating two gifts that the I.W.W. gave its apostles, its knights, its lovers—gifts that shine through a pair of stories. One is of the sheriff who shouted to a group of Wobblies, "Who's yer leader?" and got back a bellowed answer, "We don't got no leader, we're all leaders." The other is a recollection by an unidentified witness at the Chicago trial:

> Well, they grabbed us. And the deputy says, "Are you a member of the I.W.W.?" I says, "Yes," so he asked me for my card, and I gave it to him, and he tore it up. He tore up the other cards that the fellow members along with me had. So this fellow member says, "There is no use tearing that card up. We can get duplicates." "Well," the deputy says, "We can tear the duplicates too." And this fellow worker says, he says, "Yes, but you can't tear it out of my heart."

6

The Strange Affair of the Taking
of the Panama Canal Zone

BERNARD A. WEISBERGER

• The idea of an interoceanic canal somewhere across Colombia or Nicaragua intrigued adventurers, admirals, and statesmen long before the twentieth century. The military necessity of such a route was, however, finally driven home during the Spanish-American War, when the battleship Oregon had to steam for two months in order to go all around South America en route from California to Cuba. Thereafter, the United States was determined to go ahead with a canal, and under the leadership of President Theodore Roosevelt, the deed was finally accomplished in 1914.

As every school child knows, the construction of an all-water route through the swamps and insect-infested lands of Central America was an engineering feat of the first magnitude—an achievement so remarkable that even the conquering of yellow fever by Dr. Walter Reed and other Army doctors can only be regarded as a happy side effect of the task. After the earlier French failure, the successful American attempt at canal building was offered as an example of what Yankee ingenuity could accomplish.

Less well known are the political and military dealings which brought the Canal Zone to the United States. These machinations, according to Bernard A. Weisberger and many other scholars, reveals the traditional North American disdain for the sovereign rights of countries "south of the border." All over Latin America, President Roosevelt's intolerance and aggressiveness in this incident bred resentment and fear. The conviction has persisted, especially as nationalist sentiments have grown stronger, that the United States did not deal fairly with Panama.

Because a new treaty renouncing sovereignty over the Canal Zone was approved in 1978 by the United States Senate (to the great dismay of millions of Americans), it is important to review the circumstances of the original agreement.

PROLOGUE: *Washington, November 18, 1903*

As John Hay, Secretary of State of the United States of America, prepared for bed in his comfortable home just across Lafayette Park from
the White House, it must certainly have struck him that the day just
concluded had been altogether one of the most curious in his four-
year tenure in office—or, in fact, in a long diplomatic career that had
taken him as a representative of his country to London, Paris, Vienna,
and Madrid.

The hands of the clock had stood at twenty before seven when he
signed a treaty with the Envoy Extraordinary and Minister Plenipotentiary of the Republic of Panama. And extraordinary was assuredly the
word. The minister, a small man with fierce mustaches and an out-
thrust chin, was one who spoke not in sentences but in proclamations.
Hay had asked him if he had a choice between two drafts of the treaty,
which would permit the construction of an interoceanic canal by the
United States. "I am at the orders of Your Excellency," came the reply, "to sign either of the two projects which, in Your Excellency's
judgment, appears best adapted to the realization of that grand work."
And when it turned out that the minister had no signet ring to seal
the document, Hay had proffered two, one of them bearing his own
family arms. "The share which Your Excellency has in the accomplishment of this great act determines my choice," said the minister
as he reached for Hay's ring. "I shall be happy that the Treaty, due to
your generous policy, should bear at the same time your personal seal
and that of your family."

Such nobility of style was modestly ironic under the circumstances,
a point not lost to the writer's eye of Hay, who had occasionally composed novels, humorous poetry, and editorials. For one thing, the Na-
poleonic little minister represented a country that was only about the
size of South Carolina. Of its jungle-covered and mountainous terrain
only a strip of the serpentine isthmus between North and South
America was basically habitable—and the treaty had just handed over
most of that region to the absolute and sovereign control of the
United States forever.

In addition, the Republic of Panama had existed among the family of nations for precisely twelve days—brought into being by a revolt that was foreseen, aided, and just possibly arranged by the United States. Finally, in the most bizarre touch of all, the minister was not a Panamanian, or even a citizen of Colombia, from which Panama had been detached. He was a French engineer named Philippe Bunau-Varilla, whose diplomatic career was beginning and ending with this single episode.

All in all, a most unusual international pact. It would undoubtedly get through the Senate, for the canal that it would make possible was a universally popular project. But it would always remain tainted with suspicion and resentment among Panamanians, Colombians, and some Americans as well. It was not, in fact, the treaty that Secretary Hay himself had wanted. What was more, no knowledgeable observer would have predicted its achievement five years earlier. Time after time in Hay's administration of the Department of State the Panama Canal had appeared to be doomed. Yet at each point of crisis it had been rescued and put back on the long road to realization. Its history seemed to prove that despite the complexity of the world and the domination of chance and error in human affairs, a man with energy and enormous fixity of purpose could now and then shape the course of history.

ACT ONE: THE COURSE OF EMPIRE
Scene I. *Washington, December, 1898*

One of the many callers on President William McKinley in the crowded days just before the opening of the Fifty-fifth Congress was a partner in the New York firm of Sullivan and Cromwell. Though only forty-four, William Nelson Cromwell already had silvery white hair and mustaches, surprising complements to his smooth complexion and baby-blue eyes. These features could mask, for the unwary, certain other assets—a salesman's rapid tongue, a wizard with figures, and, in one reporter's observation, "an intellect that works like a flash of lightning, and . . . swings about with the agility of an acrobat."

Cromwell's specialty was corporate reorganization, and it was on behalf of a corporate client that he had presented his card at the White House. Ostensibly he merely wished to present to the President the report of an international technical commission which declared that the most practicable route for a canal linking the Atlantic and Pacific oceans—from an engineering point of view—lay through the Isthmus of Panama. But both Cromwell and McKinley knew that there was already a partially dug canal in Panama; that its right of way, equipment, concessions from Colombia, and other assets were the property of the New Panama Canal Company of Paris; and that Cromwell had recently been hired to represent that company.

The concern had called him in for what was essentially a salvage job. The original French Panama Canal Company (or Compagnie Universelle du Canal Interocéanique) had been organized nearly twenty years earlier under the leadership of Ferdinand de Lesseps, who had won world acclaim by creating the Suez Canal. In seven years the company, sometimes using as many as 14,000 workers, had managed to gouge out some eleven miles of canal in Panama, less than half of the total length necessary. Heartbreaking difficulties had been encountered—swift floods on the isthmian rivers and landslides that wiped out months of work. In addition, yellow fever and malaria, which the medical technology of the eighties could not control, were claiming over a thousand lives a year by 1885. Valor was not enough to beat these odds. More capital was required, and there was a desperate struggle for fresh money, some of it through lotteries. But in 1894 it was revealed that in the fund-raising campaign certain politicians and journalists had been bribed. The grand design collapsed in scandal, investors shut their pocketbooks, and de Lesseps died brokenhearted.

The New Panama Canal Company was created to inherit and liquidate the machinery, buildings, contracts, and good will (such as it was) of the old. Its directors correctly despaired of reawakening French interest in another long, expensive struggle with the elements. But they knew that the United States was eager to have the oceans joined, and they conceived the idea of selling their properties to the Americans. To that end they had hired Cromwell.

The conversation between the lobbyist and the President went unrecorded, but there is little doubt about the prevailing sentiment of the day, which the President probably articulated. He would shortly be pointing out, in his State of the Union message, that stunning events had taken place in the preceding twelve months. As a result of the brief war with Spain the United States would shortly acquire a protectorate over Cuba and absolute control of Puerto Rico and the Philippine Islands. She had also, in that summer of empire, annexed the Hawaiian Islands. The United States was now a colonial power with holdings in two oceans, and undoubtedly desired, needed, and planned a canal to shorten the travel time between them.

Furthermore, the entire Western world would smile on such a canal. A great seaborne traffic was in motion, carrying to the factories of the United States and of Europe the crude ores, rubber, petroleum, lumber, fibers, and foodstuffs of a colonized Africa and Asia and a weak Latin America, and returning to them manufactured goods ranging from rails and locomotives to kerosene and calico. The whole fabric of civilization would benefit from speeding up this interchange.

But, the President might have gone on, the great interoceanic highway would not necessarily go through Panama. The American Congress had, in fact, long been considering a route through Nicaragua. Mr. Cromwell might learn more about that subject from one of the Nicaraguan canal's most ardent supporters, Senator John T. Morgan of Alabama, ranking Democratic member of the Committee on Foreign Relations and that on Interoceanic Canals.

All of this was surely already known to Cromwell. His first task for his clients, therefore, in pursuit of which he had called on McKinley, was in some way to forestall a sudden, enthusiastic rush by Congress to embrace Nicaragua.

Scene II. *Washington, March 3, 1899*

As the Fifty-fifth Congress worked its way through final business in the closing hours of its life Senator Morgan was furious. It was more than thirty-three years since he had been Brigadier General Morgan, Cavalry, Confederate States of America, but he remembered enough to know that he had been outflanked.

During the winter months the aging but vigorous senator had steadily nursed along a bill for a Nicaraguan canal. Behind it he had put parliamentary and oratorical skills acquired in a classical education in Tennessee. Morgan's measure would instruct the President to open negotiations with Nicaragua to secure the right of way for such a canal, and would have the effect of giving financial support to an American organization, the Maritime Canal Company. Like the

Compagnie Universelle du Canal Interocéanique, the Maritime Company had begun its canal, dug a few miles, and then succumbed to the financial panic of 1893. Senator Morgan held stock in it.

Yet it was not merely for himself that Morgan was working. Though he had fought for the old South of cotton and slavery, he represented a new South of coal and iron and shipping and banking. He was eager to see New Orleans and Mobile and perhaps other southern ports become the centers of a lusty interhemispheric trade that would stimulate the struggling southern economy. To enhance that traffic a canal was an absolute necessity, and Nicaragua seemed, to Morgan, a logical location. It was two days closer in sailing time to American ports. It could be built so as to utilize natural watercourses, including the great expanse of Lake Nicaragua, and would therefore be cheaper and quicker to finish. Nicaragua's government, unlike that of Colombia, indicated a strong interest in dealing with Washington for the canal; so did that of neighboring Costa Rica, which would be involved for part of the route. And Nicaragua's high plateaus would be free of the pestilences that lurked in the sinister Panamanian jungles.

As the session neared an end Morgan had won Senate passage of his bill. But then something had happened. The burden of getting a Nicaraguan canal law through the House fell on Iowa's William P. Hepburn, a Republican regular serving his sixth term and elevated by seniority to the chair of the Committee on Interstate and Foreign Commerce. Hepburn was in favor of Nicaragua, too. But someone had played upon his vanity in such a way as to induce him to introduce a bill of his own rather than simply sponsoring Morgan's in the lower chamber. Because the bill contained some provisions differing from Morgan's, when it passed the House a conference committee had to be created to reconcile the discrepancies.

As the hours ticked away someone got an amendment tacked on to the committee's revised bill providing for that favorite device of compromisers, a study commission to look into all the feasible routes for a canal, Panama included. Someone got Hepburn to accept it. After a brief deadlock someone persuaded the Republican senators on the conference panel to go along, abandoning their Senate colleague Morgan for their party brother Hepburn and accepting a new canal commission.

Someone had dealt Senator Morgan a defeat and bought time for pro-Panama forces to plan and to organize. The senator was perfectly sure that the someone was William N. Cromwell. And while the attorney kept discreetly silent about it at the time, he was not choked by modesty when, much later, he submitted his firm's thumping bill (for over $800,000) to his clients. At that time he declared: "We think we are justified in stating that without our efforts the new commission would not have been created."

Whether that boast was valid or not, Cromwell's efforts continued as the oncoming Presidential election approached. They included a campaign contribution of sixty thousand dollars to the Republicans. When that party's national convention met in Philadelphia in June of 1900 to tender the garland of renomination to McKinley, it raised Cromwell's hopes by calling, in its platform, for an isthmian—not a Nicaraguan, note, but an isthmian—canal. Cynics might assume a direct connection between the gift and the declaration, but in fact, until the route-investigating commission made its final recommendation, it was a natural political act for the Republicans to hedge their bets on the canal's location.

On November 30, 1900, however, just after McKinley's re-election, Panama's prospects appeared to plummet. The investigating panel—two colonels, two professors, a lawyer, and three civil engineers, chaired by retired Admiral John G. Walker and generally known by his name—issued a preliminary report favoring the Nicaraguan route. But if, in the popular view, the Walker Commission had thereby doomed Panama, the popular view was unaware of the persistence of Mr. Cromwell or the astonishing energies of Reserve Captain Philippe Bunau-Varilla, graduate of France's Ecole Polytechnique, class of 1879.

ACT TWO: THE DOWNFALL OF NICARAGUA
Scene I. *New York, February-March, 1901*

On a brisk midwinter evening a coach with several occupants in evening dress drew up before New York's Waldorf Astoria Hotel just as a small, dapper man emerged from its front door. He and one of the men in the carriage exchanged cries of mutual recognition. "What luck to find you here!" exclaimed the passenger, who was Myron T. Herrick, a prominent Ohio Republican. "I am going to introduce you to Senator Hanna."

Thus did Philippe Bunau-Varilla get an introduction for which he had long been hoping. A consuming passion had brought him to America, and he knew that the influential Hanna, if won over, could help him realize it. The goal of Bunau-Varilla's quest was neither power, nor money, nor a woman, nor even fame for himself. It was an idea: the idea of the Panama Canal.

A Parisian, born in 1859, Bunau-Varilla grew up believing that "the greatest virtue in a Frenchman is to cultivate truth and to serve France." For him cultivating truth meant sharing in the stupendous triumphs over nature achieved by nineteenth-century engineers. When, at the age of twenty-five, he joined a contracting firm that sent him to Panama to work on the French canal, his two loyalties became fused. To join mighty oceans had been a dream of humanity for centuries. French genius had fulfilled the dream in Suez and would do so in Panama. Bunau-Varilla flung himself zealously into the work, undaunted by a bout of yellow fever in 1886. By 1889 he had risen to the superintendency of a major part of the work in the so-called Culebra Cut and had worked out what was, in his own mind, a brilliant plan of lock building that would have the waterway ready for use in a few years.

The collapse of the Compagnie Universelle du Canal Interocéanique was, for the young technician, a social, moral, and political catastrophe. The canal must be finished! As tides of scandal eddied around the project he became increasingly monomaniacal. The great work must not end in the verdict that Panama had been a swindle; history would record that to France's everlasting shame. But despite articles, interviews, letters, and petitions arranged by a nearly frantic Bunau-Varilla, France's interest in the canal had waned and died by 1900. "From that moment on," he wrote later, "I devoted myself to the single idea of saving the honour of this great creation by preserving its life." To save its life—for France's sake—Bunau-Varilla gave up on France and began to campaign for the completion of a Panama canal by the United States.

Bunau-Varilla made it his business to meet any and all Americans with an interest in isthmian affairs and canal construction. By chance he encountered two of them in Paris at a restaurant one night in 1900. Over the wine and the sauces, the voluble Frenchman poured out his usual stream of pro-Panama propaganda, with that zeal achievable only by those to whom the truth is never in doubt. Soon after, an invitation was arranged for him to come and lecture on the subject in the United States.

Arriving in Cincinnati on January 17, 1901, Bunau-Varilla lectured before that city's Commercial Club. Then a luncheon for prominent businessmen of Cleveland was set up by his friends, and it was there that he met Herrick. Back in New York, he dashed off a booklet, "Panama or Nicaragua," personally paying for the printing and distribution of fifteen thousand copies. And then more lectures—in Chicago, New York, and Princeton.

The meeting with Hanna capped these weeks of effort, especially when the Ohio senator made a date with Bunau-Varilla for an interview in Washington. Hanna was a portly Cleveland businessman, and though he was sixty-four years old, his wide eyes and slightly protuberant ears gave him something of the expression of a perpetually attentive adolescent. In 1896, as McKinley's campaign manager and fund raiser, he had been cruelly caricatured by opposition cartoonists as a fat plutocrat. But by 1901 he was committed to such modern viewpoints as accepting and recognizing labor unions—and empire. And he was one of the undisputed powers in Republican circles.

Therefore, at the interview Bunau-Varilla bombarded him hard. Did the senator know that the Panama route was shorter? Healthier? Easier to complete than Nicaragua, thanks to France's head start? Above all, safer? Nicaragua (said Bunau-Varilla, brandishing statistics) was notoriously susceptible to earthquakes and volcanic eruptions. Panama was the obvious route of choice, of necessity, of wisdom, of destiny.

Senator Hanna had no doubt heard it before, from pro-Panama members of the Walker Commission and from Cromwell. But what mattered was not who convinced Hanna but rather that, by April of 1901, he was converted. The friends of Panama had made an impressive gain.

Scene II. *Washington, July 1901*

Dr. Carlos Martinez Silva looked briefly out of the window of the Colombian embassy, then turned back to his half-packed suitcases. He would soon be off to the high, thin air of Mexico City as a delegate to the second Pan-American Congress. It would be more pleasant there

than in the sultry heat of Washington, and he would escape that
undercurrent of patronizing that any cultivated Latin-American diplomat sensed in the capital of the Colossus of the North. No matter how
formal the courtesies, one was considered a "dago" ambassador from a
powerless and insignificant state.

Nonetheless, Dr. Silva was not happy with his government for re-
moving him from Washington at a crucial stage in his negotiations. It
was undoubtedly because he had been telling them things they did not
wish to hear—a classic case of punishing the messenger with bad news.

But Silva was no ordinary envoy. A former minister of foreign relations, he was a close friend of Colombia's president, José Marroquin.
Both of them were academics: Silva held a doctorate in political science, while Marroquin, who wrote satire and poetry, was a university
professor of literature who had turned to politics late in life. Both men
represented a Colombian elite, supported by fortunes earned through
ownership (or inheritance) of Colombian coffee plantations and cat-
tle ranches.

Marroquin had been vice president but had taken power in a coup
in July, 1900. Though he was automatically assumed by the Americans' to be a dictator, he was actually in a precarious position. He took
office after two years of a civil war between Colombia's political parties
(one episode in a long history of constitutional turmoil), which had
shattered the economy and cost a toll in human life estimated at something between 100,000 and 250,000. With revenues down and costs
up, huge deficits had been incurred, leading to the usual inflationary
devices that had rapidly made the peso all but worthless. To heal these
wounds and ensure tranquillity, money was needed. And if the United
States would pay for the privilege of completing the canal through
Panama, it was urgent to find out how much and set the wheels in
motion. To do these things Marroquin had sent Silva to Washington
early in 1901.

Silva soon found, in his talks, that he faced most delicate and difficult problems. The United States might in the end close with Nicaragua and offer nothing to the Republic of Colombia or the New
Panama Canal Company. Indeed, one argument for Nicaragua was
that it was free of the added complication of negotiation with a private
concern. Secondly, if the United States did in fact elect to build a
Panama canal, it would want a degree of control over the right of way

that could be humiliating to Colombia. And thirdly, the United States,
in the end, had the power to take what it wanted; making it an offer
was something like holding out a morsel to a tiger. The tiger might
merely shake its head in the negative, or it might snap off the entire
hand.

Silva's task was made harder by the fact that, figuratively and literally, his principals were hard to reach. Bogotá was an inland capital,
several thousand feet above sea level. It had telegraphic communication
with Colón and Panama City, and from there by underwater cable to
the United States. But wire service was often interrupted, and all
steamer mail had to be unloaded and brought by mule over tortuous,
weather-vulnerable trails, a trip of several days to several weeks.

Hence the politicians in Bogotá heard little from the outside world
and suffered from a kind of parochialism that made them refer to their
city—which had poorly paved streets and almost no telephones but
had an auditorium for plays and operas—as the Athens of South America. In "Athens," in the spring of 1901, the feeling was that there was
plenty of time to negotiate with the United States. To begin with, the
United States had a half-century-old agreement with Great Britain,
known as the Clayton-Bulwer Treaty. Under it the two nations had
cooled a long rivalry in Central America by agreeing that neither would
seize exclusive control of, or fortify, any trans-isthmian canal or land
route; that both would support the neutrality of any such route; and
that neither would "occupy, fortify, colonize or exercise dominion
over" any part of Central America. That agreement would hold things
up for some time. Moreover, in 1904 the New Panama Canal Company's rights would expire and remove that distraction from the picture. The Americans might make better terms then.

Dr. Silva had labored in vain to correct these impressions. He had
written dispatches pointing out that Secretary Hay was making excellent progress with the British ambassador on a new agreement that
would abrogate Clayton-Bulwer and allow for an American-defended
canal. (The result, the Hay-Pauncefote Treaty, was, in fact, signed in
December of 1901 and soon ratified.) He had also read American
journals of opinion carefully and knew the "tiger" was not very patient.
The only result of all this caution was to provoke messages from Bogotá
telling him to go slowly, make no price concessions, and yield as little
sovereignty as possible. And finally, Bogotá was sending him on an-

other mission, though only temporarily, quite possibly to silence his negativism.

Scene III. *Washington, January 20, 1902*

William Nelson Cromwell had a lawyer's familiarity with (and distaste for) sudden and unexpected strokes of fortune that totally reversed the direction a case was taking. Yet even he could scarcely believe what he had read in the newspapers for the preceding two days. President Roosevelt was forwarding to Congress the final recommendation of the Walker Commission. It was that "the most practicable and feasible route" for an isthmian canal was "that known as the Panama route." And yet just one month earlier, to the very day, the battle had seemed hopelessly lost to Nicaragua, and Cromwell himself had been fired by the New Panama Canal Company.

The first bombshell had burst on November 16, but the fuse had been lit in the middle of the preceding month. In answer to repeated proddings from the Walker Commission, the New Panama Canal Company finally put a price tag on its properties. The sum read $109,141,500 for everything, from maps and blueprints and the forty-seven-mile-long Panama Railroad that crossed the isthmus to prospects of future profits. Admiral Walker was a New Hampshire Yankee with at least seven generations of merchants and traders behind him, and he had no difficulty in recognizing an inflated figure when he saw one. Whatever the French stockholders might think, their holdings were only, in the estimates of his experts, worth forty million dollars. His official answer to the French was in the commission's final report of mid-November. The cost of digging the Nicaragua canal was estimated at about $190,000,000. That of a Panama canal would be, to the last penny of the estimate, $144,233,358. But to go through Panama the United States would have to add the purchase price of the New Panama Company's holdings, and anything much over forty million would not only be a bad bargain but would push the Panama Canal's price beyond that of a Nicaraguan cut. Therefore it was eminently clear: the "practical and feasible route" would be through Nicaragua.

Two days later the Hay-Pauncefote Treaty was signed. With the verdict in from the commission and the green light flashing from London, Nicaragua seemed inevitable, and Panama doomed.

Swiftly, somehow, the directors of the New Panama Canal Company came to terms with the reality that they had one and only one potential customer. They wired Secretary Hay that forty million was an acceptable price to them. The news came too late to head off House passage of a new Hepburn bill for a Nicaragua canal on January 9—but not too late for Theodore Roosevelt to call the Walker Commission back into session on January 16.

Cromwell's last-minute reprieve from disaster owed much to Leon Czolgosz, who, on September 6, 1901, had fired a mortal gunshot wound into the belly of President McKinley. McKinley's death brought Theodore Roosevelt to the Presidency and changed the terms of the Panama equation. The country had never had such a President. He was only forty-three. He was well-read, knowledgeable about world affairs, a splendid if dominating conversationalist, and a supple writer of history, biography, nature lore, essays, and letters.

But there was another side to him. He was as relentlessly single-minded about some things as Bunau-Varilla (whom he later came to admire). He was restless and impulsive. A friendly observer described him as "pure act." A less flattering description came from a member of the diplomatic colony, who wrote to an acquaintance: "Always remember that the President is about six years old." And so it sometimes seemed.

With Roosevelt the canal was a top-priority item. He wanted to set the dirt flying. And, possibly through Hanna, he came into office ready to see it fly in Panama. This was worth an incalculable amount to Bunau-Varilla, Cromwell, the New Panama Canal Company, and all pro-Panama forces. He reconvened Walker's consultants on January 16, 1902; on the eighteenth they reversed their decision in the light of the new offer from the Paris directors. On the twentieth Congress was informed of their action. And on the twenty-seventh William Nelson Cromwell was rehired. Finally, on the twenty-eighth, when the Hepburn bill was brought up for consideration in the Senate, it was freighted with an amendment added by Senator John C. Spooner, an expert in business and constitutional law from Wisconsin and a most regular Republican. The Spooner Amendment directed the President to buy the properties of the New Panama Canal Company for forty million and to treat with Colombia for "perpetual control" of a canal zone in Panama, to be secured within a "reasonable" time. The final battle would turn on substituting this amendment for the original pro-Nicaragua wording. Experts believed that though Spooner's name might earn immortality through being on the amendment, the actual impetus had come from the White House and from Mark Hanna.

Scene IV. *Washington, June 19, 1902*

The newspapers agreed that there had been no such debate in the Senate since the oral pyrotechnics of the pre-Civil War giants. It was a warm June Friday, and the ninety members of the upper chamber (minus a few absentees) were moving, after two weeks of discussion, to decide on the route of the interoceanic canal. The parliamentary convolutions, as always, were confusing to the uninitiated but clear enough to the reporters and the senators themselves. The motion was to adopt a minority report of Senator Morgan's Canal Committee—one that favored Panama. If that were done, it would show that the pro-Panama group had the votes to add the Spooner Amendment to the Hepburn bill, the subject of the Canal Committee's report. And the final "Panamized" bill would automatically go through as laggards switched and jumped aboard the bandwagon. For fall elections were coming, and no one wanted to be caught without a recorded favorable vote for the "right" canal bill.

Senator Hanna watched with his usual calm. On the fifth and sixth of the month, at the start of the two-week debate, he had given what some regarded as the most impressive speech of his career. Meticulously, calmly, now and then accepting a page of figures or a chart from a secretary seated behind him, Hanna had made the Panama case: the shorter route, the fewer locks, the already existing harbors and railroad, the backlog of French experience, the lower maintenance costs. So effective was it that at least one senator, announcing that it had changed his opinion, would for the rest of his life think of the canal as the "Hannama Canal." Now Hanna sat easily, joking, awaiting the verdict.

Philippe Bunau-Varilla, back in the United States, was following the struggle and waiting for the result, too. In his mind he had furnished unanswerable arguments in response to the pro-Nicaragua case being made on the floor by Senator Morgan and others. The country was in the midst of what might have been called a volcano scare. On

May 8 Mount Pelée, an active crater on the West Indian island of Martinique, had erupted, wiping out the port of St. Pierre and forty thousand lives. To Bunau-Varilla even adversity on this gargantuan scale had its uses. In a philatelic store in Washington he picked up ninety copies of a stamp issued by Nicaragua, showing a smoking volcanic peak that could have been Mount Monotombo, only a few miles from the line of the proposed canal. He affixed each one to a sheet of paper and neatly typed underneath: "An official witness of the volcanic activity of the isthmus of Nicaragua." Then he mailed one to each senator. He counted on these "bombs, loaded with explosive truth," which arrived on the legislators' desks June 16, to do their work.

The new Colombian minister to Washington was also following the arguments intently, waiting to learn if the negotiations he had begun with Hay would reach completion. His name was Dr. Vicente Concha. He had taken over from Dr. Silva in February, and faced the same difficulties of communication. But he labored on valiantly to get a good treaty from the United States while the United States remained in a treaty-making mood.

Colombia wanted the canal zone to be ten kilometers, or about six miles, wide. She wanted to lease the zone to the United States for one hundred years and to keep a specific acknowledgment of her sovereignty. She wanted a flat payment on signing the treaty—a first suggested figure was $7.5 million—and $600,000 annually at some point after the canal had paid off its costs and was earning money from tolls, say, fifteen years after completion. She wanted the zone to be neutralized, with Colombia responsible for its defense but with the United States having the power to land troops (at Colombia's request) in emergencies. Finally, she wanted mixed Colombian and American tribunals to deal with Colombians in the zone who ran afoul of American laws.

None of this, Dr. Concha knew, would matter if Nicaragua won. All of it would be crucial if Panama prevailed. And so, like the others, he waited tensely for the results of the roll call on the minority report. Late in the day the word finally burst out of the chamber and was rushed to the wires. Enough votes had been switched from Nicaragua to carry the day for Hanna. It had been a close thing.

From there it was anticlimax. The expected rush to share credit for the amended bill took place, and Roosevelt signed the measure with a flourish of satisfaction on June 28. Only one morsel of hope had been salvaged by the Morgan-Hepburn bloc. The President was directed to pay the forty million dollars for the company's rights, to deal with Colombia for a canal zone at least six miles wide, and to build a canal usable by "vessels of the largest tonnage and greatest draft now in use, and such as may be reasonably anticipated." But if he could not achieve the first two steps in a "reasonable time," he was to proceed to build a canal in Nicaragua.

Scene V. *Panama, November, 1902*

The final act of the drama in 1902 belonged to Admiral Silas Casey, commander in chief of the United States Pacific Fleet, a Civil War veteran nearing retirement in that busy year. On November 19, bluejackets aboard his flagship, the *Wisconsin,* stood to attention, pipes shrilled, and salutes snapped as two Colombian generals, with escorts, and a cluster of high civil officials came aboard and made their way to the admiral's cabin for a conference he had arranged. The *Wisconsin's* guns overlooked the white walls, tiled roofs, piers, railroad yards, palm clusters, donkey-filled streets, and waterfront bars of Panama City, the Pacific port of the isthmus.

Some weeks earlier, in mid-September, one of the two generals, Benjamin Herrera, leading an insurgency against the government in Bogotá had been on the verge of capturing the port with his troops. Rebellions in Panama were an old story in Colombia's short history. This one, like all the others, automatically became a trigger for American military and diplomatic action under a treaty more than a half century old.

In 1846 the United States, already at war with Mexico and about to seize California, had been concerned enough about coast-to-coast communications in the future to negotiate a pact with Colombia, then known as New Granada. A pack-mule route wound its tormented way between Panama City and Colón, on the Atlantic side, and many travelers used it as a desirable if dangerous shortcut. The United States therefore agreed with New Granada-Colombia to guarantee the neutrality of the route and Colombian sovereignty over it, by force if necessary. Bogotá, in short, traded permission to the Americans to land troops in Panama to protect isthmian travelers in return for America's protection against having the province snatched away by foreign invaders or domestic rebels.

Domestic insurrection was a perennial problem. Panama was relatively isolated from the rest of the nation and as inclined to secession as the cotton states of America had once been. Early versions of Colombian constitutions even allowed Panama the privilege of peaceful separation, though the last of these escape clauses was abrogated in 1868. But there were literally dozens of outbreaks of discontent, and seven of them, between 1865 and 1901, had interrupted the "freedom of transit" seriously enough to warrant American landings, always with Bogotá's full consent.

From 1855 on the mode of transit had been a railroad, built under harrowing conditions by American engineers. It had enhanced Panamanian separatism, and it also dominated the military geography of the region. Panamian prosperity had come to depend on the road and the business life it sustained. By 1900 all of the province's leading citizens were connected, in one way or another, with the company that owned and administered the line. They included such men as Manuel Amador Guerrero, the company's doctor; Pablo Arosemena, its legal counsel; and friends of theirs like Federico Boyd, José Arango, and Ricardo Arias, landowners and businessmen who filled contracts for the line in its various activities. All of these men were intensely eager to have a canal built through Panama, of course, for it would guarantee a virtually permanent boom during and after its construction, as it brought thousands of jobs in its train.

Any attempt to win control of Panama depended entirely upon the railroad, the only possible method of moving troops and materiel between Colón and Panama City. Accordingly, when General Herrera's vanguard approached Panama City, the American government, following precedent, ordered a cruiser, the *Cincinnati*, to Colón and the *Wisconsin* to Panama City, and directed Admiral Casey to take charge of the railroad and deny it to military traffic. The first reaction of Colombian government officials was favorable. They assumed that the Americans intended to protect their control of the area.

But Admiral Casey acted with vigor and license. He refused to permit *any* troops carrying arms or munitions—loyal or rebellious—to travel on the line. Colombian commanders thought of themselves as policemen, calling in outside help to enforce the law. Instead Casey's marine guards put them on an equal footing with the "criminals" and impartially kept both from acting. Bogotá's mood turned black, and in Washington, Dr. Concha was so outraged that he lost the capacity to deal at all with the Americans and soon had to resign.

Eventually a pragmatic Colombian general, Nicolas Perdomo, persuaded the admiral to permit a modest build-up of Colombian strength. Then a change in the political situation made it possible for Perdomo and Herrera to attend the peace conference aboard Casey's ship. A true agreement was signed calling for a general amnesty and leaving outstanding problems to a meeting of the Colombian congress the following year.

The admiral had thus ended as a peacemaker. But he had demonstrated what had long been a half-formed thought in the minds of many advocates of the Panama Canal. If there was a revolt in Panama, Colombia could do nothing about it without the consent of the United States. That fact became a time bomb which began to tick away on November 19, 1902.

ACT THREE: THE MISJUDGMENTS OF COLOMBIA
Scene I. *Bogotá, August, 1903*

Arthur Beaupré, minister of the United States of America to the Republic of Colombia, sat with pencil in hand, thinking of the best possible outline for the note he was about to draft to the Colombian government. He was by now an experienced Latin-American diplomat, having gone from a law practice in Illinois to a consulship in Guatemala in 1897, a reward for Republican faithfulness. He had also been in Honduras before being assigned to Bogotá as secretary of legation. On February 12 of this year, 1903, his friend Theodore Roosevelt had boosted him to ministerial honors. Undoubtedly it was because Roosevelt wanted someone who knew how to deal politely but firmly with temperamental Latins. Talking to them was, as Secretary Hay had once remarked, "like holding a squirrel in your lap." Beaupré was prepared to hold the squirrel tightly.

The preceding six months had been crowded ones. After the resignation of Dr. Concha the new Colombian minister in Washington,

Tomas Herrán, had moved briskly. He was the son of a diplomat and had grown up, in part, in Washington and attended Georgetown University; he understood the American mentality and American politics. He knew that there was pressure from Roosevelt upon Hay to get moving and that his own room for maneuver was limited. He sparred briefly for a $600,000 annuity, but when, on January 21, Hay offered him "final" terms of a flat $10,000,000 payment and $250,000 annually thereafter, Herrán settled. The zone was to be leased for a century, was to be six miles wide, and could be "defended" by the United States. Mixed tribunals were to settle conflicts between Colombian and American laws and nationals.

The treaty was signed on January 22, with William N. Cromwell at Hay's side. Hay ceremoniously presented the signature pen to the lawyer as a well-deserved souvenir. The Senate, with unwonted speed, overrode various objections and ratified the agreement on March 17. And the nation then sat back and waited for Colombia's congress to do likewise.

And waited. And waited. And grew impatient. In the American popular mind Marroquin was a caricature—a little man with a mustache and a sombrero, who had only to snap his fingers in order to have flunkies in the "law-making body" run his errands. But in point of fact Marroquin was in full control of very little, and the United States soon moved to erode even that little.

In April, Marroquin opened negotiations with the New Panama Canal Company, looking to get for Colombia a percentage—say, a quarter—of the forty million that would be forthcoming from the American treasury. Horrified, the company directors alerted Cromwell. Cromwell spoke to Hay. By June 10 Beaupré was handing Foreign Minister Rico a sharp protest. Bogotá (it said) did not have the right to interfere in any way with the forthcoming purchase arrangements between the company and the United States by any new demands. Colombia was, it appeared, no longer sovereign over a private business firm operating on her own soil.

News of this note sharpened a dilemma that had been gnawing at Marroquin for a year. Panamanians were absolutely insisting that he close the deal quickly—something that, despite American misconceptions on the subject, he was by this time entirely willing to do. But other Colombians, running for the congress due to meet in June, were denouncing the Hay-Herrán Treaty as a shameful sellout of Colombian rights to the encroaching Yankee monster. As Herrán sadly wrote as early as mid-1902:

> History will say of me that I ruined the Isthmus and all Colombia, by not permitting the opening of the Panama Canal, or that I permitted it to be done, scandalously injuring the rights of my country.

Even in mid-April it was apparent to Beaupré, who warned Hay, that the treaty would not go through. When Colombia's congress did in fact gather, it did so among floods of antitreaty oratory that invoked national honor and denounced Marroquin in splendidly balanced phrases.

In desperations, Marroquin sent private emissaries to the American minister to see if the noose could be loosened slightly. Would Washington renegotiate the treaty to allow for a first payment of fifteen million to Colombia? And to permit her to vindicate her dignity by getting ten million from the New Panama Canal Company? Hay's answer crackled back on July 12: "Neither of the proposed amendments . . . would stand any chance of acceptance by the Senate of the United States." And two days later President Roosevelt, learning of the request, shot a note to Hay from his summer residence at Oyster Bay: "Make it as strong as you can to Beaupré. Those contemptible little creatures in Bogotá ought to understand how much they are jeopardizing things and imperilling their own future."

On the fourth of August the "contemptible little creatures" took a fatal step toward darkening their future. A study committee of the Colombian senate reported back on the Hay-Herrán Treaty, suggesting no fewer than nine amendments. All of them, in one way or another, aimed at clarifying and preserving Colombia's sovereignty over the isthmus, its residents, and its two port cities. It was in response to this development that Beaupré was composing his note. He was doing so without the benefit of fresh advice from Washington, since the telegraph company, in a dispute with Colombia's government, had shut off service to Bogotá.

Beaupré deliberated for a while and then firmly did what he knew Roosevelt and Hay unquestionably wanted him to do. His handwriting rapidly filled the blank pages that would be transcribed for delivery to

the ministry of foreign affairs on the Plaza Bolivar. The very first of
the proposed amendments, he scribbled, was "alone tantamount to
an absolute rejection of the treaty." As for the others, they would
have a hard time in the American Senate even if submitted, which
was "more than doubtful." And there was a final burst of undiplomatic
bluntness:

> If Colombia really desires to maintain the present friendly rela-
> tions existing between the two countries . . . the pending treaty
> should be ratified exactly in its present form, without any modi-
> fications whatever. I say this from a deep conviction that my
> Government will not in any case accept amendments.

Beaupré completed his work and paused for a moment of reflection.
He knew precisely what would happen. The Colombians would be
outraged at his peremptory tone, but Hay's instructions, when they
finally arrived, would support him to the limit. The Colombian senate
would also certainly reject his virtual order to sign. (Both predictions
were to prove wholly accurate.) For the moment the Panama Canal
would be dead once again. The next move would be up to the United
States. What resurrecting miracle would her leaders now attempt?

Scene II. *New York, October 20, 1903*

Dr. Manuel Amador Guerrero tried to listen patiently to the instructions of the fast-talking man who sat with him in a room of the
Waldorf Astoria. Since he had first become involved, in May, in planning a Panamanian revolution, some curious things had happened to
him, but talking with M. Bunau-Varilla always seemed especially bizarre and taxing. Amador—who was usually called by the first of his
surnames only—was due to catch a steamer in a few hours that would
take him home in seven days, and Bunau-Varilla, who seemed to have
materialized from nowhere, had taken charge of the revolution and
was telling him that it must be accomplished within five days after
Amador arrived in Colón.

Amador must have felt, like others who dealt with Bunau-Varilla,
that he was simply a chip being swept along on a tide of irresistible
purpose. At seventy years of age, Amador did not appreciate the ride.
In the entire Panama story, in fact, it often appeared that the im-

petuosity of the young—Bunau-Varilla, Cromwell, and Roosevelt, all in their forties—was overriding the desire of older men to do things in orderly and seemly fashion.

Roosevelt, for example, had received the news of Colombia's rejection of the treaty on August 12 with intense anger, though not with surprise, and had immediately begun to explore his options. There was one that was not only open to him but which was in fact required by the Spooner Act. He could wait a "reasonable time" and then turn to Nicaragua. He had no intention of doing that. A second alternative, odd as it sounded, was to claim a right to go ahead with the Panama Canal whatever the "cat-rabbits" in Bogotá might say. Roosevelt could base that claim on a "brief" prepared by Professor John Bassett Moore, of Columbia University, an expert on international law who had previously worked for the State Department, which he requested and got on the fifteenth of August.

The Moore Memorandum was a strange exercise in jurisprudence. In essence it said that under the 1846 treaty with New Granada, the United States had the right to guarantee free transit across the isthmus. Implied in the right of maintaining that freedom was the right to provide the most up-to-date and expeditious means of travel. So long as the United States kept its part of the bargain and preserved Colombian sovereignty, as it had time and time again done under the Monroe Doctrine and during rebellions, Colombia had no right to object if the United States went ahead with the canal—or, for that matter, any other mode of "transit" that was feasible. Once the canal was built, the United States would naturally own and operate it. "The ownership and control would be in their nature perpetual."

This breathtakingly broad construction of the compact of 1846 could have afforded the President some kind of lawyerlike arguments for simply seizing the isthmus and landing the steam shovels behind the troops—although, when he later tried Moore's ideas out on the Cabinet, his Secretary of War, Elihu Root, simply laughed and said: "Mr. President, do not let so great an achievement suffer any taint of legality."

But there was another avenue that might offer fewer difficulties of a diplomatic kind. That one simply involved waiting to see what would happen to various efforts to cut the slender stem that attached Panama politically to Colombia. Officially Roosevelt knew nothing of any conspiracies against the integrity of a "friendly" state. Privately he could not have been unaware of at least some of the activities in progress since June. First there had been a New York *World* story—planted by Cromwell—about the "unrest" in Panama; then a telegram came from Bunau-Varilla, in Paris, to Marroquin, warning him of Panamanian secessionism.

A few weeks later, in July, an American superintendent of the Panama Railroad had traveled up to New York on company business, which included a call on William Nelson Cromwell. When he returned, he held a meeting with Amador, Arango, Boyd, Arosemena, and other Panamanian nationalists. After this conference Amador had booked passage to New York for early Spetember, using the public excuse that he was visiting a sick son who was in the United States.

It was then that Amador's troubles had begun. Unknown to him, someone had tipped off the Colombian minister, Herrán, who had set private detectives on his trail. Through his Washington channels Cromwell found this out and went into a cautious, lawyerlike vanishing act. He did not want a Panamanian revolution traced directly to his office. So he bought a ticket for Paris, to confer with his clients. And when poor Amador, seeking instructions and help, called at the offices of Sullivan and Cromwell, there was no one there who would see him.

Then, by a marvelous coincidence, on the twenty-third of September he received word that M. Bunau-Varilla was in town and wished to talk with him. The meetings that followed were recorded for posterity by the Frenchman and not the doctor, but later investigations established that Bunau-Varilla was usually accurate in essential outline, despite imaginative flights of ego.

Amador confided to the engineer that he had come expecting to get help from Cromwell in a secret loan of six million to buy gunboats and arms for the Panamanians. Now he was at a loss as to what to do. Bunau-Varilla, who insisted that he, too, had come to the United States only on personal business, was sympathetic and brisk. He had no clients to worry about and was happily ready to jump in. "Let me reflect," he said. "I shall try to find a solution if it is at all possible." Leaving Amador to await word from him, he plunged into a zesty twenty days of activity.

Bunau-Varilla instantly and correctly dismissed the idea of a real armed struggle for Panamanian liberation as too costly, too drawn-out, and too likely to fail. The trick was a modest revolt—confined largely to the zone of the canal, which must be instantly recognized as a new nation and protected by the United States. For two solid weeks Bunau-Varilla made appointments, made telephone calls, wrote notes, and sat in waiting rooms, working every one of his excellent American contacts, until he got what he wanted. On Friday morning, October 9, he sat down across a desk from President Roosevelt. The two men, so close in age and temperament, hit it off well as they ranged over favorite subjects: the importance of the canal, the perfidy of Colombia, the Moore Memorandum (the substance of which had, by another odd coincidence, been contained in an article written by Bunau-Varilla for a Paris paper on September 2). What they said about United States action in case of a Panama revolution—if anything direct was said—would never emerge. But Roosevelt wrote to a friend, after it was all over, that he assumed Bunau-Varilla was telling the Panamanians that Washington would interfere. "He would have been a very dull man indeed had he been unable to forecast such interference, judging simply by what we had done the year before."

Bunau-Varilla was anything but dull. He rushed back to New York and summoned Amador to meet him in Room 1162 of the Waldorf on Tuesday morning the thirteenth. He told the doctor that no subsidy was forthcoming. "It is for us to act," he announced, admitting himself to the movement. Amador then raised the key question of how they could "act" with five hundred Colombian troops on the isthmus. The answer was simple for Bunau-Varilla. He knew that the soldiers had not been paid in months. Let them be bribed with twenty dollars each. Amador countered realistically: "That is not enough." He worked the figure up to two hundred apiece—a total of a hundred thousand dollars. "Well, my dear sir," said Bunau-Varilla, "it is a relatively small sum which it will be easy to find at bankers, I suppose, and if it is not to be found there, I can provide it, myself, from my own personal fortune."

For a time Amador resisted the whirlwind of Bunau-Varilla's self-confidence, then gave in and placed himself at the Frenchman's disposal. Bunau-Varilla virtually flung himself on a train to Washington, and on Friday morning was closeted with Hay. He announced to the

Secretary: "Prepare yourself for the outbreak of a revolution." So far as is known, the expression on Hay's grave, bearded face remained unchanged. He neither smiled nor winked. But he said that he, too, expected trouble and that orders were out sending cruisers toward the Gulf of Panama. That was all Bunau-Varilla wanted to know.

On Saturday morning Amador showed up again in answer to a wire that Bunau-Varilla had sent him as his train rumbled through Baltimore. This time Bunau-Varilla had an unpleasant surprise in store. Amador was assured that the revolt would be supported by the Americans. He was to show up the following Tuesday to receive a flag, a declaration of independence, a constitution, and a secret communications code. He would also get his hundred thousand dollars—half when the revolt was proclaimed and half when it was completed. But the first act of the new government must be to appoint Bunau-Varilla minister plenipotentiary.

Amador considered darkly what he was going to tell his compatriots in ten days. They were supposed to make a revolution, entirely on the assurance of an insane French civilian that the United States would safeguard them. They were to get not six million but a hundred thousand dollars from the madman, and he was to be appointed their minister plenipotentiary. Poor Amador demurred, struggled, argued feebly. Bunau-Varilla, who was at the moment Amador's only possible card to play, drew himself up. No one but he could guarantee success. "Any motive of vanity, of ambition, or even of national pride," he orated, "must yield to the imperative necessity of succeeding." Amador sighed, agreed, and made his date for the following Tuesday morning.

Bunau-Varilla, who was enjoying making revolutions as much as Theodore Roosevelt enjoyed big-game hunting, proceeded to Macy's, where he bought some colored silk. He then entrained for Highland Falls, some sixty miles up the Hudson, where he had a weekend invitation from his friend John Bigelow, former American minister to France. Ignoring the crisp outdoor delights of a pleasant fall weekend, he set to work composing his documents, assisted in English by Mr. Bigelow's secretary. The flag was sewn by Bigelow's daughter Grace and Mme. Bunau-Varilla, following an attractive design. It consisted of blue, red, and white rectangles, with a red and a blue star, presumably for the two oceans that were to be joined.

These were the creations Bunau-Varilla handed to Amador early on the twentieth as he sent him off to board the *Yucatán*. The goal was at last in sight.

Scene III. *Colón, November 3-4-5, 1903*

The day began badly and in anxiety. Great anxiety. Early in the morning the Tiradores Battalion of the Colombian army came marching into Colón. Somehow Bogotá had become suspicious and ordered the movement. The Panamanian plotters were not entirely taken by surprise. In panic Amador, only two days back from New York, rushed to the telegraph office to send Bunau-Varilla a wire in the code they had devised, which would have delighted the hearts of a boys' club: "FATE NEWS BAD POWERFUL TIGER, SMITH." It meant: "For Bunau-Varilla. More than two hundred Colombian troops arriving on the Atlantic side within five days." "URGE VAPOR CÓLON," continued Amador. ("Send a steamer to Colón.")

Bunau-Varilla, who had no authority whatever over any American VAPOR, took the train to Washington once more, asked questions, predicted disasters—but, above all, read the newspapers. He noted that the U.S.S. *Nashville* was at Kingston, Jamaica, the nearest point to Colón. His sense of the situation was that U.S. action was imminent. And so he wired back: "PIZALDO PANAMA ALL RIGHT WILL REACH TON AND A HALF OBSCURE. JONES." This went to Amador in care of a bank in Panama City, and meant that help would arrive in two and a half days.

Now it was the first Tuesday in November, the slated hour for the uprising. The two and a half days were almost gone, and the Panamanian underground in Colón looked in vain for the comforting gray hull of an American battleship, full of armed men who would land and prevent the Colombians from moving on down to Panama City.

While the hours ticked away the railroad officials worked at their part of the plot. They explained that rolling stock for conveying troops and equipment was temporarily unavailable. But perhaps General Tobar, the commander, would like to go on ahead, with his staff, in a passenger car? In Panama City there were more comfortable facilities available for them. Leaving his troops in charge of Colonel Eliseo Torres, the general accepted. He reached Panama City in midafternoon and soon found himself arrested by the forces recruited by the insurgents—the Colombian garrison, which had been promised its back pay, and the city's police and fire brigades.

With this done, a provisional revolutionary committee felt safe enough by six in the afternoon to go out to the cathedral plaza and announce to a happy crowd, which had gathered in response to rumors, that on the next day Panama would formally become independent. This news was somehow conveyed to a Colombian gunboat, the *Bogotá*, sitting in the harbor. Her commander loyally fired five shells into the town, then withdrew. They killed a donkey and a Chinese named Wong Kong Yee, the only two victims of the revolution.

The American consuls in Panama City and Colón knew what was happening. The former had already received a message from the State Department at 5 p.m.: "UPRISING REPORTED." Calmly, he cabled back: "NOT YET." Washington was unwontedly eager, possibly because President Roosevelt was due in from New York on an evening train, having gone home to Oyster Bay to vote in local elections.

The consul in Colón knew that the *Nashville* was enroute because he had already gotten cabled orders to deliver to her captain. They were, not surprisingly, to bar the railroad to all troops. Late in the afternoon the American vessel arrived. After some confusion Commander Hubbard got his directive and by 10:30 had acknowledged and executed it.

Wednesday, nonetheless, found the revolution only half completed. Hearing of its proclamation in Panama, Bunau-Varilla had sent his first cash installment. But in Colón, Colonel Torres remained stubbornly waiting for his trains. Finally one of the local revolutionary committee members took him to a hotel barroom and gently broke the news to him over a drink. Perhaps more than one drink. The colonel was outraged at the arrest of his superior and ready to do his duty as a soldier. He sent word to the American consul. Either they would get a train for his men or he would kill every American in town.

Commander Hubbard, confronted with this news at midday, sent boats out to evacuate U.S. nationals to ships in the harbor, deployed an armed landing party, and swung his cannon in a deadly arc aimed at the Colombian position. Before any shooting started, cool heads reached Colonel Torres. His patriotism was admirable, but he could not fight the United States Navy. Honor was satisfied by his gesture.

It would now be the better part of wisdom, as well as valor, to withdraw to a waiting steamer in the harbor—troops and all—and leave. A night of meditation helped Torres to see the essential logic of this view, particularly when it was reinforced by a gift of two cases of champagne and eight thousand gold dollars for himself and his men.

And so, on Thursday afternoon, the fifth of November, the Colombian troops left, and Panama was free. The New York papers had the story now, including an interview with Bunau-Varilla, who opined:

> It is a spontaneous combustion, due to the accumulation of injured feelings, and the result of the Spanish colonial system, for Panama was as much a colony of the Bogotá government as Cuba was of the grandees at Madrid.

But the more important statement was yet to come. At 10 A.M. on Friday the sixth, in Colón, in the presence of a gathering of all the foreign and local officials who could be mustered, the steering committee of the revolution announced that Panama had joined the family of nations. A United States Army officer on hand was given the honor of raising the Panamanian flag over the city hall. No sooner had he finished than official cables notified the American State Department. And at 12:51 the consuls on the isthmus had the equally official response. The people of Panama having "resumed" their independence, the United States representatives were told, and a new government having been established, "you will enter into relations with it as the responsible government of the territory."

Panama was made and recognized. That night Bunau-Varilla, after some telegraphic dickering, got his official appointment as minister plenipotentiary and sent off the final fifty thousand dollars. He had given Amador instructions on October 20. It had taken just seventeen days to carry them out.

ACT FOUR: THE BARGAIN AND THE VERDICT
Scene I. *Washington, November 13, 1903*

Wearing a uniform came naturally to Bunau-Varilla, and he looked formidably official in the one he had quickly ordered for his presentation to President Roosevelt as the official spokesman for Panama. As he waited for Secretary Hay to take him in and present him, thus converting the de facto recognition of November 6 to a de jure one, his mind was busy as always. And as always it lingered over possible plots against the future of the dream of four centuries, the Panama Canal.

Bunau-Varilla had experienced some difficult moments since assuming his new office. On November 7 he received a wire sent by the revolutionists prior to his being named minister plenipotentiary. It declared that the provisional government appointed him a confidential agent to negotiate a loan from the United States. Confidential agent indeed! The minister bristled at the very thought of the implied demotion. Fortunately, he could disregard this piece of conspiratorial "impertinence" because the higher appointment had subsequently come through.

But on Monday the ninth Hay had stunned him by asking: "What is this commission coming from Panama?" Rushing to the wires, Bunau-Varilla learned that Amador and Federico Boyd would be leaving Panama the next day to come to Washington, carrying his instructions. For Bunau-Varilla any instructions from Panama were incompatible with his dignity. He had spun his webs with an utter and delicious freedom up to then. Hay, after all, had been answerable to Roosevelt and the Senate, Cromwell to the New Panama Canal Company. Bunau-Varilla had bowed to no one, and he was not of a mind to spend a fruitless period of time in Washington rushing back and forth between Hay on the one hand and Amador and Boyd on the other. But he had only a week of freedom left. After that he would be the captive of Panamanian pride. And the Panamanians were capable of the unthinkable crime of delaying the canal by insisting on their narrow and selfish interests.

He must work fast for humanity. And he did. As he and Hay left the White House after the official reception he turned to the Secretary and delivered a tactful, almost gossamer but recognizable ultimatum:

> For two years you have had difficulties in negotiating the Canal Treaty with the Colombians. Remember that ten days ago the Panamans were still Colombians and brought up to use the hair-splitting dialectic of Bogotá. You have now before you a Frenchman. If you wish to take advantage of a period of clearness, in Panaman diplomacy, do it now! When I go out, the spirit of Bogotá will return.

Hay understood, "You are right," he said. "I wish to put the finishing touches to the project of the treaty. I shall send it to you as soon as possible."

Bunau-Varilla went back to his hotel to wait out the weekend. He was not kept in suspense for too long. On Sunday the fifteenth a messenger delivered Hay's draft to him. It was basically the old Hay-Herrán Treaty, with blanks left for possible insertion of new figures. The envoy extraordinary had perhaps three days left to retain his extraordinary liberty of maneuver.

Scene II. *Washington, November 18, 1903*

Wednesday morning in Washington. Cool weather, the town preparing for the approaching slack weekend of Thanksgiving, followed by the bustle of the opening of Congress the first week in December. Bunau-Varilla sat waiting for his telephone to ring and counting minutes.

He had worked relentlessly and purposefully, reading and rereading the treaty draft on Sunday. During the night he had slept only two hours, which he described as a "complete rest." By the time dawn was silhouetting the Capitol dome, he had worked out the problem. The prime objective was to win the approval of the Senate by making the treaty irresistible. Every American objection raised during passage of the Hay-Herrán ratification must be satisfied.

At 6 A.M. Bunau-Varilla began to scribble. The money would remain the same—a $10,000,000 flat sum, plus $250,000 per year. But the Canal Zone would be, not ten kilometers, but ten miles wide—a 60 percent increase. And it would not be leased but "granted" to the United States "in perpetuity." Naturally the United States could place its armed forces as and where it wished to defend both the canal and the independence of Panama. And as for the question of jurisdiction in the zone, Bunau-Varilla cut through all that by a simple formula:

> The Republic of Panama grants to the United States all the rights, power and authority within the zone mentioned . . . which the United States would possess and exercise if it were the sovereign of the territory . . . to the entire exclusion of the exercise by the Republic of Panama of any such sovereign rights, power or authority.

There would be no question of whose laws would be obeyed. The United States would be—save only in a technical sense—sovereign. It was fortunate that the Panamanian commissioners, on the high seas, were unaware of the conception of the national interest entertained by their envoy extraordinary. In a prewireless age, disaster did not descend so peremptorily upon statesmen.

Bunau-Varilla had asked Frank D. Pavey, an American friend and attorney, to come down and help him with the wording of the treaty. Pavey arrived, and he, Bunau-Varilla, and a stenographer labored through the day. At ten o'clock that night the Frenchman drove up to Hay's home but found it darkened. Next morning, Tuesday the seventeenth, he got his draft delivered, and then was condemned to wait for a response. Unfortunately, Amador and Boyd were due in New York that morning. By nightfall they would be on hand, and Bunau-Varilla's wings would be clipped.

But then came one of those lucky accidents that had a way of befalling Bunau-Varilla. Amador and Boyd did indeed debark in New York Tuesday morning. They immediately and naturally went to make contact with Sullivan and Cromwell. And there they learned that Mr. Cromwell himself was due, late in the afternoon or early the next morning, on his return ship from France. The two Panamanians wanted to talk to Cromwell about the future dealings of their country with his client. So they sent a cordial note to Bunau-Varilla that they would be along the next afternoon and settled into a New York hotel, still enjoying the tranquillity of ignorance as they awaited Cromwell.

Bunau-Varilla thus had a twenty-four-hour reprieve. Meantime Hay himself was not dawdling. He was sensitive to the Frenchman's time problem and eager to have the treaty wrapped up so that it might be reported in the President's State of the Union message of December, which would, as usual, become a campaign document for 1904. Roosevelt himself, that Sunday evening, had written to his son in characteristic fighting fettle:

> I have had a most interesting time about Panama and Colombia. My experiences in all these matters give me an idea of the fearful times Lincoln must have had in dealing with the great crisis he had to face. . . . Why, even in this Panama business the *Evening Post* and the entire fool Mugwump crowd have fairly suffered from hysterics; and a goodly number of the Senators even

of my own party have shown about as much backbone as so many angle worms. However, I have kept things moving just right so far.

Late Tuesday, Hay did call in Bunau-Varilla for a conference. He had busily gone over technical points with his specialists and with other members of the Cabinet, working right through lunch and, as he wrote somewhat complainingly to his daughter a day or so later, "putting on all steam." If either he or Bunau-Varilla were concerned with possible Panamanian rejection of the pact, they did not express their doubts. Both knew that the new government had little choice in the matter and had gotten at least one sop—an enlargement of their boundaries beyond the narrow strip of isthmus first envisioned. Incredible as it may seem, Bunau-Varilla may even have believed what he afterward wrote. When he thought about presenting the finished work to the Panamanians, he declared, "I did not doubt it would be received with pleasure."

At approximately 4:30 Wednesday afternoon Amador and Boyd boarded a Pennsylvania Railroad express to Washington. And sometime around that moment the long crusade of Philippe Bunau-Varilla, begun when the old French canal died in 1889, ended. He was called to come to Secretary Hay's home. There the drafts were matched. The one Hay chose was essentially Bunau-Varilla's, with minor changes in wording. Seated at a desk in a blue drawing room, Hay took a pen from an inkstand that had belonged to Abraham Lincoln. When they had finished, he handed the "precious souvenir" to Bunau-Varilla. The task was achieved. At that moment Amador and Boyd were somewhere on the track between Philadelphia and Baltimore, rolling southward.

Hay went on to supper, presumably, and Bunau-Varilla, in a glow of self-satisfaction, made his way to the railroad station. When the train carrying the Panamanians groaned to a stop, he rushed up to greet Amador, who was the first of the two commissioners to emerge.

"The Republic of Panama is henceforth under the protection of the United States," Bunau-Varilla shouted. "The Canal treaty has just been signed." To the Frenchman's surprise, the elderly physician's reaction was not joyful "He nearly fainted upon the platform," recollected the envoy.

Dr. Amador was overwhelmed by emotion and by history—by the

events that had whirled him about and perhaps by his awareness that the stream of world commerce would one day flow through his nation, even though it was to be, in effect, a country partially occupied by a greater power.

THE TREATY PROVISIONS
November 18, 1903

ARTICLE I

The United States guarantees and will maintain the independence of the Republic of Panama.

ARTICLE II

The Republic of Panama grants to the United States in perpetuity the use, occupation and control of a zone of land and land under water for the construction, maintenance, operation, sanitation and protection of said Canal of the width of ten miles extending to the distance of five miles on each side of the center line of the route of the Canal to be constructed. . . . The Republic of Panama further grants to the United States in perpetuity the use, occupation and control of any other lands and waters outside of the zone above described which may be necessary and convenient for the construction, maintenance, operation, sanitation and protection of the said Canal or of any auxiliary canals or other works necessary and convenient for the construction, maintenance, operation, sanitation and protection of the said enterprise.

The Republic of Panama further grants in like manner to the United States in perpetuity all islands within the limits of the zone above described and in addition thereto the group of small islands in the Bay of Panama, named Perico, Naos, Culebra and Flamenco.

ARTICLE III

The Republic of Panama grants to the United States all the rights, power and authority within the zone mentioned and described in Article II of this agreement and within the limits of all auxiliary lands and waters mentioned and described in said Article II which the United States would possess and exercise if it were the sovereign of the territory within which said lands and waters are located to the entire exclusion of the exercise by the Republic of Panama of any such sovereign rights, power or authority.

ARTICLE XXIII

If it should become necessary at any time to employ armed forces for the safety or protection of the Canal, or of the ships that make use of the same, or the railways and auxiliary works, the United States shall have the right, at all times and in its discretion, to use its police and its land and naval forces or to establish fortifications for these purposes.

ARTICLE XXIV

If the Republic of Panama shall hereafter enter as a constituent into any other Government or into any union or confederation of states, so as to merge her sovereignty or independence in such Government, union or confederation, the rights of the United States under this convention shall not be in any respect lessened or impaired.

7

Baseball and Politics in the Progressive Era

STEVEN A. RIESS

• Baseball has in one form or another been played for centuries in many countries. The modern version of the sport was, according to official accounts, created by Abner Doubleday in Cooperstown, New York in 1839. By 1900 baseball had become the "national game" of the United States, and as such it was an attractive investment for wealthy sportsmen with a flair for the dramatic. It was popular more generally because it was thought to be free of the double dealing and forced compromises of the working world. There on the diamond, in full view of the spectators, each game was fought to the finish—fair and square—in the American tradition.

This aura of purity and virtue surrounding the game, however, was not long, if ever, justified. A scandal in 1919 involving the top baseball team, the Chicago White Sox (before "Babe" Ruth, Lou Gehrig, and other members of the "Murderers' Row" of the New York Yankees became national symbols), was only one of the many power tactics within the game. The White Sox owner, Charles Albert Comiskey, was notoriously tightfisted—he paid superstars like outfielder "Shoeless" Joe Jackson and third baseman George "Buck" Weaver wages well below those earned by lesser players on other teams. In retaliation, eight of the White Sox conspired to lose the World Series to the inferior Cincinnati Reds. The result was the infamous "Black Sox Scandal," the banishment of the offending individuals from the game, and the beginning of a prosperous career in behind-the-scenes manipulation.

In recent years, the tarnished image of professional sport has again been visible. Famous old franchises like the St. Louis Browns, the Boston Braves, the Brooklyn Dodgers, the Philadelphia Athletics, the Washington Senators, and the New York Giants have been uprooted as though the game were musical chairs. Fan loyalty has also been tested by the apparent willingness of their heroes to abandon team mates and fans for higher salaries and stronger franchises in distant cities. And finally, baseball purists have been dismayed by the expanding number of franchises and by the tendency to play more and more games at night—even during the World Series—for reasons having nothing to do with conditions on the field and everything to do with advertising revenue.

As a result, many fans long for the pre-World War II days, when franchises and players almost never moved, "virtue" ruled the diamond, and a fierce competitor like Ty Cobb could routinely sharpen his spikes in full view of the opposing second baseman. But as Steven A. Riess reminds us in the article below, our national pastime has never been an entirely honorable vocation free from the corruption of unscrupulous and greedy men: both politicians and businessmen were conspiring to make the sport a mutually profitable endeavor even before the turn of the century.

In the Progressive Era, club owners and sympathetic journalists created a self-serving ideology for baseball. They encouraged the public to believe that the game was one of the foremost indigenous American institutions and that it epitomized the finest qualities of a bygone rural age. Many sportswriters persuaded fans to regard the baseball magnates as benevolent, civic-minded individuals, dedicated to providing their fellow townsfolk with exciting and clean entertainment. Professional baseball however was not really "dominated" by such men, but by individuals with extremely close ties to urban political leaders who were usually members of local political machines. Ironically the national pastime which was said to exemplify the best characteristics of American society was operated by men who typified some of its worst aspects. In the period from 1901 to 1920, seventeen of the eighteen American and National League baseball teams were run by people with significant political connections. These club owners included political bosses, friends and relatives of men in what we could call high political places, and political allies like traction magnates and professional gamblers. In boss-riddled Cincinnati during the early 1900s for instance, the Cincinnati Reds baseball team was owned by a syndicate which at one time included the city's Republican boss, George B. Cox, his lieutenant, Water Works Commissioner August Herrmann, and the town's mayor, Julius Fleischmann. The Baltimore Orioles were run by such men as John Mahon, the leading Democrat in Maryland, Sidney Frank, brother of a prominent city councilman, and Judge Harry Goldman. And the Philadelphia Phillies owners included several traction magnates, state senators, and a former New York City police commissioner.

The close alliance between professional baseball teams and urban politicians was not unique to cities of any particular size or geographic location. Politicos were nearly always involved in the operations of the local ball clubs. A study of the professional baseball teams in such regionally representative cities as Atlanta, Chicago, and New York, dramatically suggests the strong link between baseball and politics. New York and Chicago were the two largest American cities at the turn of the century, and after 1903 they had between them five of the sixteen major league clubs. New York's politics were dominated by the notorious Tammany organization, while in Chicago, political machines were very active on the ward level. The southern commercial center of Atlanta was a considerably smaller town, ranking forty-third among all U.S. cities in population with 89,872 inhabitants in 1900. It had just one minor league team which played in the Class B Southern League. There was apparently no important political machine in Atlanta.

By examining the ties between professional baseball and local politicians in these three cities, it becomes clear that the relationship was a mutually beneficial one. Ball clubs with political allies secured preferential treatment from city governments with regards to assessments and various municipal services; inside information about real estate and traction developments; and protection against competitors and community opposition. Politicians benefited because the ball clubs were fine investments which provided them with sources of honest and dishonest graft, patronage for their supporters, traffic for their traction routes, and favorable publicity.

The baseball franchise in Atlanta was nearly always in the hands of important politicians. In 1895 the team was controlled by a joint stock company which included Councilman Joseph E. Maddox and Alderman Joseph Hirsch, who was the team's president. These executives needed whatever political influence they could muster because the East Side residents near Jackson and Old Wheat where Athletic Park was located wanted the field shut down as a public nuisance.

The club's enemies had failed in 1894 to secure a court order preventing the team from playing at Athletic Park, but a year later the issue was brought before the city council. The fight was led by Councilman William J. Campbell, who claimed that noise from the park would disturb the residential community, crowds attending the games were of a disagreeable character, and order could not be maintained there. Joseph Hirsch tried to counter these points by guaranteeing that disorder would not be tolerated, and promising that the park would get the best possible police protection. However, the community's petition was adopted, and the Atlanta Baseball Association lost its license.

There was considerable public disapproval of this move, led primarily by the daily newspapers which strongly deprecated the council's action. The city fathers were persuaded to reconsider their decision, and a compromise was reached whereby the team was given a trial period to prove that it could keep order at Athletic Park. There were no problems there that season, but in 1896 the owners moved their team to Brisbine Park, located on the South Side at Ira and Crumley, which was said to be better serviced by public transportation. The Atlanta Traction Company had a route near the site, and it offered the franchise certain inducements to get it to move there. People living in the vicinity protested loudly but to no avail and the club had no difficulty in renewing its license.

Traction companies were always deeply tied into local politics because of their need to secure long term franchises and obtain the right of eminent domain. These firms often owned amusement parks and baseball fields since they felt that these were excellent attractions for riders, and they wanted to be sure that their routes serviced these entertainments. Transit companies were important supporters of professional baseball in all parts of the country, especially the South, and cities like Augusta, Birmingham, Charleston, Macon, Mobile, Montgomery, and New Orleans all received substantial financial backing from the streetcar lines.

The Atlanta baseball team failed to last out the 1896 season. One year later, a new team was organized by attorney W. T. Moyers, but it survived for just two months. In the winter of 1898, Moyers requested assistance from the local traction interests who were receiving large profits from the fares of fans without contributing to the upkeep of the sport. Moyers persuaded the Atlanta Street Railway Company to support him, and their superintendent, F. W. Zimmerman, purchased stock in the club and became its vice-president. The firm had made $600 on its ballpark route the year before, in spite of the abbreviated season, and Zimmerman was afraid that the streetcar line would lose money if the club failed again. He anticipated profiting by about $3,000 in 1898, but his hopes were crushed when the Southern League collapsed early that season.

Professional baseball was not resumed in Atlanta until 1902 when the Selma club of the revived Southern League was moved there by its owners E. T. Peter and Abner Powell, a former baseball player and owner of the New Orleans franchise. Powell bought out his partner a year later, and developed the enterprise into a profitable venture. He invested about $10,500 in the club, and earned $40,000 by the end of 1904. His success aroused the ire of fans who watched with distaste as the proceeds from their tickets went to an outsider. As in the case of other American cities, the Atlanta fans had a great deal of pride in their hometown team. They preferred local control because they regarded the professional club as an important local institution which represented their city in interurban competition and vividly reflected the progressive character of their community. A clique of powerful politicians decided to try to drive Powell out and replace him with Atlanta owners by raising his taxes and establishing a license fee at an inordinately high level. A bill was introduced in the city council in 1904 which proposed charging Powell a fee of $50 plus a 5 percent tax on his gross receipts, at a time when no other baseball team was taxed outside of its license fee. Abner Powell's enemies were unable to push this drastic measure through the council, and instead it was decided to set the license fee at $200 plus another $100 for police protection. In the meanwhile, the county officials also established an annual $300 assessment against the ball club.

Powell's difficulties were compounded that year because the municipality purchased the 189 acre Piedmont Park, which included the

Piedmont Baseball Park where the Atlanta club had played since 1902, as well as other amusement attractions. Powell still had one year remaining on his lease, and had just signed an option to renew with the previous owner, but he was afraid that the city would make it difficult for him in the future. He also was being plagued by the traction interests, who not only did not give him any financial assistance, but actually charged Powell five dollars before every game to guarantee their service. The owner was forced to accede to public pressure and sold his club for $20,000 to a local syndicate which included Fire Chief W. R. Joyner, the team's president in 1889, and Lowry Arnold, solicitor of the criminal court.

Walthal R. Joyner had joined the fire company in 1870 when it was still a volunteer force, and remained after it became a municipal service, serving as fire chief from 1885 until 1906, when he resigned to become mayor. As fire chief, Joyner was the highest paid city official with a salary of $4,000. Joyner's group received financial support from the Georgia Railway and Electric Company, which hoped that the sport would generate traffic along its lines. The team was moved in 1907 from Piedmont Park to a site owned by the transit company on Ponce De Leon Avenue, directly opposite its amusement park. One year later, the streetcar line purchased complete control of the team which it kept until 1915, when the company sold it for $37,500 to a group led by Councilman Frank H. Reynolds and J. W. Goldsmith, Jr. Goldsmith's father was a former Atlanta councilman, and his uncle was city comptroller. However the traction firm continued to control the ballpark.

In the midwestern metropolis of Chicago, the influence of politicians on the baseball teams was just as keen as in Atlanta. The Chicago National League club was owned by Albert G. Spalding, one of the first professional baseball players, who was also founder and head of a great sporting goods company. His partners included attorney Charles M. Sherman, Cook County Sheriff Edward Barrett, and Adrian Anson, a former star ballplayer and manager, who was elected city clerk in 1905. The baseball park was the property of the A. G. Spalding Land Association, whose officers included Spalding, James A. Hart, the president of the team, John A. Walsh, a prominent banker and politician, and Charles T. Trego, a Republican merchant and banker, and director of the Chicago Board of Trade from 1875 until 1879.

The National League team enjoyed great success in Chicago during the late nineteenth century, and their good fortune encouraged the American League, which was founded in 1900, to place a team there. The franchise was awarded to Charles Comiskey, a native Chicagoan, who had been a ballplayer and manager before he purchased the St. Paul club of the Western League in 1895. Charles was the third son of John Comiskey, an Irish immigrant who arrived in Chicago in 1852. John Comiskey became a railroad executive and later entered local politics, serving a total of eleven years as alderman. He also held other high offices, including president of the city council, county clerk, and deputy United States internal revenue collector. This family background was immediately helpful for Charles Comiskey because a late winter had slowed down construction of his grandstand in 1900, but union artisans waived many of their rules proscribing night and Sunday labor so that John Comiskey's son would have his ballpark ready for Opening Day.

In 1905 the Chicago Cubs were sold by Spalding's agent James A. Hart to Charles W. Murphy for $105,000. Murphy was a former sports editor of the *Cincinnati Enquirer*, assistant city editor of the *Cincinnati Times-Star*, and press agent for the New York Giants. Murphy had just been hired by the Cubs for a similar job when he discovered that the team was for sale. He immediately rushed to his former publisher Charles Phelps Taft, who loaned him $100,000 to complete the transaction.

Charles P. Taft was the older half-brother, and political adviser of Secretary of War William Howard Taft. Charles was an important power in Ohio Republican politics, and had once served in the United States House of Representatives. He had strong aspirations for a Senate seat, but decided instead to devote most of his attention to helping his brother get elected president. Charles P. Taft had married a wealthy heiress, and they invested a considerable amount of their money in professional baseball.

Charles Murphy's investment was a remarkable success and he quickly repaid the Taft loan, although Taft remained as a minority stockholder. In 1906, the Cubs made $165,000, or more than the price paid for the controlling shares one year before. Taft estimated that the franchise earned $1,260,000 for its stockholders between

1906 and 1915. During that decade the Cubs won four pennants (1906–08, 1910), two world championships (1907–08), and never finished worse than fourth in the league standings. Dividends on capital stock from 1907 to 1913 were an incredible 810 percent. However, competition from the Federal League and public resentment against Charles Murphy who fired his popular manager Frank Chance in 1912, and traded away several of the fans' favorite stars like Ed Reulbach and Joe Tinker in 1913, caused profits to plummet in the next two years to 20 percent and 5 percent, respectively.

There was also considerable public displeasure over Murphy's mishandling of the ticket scalping problem. Speculators never seemed to have any trouble getting tickets and fans believed that politicians were supporting and protecting them. The scalping of tickets probably received its greatest notoriety during the 1908 World Series between the Cubs and the Detroit Tigers when the Chicago fandom were unable to obtain tickets at the box office because the pasteboards had been secretly sold to speculators. Mayor Busse contemplated retaliating by forbidding the playing of the Series in Chicago on the grounds that the ballpark was unsafe, but the intercession of Corporation Counsel Edward Brundage on behalf of the Cubs owners deterred the mayor. The fans responded to the scalping scandal by boycotting the games played in Chicago.

The combination of the ticket scalping scandals, the public alienation from Murphy by his trades of popular players, and his habit of making indiscreet comments to journalists which reflected poorly on baseball, persuaded the other National League owners to oust him before the start of the 1914 season. Charles P. Taft agreed to buy Murphy's controlling interest for about $500,000 but he simultaneously announced his intention to sell the franchise as soon as possible. Several syndicates were formed to purchase the club, and they all included prominent Chicago politicians. One group consisted of William Hale Thompson, a former alderman and future mayor, James A. Pugh, a promoter, who was Thompson's political ally, Charles A. McCulloch, a taxicab executive and Republican politician, and John R. Thompson, a restaurateur and former county treasurer. Another combination included coal merchant John T. Connery, whose brothers were the city clerk and county recorder, his cousin Roger Sullivan, who was in his twenty-fifth year as a Cook County Democratic Committeeman, and was widely recognized as the dominant Democrat in the state, and Harry Gibbons, who had once run for county sheriff.

Taft did not find any of their offers acceptable, and held on to the club for two more seasons until he sold it early in 1916 for $500,000 to Charles Weeghman the owner of the Chicago Federal team, and his associates. Weeghman's partners were prominent Chicago businessmen and they included Albert D. Lasker, who was the principal stockholder, C. A. McCulloch, A. D. Plamondon, William Walker, and William K. Wrigley. They were important figures in local and national Republican politics who lunched together daily to plot strategy. Lasker was a member of the Republican National Committee, and he and William Wrigley were prominent supporters of California Governor Hiram Johnson for their party's presidential nomination in 1920. After the nominating convention, they rallied to the side of the Republican candidate, Senator Warren G. Harding of Ohio, and Lasker became his public relations director. Harding subsequently rewarded Lasker by making him head of the U.S. Shipping Board.

In Chicago, as in Atlanta, the magnates' political influence helped the teams cope with such matters as the city's building codes and licensing policies. Municipal laws generally stipulated certain requirements for the baseball club to fulfill before they received their license so that the ballpark would be kept safe for spectators and the games would not disturb the surrounding communities. Strict new building codes were written in many large cities during the Progressive Era and some of their sections had a direct impact on professional baseball. In Chicago, for instance, club owners had to obtain frontage consents for their site, and were prohibited from constructing a park within 200 feet of a hospital, church, or school. In addition, no new ballpark could be built within the city's fire limits unless it was built with fireproof materials. This condition benefited the older established franchises against potential interlopers just as other progressive regulatory legislation assisted the large firms in other industries, like meatpacking, to discourage new competition and eliminate their weaker rivals.

City inspectors were required to examine new baseball parks to make sure they were properly constructed, and then annually reexamine them to check for possible defects and safety violations. However, magnates or their contractors could utilize their political influence to secure lax enforcement of the building codes. For example, when an addition was built to the grandstands at the Cubs' West Side Park in 1908, it was inadequately inspected because the contractor Michael F. Powers was a business partner of former Building Commissioner Joseph Downey. These inspections were not intended to be punitive, unless the owners had foolishly incurred the wrath of some politico, but were aimed at discovering potentially dangerous violations which could then be rectified.

The license fee varied widely from city to city, depending, at least partly, on the amount of political power the franchise could muster. In the early 1900s, New York's standard amusement fee was $500, but in Cincinnati, where the team was operated by members of the local Republican machine, the club paid just $100 until 1912 when Mayor Henry T. Hunt's reform administration raised the levy to $750. Chicago's license fees were established on a sliding scale, which varied according to the ballpark's seating capacity. At first, the two professional clubs were assessed $300 each while the several semiprofessional clubs paid $100. Then in 1909 the amusement fees were substantially increased to a point where the Cubs were taxed $1,000 because their field seated more than 15,000 and the White Sox were assessed $700 since their smaller park seated fewer than 15,000.

After World War I when the city was nearly bankrupt, various measures were taken to raise capital, including an increase in the license schedules for baseball parks. The license fee for fields with capacities in excess of 20,000 was set at $2,000, and the impost on grounds seating between 15,000 and 20,000 spectators was made $1,500. Comiskey Park fell under the higher rate since it seated well over 30,000 people, and the Cubs were assessed the lesser amount. Then in 1921, Alderman Anton J. Cermak, the leader in the search for new sources of revenue, decided to raise previously established fees while also extending the licensing system to a variety of professions previously not covered. Cermak introduced a bill in the city council which called for a 5 percent tax on the gross receipts of the professional baseball teams. The local major league clubs were quite disturbed by the proposal, since if it had been operating one year before, the White Sox would have been taxed $30,000 and the Cubs, $20,000. Alfred Austrian, the attorney for both franchises, and a familiar figure to local politicians, met with the city council's Committee on Revenue, and tried to demonstrate the folly of Cermak's bill. Austrian convinced the aldermen not to adopt that legislation, and instead provided them with a compromise measure they later enacted, which doubled the established license fees for the major league teams.

The baseball teams expected that as taxpayers, they were entitled to police protection, both inside and outside their fields. The danger of riot or some lesser disturbance always existed whenever thousands of people gathered in one place, and crowds at ball games tended to be particularly unruly. Fans jostled with each other as they lined up for tickets, and once inside the park they tended to make themselves obnoxious by shouting caustic comments at players, umpires, and other spectators. Besides preserving peace, police officers were also needed to deter gambling inside the parks and ticket scalping outside. Chicago's municipal patrolmen were assigned to duty inside the ballparks even though it was private property. The teams were not charged for the service, which amounted to a daily savings of twenty to fifty dollars. Several bills were introduced in the city council to assess the magnates for the cost of this protection, but they were never passed.

The single most important problem that faced Chicago baseball executives in the first twenty years of the century was not recruiting ballplayers, discovering a suitable location for their ballparks, keeping taxes low, or securing police protection. Rather the principal dilemma was the disclosure in 1920 that the previous year's World Series had been fixed by several White Sox players in the interest of certain professional gamblers. Despite the rhetoric of professional baseball which claimed the sport was free of that vice, baseball was strongly tainted by gambling. In fact, several baseball owners were professional gamblers, horsemen, heavy bettors, or friends of professional gamblers. The sport served as a nexus between politics and organized crime.

While the main attraction of baseball was the action of the game, unlike horse racing for instance, the nature of the sport was highly conducive to betting, and people wagered on the outcome of ball games, the number of hits and runs, and even the probability of a batted ball being caught. Gambling on baseball was popular throughout the nation, especially in cities like Boston and Pittsburgh where there were no race tracks to interest the betting crowd. The baseball owners spoke out against pools and other betting systems because they were afraid that public gambling on the sport might harm its prestige and reputation for honesty, and thereby its appeal, by encouraging fans to believe that gamblers were fixing games.

But in spite of their rhetoric, the baseball owners did little to curtail the gambling menace. Signs were posted inside the parks which declared that betting was forbidden there, and private police roamed the stands to discourage open wagering. Only on rare occasions were any bettors evicted from the premises. Professional gamblers were seldom arrested, and rarely convicted, since it was very difficult to prove a case against them and because they were protected by influential political allies. In addition, there was no great demand for strict enforcement of the anti-betting codes because the professional gamblers were dispensing a desired service for their clients and did not harm innocent bystanders.

The gambling problem was climaxed by the revelation near the end of the 1920 season that the 1919 World Series between the Chicago White Sox and an apparently inferior Cincinnati Reds team had been fixed by eight White Sox players in the interest of the infamous Arnold Rothstein. When Charles Comiskey first became suspicious that the outcome of the Series had been prearranged, he visited with his friend, State's Attorney Maclay Hoyne, who promised to keep the matter out of the courts while Comiskey tried to clear up the affair by himself. Hoyne cooperated fully with Comiskey and did not initiate an investigation of the rumored fix until after Chicago Cubs President William Veeck, Sr. reported receiving a number of telegrams and telephone calls warning him that the Cubs game scheduled for August 31, 1920 was fixed. Hoyne then called for a special grand jury to investigate the entire matter of baseball gambling, responding both to the growing public demands for an inquiry and his own need for a campaign issue for the forthcoming primary election.

Hoyne lost his bid for reelection, but before leaving office, he stole the confessions made by several of the indicted ballplayers together with their waivers of immunity. The people behind this theft were Alfred Austrian, Comiskey's lawyer, and William Fallon, the attorney for Arnold Rothstein. The loss of that testimony severely hampered the prosecution's case, and the defendants were found not guilty. Nevertheless, Judge Kennesaw Mountain Landis, the newly appointed commissioner of baseball, refused to reinstate the athletes. In 1924, when Joe Jackson, one of the eight players involved in the scandal, sued to regain some back pay, the missing documents were conveniently produced by Comiskey to prove Jackson's complicity in fixing the World Series.

The far reaching political ties of Chicago Baseball Clubs seem almost minor in comparison to the situation in New York City where the notorious Tammany Hall organization was intimately involved in the affairs of local baseball teams since the late 1860s. The New York Mutuals, for instance, a leading amateur club of the post-Civil War period, was controlled by the unscrupulous William Marcy Tweed, who got the city government to contribute $30,000 to its upkeep. The players were ostensibly city employees, but they were really being subsidized to play baseball.

Tammany had complete control of professional baseball in New York City until 1890 when several Republican politicians established a Brotherhood League team there. That association lasted just one year, but the competition bankrupted the Tammany owners of the New York Giants, who agreed to merge their club with the Brotherhood team. The Giants were operated for the next four years by Republicans Edward Talcott, a stockbroker, Cornelius Van Cott, postmaster of New York, and General Edward A. McAlpin, a tobacconist and realtor who had been active in elective politics before becoming a leader in the Republican club movement.

The Democratic organization regained control of the franchise in January, 1895, when Andrew Freedman, a rising young realtor, purchased the controlling interest for $48,000. Freedman had joined Tammany in 1881 at the age of twenty-one, and he soon became an intimate friend of Richard Croker, the machine's future boss. Freedman was able to secure many choice business opportunities because of his close ties with Croker, and the two men cooperated in several ventures. Freedman never held any governmental position, but he did have enormous political influence through his alliance with Boss Croker and as a member of Tammany's powerful finance committee, which was its central policy making body. He also served as treasurer of the national Democratic party in 1897.

Freedman ran his baseball team as if it were an adjunct of Tammany, fighting with the baseball players and the press, encouraging rowdy baseball playing, and bullying his fellow magnates into accepting many of his demands. For instance, the league awarded him an annual grant of $15,000 just so he would continue leasing Manhattan Field which was adjacent to the Polo Grounds and was the logical site for a competing league to use for a ballpark.

Interlopers were afraid to invade New York as long as Andrew Freedman remained in baseball since he controlled most of the suitable locations for baseball fields through leases or options, and also because invaders knew that even if they did somehow secure a good lot, Freedman would use his political clout to get streets cut through their property or disrupt their transit facilities. The American League hoped to establish a New York franchise, but they were deterred by Freedman's presence. The association proclaimed itself a major league in 1901, but a New York team was essential to certify that higher status and to obtain greater profits. Thus the American Leaguers were quite interested in the outcome of the 1901 mayoralty election because experts gave the Fusion ticket a good chance to beat the machine, and the baseball people anticipated that if the election went poorly for Tammany, Freedman would lose his power to prevent them from putting a team in the borough.

Tammany was indeed soundly defeated in the elections as Seth Low was elected mayor, and William Travers Jerome was selected district attorney. Several newspapers predicted that the American League would soon establish a club in Gotham as a consequence. But in spite of the debacle, Freedman was still strong enough to forestall the efforts of the new league. However the election did harm the Giants' president's power within National League councils, by encouraging some of the other owners to finally stand up to him. An effort was actually made by the Spalding faction to ostracize him at the League's annual winter meeting in December of 1901 as a first move towards taking his franchise away from him. But enough magnates remained loyal to Freedman to prevent the move.

Nine months later, Andrew Freedman sold his team to John T. Brush, the former owner of the Cincinnati Reds, for $200,000, keeping just a few shares of stock. Freedman said he was disappointed in his investment which had never reached its potential, and was tired of the abuse being heaped upon him from all quarters. Furthermore, he had more important business matters to attend to, principally the construction of the New York subway system. He was a director of the company that built the underground, and Freedman used his influence to block the Interborough Rapid Transit Construction Company from agreeing to subsidize an American League team early in 1903. He also prevented the Fourth Avenue Line from building a station close to the Brooklyn Dodgers playing field.

John T. Brush, the new Giants owner, was a highly successful Indianapolis clothing merchant, who first got into baseball when he acquired the Indianapolis team of the American Association in 1887 for a nominal sum. Three years later he purchased the Cincinnati Reds for $25,000, and then sold them in 1902 for $146,000. A newspaper story was published several years later which asserted that Cincinnati's Republican political machine had apparently forced Brush to sell his club to them. The journalist alleged that a rumor had reached Brush that York Street was going to be extended through the ballpark as part of a series of municipal improvements. Brush was perturbed by the gossip and met with a local politician who advised him to sell the team to the Republican organization for a fraction of its real worth. Brush denied the story, but he did sell the franchise to a consortium comprised of Boss George B. Cox, Mayor Fleischmann, and August Herrmann.

New York at this time had a second National League team, the Brooklyn Dodgers, as a result of the city's annexation of Brooklyn in 1898. The owner of that team was Charles Ebbets who had just purchased the club. He had been a printer until 1883 when he was hired by the Brooklyn franchise as a sort of general factotum, and his duties included printing scorecards and selling tickets. In 1898 Ebbets moved his enterprise from its distant site in Brownsville to its original location near the Gowanus Canal in Red Hook where the team was much more accessible to its fans. He received considerable financial support in this venture from streetcar magnate Al Johnson, bother of Cleveland's future mayor, Tom Johnson. The traction executive had routes located near the old site which he expected would benefit from the traffic of fans attending games. Fifteen years later, Ebbets moved his team to another spot in Flatbush, where he nearly went bankrupt building a modern fireproof stadium. Consequently he had to take in the McKeever brothers, who were prominent Brooklyn contractors, as partners. They were active in politics, and Steven McKeever had served a term in the city council.

Charles Ebbets himself, was a notable political figure, having served several years as an alderman and a term in the state assembly. In 1904 he ran for the state senate but was defeated in the Roosevelt landslide. Ebbets tried to put his political skills to practical use by campaigning for reform of the blue laws which proscribed Sunday baseball in New York. Sunday reform received substantial Tammany backing for it was a popular measure among its constituents. Ebbets hoped to secure Sunday baseball by staging Sabbath games in 1904, 1905, and in 1906, by circumventing the prohibitory laws. He did not sell tickets of admission to games, but admitted fans free if they purchased programs or magazines for fifty cents or seventy-five cents or if they volunteered a 'donation'. He received cooperation from the police who rarely made arrests for violations, and from magistrates who rarely convicted anyone tried in their courts. However the vigorous Sabbatarian organizations prevailed because they secured redress in higher courts, and got a reform police commissioner to force Ebbets to cease his efforts at evading the law. Charles Ebbets and his allies then turned to the state legislature where they hoped to repeal the blue laws. Sunday reform bills had been introduced in Albany each year since 1897, but upstate rural Republicans controlled both chambers, and the Democrats rarely even got their bills out of committee. Only after World War I, when a broad coalition of labor leaders, veterans organizations, reformers, and Tammanyites was established, did the "repressive" Sabbath laws get amended to permit Sunday baseball. The results of this crusade indicated that the urban political machines were not omnipotent and could not do everything they wished.

New York became the site of a third major league team in March, 1903, when the American League finally succeeded in placing a franchise there. American League President Ban Johnson had tried for some time to find a group of non-Tammanyites who had sufficient influence to counter Andrew Freedman and obtain a suitable site for a ballpark. But he was unsuccessful, and in desperation acceded to Tammany and granted the franchise to some politicos who found a location for a baseball field that Freedman did not control. The syndicate was ostensibly headed by Joseph Gordon, a former owner of the New York Giants, who had been an assistant district leader, state assemblyman, and city buildings superintendent. The real owners, though, were Frank J. Farrell, a leading gambler, and William Devery, a former police chief. Tom Foley, the leader of the Second District, and a future sheriff, was a minor stockholder. The lucrative construction contracts were awarded to Thomas McAvoy, the Tammany leader in Washington Heights where the new field was located.

Frank Farrell was said to be the head of New York's gambling trust in 1901, which allegedly included Chief Devery, Police Commissioner Joseph Sexton, City Clerk J. F. Carroll, Mayor Van Wyck, and Tim Sullivan, the powerful leader of the Third District. Farrell had important interests in several local poolrooms, and he owned a luxurious casino, designed by the noted architect Stanford White, which was frequented by members of high society. He also had substantial holdings at the Saratoga Springs resort, and was a partner with Julius Fleischmann in a major racing stable.

Farrell's associate, William Devery, had joined the police force in 1878, and he advanced rapidly through the ranks, aided by his political friends, Richard Croker and Tim Sullivan. Devery was appointed police chief after a turbulent twenty-year career during which he was repeatedly castigated for taking bribes to permit gamblers and keepers of disorderly houses to operate. Throughout his flamboyant tenure, Devery could usually be found at the corner of Twenty-eighth Street and Eighth Avenue, meeting with bailbondsmen, dive owners, and pool room operators. His regime was so blatantly corrupt that the state legislature decided in 1901 to abolish his position and replace it with a commission system. However, Tammany circumvented the intent of that reform by getting the new police commissioner to appoint Devery as his deputy, and then the commissioner left the department in his hands. When the Fusion mayor Seth Low took office on January 1, 1902, one of the first things he did was relieve Devery of his post.

After the disastrous election in the fall of 1901, William Devery broke with the Croker wing of Tammany which had blamed him for their defeat. He ran for district leader of the Ninth Ward in 1902 and defeated the regular organization's handpicked candidate. Tammany's executive committee then issued him an unprecedented rebuff when they refused to accept his claim for admission to the central committee as the duly elected leader of the Ninth District. Miffed by this rebuke, he left the regular party and established his own district organization which was strong enough to elect an assemblyman.

Buoyed by this success, Devery ran for mayor on an independent slate in 1903, but was soundly thrashed.

The close relations between the owners of the New York baseball clubs and Tammany Hall helped the teams obtain favored treatment from the police department, which not only maintained order outside the playing fields, but also patrolled the environs of the ballparks. In 1907, however, this service was discontinued by the reform police commissioner, General Thomas A. Bingham, who decided to enforce the law which prohibited the use of municipal police within private property unless there was some manifest danger present. Bingham's decision was immediately tested by the New York Giants, who publicly announced that they would not engage any private police for the Opening Day game that year and warned Bingham that he would be responsible for the consequences. The result was a riot when many of the 17,000 spectators swarmed over the field at the beginning of the ninth inning. After fifteen minutes of chaos, the management appealed to police officers outside for assistance, but the constables refused to go inside and help quell the disturbance.

Bingham's action was supported by the *New York Times* which noted that the law was quite clear in its proscription of the use of city patrolmen to police private grounds. Bingham had previously complained of the way his staff was often weakened whenever officers were detailed to perform work that should have been done by special police at the expense of individuals running the particular event. He felt entrepreneurs should be made to realize that the cost of protection was a necessary and expected expense, and that people who assembled crowds for their own private financial gain should pay for the safeguarding of the affair out of their profits.

After this confrontation, the Giants decided to hire a number of uniformed Pinkerton agents to keep order at the Polo Grounds. The New York Americans retained retired policemen for their field. As long as there was no disorder, these operatives were adequate. But on those occasions when the fans did get out of control, the special policemen were virtually useless because they did not have any legitimate authority or power, and the spectators refused to listen to them. Besides, the guards were probably more frightened of the spectators than the fans were of them, and they were careful not to antagonize the crowds. The owners continued for some time to try to reverse Bingham's decision and get uniformed policemen to patrol their events, but the city government only relented on rare occasions. This was another of those rare instances when the political machine failed to assist the local ball clubs.

The police continued to work outside the ballparks, and as in Chicago, one of their biggest problems was ticket scalping. Extensive preparations were announced by the New York police to eliminate scalping at the 1912 World Series. Plainclothesmen and other officers were detailed to keep known speculators from obtaining extra tickets at the public sale, and an area was cordoned off for fans waiting in line for tickets. The first one hundred individuals in line were recognized as either plainclothesmen, uniformed officers, or speculators, and people with pull were seen going through the ticket offices several times. Instead of going to the end of the queue, these repeaters returned to the front where policemen helped them back into line. Scalpers also obtained additional paste boards by buying them from people who had waited in line or by bringing boys and women with them to purchase tickets. One leading sportswriter estimated that a quarter of the reserved seats were sold to speculators.

In 1915 and 1919, respectively, the Yankees and Giants were sold to men with substantial influence in Tammany Hall. William Devery and Frank Farrell sold their club for $460,000 to Jacob Ruppert, Jr., the heir to the Ruppert Breweries fortune, and Tillinghast Huston, a civil engineer who made his fortune in Cuba after the Spanish-American War. The old owners had become estranged from each other as they bickered over the disappointing performance of their team on the field and at the box office, especially in comparison to their rivals, the Giants. Furthermore, they were both in dire need of funds.

Jacob Ruppert, the principal figure in the new Yankee management, was an important Tammanyite. He joined the organization in 1888 at the age of twenty-one, in search of prestige, power, and protection for the family business. Ruppert eventually became a sachem of the association and served as a member of its finance committee. He was personally selected by Boss Croker in 1897 to run for the presidency of the city council in order to balance the ticket with a German candidate. However Croker had to withdraw the nomination because it failed to placate the German-Americans who had expected the mayoralty nomination and because it aroused the jealousy of the other New York brewers. As a reward for his party loyalty, Ruppert was nominated for Congress from a Republican district in 1898. He was elected in an upset and served in that position until 1907.

The New York Giants were sold by the Brush family in 1919 to Charles Stoneham for one million dollars. Stoneham was a member of Tammany Hall and counted Al Smith and Tom Foley among his political allies. He was a curb market broker of dubious integrity who had several brushes with the law because of his shady business transactions. Charles Stoneham had two minor partners in the baseball team, John J. McGraw, the Giants' manager, and Magistrate Francis X. McQuade, who was a leading figure in the movement for Sunday baseball. McQuade had handled several cases involving baseball playing on the Sabbath in his capacity as a judge, and he always released the defendants and urged reform of the antiquated codes. Stoneham's investment was quite profitable as the club made $296,803 in 1920, which was the most any National League club made that year. But the Yankees, who were Stoneham's tenants at the Polo Grounds did even better, earning $373,862.

The close ties that existed between local politicians and the professional baseball teams in Atlanta, Chicago, and New York, were typical of the relationship that existed between most franchises and their communities in the Progressive Era. A ball club's political associations were often direct, in which case the team's executives were themselves party leaders or elected officials. In other instances, the political elite were friends of the owners or else they were closely tied to a traction company which supported the ball club. Political connections were useful for the baseball teams because they received preferential treatment from the city governments in matters relating to taxation and municipal services, their owners were privy to confidential information about real estate and traction developments, and they were protected against potential competitors and other enemies. In return, the politicos manipulated the local baseball for their benefit in several ways. They used the franchise as a source of honest graft and patronage, as an inducement to encourage people to travel on the traction routes they operated, and to improve their public image.

The domination of professional baseball by urban politicians reflected their ubiquitous presence in all aspects of city life. Businessmen and leaders of various public institutions had to come to terms with them if they wished to be successful. However, even though the machines were extremely powerful, they were not omnipotent, as the New York magnates discovered when they attempted to play Sunday baseball or when they tried to prevent a reform police commissioner from withdrawing police protection inside their ballparks. The preeminence of politicos in the national pastime created an interesting paradox since contemporaries regarded baseball as an institution which epitomized the finest qualities of a bygone age, like individualism, honesty, competitiveness, courage, and fairmindedness, and which certified the relevancy of these values in an urbanized, industrialized, and bureaucratized era. Yet the sport was controlled by urban bosses, the enemy of the old-stock Americans who believed in these traditional American values. The machine politicians symbolized to them all that was evil in American society.

MATURE NATION
1920–1979

8

The New Woman: Historians' Interpretations of Women in the 1920s

ESTELLE B. FREEDMAN

> • Although the end of World War I ushered in a new era in
> the women's movement, historians long regarded the period
> between the passage of the nineteenth amendment in 1920
> and the publication of Betty Friedan's The Feminine Mys-
> tique in 1964 as one of relative quiescence in the struggle for
> full equality by the "second sex." The explanation for the
> lack of forward thrust was that the very success of the suffrage
> movement convinced many people that there was no longer
> much purpose in or need for women's rights.
>
> By the late 1960s, such an analysis had become unsatisfac-
> tory to many historians. The increasing attention focused on
> existing sexism in contemporary society forced a reevaluation
> of women's history in previous decades. Perhaps nowhere was
> this more fruitful than in accounts of the 1920s, the symbols
> of which have long been speakeasies, flappers, rumble seats,
> and prosperity. Younger historians challenged the notion that
> women had won full equality by virtue of the nineteenth
> amendment, and they suggested a number of fresh perspec-
> tives on feminist issues during that period. Professor Estelle
> B. Freedman of Stanford University, whose major research
> effort has focused on women's prisons, has been in the fore-
> front of the effort to reinterpret women's history in light of
> new findings and methods of analysis. In the following essay,
> she evaluates interpretations of the 1920s that touch on the
> role of women in a transition era.

In his suggestive article, "What Happened to the Progressive Movement in the 1920s," Arthur S. Link analyzed the legacy of the pre-
World War I "progressive coalition" of businessmen, farm groups,

From the *Journal of American History* LXI (Sept. 1974), 372-393. Reprinted
by permission.

labor unions, and "advocates of social justice." However, he neglected to mention the fate of the feminists, either those women active in the suffrage movement, or those involved in broader areas of social reform. Despite Link's inattention to women reformers, the question he posed about the progressive movement in the twenties should be asked of the women's movement as well. What happened to feminism during the decade after the political goal of suffrage had been achieved?

Failure to consider the women's movement in the nineteen-twenties is not an uncommon oversight among historians. Even students of women's history, such as Eleanor Flexnor, Andrew Sinclair, and Aileen Kraditor, conclude their accounts with the passage of the nineteenth amendment. Until very recently, this tendency to ignore post-1920 women's history has fostered the repetition of a standard image of American women in the twenties. Frederick Lewis Allen's 1931 account is representative:

> The revolution [in manners and morals] was accelerated . . . by the growing independence of the American woman. She won the suffrage in 1920. She seemed, it is true, to be very little interested in it once she had it; she voted, but mostly as the unregenerate men about her did. . . . Few of the younger women could rouse themselves to even a passing interest in politics: to them it was a sordid and futile business, without flavor and without hope. Nevertheless, the winning of the suffrage had its effect. It consolidated woman's position as man's equal.

William E. Leuchtenburg reached a similar conclusion nearly three decades later:

> The new woman wanted the same freedom that men had and the same economic and political rights. By the end of the 1920's she had come a long way. Before the war, a lady did not set foot in a saloon; after the war, she entered a speakeasy as thoughtlessly as she would go into a railroad station . . . In the business and political worlds, women competed with men; in marriage, they moved toward a contractual role . . . Sexual independence was merely the most sensational aspect of the generally altered status of women.

These and other accounts have attributed the following characteristics to the "New Women" of the 1920s: they failed to vote as a block or in greater numbers than did men; their manners and morals differed sharply from those of previous generations; and their legal and economic position had so improved that for the first time in history, women had become the social and economic equals of men.

An examination of the record, however, reveals that historians have repeated these descriptions not because research and analysis have confirmed their validity, but because no new questions have been asked about women in the 1920s since the initial impressionistic observations were made. The fact that these interpretations have been handed down for forty years with very little modification makes them suspect, and closer analysis confirms that several important historical questions have remained unanswered. Who precisely was the New Woman; what was her fate after 1920; and how does her history relate to that of the women's movement? Specifically, historians need to clarify when and why the organized women's movement lost its influence; whether enfranchisement affected women's efforts for social reform and for equal rights for their sex; precisely what economic gains women made; and how widely and deeply the moral revolution reached.

Original and creative use of primary resources is obviously necessary to answer these questions. But before this research is undertaken, it is essential to understand what has already been written about women in the twenties. This essay will provide such an historiographical framework by tracing interpretations of the new woman from the 1920s to the early 1970s. The influence of historical events will be of central concern, as will the shift of conceptual frameworks from the analysis of the 1920s to the contemporary revival of women's history.

For years, historians agreed with Mary Beard's claim that women are a positive "force in history." They praised the post-1920 woman as an active participant in American politics and economic life, as if trying to correct what Arthur Meier Schlesinger had termed "the pall of silence which historians have allowed to rest" over women's "successes and achievements." Women's history was merely an effort to include more women and their successes in the history books. In later years after social scientists rediscovered the "woman question" in the 1950s, historians groped towards a feminist perspective. This approach to women's history, as Gerda Lerner has explained, finds that women have been unable to contribute fully to American society—even after suffrage—because they have remained the oppressed victims of history. If the latter view prevails, women's history must become the study of a unique interest group, a study which requires new forms of research and new conceptual models.

Since historians were relatively silent on the question of the new woman during all but two periods—from approximately 1927 to 1933 and from 1964 to the present—broad accounts and textbooks must suffice as evidence for parts of this review of the literature. Towards the end of the long period of neglect, scholars in other disciplines began to question the validity of the image of women in post-World War I America. By the time a revival of interest in the subject had reached popular dimensions (coincident with but not necessarily related to the 1963 publication of *The Feminine Mystique*), historians too had begun to review their conceptions of the new woman. Numerous revisionist interpretations can now be expected; from what historiographical traditions do they proceed?

Social commentators of the late 1920s and early 1930s reached mixed conclusions in their evaluations of the first decade of woman suffrage. Concentrating on political and economic measures of emancipation, they praised women's participation in American society, in spite of strong indications that women had not, in fact, achieved equality.

As might be expected, many analyses reflected presuffrage positions. In a 1927 *Current History* symposium on "The New Woman," Charlotte Perkins Gilman found extensive evidence of women's political, literary and economic achievement since enfranchisement, and Carrie Chapman Catt wrote that the vote had been used profitably to remove discrimination on the state level and to improve legislation for women and children. Former opponents of woman suffrage found very little to praise in articles decrying "Woman's Encroachment on Man's Domain," and the "Evils of Woman's Revolt Against the Old Standards." Ida Tarbell, an "anti" in the early suffrage debate, wrote in 1930, "I don't feel that women have contributed anything new or worthwhile . . . I maintain that this ten years experience has proved that women have become the tools of party leaders, just as men have."

Positive but apologetic evaluations of women's progress appeared in a special 1929 issue of the *Annals of the American Academy of Political and Social Science* devoted to "Women in the Modern

World." A regional director of the League of Women Voters argued that it would take more than eight years to break a tradition of exclusion from public affairs. Therefore the contribution of women should not be measured by the size of their vote. Another contributor proclaimed that already "women have successfully stepped from social life into the political realm," even as she felt it necessary to assure her readers that women politicians did not shirk their domestic duties.

Journalists, too, concentrated on political progress. Although generally favorable, their analyses were usually qualified by an apologetic tone. "Not many of our editors seem enthusiastic over the showing made under the Nineteenth Amendment," a *Literary Digest* survey found; "Yet on the other hand, few are pessimistic." A representative editorial comment came from the Winston-Salem *Journal:*

> The women have acquitted themselves well during this first ten years of their political enfranchisement. But even greater results will be expected during the next decade. During the ten years just passed the women have been laying a foundation. The superstructure of achievement now remains to be built.

Social scientists reported few substantive gains for women since suffrage, but they were not without sympathy for the problems the new voters faced. The authors of a statistical study of the 1920 election found that women had not utilized the ballot to the same extent as men, nor had they voted predictably. However, they suggested that women were politically handicapped—not by a psychological incapacity for politics, as some critics claimed, but only by lack of experience. "When participating in politics has become through habit as natural to women as to men . . . women will undoubtedly participate in all phases of political life on a basis of actual as well as nominal equality with men."

Although most authors stressed political progress, a few also evaluated women's economic and personal rights. Editor V. F. Calverton believed that "woman's economic independence has been a far more important item in her emancipation than [has] her political enfranchisement." He was impressed by the increasing number of married women who were working and by the effects of the growing women's labor force in fortifying single women's desires for independence. However, he duly noted the pervasive discrimination against women workers, particularly that of organized labor against married women in industry.

Other writers who explored the possibilities of social and cultural emancipation of women in the twenties found, like Calverton, that antifeminist attitudes persisted. George Britt wrote that "it is possible for the Southern girl now to an extent never permitted before to . . . become a person and not just another woman." But, after citing individual examples of professional women in the South, the growth of women's clubs during the 1920s, the changes in personal habits such as smoking, and the involvement of women in social reform, Britt concluded: "The Southern girl may like to earn a little money and have her fling, but the ideal in the back of her head is a nice house in the home town and a decorative position in society."

Former Judge Ben Lindsey drew on his experiences counselling youth in the 1920s to evidence a moral revolution: premarital sex, birth control, drinking, and contempt for older values. Yet almost every case he cited revealed a strong conflict between the appeal of flamboyant freedom and the sense of sin it still engendered. Lindsey suspected that in a few years each lively flapper would become "a happy, loyal wife with several children."

In spite of indications that only a few political rights and not many broader feminist goals had been achieved in the 1920s, the optimistic writers of the decade generally hailed the end of discrimination against women. Typical of their strained efforts was a 1930 essay by feminist Chase Going Woodhouse. She maintained an overly enthusiastic tone, even as her evidence wore thin. Women had made significant advances in education, Woodhouse wrote, particularly "outstanding improvements in nursing education," but Harvard still refused to train women for law and medicine. Employment figures "increased steadily," she claimed, although for the period after 1919 she had to juggle figures to include housewives among the "gainfully employed." Women advanced in the professions, but mainly in teaching, and mostly before 1920. Despite the fact that in education, industry and politics, "despair and resentment" characterized women's responses, Woodhouse claimed "steadily gained recognition" for women.

Certainly women had made some advances by the end of the 1920s, although few commentators explained how their economic and political gains measured in comparison to the previous decades or with feminists' larger goals of economic and social equality. In politics, women writers claimed significant progress, while men graciously excused women's supposedly poor voting record. Most observers ignored entirely women's legislative achievements of the early 1920s. A few writers recognized the limitations of women's roles, but most strained to emphasize the positive, although often superficial, aspects of women's history in the twenties—slight increases in political office holding and nonprofessional jobs, and greater sexual freedom. Nevertheless they confidently portrayed the period as one in which feminist goals were well on their way to fulfillment. By proclaiming emancipation a *fait accompli* and denying the existence of discrimination, they helped to discourage further efforts for social change.

Meanwhile, historians began to incorporate the 1920s into their works. They too stressed positive roles and women's increased participation in American history. Although published in the early 1930s, the first histories reflected the tone of the years before the crash rather than that of the depression. Charles and Mary Beard, Frederick Lewis Allen, and Preston William Slosson echoed the feelings of the generation which had seen both the presuffrage woman and the new woman, and their predepression accounts emphasized the changes in woman's social position during the 1920s.

"Women," the Beards wrote in *The Rise of American Civilization,* "now assumed an unquestioned role in shaping the production of goods, material, humanistic, literary and artistic." The ballot had enlarged women's influence in politics, while economic power, education and social freedom had made women "powerful arbiters in all matters of taste, morals and thinking." The Beards seemed pleased with these successes, but they were also apprehensive about some of the consequences of women's emancipation—the decline in the authority of fathers, defiant and divorce-prone women, and the "more intransigent" demand for " 'absolute and unconditional equal opportunity' in every sphere" of an equal rights amendment.

Preston William Slosson reported in *The Great Crusade and After* the "complete acceptance of American women in political life" and even greater progress, if that was possible, in economic status and social prestige. But Slosson's main concerns were topics traditionally defined as part of women's sphere. In a chapter entitled "The American Woman

Wins Equality," Slosson devoted six pages to economics and politics and twenty-two pages to the family, home, and fashions. Shorter skirts, more comfortable undergarments, shorter hair, the use of cosmetics, smoking, drinking, and the "breezy, slangy, informal" flapper characterized the era for him. As suffrage "disappeared from politics," women became content, he wrote, with the exception of "the more doctrinaire type" who pressed for equal rights. Women's history was reverting to women's spheres of home, fashions, and sex and finding there little or no oppression.

According to Frederick Lewis Allen, women did not vote in the 1920s, but they did work, if not in offices or factories, then as "professional" homemakers. But the job, or the potential for earning, created a feeling of comparative economic independence in women, which, for Allen, threatened husbandly and parental authority. Even with all of this, woman wanted more: "She was ready for the revolution"—sexual freedom, as enhanced by Sigmund Freud, the automobile, and Hollywood. Changes in fashion, Allen implied, were signs of deeper changes in the American feminine ideal.

With these three historical views, women in the 1920s began to be presented as flappers, more concerned with clothing and sex than with politics. Women had by choice, the accounts suggested, rejected political emancipation and found sexual freedom. In the long run, however, they settled down to home and family. The term feminism nearly disappeared from historical accounts, except in somewhat pejorative references to the Woman's Party. While critics claimed that women had achieved equality with men, they issued subtle warnings of moral and family decay.

At the same time, many women who wrote about the 1920s were more concerned about political and economic equality than the flapper and the moral revolution. In 1933, Inez Haynes Irwin offered *Angels and Amazons*, an all too glowing chronicle of the advancement of women in American history. Looking back over the first decade of new freedom, Irwin found four organized feminist activities "worth remembering": work for child welfare, self-education as voters, influence on world peace, and the struggle for equal legal status for women. None of these subjects had been discussed yet by historians, and Irwin left the moral revolution entirely to them.

In the same year Sophonisba Breckinridge, a social scientist from the University of Chicago, offered a more sophisticated approach to women's history. In a monograph prepared for the President's Commission of Recent Social Trends, a document which Henry F. May has called a "monument of the chastened social science of the thirties," she quantified and analyzed women's organizations, occupations, and politics. The volume, *Women in the Twentieth Century,* is an invaluable aid for the study of American women and a sobering contrast to the superficial treatment of the topic in other texts.

Breckinridge's conclusions suggested that perhaps women were not the emancipated, satisfied participants in American society that historians were describing. While an increasing number of women worked, she found that they were severely restricted in their range of employment. In the realm of public activity, Breckinridge reported that "the moment seems an unhappy one at which to attempt to take account of stock." Women had become disillusioned with the ballot and had to turn to government agencies and educational institutions for bases of emancipation. They had not as yet been successful in obtaining political power. Breckinridge described women's lobbying efforts and their roles in the national parties, but her picture is nowhere as promising as either Irwin's account of public life or the "progress" implied in Slosson's or Allen's description of the flapper. The Breckinridge study provided the data which might have prompted historical revisions on women's emancipation in the 1920s. On the contrary, with one exception in the mid-1930s, her work seems to have been unconsulted for several decades. The new woman remained an assumption rather than a subject for historical inquiry.

The one exception was *The American Woman: The Feminine Side of a Masculine Civilization* (1937) by Ernest R. Groves, a sociologist of marriage and the family who stressed the economic roots of feminist activity. Groves outlined the effects of industrial employment during World War I in raising women's expectations and in "heightening of the feelings of self-interest." Groves was aware that the growth of a female labor force did not automatically change attitudes towards working women and the family. He suggested that the continued existence of a temporary female work force contributed to the exploitative double standard of wages geared to nonpermanent help. While the vote had quickened the trend to legal equality and reinforced lobbying activities, women were not yet, in Groves' view, active and equal subjects in history. Later writers would agree with him that women were a special class, treated unequally, the "feminine side of a masculine civilization."

From the mid-1930s through the late 1940s feminism was not a popular subject among historians. A country struggling through a prolonged depression viewed woman's emancipation and her entry into the job market in a very different light than had an earlier, more prosperous society. Working women were being asked, if not forced, to leave their newly acquired positions and return to the home, either to allow men to take up their jobs or at least to offer moral support to families in a time of crisis. When rearmament and the war provided new jobs for women, American society had ample reason to readjust to working women; but by no means had a consensus been reached on the proper place of women in American society. The postwar years witnessed renewed debate over women's roles.

It is not surprising that during these crisis-ridden years, historians were either silent or ambivalent about the emancipation of women. The only sense one can get of their interpretations must come from textbooks and broad surveys of American thought, most of which contained brief sections on the new woman. While no one seemed to doubt that emancipation had occurred, several historians were unsure whether to welcome or denounce the new woman.

Historians often cited the relationship between urbanization and the emancipation of women to explain economic opportunities in the 1920s. A rising standard of living, more household appliances, and compulsory public education provided women with unprecedented leisure time which enabled them to join women's clubs or to enter the work force. These developments in turn influenced family life, the texts claimed, as evidenced by a declining birth rate and a climbing divorce rate. At this point historians often highlighted woman's new role of "professional homemaker." For example, Dwight Lowell Dumond's 1937 college text explained that feminists in the nineteenth century had made only small gains, but "Since then household electrical appliances have done more to emancipate women than all the generations of agitation by militant suffragettes." Consequently, "Women were living in a new and happier world. . . . The joy of homemaking replaced the drudgery of housekeeping. . . ." Merle Curti's image of women in the 1920s displayed ambivalence toward working women. While he found that women's magazines devoted space to careers "in the big world outside the home," he added that they "naturally" gave more space to the efficient management of the home. Foster Rhea Dulles's one page on the emancipation of women related increasing opportunity in business and professions to divorce rates, as well as to the development of independent social lives for women. Harvey Wish discussed women's employment outside the home and then cited Robert and Helen Lynds's Middletown study to demonstrate the weaknesses in modern marriage—the loss of companionship in marriage, the use of birth control, and the new manners (smoking, drinking, and masculinized fashions) of women.

These authors may not have intended to link working women with family decline, but often the proximity of the two statements, if not an explicitly drawn connection, brought them together in the mind of the reader. Similarly, historians in the 1930s and 1940s viewed the "moral revolution" in more negative terms—as a threat to the family—than it had been seen in the late twenties. Then the short skirt and bobbed hair had been used as symbols of emancipation.

Once again, historians disagreed about the political effects of enfranchisement. Some believed that voting rights for women had little or no effect. Others claimed that women had won total equality, as in John D. Hicks's statement that even before 1920, "Legal discrimination against women, aside from suffrage, were brought near the vanishing point." Similarly, Henry Steele Commager wrote that while the emancipation of women had begun in the 1890s with the typewriter, telephone exchange, and labor saving devices, it was "dramatized by the vote, and guaranteed by birth control." Dwight Dumond pointed to women's political roles in the Women's Joint Congressional Committee and stated that "Their successes in securing state legislation for child welfare, women's legal rights, social hygiene and education have been little less than phenomenal." A 1950 textbook by Curti, Richard Shryock, Thomas Cochran and Fred Harvey Harrington also acknowledged women's fight for progressive legislation and local good government in the twenties. Contrary to Dumond, however, it claimed that women rarely entered the political parties.

Throughout the 1930s and 1940s, then, historians suggested that women in the 1920s were emancipated by the vote and by an urbanized, industrialized society, but chose to remain for the most part in the home. Textbook portrayals of satisfied professional housewives or unstable career women were doubtless both products of and reinforcements for the depression psychology which sought to take women out of the work force. While legal and political equality won praise, social and cultural emancipation evoked gentle reproaches. Rarely, however, did even the most liberal male historians recognize the persistence of discrimination against women.

Post-World War II American society faced a dilemma of women's roles: Would the many women who had gone to work during the war return to their homes? Popular literature on "woman's place" abounded after 1947. Scholars, too, began to question women's roles in a way that would eventually change the direction of historical writing on the new woman. Once the existing discrimination against women was exposed, historians would have to reexamine their portrayal of the past decades as periods of emancipation.

Evidence of a reemerging intellectual curiosity about women can be found in the publications and reviews of the early 1950s. Alfred Kinsey's report on *Sexual Behavior in the Human Female* (1953) raised dormant issues of women's sexuality. More provoking, perhaps, was the 1953 English translation of Simone de Beauvoir's *The Second Sex*, which produced new hopes and fears of a revitalization of feminism. In the same year, Mirra Komarovsky defended equal education for women in *Women in the Modern World*, and another sociologist, Sidney Ditzion, published *Marriage, Morals, and Sex in America: A History of Ideas*. If these offerings were not sufficient to bring women to the attention of intellectuals, the very title of Ashley Montagu's essay, *The Natural Superiority of Women*, must have raised a few eyebrows (though probably not much consciousness).

These precursors of the new feminism appeared in the 1950s for several reasons. American women were ready for a revival of feminism. They had weathered the years of the depression and war without making new demands for equality. They now lived in an increasingly affluent society which was beginning to turn its attention to the question of racial equality, a subject which has historically heightened feminist concerns. Furthermore, the generation of women which came to maturity in the 1950s had not lived through and tired of an earlier feminist movement. These women were at a crossroads; would they return to the long interrupted battle for equality, or would they be seduced by the security promised to homemakers? Scholars looked back to the 1920s for clues and although they discussed politics, they emphasized social and cultural forces which defined women's roles.

In 1950, for example, Arnold W. Green and Eleanor Melnick asked "What Has Happened to the Feminist Movement?" They found that feminism had achieved the specific goals of suffrage and career opportunity, and it had given impetus to "the steady nurturing of the philosophy of the service state." But the feminist movement, they believed, had in a larger sense failed, for "about thirty years ago, in both politics and the job world, a fairly stable level was reached which the further passage of time has only indeterminately altered." Three factors hampered women's efforts for further advancement. First was the "residue of prejudice against working women," especially in nontraditional women's occupations. In addition the feminists were ignorant "of the fundamental changes in social structure which must precede women's assuming positions of leadership." Finally were the class cleavages in the women's movement, which were exacerbated by the conflict over the equal rights amendment (the upper-class and professional women of the National Woman's Party supported the amendment, while lower- and middle-class women wanted protective legislation).

The views that women had not yet achieved full equality and that social prejudices were at least partially responsible found even fuller expression in 1951 in a pivotal article by sociologist Helen Mayer Hacker. Elaborating on Gunnar Myrdal's comparison of woman's social position with that of Negroes, Hacker viewed women as a minority group that suffered collective discrimination, received separate socialization, and generally fit sociological definitions of minority group status and behavior. Of particular interest to historians was Hacker's conceptualization of a "sex relations cycle," comparable to the race relations cycle hypothesized by Robert Park. She believed that the latter stages of the cycle of competition, conflict, accommodation, and assimilation had been reached with passage of the suffrage amendment. Hacker suggested prophetically that a new era of women's dissatisfaction was approaching.

The analogy of women with minority groups later appeared elsewhere, including Sidney Ditzion's *Marriage, Morals, and Sex* and in a reinterpretation of the flapper by B. June West. Rejecting the traditional view that women's fads and fashions in the 1920s were manifestations of freedom, West's literary analysis suggested that women's fashions were an aping of men, "as minority groups have always done . . . to the so-called superior group." Although the plays and novels of the 1920s depicted women in a variety of masculinized roles—the aggressor in sex, the divorcee—West cautioned that the literature "implied a moral disintegration that was quite likely more publicized than actually existent."

Another reinterpretation of changes in women's roles in the 1920s which questioned historians' assertions of sex equality was *Women and Work in America* (1959) by Robert W. Smuts. The legal status of women, he found, shifted not after World War I but earlier with the passing of the frontier. By the end of the war the feminist movement was "rapidly subsiding." The war had led to a "remarkable liberalization of views about women's abilities and the propriety of their working outside the home," but the postwar decades were marked by women's lack of interest in many of the victories they had won. As evidence Smuts described a low level of interest in politics, a small increase in women working for pay, retirement from work at marriage, indifference of young women to feminism, and a failure to make significant gains in careers other than teaching and nursing. His explanation for this demise of feminism in the 1920s was that feminists, never more than a small minority of women to begin with, had won their primary goals; their demands became less important as the status of men and women became less differentiated. Thus the women's rights movement had failed only in succeeding too well, and women turned from a search for political and economic equality to one for sexual and social identity.

How did historians initially respond to the postwar interest in the social roles of women? A few studies appeared, some inspired by the centennial of the Seneca Falls Convention, some worthless, and some very suggestive, such as Carl N. Degler's 1956 article on Charlotte Perkins Gilman. For the most part, however, historians maintained the older view that women had lost interest in politics after attaining legal equality. Historians' interests in social emancipation remained confined to the "revolution in morals" concept.

Eric Goldman's 1952 history of reform, *Rendezvous with Destiny*, stated little more than that women's suffrage had made no difference, women failed to use the ballot, and when they did vote they didn't vote as women. Arthur Link's 1955 text repeated the story of the revolution in manners and morals, claimed that women had achieved political and economic equality after 1920, and seemed relieved to announce that the "revolution in morals and customs had run its full course by 1930 [when] . . . [t]here seemed to be certain signs of returning sanity." William Leuchtenburg argued in *The Perils of Prosperity* (1958) that "women's suffrage had few consequences, good or evil." Although millions voted and some held office, "the new electorate caused scarcely a ripple in American political life." Yet in business and social life Leuchtenburg described a period of accomplishment.

Once again, these accounts are not necessarily mistaken, but they are glaringly inconsistent in their evaluations of the progress towards women's emancipation that was made in the 1920s. What is most interesting is that historians had not yet defined and attempted to resolve the controversies over the women's movement and the history of women after suffrage. Previous writers had claimed all things and nothing for women in the 1920s: that the vote was not used, that it had brought equality; that women became men's equals in the world of work, that they had remained in traditionally female occupations; that the sexual revolution had changed women's lives, that the revolution was more literary than actual. Either historians were indifferent to these issues in the early postwar years, or, perhaps, while other scholars pointed to new conceptual frameworks for viewing women's history, historians were contemplating the issues and beginning to design the research which was to take form in the next decade. If the latter was the case, it was a long time before their thoughts actually reached the public, for one must skip to the early 1960s to find them in print. By this time, concern about discrimination against minority groups was widespread. President John F. Kennedy had established a Commission on the Status of Women and several states and localities had followed suit. Civil rights legislation was being applied to women's rights. The Negro rights movement was about to turn toward Black Power. And, in 1963, Betty Friedan published *The Feminine Mystique*, a journalistic polemic which was to sell over a million copies and help spark a revival of feminism in America.

As if to mark the beginning of serious interest in women in American history, two established historians published essays on the subject in 1964. Both works indicated a significant shift away from the view that women's emancipation had been completed in the 1920s and toward one that recognized the persistence of discrimination against women.

David Potter's comments on "American Women and the American Character" credited the city, the business office, and mechanization with the promotion of sexual equality, but acknowledged the barriers to full equality. Most important was the conflict between women's dual roles of career and domestic life, which made women's emancipation different from that of other oppressed groups. Carl Degler also linked feminism with industrialization and urbanization. At first, Degler agreed with earlier commentators about the advances women had made. However, he retreated from unqualified congratulations by noting that no permanent increase in the female labor force was made after World War I, that women's occupational gains were not great in the professions, that sexual divisions of labor remained, and that women's educational position later regressed. Why, an historian finally asked, did feminism fail to consolidate and increase its gains after the 1920s? Changes in women's status, he explained, had occurred more through chance of war, depression, and technological change than through planned efforts. American women, "like American society in general, have been more concerned with individual practice than with a consistent feminist ideology." Thus, he suggested that only a strong ideological stand would enable feminists to recognize their goals consistently and continuously.

At the time that Degler and Potter made these generalizations about women, a small number of historians began investigating more closely women's political and social activities in the post-World War I decade. They discovered that there was more to the new woman than the image of the flapper had revealed, and their works offered compensatory balance to former interpretations. Harking back to emphasis on women's political activities during the late 1920s, the new studies still did not elaborate on the theme of women as an oppressed group, but they did present valuable discussions of women's political efforts and incidentally acknowledged the social barriers impeding emancipation.

One revision was implicit in Clarke A. Chambers's 1963 study of social service reforms. Chambers did not discuss feminism *per se*, but he did find women in the 1920s actively working in settlement houses, lobbying for wages and hours regulations and for safeguards for earlier protective legislation, and educating women workers. Chambers proposed that progressive thought did not end in the 1920s, but was tempered, to be drawn on heavily by the New Deal. Anne Firor Scott's study of Southern women confirmed that women advanced Progressivism in the 1920s and weakened the historians' monolithic interpretation of the new woman as flapper. Suffrage, she found, greatly encouraged the political life of Southern women and prompted efforts for social and political reform. In several states Scott found women's organizations investigating labor conditions, securing children's and women's legislation, and even organizing for interracial cooperation. In Georgia, Tennessee, Virginia, and Kentucky, women's groups pursued state and municipal government reform. At odds with entrenched politicians, Southern women's political progress was "not one to gladden Mrs. Catt's heart," yet their efforts persisted through the decade. However, the 1920s did not witness a new morality in the South: "Through it all the outward aspect of the Southern lady was normally maintained as the necessary precondition of securing a hearing."

James Stanley Lemons's book, *The Woman Citizen* (1973), showed how the women's movement "advanced progressivism in the period from World War I to the Great Depression." He cited successes such as the Sheppard-Towner Act, new marriage and divorce laws, independent citizenship (the Cable Act), and municipal reform, as well as organizations such as the National Women's Trade Union League, the National League of Women Voters, and the National Consumer's League and various professional women's groups. The list of legislation which the Women's Joint Congressional Committee influenced successfully is a lengthy one, but most of its entries are dated

before 1925, for, as Lemons shows, forces of reaction after 1925
shifted the emphasis of women's activities from goals of social justice
to goals of efficiency. Red-baiting, the defeat of the child labor amendment, decisions of the Supreme Court barring protective legislation,
and the rejection of the Progressive Party in the 1924 election placed
progressive women on the defensive. The equal rights amendment,
Lemons believed, was "the hallmark of impatience in the 1920s, and
it was an issue which helped fragment the women's movement and
weaken the progressive impulse." Although the newly enfranchised sex
had achieved no great political gains in public office or party politics,
women had continued to push for reforms, laying the groundwork for
the New Deal.

Not unrelated to these new interpretations of women in the 1920s
was an essay by James R. McGovern, which called into question earlier historians' periodization of the revolution in morals. McGovern
cited Sophonisba Breckinridge's statistics on the prewar occupational
status of women, pre-1910 advertisements depicting women, changing
hair and cosmetic styles in the Progressive era, dance crazes, the
practice of birth control, and use of automobiles to show that the
flapper had been predated by events of the first decades of the century. If, as McGovern suggested, a moral revolution occurred before
World War I, were the 1920s as "revolutionary" as they had been
depicted, or in fact had a reaction taken place in which women returned to home and family?

The works of Scott on the Southern woman's new political awareness, Chambers and Lemons on progressivism and women in the
twenties, and the reinvestigations of the moral revolution by McGovern and others may differ on many counts, but they all point to a new
attitude toward women's history. Prompted in part by the political
and social movements of the 1960s, these authors looked more closely
at the political lives of post-World War I women and more critically
at the supposed moral revolution. While they were eager to praise
the role women had played in political movements, their researches
laid the foundation for recent works which are critical of the failures
of the women's movement to achieve lasting reform. Two recent
studies evidence the shift in view from woman as emancipated historical actor to woman as the victim of discrimination. William
O'Neill places the bulk of the blame for feminism's demise on women;

William Chafe faults American society for oppressing the "second sex."

Everyone Was Brave (1969), O'Neill's history of feminism, was originally subtitled "the rise and fall of feminism in America," a phrase indicative of the author's view of the 1920s:

> The women's rights movement expired in the twenties from ailments that had gone untreated in its glory days. Chief among them was the feminists' inability to see that equal suffrage was almost the only issue holding the disparate elements of the woman movement together.

O'Neill found that politicians abandoned the women's movement when no female voting bloc appeared. He also offered several criticisms of women's political activity. The author quoted—and made clear his agreement with—a blatantly antiwoman assessment of suffrage which claimed that the vote had done little more than to bring out such undesirable female traits as fussiness, primness, bossiness, and the tendency to make unnecessary enemies. O'Neill also claimed that although the radicals of the Woman's Party correctly understood the discrimination against women which existed after 1920, their "knowledge did them little good because the passions that led them to demand a feminist revival kept them from effecting it."

Outside of politics as well, O'Neill noted little progress towards emancipation after 1920. The moral revolution had been rooted in the prewar years, and "sexual freedom had little effect on the life styles of most women," who still preferred the stability of home and family to the life of the flapper. Professionalism among women declined by the mid-twenties, he explained, because the novelty and "glamour" of the career experience was wearing out, discrimination in salaries and promotions became apparent to women, and the struggle between home and career exhausted working women.

O'Neill believed that the feminine mystique of fulfillment through motherhood and home originated in the 1920s, when "feminism" came to mean merely sexual liberation within the confines of domesticity. Home economics became woman's professional realm, and femininity became the watchword for the "privatized young women." Although the ideas of earlier feminists were kept alive by individuals such as Charlotte Perkins Gilman, Dorothy Bromley, Alice Beal Parsons, and Suzanne La Follette, by 1930 feminism had fallen, to remain dormant until the present revival.

The second recent interpretation and one of greater usefulness is Chafe's study, *The American Woman* (1972). In an effort to correct what Degler called the "suffrage orientation of historians of women's rights," Chafe began after suffrage. He has provided a broad and preliminary investigation of women in politics, industry, the professions, and other aspects of American life. Drawing on several of the studies discussed above, he explored the progressive legislative successes of women in the early 1920s and acknowledged the individual accomplishments of women in the peace movement, in the struggle for social welfare legislation, and in municipal government reform. But in general, Chafe found that women had failed to achieve political equality. After surveying the political and sociological literature on voting behavior, he attempted to explain women's political failure in terms of social forces—the cross-group pressures on women, discrimination rooted in the authoritarian family structure and the sexual division of labor, and the absence of a strong women's issue for the new voters to focus upon. Chafe acknowledged that economic advances by women were minimal. Although he believed that sexually women had "substantially increased the amount of equality," he realized that "shifts in manners and morals did not interfere with the perpetuation of a sexual division of labor." He dated the shift in emphasis from careers to homemaking at 1930 and suggested that the Depression merely wielded the final blow to feminist hopes for equality. Although Chafe placed part of the blame for the decline of feminism on the feminists themselves, especially their factionalism over the equal rights amendment, his analysis emphasized social barriers to emancipation. "For economic equality to become a reality," he wrote, "a fundamental revolution was required in the way men and women thought of each other, and in the distribution of responsibilities within marriage and the family."

In the last few years, the literature on women in the 1920s has reached a new level of historical inquiry. Historians are now trying to understand the decline of feminism rather than to deny the need for further emancipation. Although the revised version finds that women were politically active in lobbying for reforms in spite of failures at

the polls, the latest accounts recognize that the 1920s were not the
years of economic prosperity for women described so proudly earlier:
professional gains were minimal, industrial wages discriminatory, and
unionization difficult. Marriage and motherhood brought most women
out of the labor force and, supposedly, home to domestic and sexual
fulfillment. Historians have generally retained the notion of the revolution in manners and morals, although research on the prewar years
and on literary stereotypes may indicate a need for revision. How the
social freedom in clothing, manners, and sex contributed to deeper
social change must be questioned further in light of the new view of
women's history. Rather than proclaiming the contributions of
"women as force" in recent history, historians now explain feminism's
decline in terms of societal forces, such as family structure and political trends, the weaknesses inherent in the pre-1920 suffrage coalition,
and legal and social discrimination against women as a group.

By further investigations of women's lives, historians can continue
to correct their past errors, not only for the sake of historical accuracy, but also to begin to compensate for the disservice which earlier
writings have rendered. The portrayal of the 1920s as a period of full
equality, when actually discrimination in education, hiring, salaries,
promotions, and family responsibilities was abundant, has perpetuated
a myth of equality, one which has helped undermine women's attain-
ment of group consciousness. Similarly, to write and teach—on the
basis of insubstantial observations—that women were politically apathetic but sexually active during the 1920s is to provide sexually
stereotyped historical roles for women. Historians' use of the "sexual
revolution" as an explanation for women's history in the 1920s was,
perhaps, an extension of their own inability to conceive of women
outside of sexual roles. Furthermore, if the admittedly minimal evidence on writings in the 1930s and 1940s is substantiated, American
historians' emphasis on woman's place in the home rather than her
capacities for nondomestic careers may have contributed to the perpetuation of cultural stereotypes which helped weaken feminism since
1920.

The works of recent writers have begun the long overdue revision of
historical attitudes towards women. Since 1970, studies by Lois Banner,
William Chafe, Paula Fass, Peter Filene and Mary Ryan have shown
the complexities of the historical experiences of women in the 1920s.

Younger scholars are heeding the advice of the pioneering modern
historian of American women, Gerda Lerner, to study women both as
a group and as members of specific racial, class, regional and ethnic
cultures. Only after investigating the lives of numerous women of the
1920s will historians discover patterns of women's history which will
enable us to generalize about the new woman. Only then can we begin to judge the impact of suffrage and the extent to which women
became active participants or struggling victims in American history.

BIBLIOGRAPHY

Allen, Frederick Lewis. *Only Yesterday: An Informal History of the Nineteen-
Twenties.* New York, 1931.
Banner, Lois W. *Women in Modern America: A Brief History.* New York,
1974.
Beard, Charles A. and Mary R. *The Rise of American Civilization.* New York,
1930.
Beard, Mary R. *Woman as Force in History.* New York, 1946.
Breckinridge, Sophinisba P. *Women in the Twentieth Century: A Study of
the Political, Social and Economic Activities.* New York, 1933.
Britt, George. "Women in the New South," *Woman's Coming of Age,* eds.
Schmalhausen and Calverton. New York, 1931.
Calverton, V. F. "Careers for Women: A Survey of Results," *Current His-
tory,* XXIX, 1929.
Calverton, V. F. and Samuel Schmalhausen. *Woman's Coming of Age: A
Symposium.* New York, 1931.
Catt, Carrie Chapman. "Suffrage Only An Epic in Age-Old Movement," *Cur-
rent History,* XXVII, 1927.
Chafe, William H. *The American Woman: Her Changing Social, Economic,
and Political Roles, 1920-1970.* New York, 1972.
Chambers, Clarke A. *Seedtime of Reform: American Social Service and Social
Action, 1918-1933.* Minneapolis, 1963.
Commager, Henry Steele. *The American Mind: An Interpretation of Ameri-
can Thought and Character Since the 1880's.* New Haven, 1950.
Curti, Merle. *The Growth of American Thought.* New York, 1943.
Curti, Merle, et al. *An American History.* New York, 1950.
de Beauvoir, Simone. *The Second Sex.* New York, 1953.
Degler, Carl N. "Charlotte Perkins Gilman on the Theory and Practice of
Feminism," *American Quarterly,* VIII, 1956.
Degler, Carl N. "Revolution Without Ideology: The Changing Place of
Women in America," *The Woman in America,* ed. Lifton. Boston, 1967.
Ditzion, Sidney. *Marriage, Morals, and Sex in America: A History of Ideas.*
New York, 1953.
Dulles, Foster Rhea. *Twentieth Century America.* Cambridge, Mass., 1945.

Dumond, Dwight Lowell. *Roosevelt to Roosevelt: The United States in the Twentieth Century.* New York, 1952.

Fass, Paula, *The Damned and the Beautiful: American Youth in the 1920s.* New York, 1977.

Filene, Peter. *Him/Her/Self: Sex Roles in Modern America.* New York, 1974.

Flexner, Eleanor. *Century of Struggle: The Woman's Rights Movement in the United States.* Cambridge, 1959.

Friedan, Betty. *The Feminine Mystique.* New York, 1963.

Goldman, Eric F. *Rendezvous with Destiny: A History of Modern American Reform.* New York, 1952.

Green, Arnold W. and Eleanor Melnick. "What Has Happened to the Feminist Movement?," *Studies in Leadership: Leadership and Democratic Action,* ed. Gouldner. New York, 1950.

Groves, Ernest R. *The American Woman: The Feminine Side of a Masculine Civilization.* New York, 1937.

Hacker, Helen. "Women as a Minority Group," *Social Forces,* XXX, 1951.

Hicks, John D. *The American Nation: A History of the United States from 1865 to the Present.* Boston, 1949.

Irwin, Inez Haynes. *Angels and Amazons: A Hundred Years of American Women.* Garden City, New York, 1933.

Kinsey, Alfred, et al. *Sexual Behavior in the Human Female.* Philadelphia, 1953.

Komarovsky, Mirra. *Women in the Modern World: Their Education and their Dilemmas.* Boston, 1953.

Kraditor, Aileen S. *The Ideas of the Woman Suffrage Movement, 1890-1920.* New York, 1965.

Lemons, James Stanley. "The New Woman in the New Era: The Woman Movement from the Great War to Great Depression," doctoral dissertation, University of Missouri, 1967.

Lerner, Gerda. "New Approaches to the Study of Women in American History," *Journal of Social History,* 3, 1969.

Leuchtenburg, William. *The Perils of Prosperity: 1914-1932.* Chicago, 1958.

Lindsey, Ben. "The Promise and Peril of the New Freedom," *Woman's Coming of Age,* eds. Schmalhausen and Calverton. New York, 1931.

Link, Arthur S. *American Epoch: A History of the United States Since the 1890's.* New York, 1955.

Link, Arthur S. "What Happened to the Progressive Movement In the 1920's," *American Historical Review,* 64, 1959.

McGovern, James R. "American Woman's Pre-World War I Freedom in Manners and Morals," *Journal of American History,* LV, 1968.

Moncure, Dorothy Ashby. "Women in Political Life," *Current History,* XXIX, 1929.

Montagu, Ashley. *The Natural Superiority of Women.* New York, 1953.

O'Neill, William. *Everyone Was Brave: A History of Feminism in America.* Chicago, 1971.

Potter, David. "American Women and American Character," *American Character and American Culture: Some Twentieth Century Perspectives,* ed. Hague. DeLand, Fla., 1964.

Rice, Stuart A. and Malcolm M. Willey. "American Women's Ineffective Use of the Vote," *Current History,* XX, 1924.

Ryan, Mary P. *Womanhood in America: From Colonial Times to the Present.*
    New York, 1975.
Schlesinger, Arthur Meier. *New Viewpoints in American History.* New York,
    1922.
Scott, Anne Firor. "After Suffrage: Southern Women in the Twenties," *Jour-
    nal of Southern History,* XXX, 1964.
Sinclair, Andrew. *The Emancipation of the American Woman.* New York,
    1965.
Slosson, Preston William. *The Great Crusade and After: 1914-1928.* New
    York, 1931.
Smuts, Robert W. *Women and Work in America.* New York, 1959.
"Ten Years of Women Suffrage," *Literary Digest,* 105, 1930.
Wells, Marguerite. "Some Effects of Woman Suffrage," *Annals of the Ameri-
    can Academy of Political and Social Science,* CXLIII, 1929.
West, B. June. "The 'New Woman'," *Twentieth Century Literature,* I, 1965.
Wish, Harvey. *Society and Thought in Modern America: A Social and Intel-
    lectual History of the American People from 1865.* New York, 1952.
Woodhouse, Chase Going. "The Status of Women," *American Journal of
    Sociology,* 35, 1930.

9
Roosevelt and Hitler .

THE NEW DEAL, NATIONAL SOCIALISM,
AND THE GREAT DEPRESSION

JOHN A. GARRATY

• No other single individual in this or any other century has
been responsible for as much hatred and horror as Adolf
Hitler. Born in Austria in 1889, he won the Iron Cross in
World War I as a corporal in the Bavarian Army. He was enraged by the Treaty of Versailles and blamed German defeat
on betrayal by Jews and Bolsheviks. In the early 1920s, he became the leader of the militant "brown shirts," a paramilitary
group known officially as the National Socialist German
Workers' party, and, more popularly as the Nazis. On November 8, 1923, Hitler attempted a coup in Munich designed
to bring Germany under Nazi control with the support of the
army. But the "beer-hall putsch" failed, and Hitler was forced
to serve nine months in the Landsberg prison. While incarcer-
ated, he wrote a book, Mein Kampf (My Struggle), which
outlined his notions of racial purity, anti-Semitism, and national destiny. The book was turgid and rambling, but as an
orator Hitler was a wizard, and his strong sense of purpose
impressed many Germans who were troubled by the economic and political dislocations which beset their nation. On
January 30, 1933, a fateful day in the history of the world,
Adolf Hitler became the chancellor of Germany. Within
months the Fuehrer had assumed absolute power.

According to Hitler, the "Third Reich" was to last for a
thousand years, and a monumental Berlin was to become the
nerve center of the earth. For a time, the highly trained and
tightly disciplined German Army pushed aside smaller nations, and Austria, Czechoslovakia, Poland, Denmark, Hol-
land, Norway, and Belgium came under Nazi control. Unbe-
lievably, the renowned French Army surrendered in less than
two months of fighting. In the end, however, the Nazis were

crushed between the Soviet Union on the east and the
United States and Great Britain on the west. Instead of a glit-
tering capital, Berlin became a smoking ruin, and Hitler was
forced to take his own life to avoid being carried to Moscow
in a cage.

In the following selection, one of the most distinguished
and prolific of American historians, John A. Garraty of Columbia University, compares the responses of Adolf Hitler
and Franklin D. Roosevelt to the world-wide depression of
the 1930s. Both leaders came to power at almost precisely the
same time, both were confronted with unprecedented unemployment in highly advanced nations. They shared a similar
goal of economic recovery although the tactics and the result
were initially different. Professor Garraty does not discount
the suffering that Hitler inflicted on innocent people in
Auschwitz, Mauthaussen, Buchenwald, and a dozen other
death camps, but he argues that the atrocities caused by Hitler should not preclude a scholarly analysis of those areas in
which the German dictator acted more reasonably and
responsibly.

The Great Depression of the 1930s was a unique phenomenon in that
it happened simultaneously over almost the entire globe. It was experienced directly, not merely through its repercussions, by the people of
nearly every nation and social class. Neither of the so-called world wars
of this century was so pervasive, and while many distinct combinations
of past events, such as the French Revolution, may be said to have had
global results, these usually have been felt only over extended periods
of time, long after the "event" itself has ended. The depression therefore presents a remarkable opportunity for historians interested in comparative study and analysis. It provides a kind of independent variable;
when we look at how different nations or groups of people responded
to the Great Depression, we can be sure, at least in a sense, that we are

From "The New Deal, National Socialism, and The Great Depression," American Historical Review, 78 (October 1973), 907-44. Reprinted by permission.

examining one single "thing," the existence of which was universally recognized at the time. Contemporaries disagreed among themselves about the causes of the depression (to say nothing of their disagreements about how it might be ended), but that there *was* a world-wide depression and that their own depression was related directly to those of their fellows, few denied.

In this article I shall compare the response to the depression in the United States and Germany during the period from 1933 to about 1936 or 1937—that is, during the early years of the regimes of Franklin Roosevelt and Adolf Hitler. The choice is neither capricious nor perverse. I hope to demonstrate that Nazi and New Deal antidepression policies displayed striking similarities. Since the two systems, seen in their totality, were fundamentally different, these similarities tell us a great deal about the depression and the way people reacted to it.

The differences between nazism and the New Deal scarcely need enumeration; within the context of Western industrial society two more antithetical systems would be hard to imagine. The Nazis destroyed democratic institutions. They imprisoned and murdered dissidents, even those, such as the Jews, who simply did not fit their image of a proper German. The New Dealers, whatever their limitations, threw no one in jail for his political beliefs and actually widened the influence of underprivileged elements in the society. Furthermore the historical experience, the traditions, and the social structure of the two nations could hardly have been more unlike. The Great War and its aftermath affected them in almost diametrically opposite ways. All the major economic groups in the two countries—farmers, industrialists, factory workers, and so on—confronted the problems of the depression with sets of expectations and values that differed greatly.

But these were the industrial nations most profoundly affected by the Great Depression, measured by such criteria as the percentage decline of output, or by the degree of unemployment. When Hitler and Roosevelt came to power both nations were in desperate straits; Hitler and Roosevelt followed leaders who had spectacularly failed to inspire public confidence in their policies. Both the severity of the depression and the sense of despair and crisis that existed in Germany and America in early 1933 set the stage for what followed.

I have focused on the early New Deal and Nazi years because at that time the new governments were primarily concerned with economic problems resulting from the depression. Hitler's expansionist ambitions no doubt existed from the beginning, but it was not until after the adoption of the Four Year plan in 1936 that he turned the German economy toward large-scale preparation for war. Similarly, although his motive was clearly defensive, after 1937 Roosevelt also began to be influenced by military considerations.

Needless to say, by considering the similarities in American and German experiences during the depression, I do not mean to suggest that the New Deal was a form of fascism or still less that nazism was anything but an unmitigated disaster. I slight the basic differences between the New Deal and Nazi experiments here partly because they are well known but also because the differences did not affect economic policy as much as might be expected. The worse horrors of nazism were unrelated to Nazi efforts to overcome the depression. Hitler's destruction of German democracy and his ruthless persecution of Jews had little impact on the economy as a whole. Discharging a Jew and giving his job to an "Aryan" did not reduce unemployment. The seizure of Jewish property merely transferred wealth within the country; it did not create new wealth. Moreover, actions undertaken by New Dealers and Nazis for different reasons often produced similar results. My argument concentrates on policies and their effects, not on the motives of the policy makers.

Finally, the fact that countless Germans were deluded by Nazi rhetoric (or that large but lesser numbers were repelled by the system) does not mean that nothing the Nazis did helped anyone but themselves and their sympathizers. Moral abhorrence should no more blind us to the success of some Nazi policies than should admiration of the objectives of the New Deal to its failures. As the English economic historian C. W. Guillebaud warned in *The Social Policy of Nazi Germany*, written in the midst of the Battle of Britain, "Modern Germany is a highly complex phenomenon, with much that is good and bad in it, and nothing is achieved except distortion and absence of reality by any attempt to reduce it to a simple picture of a vast population deluded and oppressed by a small number of brutal gangsters."

Consider first how the two governments dealt with poverty and mass unemployment. Both combined direct relief for the indigent with public-works programs to create jobs. The Americans stressed the

former, the Germans the latter, with the result that while acute suffering was greatly reduced in both nations, unemployment declined much
more rapidly in Germany. Congress appropriated $3.3 billion for pub-
lic works in 1933, but Roosevelt, unconvinced that public works would
stimulate the economy and fearful of waste and corruption, did not
push the program. Briefly, during the winter of 1933-34, he allowed
Harry Hopkins to develop his Civil Works Administration, which
found jobs for over four million people, but in the spring the program
was closed down to save money. Only in 1935 did federal public works
become important. Then, under Hopkins's Works Progress Administration and Harold L. Ickes's Public Works Administration, countless
roads, schools, bridges, dams, and public buildings were constructed.
The Germans, on the other hand, immediately launched an all-out
assault on unemployment. Expanding upon policies initiated under
Franz von Papen and Kurt von Schleicher, they stimulated private industry through subsidies and tax rebates, encouraged consumer spending by such means as marriage loans, and plunged into the massive
public-works program that produced the autobahns, and housing, railroad, and navigation projects. If some New Deal projects seemed to
critics wasteful and unnecessary, so did the Nazi penchant for gigantic
stadiums and other public buildings, as described in Albert Speer's
memoirs. The American boondoggle had its parallel in what the Germans called *Pyramidenbau*, pyramid-building.

It is fashionable, and not of course inaccurate, to note the military
aspect of German public-works policies, although in fact relatively little was spent on rearmament before 1935.[1] It is less fashionable, but
no less accurate, to point out that the aircraft carriers *Yorktown* and
Enterprise, four cruisers, many lesser warships, as well as over one hundred army planes and some fifty military airports (including Scott
Field in Illinois, the new Air Force headquarters) were built with
Public Works Administration money—more than $824 million of it.[2]
There was, furthermore, little difference in appearance or intent between the Nazi work camps and those set up in America under the
Civilian Conservation Corps. Unlike the public-works programs, these
camps did not employ many industrial workers who had lost their jobs,
nor were they expected to have much of a stimulating effect on private
business. Both employed enrollees at forestry and similar projects to
improve the countryside and were essentially designed to keep young

men out of the labor market. Roosevelt described work camps as a means for getting youth "off the city street corners," Hitler as a way of keeping them from "rotting helplessly in the streets." In both countries much was made of the beneficial social results of mixing thousands of young people from different walks of life in the camps and of the generally enthusiastic response of youth to the camp experience.[3]

Furthermore, both were organized on semimilitary lines with the subsidiary purposes of improving the physical fitness of potential soldiers and stimulating public commitment to national service in the emergency. Putting the army in control of hundreds of thousands of young civilians roused considerable concern in the United States. This concern proved to be unfounded; indeed, the army undertook the task with great reluctance and performed it with admirable restraint. It is also difficult to imagine how so large a program could have been inaugurated in so short a time in any other way. The CCC program nevertheless served para-military and patriotic functions not essential to its announced purpose. Corpsmen were required to stand "in a position of alertness" while speaking to superiors and to address them as "Sir." Camp commanders possessed mild but distinctly military powers to discipline their men, including the right to issue dishonorable discharges. Morning and evening flag-raising ceremonies were held as "a mark," the civilian director of the CCC, Robert Fechner, explained, "of patriotism, of good citizenship and of appreciation by these young men of the thoughtful care being given them by their government." Army authorities soon concluded that six months' CCC service was worth a year's conventional military training, and Secretary of War George Dern claimed that running the camps provided the army with the best practical experience in handling men it had ever had. Summing up the military contribution of the CCC, John A. Salmond, the most sympathetic historian of the agency, wrote:

> To a country engaged in a bloody war, it had provided the sinews of a military force. It had given young officers valuable training in command techniques, and the nearly three million young men who had passed through the camps had received experience of military life upon which the Army was well able to build.

New Deal and Nazi attempts to stimulate industrial recovery also resembled each other in a number of ways. There was at the start much jockeying for position between small producers and large, between manufacturers and merchants, between inflationists and deflationists, between planners, free enterprisers, and advocates of regulated competition. In Germany the great financiers and the leaders of the cartelized industries, most of them bitterly opposed to democratic institutions, demanded an authoritarian solution that would eliminate the influence of organized labor and increase their own control over the economy, whereas small operators, shopkeepers, and craftsmen wanted to reduce the power of bankers and to destroy not only the unions but also the industrial monopolies and chain stores. The former sought to manipulate the Nazis, the latter comprised, in the main, the Nazis' enthusiastic supporters, but Hitler and the party felt and responded to pressures from both camps.[4] In the United States most big business interests had no open quarrel with the existing order, but by 1933 many were calling for suspension of the antitrust laws in order to end the erosion of profits by competitive price cutting. Other interests wanted to strengthen the antitrust laws, still others favored various inflationary schemes, still others some attempt at national economic planning. All clamored for the attention of the new administration.

The ideas of these groups were contradictory, and neither Roosevelt nor Hitler tried very hard to resolve the differences. Roosevelt's method was to suggest that the contestants lock themselves in a room until they could work out a compromise. But Hitler, who freely admitted to being an economic naïf, was no more forceful. "I had to let the Party experiment," he later recalled in discussing the evolution of his industrial recovery program. "I had to give the people something to do. They all wanted to help. . . . Well, let them have a crack at it."

Out of the resulting confusion emerged two varieties of corporatism, a conservative, essentially archaic concept of social and economic organization that was supposed to steer a course between socialism and capitalist plutocracy. Corporatist theory argued that capitalists and workers (organized in industry-wide units) should join together to bring order and profit to each industry by eliminating competition and wasteful squabbling between labor and management. These associations should be supervised by the government in order to protect the public against monopolistic exploitation. In 1933 corporatism was already being experimented with by the Portuguese dictator Antonio de Oliveira Salazar and more tentatively by Benito Mussolini. It also had roots in American and German experience. The American trade association movement of the 1920s reflected basic corporatist ideas (with the important exception that industralists were opposed to government representation in their councils). When the depression undermined the capacity of these "voluntary" associations to force individual companies to honor the associations' decisions, some trade association leaders became willing to accept government policing as a necessary evil. Among others, Gerard Swope of the General Electric Company attracted considerable attention in 1931 with his Swope Plan for a nationwide network of compulsory trade associations supervised by the Federal Trade Commission. President Herbert Hoover, who had been among the most ardent supporters of trade associations, denounced the Swope Plan as both a threat to industrial efficiency and "the most gigantic proposal of monopoly ever made." He considered all such compulsory schemes fascistic. But a number of early New Dealers—Hugh Johnson, Donald Richberg, and Lewis Douglas among others—found corporatism appealing. In Germany the concept of government-sponsored cartels that regulated output and prices had a long tradition, but the existence of powerful trade unions precluded the possibility of a truly corporative organization before 1933. Hitler's success changed that swiftly. Nazi ideologues such as Gottfried Feder combined with big industrialists like Fritz Thyssen and leaders of small business interests like Dr. Heinrich Meusch to push the corporative approach. The works of one of the leading theorists of corporatism, Professor Othmar Spann of the University of Vienna, were widely discussed in Germany in 1933, and the Nazis established a complex system of "estates" governing all branches of industry.

In America the process went not nearly so far, but the system of self-governing industrial codes established under the National Recovery Administration was obviously in the same pattern.[5] Production controls, limitation of entry, and price and wage manipulation were common characteristics of government policy in both countries. So were the two governments' justifications of drastic and possibly illegal or unconstitutional[6] changes in the way the economy functioned on the ground that a "national emergency" existed, and the enormous propaganda campaigns they mounted to win public support.

The drafters of the National Industrial Recovery Act were not deliberately imitating fascist corporatism (although Hugh Johnson, a key figure among them, was an admirer of Mussolini). *Fortune*, which devoted an entire issue in 1934 to an analysis of the Italian system, was scarcely exaggerating when it stated that corporatism was "probably less well known in America than the geography of Tibet." As Gilbert H. Montague, a lawyer who had played a small role in the design of the code system, later wrote, the NRA was only "unconsciously" fascistic. It would be hard to find a better illustration of the common impact of the depression on two industrial nations committed to the preservation of capitalism.

During the early stages big business interests dominated the new organizations and succeeded in imposing their views on government. In Germany the radical Nazi artisan socialists who wanted to smash the cartels and nationalize the banks, led by Gregor Strasser and Gottfried Feder, lost out to the powerful bankers and industrialists, represented by Hjalmar Schacht. In the United States victory went to the large corporations in each industry, which dominated the new code authorities.

But bewildering crosscurrents of interest and faction hampered the functioning of corporatism. In theory the system promised harmony and efficiency within industries, but in practice it seldom provided either. It did not even pretend to solve interindustry conflicts, yet these were often more disturbing to government authorities. Under corporatism workers were supposed to share fairly in decision making and in the rewards resulting from the elimination of conflict and competition; in both countries industrialists resisted allowing them to do so, with the consequence that the governments found themselves being pushed to enforce compliance. In America workingmen were a potent political force and a vital element in the New Deal coalition. German workers did not count as voters after 1933, but their cooperation and support remained essential to Nazi ambitions. Small businessmen also maintained a steady drumfire of complaint, and both New Dealers and Nazis were sensitive to their pressure. Even the great industrialists were sometimes at odds with the system. Many German tycoons objected to sharing authority with labor and small producers, others to particular decisions imposed on the new estates by the government. German steel and chemical manufacturers like the Krupps and the I. G. Farben interests benefited from Hitler's emphasis on building up war-oriented industry and backed him enthusiastically, but producers dependent upon foreign raw materials or primarily concerned with the manufacture of consumer goods suffered from Nazi trade and monetary policies and held back. And as for the American industrialists, however much they profited under NRA codes, most of them came increasingly to resent the regimentation that codes entailed and to fear the growing interference in their affairs by bureaucrats.

To the Nazis corporatism seemed at first compatible with the political process called *Gleichschaltung*, or coordination, a process by which nearly every aspect of life in their totalitarian state was brought under the control of Hitler and the party. It quickly became apparent, however, that the autonomous character of any corporatist organization made direct control from above difficult. America, fortunately, was never *gleichgeschaltet*. But, in any case, by 1935 and 1936 the Roosevelt and Hitler governments were abandoning corporatism and taking a more anti-big-business stance. In America this meant, aside from the demise of the NRA, more support for industrial labor, stricter regulation of public utilities, higher taxes on the rich and on corporations, rhetorical attacks on "economic royalists," and—by 1938—revived enforcement of the antitrust laws. In Germany, although the traditional cartel structure was retained, it involved limitations on corporate dividends; forced reductions in the interest rates paid on government bonds; government construction and operation of steel, automobile, and certain other facilities in competition with private enterprise; and higher taxes on private incomes and on corporate profits. As in the United States, but to a much greater degree, freedom of managerial decision making was sharply curtailed.

The success or failure of American and German efforts to stimulate industrial recovery is a separate question not central to my argument here. What is central to the argument is this: both were marked by vacillation, confusion, and contradictions, by infighting within the administering bureaucracies, by an absence of any consistently held theory about either the causes of the depression or how to end it. Both also subordinated economic to political goals. The "primacy of politics" in Nazi Germany is a commonplace, its most glaring expression occurring in 1936 when shortages of raw materials and foreign exchange led Hitler to choose between guns and butter. He chose, of course, guns. The problem could be solved by an act of will, he insisted; it was the task of the economy to supply the military needs of the state—so be it!

When Schacht, his chief economic adviser, urged a more balanced use of available resources, the Führer fired him. Such ruthless subordination of economic interests to the state did not occur in the United States, although when military considerations began to dominate American policy after 1939 Roosevelt was also prepared to substitute guns for butter. I need only mention his famous announcement that he was replacing "Dr. New Deal" with "Dr. Win the War" as his prime consultant.

But conventional "politics"—the accommodation of political leaders to the pressures of interest groups—affected economic policy in both nations. Beset by business interests seeking aid, by trust busters eager to break up the corporate giants, by planners brimming with schemes to rationalize the economy, the Roosevelt administration survived in a state of constant flux, making concessions to all views, acting in contradictory and at times self-defeating ways. "The New Dealers," writes Ellis W. Hawley, "failed to arrive at any real consensus about the origins and nature of economic concentration." Nor did they follow any consistent policy in the fight against the industrial depression. And Roosevelt's inconsistency, as Hawley also notes, "was the safest method of retaining political power, . . . a political asset rather than a liability." The Nazis, as I have shown, also permitted pressures from various economic interests to influence policy. They did so partly because even a totalitarian dictatorship could profit from the active cooperation of powerful economic groups and partly because the Nazi party had no fixed economic beliefs. Roosevelt responded to pressure groups, Hitler for a time suffered them to exist—a most vital distinction—but the practical result was the same. Put differently, Hitler had a clear political objective—it was actually an obsession—but he was almost as flexible about specific economic policies as Roosevelt. "As regards economic questions," he boasted in 1936, "our theory is very simple. We have no theory at all."[7]

New Deal and Nazi labor policies were also shaped by the Great Depression in related ways. On the surface this statement may appear not simply incorrect but perverse, but only because of our tendency to identify labor with unionization. It is true that Hitler totally destroyed the German unions and that Roosevelt, in part unwittingly and surely with some reluctance, enabled American unions to increase their membership and influence enormously. But New Deal and Nazi policies toward unions had little to do directly with the depression and threw little light on the national policies toward workingmen. Hitler would no doubt have destroyed the Weimar unions as autonomous organizations in any case—he destroyed all autonomous organizations in Germany. But it was because they were anti-Nazi that he smashed the unions so quickly. Roosevelt was at first indifferent to organized labor; he encouraged the American unions in order to gain labor's support, not to speed economic recovery. In each instance the decision was essentially political.

It is not difficult to demonstrate Nazi concern for industrial workers. The "battle against unemployment" had first priority in 1933, and it was won remarkably swiftly; by 1936 something approaching full employment existed in Germany and soon thereafter an acute shortage of labor developed. Of course the military draft siphoned thousands of men out of the German labor market, contributing to the shortage, but this was also true in the United States after 1940. Certainly full employment was never approached in America until the economy was shifted to all-out war production.[8]

Moreover, Nazi ideology (and Hitler's prejudices) inclined the regime to favor the ordinary German over any elite group. Workers—as distinct from "Marxist" members of unions—had an honored place in the system. To the extent that the Nazis imposed restrictions on labor, they did so for the benefit of the state, not of employers. In a sense the Nazi Courts of Social Honor may even be compared with the New Deal National Labor Relations Board. These courts did not alter power relationships between capital and labor as the NLRB did; they represented the interests of the Nazi party rather than those of labor. But they did adjudicate disputes between workers and bosses, and there is considerable evidence that the Courts of Social Honor tended more often than not to favor workingmen in these disputes. Furthermore the very existence of these courts put considerable psychological pressure on employers to treat labor well.

It is beyond argument that the Nazis encouraged working-class social and economic mobility. They made entry into the skilled trades easier by reducing the educational requirements for many jobs and by expanding vocational training. They offered large rewards and further advancement to efficient workers, and, in the Strength Through Joy movement, they provided extensive fringe benefits, such as subsidized housing, low-cost excursions, sports programs, and more pleasant factory facilities. Eventually the Nazi stress on preparation for war meant harder work, a decline in both the quantity and quality of consumer goods, and the loss of freedom of movement for German workers, but the hierarchy imposed these restrictions and hardships belatedly and very reluctantly because of its desire to win and hold the loyalty of labor. If the question is: "Did the Nazi system give workers more power?" the answer of course is that it did not. But that question, albeit important, has little to do with the actual economic position of workingmen or with the effectiveness of the Nazi system in ending the depression.

New Deal and Nazi methods of dealing with the agricultural depression also had much in common. Both sought to organize commercial agriculture in order to increase farm income, under the New Deal Agricultural Adjustment Act through supposedly democratic county committees to control production, in Germany through the centralized Estate for Agriculture. The purpose was to raise agricultural prices and thus farm income through a system of subsidies, paid for in each instance by processing taxes that fell ultimately on consumers. Both governments also made agricultural credit cheaper and more readily available and protected farmers against loss of their land through foreclosures.

These similarities are not remarkable; nearly every nation sought, more or less in these ways, to bolster agricultural prices and protect its farmers. What is interesting, given the profound differences between American and German agriculture, is the attitudes of the two governments toward the place of farmers in the society and toward rural life. Although there was no American counterpart to Hitler's racist, anti-intellectual glorification of the German peasantry, Nazi thinking was at least superficially similar to that of generations of American farm radicals. (David Schoenbaum has aptly called Gottfried Feder "a kind of Central European William Jennings Bryan.") The typical American farmer was no more like a German peasant than the owner of a Southern plantation was like a Junker, but under the impact of the depression farmers large and small in both countries were expressing the same resentments and demands, and these affected Nazi and New Deal policies in related ways. Furthermore, the ideas of Roosevelt and Hitler about farmers were quite alike. Both tended to romanticize rural life and the virtues of an agricultural existence. They hoped to check the trend of population movement to the cities and to disperse urban-centered industries. Roosevelt spoke feelingly of the value of close contact with nature and of the "restful privilege of getting away from pavements and from noise." Only in the country, he believed, did a family have a decent chance "to establish a real home in the traditional American sense." He did not deny the attractions of city life, but he argued that electricity, the automobile, and other modern conveniences made it possible for rural people to enjoy these attractions without abandoning the farm. While governor of New York he set up a program for subsidizing unemployed city families on farms so that "they may secure through the good earth the permanent jobs they have lost in over-crowded cities and towns."[9]

Hitler called the German peasantry "the foundation and life source" of the state, "the counterbalance to communist madness," and "the source of national fertility." The superiority of rural over urban life was a Nazi dogma—especially the life of the self-sufficient small farmer, free from the dependency and corruption of a market economy. "The fact that a people is in a position to nourish itself from its own land and through that to lead its own life independent of foreign nations has always in history been significant," a Nazi agricultural expert wrote in 1935. "Families on the land also have the biological strength to maintain themselves and to compensate for population losses resulting from migration to cities and from war." Nazi leaders referred to Berlin as "Moloch Berlin" and deplored the influx of Germans from the east into the capital. The Nazis' housing policy sought to stimulate suburban development in order to bring industrial workers closer to the land and to reduce urban crowding. They placed all construction under government control, made funds available for low-interest, state-guaranteed mortgage loans, and provided tax relief to builders of small apartments and private homes.

The Tennessee Valley Authority and the rural electrification program made important progress toward improving farm life, but efforts to reverse the population trend yielded very limited results. As president, Roosevelt dreamed of decentralizing industry and of relocating a million families on small farms, but during the whole of the New Deal his Resettlement Administration placed fewer than 11,000 families on the land; even the best-known of the settlements, Arthurdale in West Virginia, which benefited from the particular interest and financial support of Eleanor Roosevelt never became a viable community until the outbreak of the war. That the Resettlement Administration was run by Rexford Tugwell, who considered the back-to-the-land movement impracticable, contributed to the ineffectiveness of this program, but the agency's greenbelt town program of planned suburban development, which Tugwell did think practicable, also produced minuscule results—only three of the sixty originally planned greenbelt towns were built.

Although Nazi ideologues hoped to reverse Germany's urban-rural ratio, which was seventy percent urban in 1933, their rural resettlement and "urban" programs proved equally disappointing. Between 1933 and 1938 the Nazis resettled about 20,000 families, but this was scarcely more than half the number the Weimar government had managed to relocate between 1927 and 1932. Nor did the German "rurban" development program ever get very far off the ground. In both the American and German cases efforts to check the movement of population to the cities foundered on the opposition of real-estate and construction interests and still more on the conflicting objectives of government policy makers and their unwillingness to allocate sufficient funds to enable much progress to be made. In 1937 Roosevelt established the Farm Security Administration to coordinate the various New Deal rural rehabilitation programs, but again relatively little was accomplished. Large sums were made available to help tenants buy their own farms, but local agents, concerned for the sake of their own records with making sure that the money was repaid, tended to make loans to tenants who were better off rather than to the most poverty stricken. While many families benefited, the overall impact upon American agriculture was negligible. The sums spent were measured in the millions, whereas, as one critic put it, only if billions had been appropriated could "the drift into tenancy and degradation be stopped and reversed." In Germany the very success of the Nazis in ending unemployment and their post-1936 drive to build their war machine created a shortage of industrial labor that made a meaningful back-to-the-soil movement impossible.

There were significant differences between the objectives of American and National Socialist agricultural policies, the former, for example, seeking to limit output, the latter to increase it. All in all, the New Deal was the more successful in solving farm problems; far less was accomplished in Germany toward modernizing and mechanizing agriculture during the thirties. On the other hand, Nazi efforts in behalf of farm laborers were more effective than those of the New Deal; the AAA programs actually hurt many American agricultural laborers and also tenants and sharecroppers. In both nations agricultural relief brought far more benefits to large landowners than to small.

The complications of German and American monetary and fiscal policies during the depression and of questions relating to foreign trade preclude their detailed discussion here. I shall only mention a few common themes. Both nations increased government control of the banking system but did not nationalize the banks. Both, following the precepts of economic nationalism, sought to improve the competitive position of their export industries, the Americans by devaluing the dollar, the Germans by subsidies, both by sequestering the national gold supplies and prohibiting the export of gold. Both paid most of the costs of their recovery programs by deficit financing. However, both also ignored the newly developing Keynesian economics and remained inordinately fearful of inflation.

Nazi and New Deal policies were not essentially different from those of other industrial nations in these respects. However, they adopted them sooner and pursued them more vigorously than, for example, the British or the French. Thus when Roosevelt decided against international stabilization of foreign exchange rates and thus "torpedoed" the London Economic Conference, the British and French were bitterly disappointed but the Germans were delighted. Roosevelt's opinion, expressed in his "bombshell" message, that "the sound internal economic situation of a nation is a greater factor in its well-being than the price of its currency," was Nazi orthodoxy. In a radio message beamed to the United States the German foreign minister, Konstantin von Neurath, praised Roosevelt's "fearlessness" and spoke of the "heroic effort of the American people . . . to overcome the crisis and win a new prosperity." Reichsbank president Hjalmar Schacht told a *Völkischer Beobachter* reporter that FDR had adopted the philosophy of Hitler and Mussolini: "Take your economic fate in your own hand and you will help not only yourself but the whole world."

In the early months of the New Deal Roosevelt toyed with the idea of stimulating exports by means of subsidized dumping and by barter agreements, trade tactics that the Nazis adopted wholeheartedly. A mighty behind-the-scenes battle was fought within the administration in 1933 and 1934 between supporters of this approach and those who believed in lowering tariff barriers by making reciprocal trade agreements based on the unconditional most-favored-nation principle. Rexford Tugwell, Raymond Moley, and George W. Peek argued the former position; the secretary of state, Cordell Hull, and the secretary of agriculture, Henry Wallace, the latter; and the president—after one of his typical attempts to get the protagonists to reconcile the irreconcilable—finally sided with Hull and Wallace. Roosevelt nevertheless continued for some time to flirt with the idea of bilateral agreements, especially one suggested by Schacht involving 800,000 bales of American cotton. The rejection of this and similar proposals resulted more from Roosevelt's growing political and moral distaste for Hitlerism than from economic considerations. But despite Roosevelt's antifascism and the internationalist, free-trade rhetoric of the reciprocal trade program, it seems clear that New Deal foreign policy was as concerned with advancing national economic interests as was German policy. State Department alarm at Nazi "penetration" of Latin America, publicly expressed in strategic and moral terms, had a solid base in lost and threatened markets for American exports.[10]

There remains the question of leadership, that is, of the personal roles of Roosevelt and Hitler in their nations' campaigns against the Great Depression. To overemphasize Roosevelt and Hitler as individuals would be to approach the problem simplistically, but certain parallels merit examination. It cannot be proved that neither would have achieved national leadership without the depression, but the depression surely contributed to the success of each. Yet on the surface they seem most improbable leaders of the two countries at that particular time. In an economic crisis of unprecedented severity, neither had a well-thought-out plan. Both lacked deep knowledge of or even much interest in economics.[11]

It is no less than paradoxical that the American electorate, provincial in outlook, admiring of self-made men and physical prowess, and scornful of "aristocrats," should, at a time when millions were existing

on the edge of starvation, choose for president a man who lived on inherited wealth, who came from the top of the upper crust, who had
been educated in the swankest private schools, who had a broad cosmopolitan outlook, and (to descend to a lesser but not politically unimportant level) who was a cripple. But no more a paradox than that a
country whose citizens were supposed to have an exaggerated respect
for hard work, for education and high culture and family lineage, and
who had a reputation for orderliness and social discipline should follow the lead of a high-school dropout, a lazy ne'er-do-well, a low-born
Austrian who could not even speak good German, the head of a rowdy
movement openly committed to disorder and violence. Equally strange,
Roosevelt and Hitler appealed most strongly to their social and economic opposites: Roosevelt to industrial workers, to farmers, to the
unemployed and the rejected; Hitler to hard-working shopkeepers and
peasants, and, eventually, to industrialists, great landowners, and the
military.

It may of course be true that these seeming contradictions are of no
significance. Probably any Democrat would have defeated Hoover in
1932, and although Hitler became chancellor in a technically legal way,
his subsequent seizure of total power was accomplished without the
consent, if not necessarily without the approval, of a majority of the
German people. Yet the personal impact of Roosevelt and Hitler on
the two societies in the depths of the Great Depression was very large.
Their policies aside, both exerted enormous psychological influence
upon the citizenry. Roosevelt's patrician concern for mass suffering, his
charm, his calm confidence, his gaiety, even his cavalier approach to
the grave problems of the day had, according to countless witnesses, an
immediate and lasting effect upon the American people. Hitler's resentment of the rich and well born, however psychotic in origin, appealed powerfully to millions of Germans. His ruthless, terrifying
determination, always teetering on the edge of hysteria, combined with
the aura of encapsulated remoteness that he projected to paralyze those
who opposed him, to reduce most of his close associates to sycophancy,
and to inspire awe among masses of ordinary Germans. Both the eu-
phoria of the Hundred Days and the nationalistic fervor that swept
Germany in the early months of 1933 made millions almost incapable
of thought, let alone of judgment. Bills swept through Congress ill
drafted and scarcely debated, basic rights were abolished in Germany

without even an attempt at resistance, and both were possible largely because of the personalities of the two leaders.

Much of this was probably spontaneous, but not all. Roosevelt and Hitler employed the latest technologies to dramatize themselves and to influence public opinion. Roosevelt's flight to Chicago to accept the Democratic nomination and Hitler's whirlwind tours testify to their swift grasp of the psychological as well as the practical value of air travel to politicians. And no greater masters of the radio ever lived—Roosevelt with his low-keyed, fatherly, intimate fireside chats, Hitler with his shrill harangues beneath the massed swastikas at Nuremberg. Both were terrible administrators in the formal sense but virtuosos at handling subordinates. Their governments were marked by confusion, overlapping jurisdictions, and factional conflicts, yet somehow they transformed their inadequacies into political assets—symbols not of weakness or inefficiency but of energy and zeal in a time of grave emergency.[12]

Both also made brilliant use of the crisis psychology of 1933, emphasizing the suffering of the times rather than attempting to disguise or minimize it. "The misery of our people is horrible," Hitler said in his first radio address after becoming chancellor. "To the hungry unemployed millions of industrial workers is added the impoverishment of the whole middle class and the artisans. If this decay also finally finishes off the German farmers we will face a catastrophe of incalculable size." Roosevelt's personal style was more reassuring than alarmist, but he also stressed the seriousness of the situation and the urgent need for decisive action: "Action, and action now," as he put it in his inaugural.

Both the Roosevelt and Hitler governments tried to influence public opinion in new and forceful ways. Roosevelt did not create a propaganda machine even remotely comparable to Goebbels's, but under the New Deal the government undertook efforts unprecedented in peacetime to sell its policies to the public. The NRA slogan "We Do Our Part" served the same function as the Nazis' incessantly repeated *Gemeinnutz geht vor Eigennutz*. With Roosevelt's approval, General Hugh Johnson, head of the NRA and designer of its Blue Eagle symbol, organized a massive campaign to rally support for the NRA. "Those who are not with us are against us," Johnson orated, "and the way to show that you are a part of this great army of the New Deal is to insist on this symbol of solidarity." Johnson denounced "chiselers" and "slackers"; his office plastered the land with billboard displays; distributed posters, lapel buttons, and stickers; dispatched volunteer speakers across the country; and published *Helpful Hints* and *Pointed Paragraphs* to provide them with The Word. Roosevelt himself, in a fireside chat, compared the Blue Eagle to a "bright badge" worn by soldiers in night attacks to help separate friend from foe. Placed beside the awesome Nazi displays at Nuremberg, even the ten-hour 250,000-person NRA parade up Fifth Avenue in September 1933 may seem insignificant, but it and other NRA parades and hoopla were designed to serve the same functions: rousing patriotic feelings and creating in the public mind the impression of so extensive a support for government policies as to make disagreement appear close to treason. As Johnson himself explained, the purpose was to "put the enforcement of this law into the hands of the *whole* people."[13]

Another example of New Deal propaganda is provided by the efforts of the Resettlement Administration and the Farm Security Administration under Rexford Tugwell. Because Pare Lorenz's government-sponsored films, *The Plow That Broke the Plains* (1936) and *The River* (1938), and the still photographs of Dorothea Lange, Walker Evans, Margaret Bourke-White, Gordon Parks, and others were esthetic achievements of the highest order, we tend to forget that they were a form of official advertising designed to explain and defend the New Deal approach to rural social and economic problems. They differed from Leni Riefenstahl's *Triumph of the Will* (also a cinematic masterpiece) and the annual volumes of photographs celebrating National Socialism chiefly in style—"soft" rather than "hard" sell—and point of view.[14]

The New Deal efforts at mass persuasion were unparalleled among democracies in peacetime—nothing comparable was attempted in France or Great Britain before the outbreak of war in 1939. They reflect the attitude of the Roosevelt government, shared by Hitler's, that the economic emergency demanded a common effort above and beyond politics. The crisis justified the casting aside of precedent, the nationalistic mobilization of society, and the removal of traditional restraints on the power of the state, as in war, and it required personal leadership more forceful than that necessary in normal times. That all these attitudes were typical of Hitler goes without saying, but Roosevelt held them too. Consider this passage in his first inaugural:

> I assume unhesitatingly the leadership of this great army of our people. . . Our true destiny is not to be administered unto but to minister to ourselves. . . . In the event that Congress shall fail . . . I shall ask the Congress for the one remaining instrument to meet the crisis—broad executive power to wage a war against the emergency, as great as the power that would be given to me if we were in fact invaded by a foreign foe.[15]

Roosevelt was neither a totalitarian nor a dictator, real or potential, but his tactics and his rhetoric made it possible for anti-New Dealers and outright fascists to argue that he was both. Many of the accusations of conservatives and Communists in the United States were politically motivated, as were, of course, Nazi comments on the president. But during the first years of the New Deal the German press praised him and the New Deal to the skies. Before Hitler came to power he was, although impressed by Henry Ford's automobiles and the racially oriented American immigration laws, basically contemptuous of the United States, which he considered an overly materialistic nation dominated by Jews, "millionaires, beauty queens, stupid [phonograph] records, and Hollywood." Nevertheless, he and his party were impressed by New Deal depression policies. "Mr. Roosevelt . . . marches straight to his objectives over Congress, lobbies, and the bureaucracy," Hitler told Anne O'Hare McCormick of the New York *Times* in July 1933. In July 1934 the *Völkischer Beobachter* described Roosevelt as "absolute lord and master" of the nation, his position "not entirely dissimilar" to a dictator's. Roosevelt's books, *Looking Forward* (1933) and *On Our Way* (1934) were translated into German and enthusiastically reviewed, the critics being quick to draw attention to parallels in New Deal and National Socialist experiences.[16]

A friendly German biography, *Roosevelt: A Revolutionary with Common Sense,* by Helmut Magers, appeared in 1934. Magers described the New Deal as "an authoritarian revolution," a revolution "from above," and pointed up what he called the "surprising similarities" it bore to the Nazi revolution. That there appeared to be some basis for this view at the time is suggested by the fact that Ambassador William E. Dodd wrote a foreword to Mager's book in which he

praised the author's "outstanding success" in describing both conditions in the United States and the nation's "unique [*einzigartig*]
leader" and spoke of the "heroic efforts being made in Germany and
the United States to solve the basic problem of social balance."

Dodd was vehemently anti-Nazi, but he hoped that German mod-
erates like Schacht and Neurath would be able to overthrow Hitler or
at least restrain him. He considered the Magers volume an "excellent,
friendly, unpartisan book . . . without a sentence that could have
been quoted to our disadvantage" and allowed his foreword to be published despite State Department objections. The Germans, for their
part, went out of their way to welcome Dodd. A throng of reporters
and Foreign Office officials greeted him when he arrived in Berlin. He
was put up in the six-room royal suite of the Hotel Esplanade and
charged only ten dollars a day. He was invited to lecture at the University of Munich. Hitler assured him that Germany had no warlike
intentions. When he criticized authoritarian rule and economic nationalism in a speech, the German press reported his remarks fairly and
accurately.

At the end of Roosevelt's first year in office Hitler sent him a message through diplomatic channels offering sincere congratulations for
"his heroic efforts in the interests of the American people. The President's successful battle against economic distress is being followed by
the entire German people with interest and admiration," Hitler announced. In November 1934 the *Völkischer Beobachter* characterized
Democratic gains in the Congressional elections as an "exceptionally
personal success" for Roosevelt. The tone of this article was almost
worshipful, the rhetoric hyperbolic. The president (a man of "irre-
proachable, extremely responsible character and immovable will"
[*tadelsfreie verantwortungsvolle Gesinnung und . . . unverrückbarer
Wille*]) had shown himself to be a "warmhearted leader of the people
with a profound understanding of social needs" as well as an energetic
politician. This attitude ended in 1936, although even after Roosevelt's
"quarantine" speech the Nazi propaganda machine refrained for tactical reasons from attacking him personally. It is clear, however, that
early New Deal depression policies seemed to the Nazis essentially
like their own and the role of Roosevelt not very different from the
Führer's.[17]

The importance of these leaders in the fight against the depression lies less in what they did to revive the economy than in the shift in public mood they triggered. In early 1933 that mood was profoundly pessimistic. For four years business conditions had been growing almost steadily worse. The promises and optimstic predictions of innumerable political and business leaders that the tide would turn had all proved illusory. Millions had lost not merely their jobs and savings, but hope itself. It was the duration more than the depth of the decline that was truly depressing.

The Great Depression was totally unlike any earlier economic slump. Men had noted as early as the eighteenth century that economic activity tended to rise and fall in recurrent patterns, and during the nineteenth century the concept of the business cycle was firmly established. Cycles were variously explained, and the terminology was not precise, but it was accepted that the world economy moved in an irregular but unending path through periods of expansion, crisis or panic, recession or depression, and then returned to expansion. Before the collapse of the 1930s a cycle was usually identified by its most dramatic phase, the crisis or panic: witness the American "panics" of 1819, 1837, 1857, 1873, 1893, and 1907. The business slump that followed panics was characteristically precipitous but mercifully brief. In his classic study of *Business Cycles* (1913), Wesley Clair Mitchell wrote: "The lowest ebb of the physical volume of industrial production usually comes in either the first or the second year after a severe crisis."[18] The German and French words *die Krise* and *la crise* reflect this same focus on the panic aspect of the "normal" business cycle. However, the recession that came after the "panic of 1929" did not follow the expected pattern. Interminably, or so it seemed, it continued. By the end of 1932 industrial production in both the United States and Germany was scarcely more than half of what it had been in 1929.

By the early 1930s professional economists were beginning to realize that the character of business cycles was changing. The first edition of the *Encyclopedia of the Social Sciences*, published between 1930 and 1935, contains an article on *crises* by Jean Lescure, a French expert on business cycles. "A crisis," Lescure wrote, "may be defined as a grave and sudden disturbance of economic equilibrium." Lescure went on to discuss the nature and history of crises, paying special attention to the impact of industrialization and of the growth of cartels and trusts, which he believed had reduced the acuteness of crises but also delayed the process of recovery. "It would seem," he concluded, "that for the term crisis one may henceforth substitute that of depression; it is reasonable to speak today of a world depression rather than of a world crisis."

Lescure's emphasis on the word "depression" highlights the psychological impact of the long economic decline, the pessimism, the sense of hopelessness that had little to do with the size of an individual's pocketbook. A constricting pall appeared to have descended upon the world. Among economists, stagnation theorists flourished and learned authorities spoke of a "mature" economy and the end of the era of economic growth spawned by the Industrial Revolution. Many recommended what the French called a "Malthusian" approach, the reduction of output to the current level of consumption rather than the attempt to increase consumption. Governments, faced with the most extended fall in prices since the 1890s, responded not with inflationary measures but by adopting deflationary monetary policies and by slashing shrunken budgets. Businessmen feared to make new investments. Trade languished. Unions dealt with mounting unemployment by urging that youths be kept longer in school, that working women return to the home, that older men retire early. The mood of unemployed workers, some twenty million in the United States and Germany alone by early 1933, was more apathetic than rebellious. It was this general pall of despair and listlessness that the New Deal and the Nazi revolution, personified by Roosevelt and Hitler, dispelled. Long before their economic policies had much effect on the stalled business cycle, they had revitalized the two societies.

Comparison with Great Britain and France is suggestive. Economic historians disagree about the character of Britain's economic recovery in the 1930s, but the argument concerns the growth *rate* and its causes, not the fact of expansion. By 1937 industrial output was over thirty percent larger than in 1933, and unemployment had been almost halved. Even allowing for the facts that the British economy had been sluggish in the 1920s, unemployment extremely high, and, therefore, that the world depression seemed a less dramatic collapse in Britain than it did in the United States or Germany, the improvement between 1933 and 1937 marked a very substantial change.

Furthermore, during these years the British government made many efforts to improve conditions. To aid industry it adopted tactics strikingly similar to those of the NRA. It allowed coal operators to limit and allocate output, fix prices, and amalgamate companies; it encouraged cotton textile manufacturers to scrap inefficient machinery, and the steel industry to cartelize its operations. Both the ailing shipbuilding industry and the healthy automobile industry received government subsidies. Electric utility companies were assisted in consolidating their activities by the Central Electricity Board. The remarkable British housing boom, it is true, was largely the work of private enterprise, but government construction was significant—and focused where it was most needed, on slum clearance and homes for the poor. Agriculture was also assisted through a complex mixture of import quotas, tariffs, subsidies, and marketing schemes.

The government also acted to help British labor. Unemployment insurance and relief services were well established long before 1933, but beginning with the Unemployment Act of 1934 the system was considerably improved. Insurance was put on a sounder financial basis, and an Unemployment Assistance Board was set up to administer the relief program. In 1936 half a million agricultural wage earners were brought into the insurance system. Other laws sought to encourage the movement of labor from the economically stagnant north and west to the more prosperous southeast, and manufacturers willing to build factories in the depressed areas received subsidies. Economic recovery was thus accompanied by considerable social reform; by 1937 the combination of a progressive tax structure and extended social services was transferring five or six percent of the national income from rich to poor, raising the real income of the working classes by some eight to fourteen percent. In the United States, by way of contrast, New Deal legislation had almost no measurable effect on income distribution.

Yet the people of Great Britain had no sense of experiencing a new era. It seems clear (although such things are difficult to measure) that the national mood remained depressed, despite economic progress. No political leader was able to generate a sense of common commitment to the battle against the depression. When David Lloyd George announced a plan for a "New Deal for Britain" in 1935—it was little more than a rehash of proposals he had made repeatedly in the 1920s —Ramsay MacDonald's cabinet was thrown almost into a panic and gave serious consideration to inviting both Lloyd George and Winston Churchill to join the government, but it did not do so. Chancellor of the Exchequer Neville Chamberlain wrote in his diary at this time: "The P.M. [MacDonald] is ill and tried, S[tanley] B[aldwin] is tired and won't apply his mind to problems." (Contrast this state of mind with the mood in government circles in Washington and Berlin.) "It is certainly time there was a change," Chamberlain also wrote, having himself in mind as the person to institute it. But after Chamberlain became prime minister in 1937, the national mood was no different. Chamberlain was a conservative of the finest type, hard working and public spirited; no one in Great Britain contributed more to social reform in the interwar years. But he was by this time also aging and ailing—unable to inspire public enthusiasm. As he said of himself, he could not "unbutton."

Thus the 1930s passed into memory in Great Britain as a time of inactivity and decline—the Great Slump. "The man in the street's view of Britain's experience . . . is that activity was stagnant and very depressed," the economic historian Harry W. Richardson writes—this even though "any glance at the evidence shows it to be a misconception." Surely this helps to explain why fascism became a more formidable force in Britain than in the United States, despite economic recovery and the far more serious and immediate threat that the Nazis posed to the British.

The French experience provides another opportunity to study this aspects of the depression. Its full force struck France late, but by 1935 conditions were very bad. Farm prices had collapsed. Industrial output was down sharply. French workers were probably worse off than those of any other industrial nation: wage rates as low as eighty centimes an hour (the franc was worth about five cents) were not unknown; employers were autocratic, superficially well organized, and adamantly opposed to collective bargaining; unemployment was increasing rapidly and was far greater than French statistics indicated. Over 503,000 persons were receiving relief payments in February 1935, an increase of more than 150,000 in one year, and many of the unemployed were unable to meet all the eight "general conditions" required to qualify for aid. Furthermore, in counting the unemployed the French government made no allowance for those who had given up looking for work, for individuals who had lost their jobs and returned to family farms, or for unemployed foreigners who had no work permits. The Ministry of Labor, which compiled the unemployment statistics, itself confessed that the number of *employed* Frenchmen had declined by 1,880,000 since 1930, and this estimate was probably too low.

Moreover, French governments, aside from the fact that no party or coalition was capable of staying in power for more than a few months, were not merely ineffective but complacent in dealing with the problems of the depression. In 1935, when organized business sought a law (*le projet Marchandeau*) much like the NRA codes enforcing restrictive trade agreements, the bill was defeated. The official position of the Ministry of Labor on unemployment, repeatedly enunciated in its annual reports, ran as follows: "The state cannot pretend to be able to eliminate or diminish unemployment since its activities do not get at the causes of the evil." The minister's report of June 22, 1936, praised local relief officers for their "very important" services in "not allowing unemployed workers to get aid unless they met all the requirements." Thus "public funds have been safeguarded."[19]

Then quite suddenly in the spring of 1936 the electoral victory of the Popular Front unleashed a spontaneous, grass-roots outburst of protest, signalized by a wave of sit-down strikes that brought the economy to a standstill. Thoroughly alarmed, the leaders of industry swiftly capitulated, throwing themselves on the mercy of the new Socialist premier, Léon Blum. Within a matter of days a new system of labor-management relations, buttressed by a host of laws similar to those of the New Deal, was hammered out by representatives of big business and the unions and pushed through parliament by the Blum government: state-supervised collective bargaining, large wage increases, a forty-hour week, and paid vacations, along with banking reform and a program to support agricultural prices were all instituted in one hectic burst of activity.

This transformation was, of course, shortlived; by 1939 France was more divided and lacking in any sense of commitment to common national purposes than in 1935. To what extent a lack of leadership and particularly Léon Blum's personal inadequacies caused this reversal is a very difficult question. Blum's performance can be criticized from two perspectives. First of all, should he, as a lifelong socialist, have attempted to use the crisis to change France more radically? In a brilliant article, *"Tout est possible,"* the left-wing socialist Marceau Pivert urged him to try. "The masses are much more advanced than we imagine," Pivert insisted. They are ready not merely for "an insipid cup of medicinal tea," but for "drastic surgery," including the nationalization of banks, utility companies, and "trusts," and the confiscation of the wealth of "deserters of the franc." Blum rejected these proposals, being backed by most of the Socialists and also by the Communists, the union leaders, and the Radicals who made up his coalition. He did so on the reasonable, indeed honorable ground that the Popular Front parties, having campaigned on a platform of moderate reform within the capitalist system, had no mandate for revolutionary change. "Our duty," he later said, "was . . . to show ourselves scrupulously faithful to the program." He felt that he must "keep loyally, publicly, the promise that I had made." But it can be argued that the upheavals of 1936 *were* revolutionary, even that (as Pierre Mendès France said many years later) the election of 1936 was not a plebiscite for any particular reform but "an affirmation of a popular desire to see the country break out of its deflationary rut and conservative structures." Socialist critics, re-reading some of Blum's modest and diffident comments about the responsibilities of his high office, have been impressed by a "crushing masochism" in his character, a defeatist attitude, an exaggerated concern for punctilio. Blum was too much the "grand bourgeois," Pivert recollected, "too subtle, too refined to be a revolutionary leader." Georges Lefranc, both a participant in and one of the leading historians of the events of 1936, put the question this way: perhaps everything was not possible, "but can one say that everything that was possible was tried?"

One can reject this line of argument, but it remains true that Blum failed not merely to build upon the reforms of 1936 but even to protect them adequately against counterattack. He of course faced staggering difficulties: the antediluvian mentality of French industrialists, the doctrinaire rigidity of union leaders, the slavish commitment of the Communists to the policies of the Soviet Union, the tragic divisions resulting from the Spanish Civil War, the noisy rightist "patriotic" groups, the perverse individualism of nearly every Frenchman. Probably no political leader could have overcome the shortsighted selfishness and inertia or resisted the splintering factionalism that plagued French society in the late thirties.

Yet Blum's efforts were pitifully inadequate, no better or worse than

those of the uninspired premiers who preceded and followed him. Long
years of balancing his socialist principles against his political ambitions
and responsibilities had made him, in Joel Colton's words, a "tight-
rope-walker." Before the formation of the Popular Front he had, when
forced to make a choice, always put his socialism above political accommodation. After he finally made the other choice in 1936, he became too much the politician, telling workers, despite the still-lagging
French economy, that it was time for a "pause," that they must exercise "moderation and patience." It was not of central importance that,
as the historian Alfred Sauvy has said, Blum's ignorance of economics
was matched only by his sincerity. He could muster neither the flexibility of Roosevelt (whom he greatly admired) nor the ruthlessness of
Hitler (whom he detested).[20]

During Blum's brief second term as premier, he revised his economic
thinking. Aided by Georges Boris, author of an admiring study of the
New Deal, *La Révolution Roosevelt* (1934), and one of the few
Frenchmen familiar with the new Keynesian economics, Blum drafted
a comprehensive program involving tax relief and government credits
for defense industries, tax relief for the construction industry and small
business, suspension of redemptions of the national debt, a special
capital levy on the rich, a more progressive income tax, and rudimentary exchange controls. A massive common effort was necessary, he
said, in order to build up French defenses, expand production, and
maintain "social solidarity." The Assembly supported Blum's plan, but
when the Senate voted it down he meekly resigned without even demanding the vote of confidence that might have compelled the Senate
to yield. "To make the project succeed," Sauvy writes, "would have
required a resounding appeal to all the forces of a country threatened
with collapse. Unfortunately, Blum was not capable of such an effort."

What he lacked was not courage but firmness, and the daring to step
beyond the comfortable security of conventional political procedures.
After the fall of his second government he confessed: "Perhaps, if I
committed errors it was because of not having been enough of a
leader." None of this proves that a Blum like Roosevelt or—God forbid
—Hitler could have provided France with the kind of *élan* that developed in the United States and Germany. It does, however, point up
the psychological importance of Roosevelt and Hitler in their own
countries.

These parallels suggest a number of generalizations about how the Great Depression influenced the United States and Germany. They do not, as I said at the start, indicate that the New Deal was a variant of fascism. The extraordinary expansion of the role of the federal government that took place in America cannot be equated with the Nazi totalitarian system, nor Hitler's despotism with the new executive power that Roosevelt exercised. The differences are qualitative not merely quantitative. But both governments experienced the depression as a tremendous crisis, and this fact shaped their responses in related ways. Furthermore the two regimes suffered from common intellectual, emotional, and organizational limitations that also led to analogous re-actions to the depression.

Before Hitler and Roosevelt achieved power, more rigid and con-servative leaders had tended to see the depression as a world-wide dis-ease that would yield to international rather than national cures and indeed as one that governmental medicines could not alone eradicate. Hoover, despite his belief that European selfishness and shortsighted-ness had caused the depression, proposed his moratorium of 1931 "to give the forthcoming year to the economic recovery of the world," and Heinrich Brüning defended what he himself called his "draconian" emergency decrees as necessary to enable Germany "to meet its inter-national obligations" and "conquer the economic crisis." Brüning, like Hoover, also believed that governmental policies of any kind could in-fluence the economy relatively little. After the disastrous German elec-tions of 1930, which made the Nazis a formidable political force, Brüning informed Hitler complacently: "According to our estimation, the crisis will last about four or five years more." And in a message on New Year's Day, 1931, he told the nation: "I am anxious to stress the limitations of any policy so that you will not indulge in any illusions."

Nazis and New Dealers adopted more parochial but also more in-tense tactics, placing the economic well-being of their own societies ahead of world recovery and taking a far more optimistic view of what government could accomplish. While assuming the continuance of capitalism and in many ways adding to the wealth of private business groups, each nation sharply restricted the individual's freedom to pursue his economic interests and construed the power of government, and of executive power within the political system, in very broad terms. In addition, New Dealers and Nazis insisted that economic recovery could not be achieved without a certain amount of social restructuring and, furthermore, that society could be changed without exacerbating class conflicts. Indeed in both cases social reform was supposed to moderate such conflicts. But in both Roosevelt's America and Hitler's Germany economic and social objectives were subordinated whenever necessary to political aims.

That other nations adopted many of the tactics employed by New Dealers and Nazis scarcely needs demonstration. Depression policies everywhere were certainly based on national self-interest narrowly conceived, despite the obvious fact that the same plague was ravaging all. The tendency of governments to extend their sway in economic affairs and of leaders to be heavily influenced by political considerations was virtually universal. Whether conservative, moderate, or radical, few if any of the statesmen of the thirties remained indifferent to the suffering of their constituents or unwilling to sanction changes designed to alleviate it. The difference between the American and German depression experiences and those of other nations was in large measure psychological, resulting from Roosevelt's and Hitler's personal qualities of leadership and from their responses to the particular conditions in the two countries.

Again the comparison with Hoover and Brüning is at least suggestive: both lacked political tact and the ability to project an impression of warmth, sympathy, and self-assurance. In 1931 Walter Lippmann described Hoover as "indecisive and hesitant in dealing with political issues," and Arthur Krock commented on his "awkwardness of manner and speech and lack of mass magnetism." A recent student of the Hoover administration, Albert U. Romasco, remarks on his "inability to master the political techniques of leadership." As for Brüning, the historian Theodore Eschenburg, who knew him personally and considered him a "statesman of the highest intellectual gifts," admits that he had neither "the psychological talent" to win public backing nor "the tactical ability" to manage politicians. "He thought in terms of policy, not of human beings." And Andreas Dorpalen, another historian who lived through the Brüning period as a student in Germany, describes him as a "shy, withdrawn man [who] was unable to arouse the nation," a person lacking in warmth and imagination. Dorpalen's statement that the German public "mistook the chancellor's sober factualness for cynical coldness" could as well be applied to Hoover.

So far as the depression is concerned, Roosevelt and Hitler, the one essentially benign, the other malevolent, justified far-reaching constitutional changes as being necessary to the improvement of economic con·ditions in a grave emergency but used change also as a device for mobilizing the psychic energies of the people. Yet both their administrations were plagued by infighting and confusion, partly because of genuine conflicts of interest and philosophy within the two diverse societies, but partly because of ignorance. No one really knew how to end the depression or even how best to serve the different interests the governments presumed to represent. Time after time major American and German policies produced results neither anticipated nor desired, some of them—the effect of New Deal farm policy on share croppers and of its public housing policy on racial segregation, and that of Nazi rearmament on urban concentration, for example—directly contrary to the leaders' intentions.

Hitler papered over confusion, doubts, and rivalries with the *Führerprinzip*, unquestioning obedience to the leader, who was presumed to know what was best. Roosevelt, on the other hand, made a virtue of flexibility and experimentation. Both, however, masterfully disguised the inadequacies and internal disagreements in their entourages and to a remarkable extent succeeded in convincing ordinary citizens of their own personal wisdom and dedication.

The differences in the degree and intensity with which psychological pressures were applied by Nazis and New Dealers were so great as to become differences in kind—leaving aside the brute Nazi suppression not merely of those who resisted or disagreed, but of all who did not fit the insane Hitlerian conception of the proper order of things. The two movements nevertheless reacted to the Great Depression in similar ways, distinct from those of other industrial nations. Of the two the Nazis were the more successful in curing the economic ills of the 1930s. They reduced unemployment and stimulated industrial production faster than the Americans did and, considering their resources, handled their monetary and trade problems more successfully, certainly more imaginatively. This was partly because the Nazis employed deficit financing on a larger scale[21] and partly because their totalitarian system better lent itself to the mobilization of society, both by force and by persuasion. By 1936 the depression was substantially over in Germany, far from finished in the United States. However, neither regime solved the problem of maintaining prosperity without war. The German leaders wanted war and used the economy to make war possible. One result was "prosperity": full employment, increased output, hectic economic expansion. The Americans lacked this motivation, but when war was forced upon them they took the same approach and achieved the same result.

NOTES

1. Through 1934 Nazi expenditures for armaments totaled 4.9 million marks.

2. The first New Deal authorization for public works was part of the National Industrial Recovery Act and provided for "the construction of naval vessels within the terms and/or limits of the London Naval Treaty of 1930 and of aircraft required therefore and construction of heavier-than-air aircraft and technical construction for the Army Air Corps and such Army housing projects as the President may approve, and provision of original equipment for the mechanization or motorization of such Army tactical units as he may designate."

3. Roosevelt stressed "the moral and spiritual value" of camp life, Hitler its "class reconciling" function.

4. Arthur Schweitzer, *Big Business in the Third Reich*, writes: "We must give up the notion of the [Nazi] state as a unified . . . entity developing an economic policy. . . . Instead we must see who stood behind the state and who originated each economic goal and supported the subsequent economic policy (p. 4)."

5. When a reporter asked Roosevelt in November, 1933, for his opinion of an updated version of the Swope plan, he replied: "Mr. Swope's plan is a very interesting theoretical suggestion in regard to some ultimate development of N. R. A."

6. Although many Supreme Court decisions declaring New Deal laws unconstitutional reflected the unreasonably narrow views of five conservative justices, much of the early "emergency" legislation was very loosely worded. Furthermore, the decision invalidating the NIRA (*Schechter Poultry Corp.* v. *United States*, 295 U.S. 495) was a unanimous one.

7. This does not mean, of course, that the ideas of American and German economists were not taken up by the politicians. Roosevelt was influenced by dozens of them; he did not, however, adopt any consistent line of economic reasoning. Both the Nazi program to create work and their post-1936 autarchic policies were apparently anticipated in Robert Friedlaender-Prechtl's *Die Wirtschaftswende* (Leipzig, 1931), although Friedlaender-Prechtl, whose father was Jewish, was unable to publish or exert any direct influence on economic policy after 1933.

8. American unemployment never fell much below 8 million during the New Deal. In 1939 about 9.4 million were out of work, and at the time of the 1940 census (in March) unemployment stood at 7.8 million, almost fifteen percent of the work force.

9. "Is it worthwhile," Roosevelt asked in a radio address late in 1931, "for us to make a definite effort to get people in large numbers to move out of cities . . . ? It seems to me that to that question we must answer an emphatic YES."

10. The reciprocal trade program, despite the high hopes of its supporters, had little effect upon American trade or the world economy. Furthermore the argument of Secretary Hull and others that the "non-discriminatory" reciprocal trade policy was particularly high-minded and that bilateralism and barter agreements were, per se, destructive of the interests of underdeveloped nations makes little sense.

11. Roosevelt's opinion is perhaps revealed in a remark he made to Marriner Eccles after listening to a debate between Eccles and a conservative senator: "You made the problem so simple that even I was able to understand it." Hitler said in 1934: "Don't allow yourself to be deceived by cut-and-dried [economic] theories. Certainly I know less today about these matters than I thought I knew a few years ago."

12. Judgments of Roosevelt's and Hitler's abilities as administrators are of course highly subjective. Furthermore, the internal workings of any government seem confused when examined in detail. It is clear, nevertheless, that both Roosevelt and Hitler were exceptionally prone to set up confused lines of responsibility among their subordinates and to tolerate and at times encourage interdepartmental and intra-departmental rivalries. Waste and ineffectiveness frequently resulted.

13. A 1935 Brookings Institution study of the NRA put it this way: "The work of 'selling' it [the NRA] to the country brought into play demonstrations of emotionalism, pageantry, and oratorical appeals usually associated with war-time propaganda rather than with the ordinary functionings of peace-time government."

14. In 1934 Harry Hopkins negotiated a contract with Pathé News for a series of short commercial films for the WPA. This led Newsweek to comment: "New Deal Goes Hollywood."

15. This last sentence evoked the loudest cheering Roosevelt's speech produced. Eleanor Roosevelt found the response "a little terrifying." Commenting on it later, she said: "You felt they would do anything—if only someone would tell them what to do."

16. Mussolini wrote a widely publicized review of Looking Forward in which he noted a number of similarities between Roosevelt's thinking on economic policy and his own. He concluded, however, that while Roosevelt's ideas were superficially related to "fascist Corporatism . . . it would be an exaggeration to say anything more."

17. In May, 1940, Das Reich published an article comparing Nazi and New Deal policies to combat the depression. "Hitler and Roosevelt. A German Success—An American Attempt." The anonymous author blamed what he called the weaknesses of the New Deal not on Roosevelt but on the "sacrosanct Constitution" of the United States and on the "parliamentary-democratic system" that forced Roosevelt to cater to conflicting interests. "We began with an idea and carried out the practical measures without regard for consequences. America began with many practical measures that without inner coherence covered over each wound with a special bandage."

18. The general acceptance of this theory helps to explain President Hoover's often-derided optimistic prognostications in 1930 and 1931.

19. In February, 1935, Premier Flandin explained his unemployment "policy" to the National Assembly: Large-scale direct relief on the model of the British dole would be impossible in France because of the rapid increase in French unemployment, because France "lacked the resources" of Britain, and because it would unbalance the budget. Extensive public works on the American model would not work because "the future earnings" of such projects would not equal their cost, because France lacked the necessary capital and was too deeply in debt to borrow it, and because France did not need more public works. Yet Flandin admitted that he was receiving "hundreds of heart-rending letters each day" from unemployed workers. He professed to be feeling *"une angoisse quotidienne . . . de jour et de nuit."*

20. It is ironic that flexibility was the Rooseveltian quality that Blum admired most. On May 29, 1936, a few days before he assumed the premiership, Blum told Léon Jouhaux, head of the French labor unions: "What inspires me at the present moment is the example of Roosevelt . . . and especially his boldness, which has enabled him to change his methods when he realizes that they are not working out as planned."

21. Between 1933 and 1939 the German national debt increased from 12.9 billion marks to 42.7 billion, the American from $22.5 billion to $40.4 billion.

IO

A Klansman Joins the Court:
The Appointment of Hugo L. Black

WILLIAM E. LEUCHTENBURG

• Fear of blacks and foreigners was largely responsible for the enormous popularity of the Ku Klux Klan in the early 1920s. The secret order got its start in 1915 when "Colonel" (the title was honorary in the "Woodmen of the World") William Joseph Simmons, a tall, clean-shaven, two hundred pound fraternal organizer, persuaded fifteen fellow Atlantans to motor out to nearby Stone Mountain to burn a cross, raise an American flag, and read a few biblical verses. The small group swore allegiance to the Invisible Empire, Knights of the Ku Klux Klan.

For almost five years, the "Invisible Empire" remained confined to the Peachtree State and neighboring Alabama, and could best be described as just another indolent southern fraternal group. In the spring of 1920, however, two enterprising promoters took a long, interested look at the Klan, recognizing its financial, as well as patriotic, possibilities. Edward Young Clarke, an unimposing dark-haired man in his early thirties, and Mrs. Elizabeth Tyler, a crafty, voluptuous divorcee, noticed the secret order's floundering condition and reasoned correctly that it could greatly broaden its appeal by exploiting the fears and prejudices of uncritical minds against the Catholic, the Jew, the Negro, the Oriental, and the recent immigrant. They formed the Southern Publicity Association and entered into negotiations with Simmons, who despite his title as Imperial Wizard, was richly endowed with neither character nor ability. According to the contract, Clarke would be appointed Imperial Kleagle and receive two dollars and fifty cents for each new recruit. It was a tidy arrangement and would occasionally yield him thirty thousand dollars per week.

Once free to put their booster techniques into practice, Clarke and Tyler quickly transformed the little society into the militant, uncompromising instrument that soon scourged the nation. By 1925 about two million persons had paid the ten dollar initiation fee to become a citizen of the Invisible Empire, which by that time was being described by Stanley Frost as "the most vigorous, active and effective organization in American life outside business." Strongest in Indiana, Ohio, Texas and in such big cities as Chicago, Portland, Denver, Indianapolis, and Dallas, the Klan was particularly successful in the political arena and for a time claimed a half dozen governorships, including those of Oregon, Indiana, and Colorado. It had only a minor impact upon presidential politics, but its divisiveness as a national issue was well illustrated by the appointment of Hugo L. Black to the United States Supreme Court. Soon after President Franklin D. Roosevelt announced the nomination, Black's involvement with the Birmingham chapter of the Invisible Empire became known. In the article below, one of the nation's most eminent historians, William E. Leuchtenburg of Columbia University, discusses the ironies involved in the selection of a Klansman who was to become one of the country's leading exponents of civil liberties.

I. THE NOMINATION

On August 12, 1937, Franklin Delano Roosevelt, rebounding from the worst setback of his long Presidency, took the first of a series of steps toward creating what historians would one day call "the Roosevelt Court." Galling defeat had come less than a month before when the Senate had killed his scheme to add a Justice to the Supreme Court for every member aged seventy or over who did not resign or retire. The original plan would have allowed the President to name as many as six new Justices, but after a bitter 168-day fight, the measure was buried, amid loud rejoicing from FDR's opponents. Roosevelt was not

From the *University of Chicago Law Review*. © 1973 by the University of Chicago.

finished yet, however, for one legacy of the protracted struggle was the creation of a vacancy on the Supreme Court, and it was the President's prerogative to nominate a successor. The choice he finally made would trigger an acrimonious controversy and would have a momentous impact on the disposition of the Court.

The vacancy resulted, at least indirectly, from Roosevelt's "Court-packing" plan. The President had advanced his bold proposal in February because he was frustrated by the performance of the Supreme Court, particularly the conservative "Four Horsemen"—Willis Van Devanter, Pierce Butler, James McReynolds, and George Sutherland. In May, during the congressional battle, Van Devanter announced his retirement in what some thought was a well-timed move to dispose of the plan. Roosevelt was urged to drop the Court bill, since replacing Van Devanter with a liberal would give the Administration a decisive margin in most cases. As soon as Van Devanter's communication was made known on the Senate floor, however, the senators crowded around their colleague, Joseph T. Robinson, to congratulate him on his impending nomination for Van Devanter's seat. They all but usurped the power of appointment from Roosevelt, who knew that he could not avoid honoring the Majority Leader without inciting an uprising. Unfortunately for the New Dealers, Robinson was a 65-year-old conservative who had close connections to private utility interests. So the fight went on into June and July with tempers growing short in the brutal Washington heat. In July, at a critical point in the Great Debate, Robinson died. His death doomed the President's Court-packing scheme, but it left Roosevelt with an opportunity that his opponents had hoped to deny him—naming the first Justice of his own choosing to the Supreme Court.

The battle over the Court plan, Joseph Alsop and Turner Catledge have written, "conferred a strange, almost a lurid importance on the President's choice for the Supeme Court vacancy." As he had done in February while preparing his Court-packing message, Roosevelt moved in a covert manner that put Washington on edge. Each day it was expected that he would send a name to the Senate, but July ran its course without a decision and Congress, which had hoped to go home in June, found itself in the sultry capital in August with adjournment near and still no word from the White House.

In early August, a *New York Times* correspondent noted that "an unusually fierce attack of nervous irritability has seized the 529 legislators." "You have to see the shaking hands and the quivering facial muscles, hear the rage-quavers of the voices" of Congressmen as they spoke to appreciate "the violence of the nerve tension." They "snap at each other over trifles in floor debates" and were biting the heads off secretaries, prompting the correspondent to report "a new high in headless . . . secretaries." One secretary remarked, "Yesterday morning I had to phone six Senators, all of them my friends, and remind them of a subcommittee meeting. Five of them bawled me out for it, and the sixth hung up on me." Another secretary said: "The boss came back from a subcommittee row over a technicality the other day so ill that I had to nurse him and dose him for an hour and then call a doctor. It's the first time I've ever known him to be sick without a hangover for eleven years."

Roosevelt had added to this anxiety when, at a press conference on July 27, he said that he was exploring the possibility of making the appointment after the Senate had adjourned. Mutinous legislators were incensed at the prospect of not having a chance to act on Roosevelt's selection until after the nominee had donned the black robes of a Justice and taken part in the Court's decisions. The President's declaration also indicated that he might be contemplating a particularly offensive nomination, making it desirable for him to bypass the Senate. Attorney General Homer Cummings assured Roosevelt that he could fill a vacancy at any time, even when the Senate was not in session, although, of course, any designee would ultimately have to be confirmed. The historical record on this point, however, did not give the President as much comfort as he wanted, and the Senate was kicking up a storm. By early August he had resolved to settle on a nominee before the Senate adjourned.

Although Roosevelt may have been needling the senators with his talk of a recess appointment, he did have a valid reason for his inquiry. On August 4 Stephen Early, the White House press secretary, reviewed the situation for a Scripps-Howard columnist, Raymond Clapper. Early explained that the President did not know how long Congress would remain in session, and he needed two to four more weeks to make up his mind. It had not been clear until the Senate killed the Court bill in late July that he would have only one seat to fill. It might be supposed, Early said, that Roosevelt could easily come up with one name since he had originally sought to choose six, but in fact it was harder to pick one, because he could not submit a balanced group and had to "make it a bull's eye." Clapper summarized the President's position in his diary: "been sixty to 75 names recommended since Robinson died. All have to be carefully investigated. Is serious matter and Rvt [Roosevelt] would be in bad spot if he sent up a name and then the opposition dug out some dumb chapter in his record. . . . Opposition which has been complaining that Rvt is slapdash would leap on him and say this is the kind of dumb[b]ell or bad actor he would have given us six of."

As the tension mounted, congressmen and reporters made book on whom the President would pick, but they had little to go on. Although it was expected that Roosevelt would try to heal the breaches within his party and the Senate by making an especially judicious choice, he gave no sign of where his favor might light. Even veteran Administration senators like James F. Byrnes remained in the dark. "I haven't the slightest idea who will be appointed to the Supreme Court, nor has anybody in Washington other than the President," Byrnes wrote a South Carolina friend on August 10. "The President certainly has not consulted anybody in the Senate about it. The only information we have is that contained in the Press; namely, that Sam Bratton of New Mexico, now a Judge of the Circuit Court of Appeals and formerly a member of the Senate, is receiving serious consideration. It may be that it is because the Senators have such a high opinion of Bratton that they think he has a good chance."

When Roosevelt finally made his decision, he moved in the same furtive manner he had used in preparing the Court plan. On the night of August 11 the President startled the man he had finally chosen by summoning him to the White House after dinner and, upon informing him of the honor in store for him, pledged him to silence. Not even the White House staff knew what had transpired. The next morning Stephen Early indicated that Roosevelt was still considering a list of sixty or seventy names and that a selection might not be made during the current congressional session. Two hours later the President sent a courier to Capitol Hill with a notice of appointment that Roosevelt had written in his own hand. The President kept the secret almost to the very end, but it had become too much for him. Like "a small boy waiting for his surprise to be revealed," as Virginia

Hamilton has written, he had to blurt out the news to someone. Before the messenger reached the door of the Senate chamber, Roosevelt told Early the name of the nominee. "Jesus Christ!" Early exploded. FDR grinned.

II. THE SENATE CONSENTS

The words "I nominate Hugo L. Black . . . ." sent the Senate into a state of shock. Senator Black, who had not let on at any point that he knew what the message contained, now slumped in his seat, white-faced and wordless, and nervously shredded a sheaf of papers. A few liberal colleagues came over to congratulate the Alabama senator, but other legislators did not try to hide their unhappiness. The House of Representatives responded more volubly. One reporter noted, "From the House press gallery it was quite a show to watch the reactions of the Congressmen as the news swept across the floor. A great buzzing as the name of Black was passed from lip to lip."

If Roosevelt anticipated immediate acquiescence from the Senate, he was reckoning without the diehards. Henry Fountain Ashurst, the eloquent chairman of the Judiciary Committee, rose on behalf of the administration and asked the senators to confirm instantly the appointment of this "lawyer of transcendent ability, great, industrious and courteous in debate, young, vigorous, of splendid character and attainments." Ashurst contended that there was "an immemorial rule of the Senate that whenever the Executive honors this body by nominating a member thereof, that nomination by immemorial usage is confirmed without reference to a committee for the obvious reason that no amount of investigation or consideration by a committee could disclose any new light on the character or attainments and ability of the nominee, because if we do not know him after long service with the nominee no one will ever know him." When Hiram Johnson of California and Edward Burke of Nebraska objected, however, Ashurst was compelled to name a subcommittee to consider the nomination. Not since 1888, when President Grover Cleveland nominated Lucius Quintus Cincinnatus Lamar to the Supreme Court, had a proposed appointment of a senator or former senator been sent to committee.

Roosevelt could hardly have made a choice that would have discomforted his opponents more. Black was an ardent New Dealer and had been a strong supporter of Court-packing; indeed, it was said that he was one of the few senators who actually believed in the plan. Most people had expected that Roosevelt would take pains to name some-one like a federal judge, but Black's only judicial experience consisted of eighteen months as a police court judge in Birmingham. Little about him suggested the judicial temperament, and he had especially incensed conservatives by his performance as an exceptionally vigor-ous prosecutor on Senate committees. As one biographer described it, "The paths of his investigations had been lurid with charges and coun-tercharges, *subpoenas duces tecum*, searches and seizures, and con-tempt proceedings," and the political scientist Earl Latham has noted that "Senator Black in 1936 was the kind of legislator Justice Black had no use for twenty years later."

A year before the nomination Newton D. Baker, a onetime progres-sive leader who had become a prominent corporation attorney, had written a friend: "I heard last week that the incredible Senator Black with his eavesdropping, peeping-Tom committee had secured from the Western Union Telegraph Company all the telegrams sent out of my office in a year. As I run a law office and not a criminal conspiracy, I am entirely indifferent as to what he discovered from the telegrams, but the oftener I permit myself to reflect on this outrage, the more violent I become. Man of peace as I am, I am quite sure I could not keep my hand off the rope if I accidentally happened to stumble upon a party bent on hanging him."

Conservatives outdid themselves in expressions of indignation. "If the President had searched the country for the worst man to appoint, he couldn't possibly have found anyone to fill the bill so well," grumbled one senator. "Mr. Roosevelt could not have made a worse appointment if he had named John L. Lewis," wrote the columnist David Lawrence, and Herbert Hoover protested that the court was now "one-ninth packed." The most devastating critique appeared on the editorial page of the *Washington Post*:

Men deficient in the necessary professional qualifications have occasionally been named for the Supreme Court. And qualified men have sometimes been put forward primarily because they were also politically agreeable to a President. But until yesterday students of American history would have found it difficult to refer to any Supreme Court nomination which combined lack of training on the one hand and extreme partisanship. In this one respect the choice of Senator Black must be called outstanding.

. . . .

If Senator Black has given any study or thought to any aspect of constitutional law in a way which would entitle him to this preferment, his labors in that direction have been skillfully concealed. If he has ever shown himself exceptionally qualified in either the knowledge or the temperament essential for exercise of the highest judicial function, the occasion escapes recollection.

Although Black came from Alabama, no group was unhappier about his nomination than the Southern congressmen. A sharp-tongued, unrelenting partisan who kept too much to himself, Black had never been a member of "the club." More important, he was a Southern liberal, and his selection signaled Roosevelt's determination to back those who were attempting to transform the conservative structure of Southern politics, an inclination that was later manifested in the 1938 purge. A Georgia congressman called the nomination of Black "the worst insult that has yet been given to the nation"; a Texas congressman said, "I wouldn't appeal a case with him there." Black had particularly antagonized Southern conservatives by sponsoring the wages and hours bill, which they claimed was denying their constituencies a competitive advantage granted by God. When reporters asked the veteran Virginia Senator Carter Glass for a comment on Black, he replied, "Don't start me off again."

Yet Roosevelt knew very well that there was not a thing they could, or would, do about it. Black was a senator, and the sense of collegiality was so strong that it was inconceivable that the Senate would fail to confirm one of its members. As the President told Democratic Chairman James A. Farley, "They'll have to take him."

The Senate proved unwilling to entertain the real objections many felt to Black's nomination. It would not consider the assertion that Black was too liberal, because ideological differences were not regarded as proper grounds for refusing to confirm a fellow senator; nor was Black's lack of judicial background explored, since it could not be conceded that any member of the Senate might be unqualified to sit on the Supreme Court. The little consideration given the appointment therefore focused on technical matters. Senator William E. Borah of Idaho claimed that since Van Devanter had taken advantage of legislation passed earlier in the session allowing retirement rather than resignation, he was still a member of the Court, and there was no vacancy for Black to fill. Ashurst retorted that if all nine Justices retired or went mad, according to Borah's reasoning, there would be no Court; even Van Devanter thought the argument was nonsense, since he had no intention of ever returning to the bench. Others speculated that Black was ineligible for another reason: since the retirement legislation also guaranteed the pensions of retiring Justices, Congress had increased their emoluments, and the Constitution forbade any member of Congress to accept a post under such circumstances. Few people thought much of that argument either.

Two days after the nomination, a more explosive consideration arose—it was said that Black, at the outset of his career, had been associated with the Ku Klux Klan. The National Association for the Advancement of Colored People and the Socialist Party each urged the Senate to explore Black's racial attitudes. The Socialist leader Norman Thomas also asked the Judiciary Committee to investigate Black's opposition during the Hoover administration to proposals to equalize relief between Whites and Negroes, his hostility to antilynching legislation, and his silence about the "Scottsboro boys," a group of Negroes convicted in Alabama in what appeared to be an outrageous miscarriage of justice. "We fully appreciate Senator Black's championship of labor legislation," Thomas said, but "no other excellence can fit a man for the Supreme Court whose record is marred by race prejudice."

Despite these reservations the nomination moved quickly through committee, but not without occasioning some animosity. Matthew Neely of West Virginia, an Administration stalwart, allotted the matter only two hours in a meeting of his subcommittee on Friday, August 13, the day after the nomination; the subcommittee then reported the recommendation by a vote of 5–1, with only Warren Austin of Vermont dissenting on constitutional grounds. On the following Monday, as the Judiciary Committee convened behind closed doors, William Dieterich of Illinois accused certain committee members of trying to "besmirch" their colleague by linking him to the Ku Klux Klan. Dieterich's tirade nearly resulted in a fist fight with a fellow Democrat when Senator Burke charged at him. Although "tempers flared to white heat," the committee approved the nomination 13–4.

When the full Senate took up the Black appointment on August

17, Senator Royal S. Copeland of New York opened the debate by asserting that his Alabama colleague's first election to the Senate in 1926 had been supported by the Klan. Before crowded public galleries, Copeland read a *New York Times* report on Black's exploitation of anti-Catholic sentiment in attacking the Presidential ambitions of Alfred E. Smith. Copeland asserted, "We are free because we are guarded by the Supreme Court. Catholics, Protestants, Negroes, Jews, Gentiles, all of us, are guarded by the Supreme Court. But what will happen if a half dozen men of the mental bias of the nominee should be seated on the bench? . . . Does the leopard change his spots? Will Mr. Justice Black be any different from Candidate Black? . . . Naturally we wonder what Mr. Justice Black would do were another Scottsboro case appealed to the Supreme Court."

Copeland made no headway with his charges, because they were regarded as blatantly political and because the Senate received reassurances. Many believed that Copeland, an anti-New Deal Democrat who was running for Mayor of New York City, was exploiting the Klan issue to curry ethnic voters. Although Black left the question unresolved when cornered by some of his supporters during the debate, the unpredictable Borah came to his aid. The Idaho maverick, who eventually voted against confirmation on the technical ground of ineligibility, conceded that senators had received thousands of telegrams about Black and the Klan, but insisted, "There has never been at any time one iota of evidence that Senator Black was a member of the Klan. . . . We know that Senator Black has said in private conversation, not since this matter came up but at other times, that he was not a member of the Klan." When Copeland asked Borah how he would vote if he knew that Black was or had been a Klansman, the Idaho senator replied, "If I knew that a man was a member of a secret association organized to spread racial antipathies and religious intolerance through the country, I should certainly vote against him for any position."

Late in the afternoon of August 17, just five days after the Black nomination was made and after only six hours of debate, the Senate confirmed the appointment by the lopsided margin of sixty-three to sixteen. Of the Republicans present all but three voted "nay," as did six Democrats, including Burke and Copeland. However, some of the most reactionary Southern Democrats, who had bitterly fought the Court plan, ended up supporting the administration. Ickes recorded,

"Even 'Cotton Ed' Smith, of South Carolina, who 'God-damned' the nomination all over the place when it was first announced, didn't have the courage to stand up and vote against a fellow Senator from the Deep South." The Klan issue had fizzled, but it left some uneasiness. In Washington, a one-liner went from mouth to mouth: "Hugo won't have to buy a robe; he can dye his white one black." Despite the rumbling about the KKK, Roosevelt and the New Dealers had apparently won a stunning victory, less than a month after the opposition thought FDR was on the ropes. Ickes concluded: "So Hugo Black becomes a member of the Supreme Court of the United States, while the economic royalists fume and squirm, and the President rolls his tongue around in his cheek."

The outcome left conservatives disconsolate. When Carter Glass heard the nomination called a triumph for the common man, he snapped, "They must be Goddam common!" Senator Peter Gerry of Rhode Island explained to Canada's prime minister, "His legal experience was not considered sufficient and he hasn't a judicial attitude of mind. He is a prosecutor and not a judge." An Oregon editor went even further: "His appointment of Black was the grossest insult to the Supreme Court and the American people that we have ever been called upon to accept." Roosevelt's former adviser Raymond Moley commented, "There have been worse appointments to high judicial offices; but . . . I can't remember where or when."

After Congress adjourned, Hiram Johnson wrote a confidant in California: "This was a most unsatisfactory session. We wound up by confirming Black, who is unfit to be a Supreme Court Justice. . . . Had it not been for me, Black's nomination would have gone through with a 'Hurrah!' . . . Borah and other distinguished patriots wished it so, but I had 'guts' enough to stop it. I accomplished nothing —save that sixteen men in the Senate showed their feeling of his unfitness. I understand he was a member of the Ku Klux Klan when first elected to the Senate. He never dared say anything about it subsequently, and Borah and his other friends, saw to it that he was not called as a witness."

Once Black was confirmed, the hubbub died down. Congressmen left the capital, and Black sailed with his wife to Europe for a vacation. His name soon disappeared from the newspapers, and the controversy appeared to be at an end.

III.   THE REVELATION

On September 13 the Pittsburgh *Post-Gazette* detonated a bombshell. It published the first of six articles by Ray Sprigle, an enterprising reporter who had dug up original materials, including the transcript of a Klan meeting, conclusively connecting Hugo Black to the Ku Klux Klan. The series grabbed front page headlines in newspapers throughout the country.

Sprigle began, "Hugo Lafayette Black, Associate Justice of the United States Supreme Court, is a member of the hooded brotherhood that for ten long blood-drenched years ruled the Southland with lash and noose and torch, the Invisible Empire, Knights of the Ku Klux Klan." Since it was generally suspected that Black had once had a KKK relationship, that allegation hardly constituted news. Sprigle developed three points in his series, however, that were very damaging. First, he demonstrated that Black had not merely run with Klan backing, but had actually been a member of the organization. He gave an account of the night of September 11, 1923, when Black pledged that he would never divulge, even under threat of death, the secrets of the Klan; surrounded by white-robed members of the Robert E. Lee Klan No. 1 in Birmingham, Black had vowed, "I swear that I will most zealously and valiantly shield and preserve by any and all justifiable means and methods . . . white supremacy."

Second, Sprigle recounted vivid examples of the views held by the Klansmen with whom Black had associated. In a meeting on September 2, 1926, the Imperial Wizard Hiram Wesley Evans said, "We find that America up to now has done all that has been worthwhile under the leadership of native-born, white, gentile, Protestant men. . . . There isn't a Negro in Alabama that dares open his mouth and says he believes in social equality of the black man. . . . I mean to tell you any time they propose to produce equality between me and a certain said Negro they are simply going to have to hold a funeral for the Negro." The Imperial Wizard added that Northern Negroes "will be murdered by the Yankees that have gotten all the sass from the Negroes that they want." On that same occasion the KKK's Imperial Legal Adviser in Washington observed, "To come down here now and find that you have given us a man named Black who wears 'white'—do you get that boys—to occupy a seat in the Senate of the United States is like getting an inspiration before baptism." Turning to Bibb Graves, who had just won the Democratic nomination for Governor, tantamount to election, he added, "I am so glad that you have a man, all but elected Governor, who comes from a town that, prior to his advent as Exalted Cyclops of the local Klan, I am told was owned by the Jews, controlled by the Catholics and loved by Negroes [Laughter and applause]. Now he tells me that the Jews have a foreclosure sale at bankruptcy, selling out, the Catholics are on the run, and the Negroes are in hiding [Applause]."

Most of Black's own remarks that afternoon were unexceptionable. In fact he spoke of the "principles of liberty which were written in the Constitution of this country" and the ideal of loving one's enemies. But he also assured the assembled Klansmen, "I realize that I was elected by men who believe in the principles that I have sought to advocate and which are the principles of this organization," and said to them and to the Grand Dragon, "I thank you from the bottom of a heart that is yours."

Finally, Sprigle made a third and critical contribution—he established that, on the same afternoon in 1926, Black, who had resigned from the Klan in the summer of 1925 for reasons of political expediency, had been awarded a special life membership, a gold "grand passport." Black had thanked the Klan for this honor, which only a half dozen men in the United States had received. Most important, the card was presumably still valid because there was no evidence in the Klan archives that it had been returned. In short, Sprigle was saying not merely that Black had been elected with Klan backing, not merely that Black had thanked the Klan leaders for their aid, but that Black was *still* a member of the Ku Klux Klan.

Sprigle's articles prompted denunciations of Black and Roosevelt that far exceeded, in both volume and vehemence, the protests that had greeted the nomination. Cartoonists had a field day depicting the members of the Supreme Court assembled in their silk, eight in black and the ninth in the white robe and hood of the KKK. In the pages of the *American Mercury* the mordant critic Albert Jay Nock called Black "a vulgar dog" and wrote that Roosevelt's appointment "was the act of a man who conceives himself challenged to do his very filthiest."

Several senators who had voted to confirm Black hastened to declare that if they had known of his Klan connection they would have opposed his elevation to the Court. Some thought they had been duped, since Black had temporized when the KKK rumors surfaced in August, and others had given assurances that there was no foundation to the allegations. Democratic senators from New Jersey and South Dakota charged that John Bankhead of Alabama had deliberately misled them by stating that Black had not been a member of the Klan. "I feel that not only I but the rest of the Senators were deceived and imposed upon," complained Clyde Herring, and his Iowa colleague, Guy Gillette, added, "I hope something is done to keep Black from the high court bench."

The issue hit directly at the core of Roosevelt's urban coalition since the main targets of the KKK had been Catholics and Negroes. The revelations also embarrassed Northern Democratic senators with large ethnic constituencies who had voted for Black. Groups like the Ancient Order of Hibernians demanded that Black resign or be removed; the Catholic Club of the City of New York deemed the appointment "a direct affront to the more than 20,000,000 Catholic citizens of the United States as well as to countless numbers of other citizens." In New Hampshire the Knights of Columbus adopted resolutions castigating Senator Fred Brown for supporting confirmation, and a member of the staff of Senator Theodore Green of Rhode Island noted, "At a very large meeting of the Hibernian County Convention last night a great many Democrats were denouncing Roosevelt. Very severe criticism among the Democrats.

Irish Catholic politicians played a numerically disproportionate role in the campaign to get rid of Black. Representative John J. O'Connor, chairman of the House Rules Committee, reported he had been canvassing congressmen about instituting impeachment proceedings and had found no one opposed to such a move. "If Mr. Justice Black was a member of the Klan when nominated and confirmed, his silence constituted a moral fraud upon the American people," said Representative Edward L. O'Neill, a New Jersey Democrat. Lieutenant Governor Francis E. Kelly of Massachusetts drafted a resolution asking the President to insist upon Black's resignation, and Senator David I. Walsh, who favored the same course, declared, "There are two counts against him, one that Black, for political advantage joined the Klan and took the oath of a Klansman and subscribed to its creeds; two, that Black obtained his nomination and confirmation by concealment and thereby deceived the President and his fellow-Senators, especially the latter."

Sprigle's articles appeared just as the campaign for the mayoralty in New York City was reaching a climax, and Senator Copeland took full advantage of the opportunity. He told a Carnegie Hall audience: "I never expected to see the day when a member of that organization, sworn to bigotry and intolerance, should become a member of the court. Shame upon him that he did not have the courage and decency to tell his colleagues in the Senate that the suspicion of his affiliation was a reality." Copeland accused his rival, Jeremiah T. Mahoney, of approving Roosevelt's action in the "placing upon the court of a Klansman who wears a black robe of court by day and a white robe of the Klan by night." "Imagine a man named Mahoney being mixed up with the Klan," his opponent spluttered. "Show me a Ku Klux Klanner and I promise he won't be alive a minute after I see him!"

Negro spokesmen joined in the hue and cry. The National Association for the Advancement of Colored People urged the President to call upon Black "to resign his post in the absence of repudiation and disproof of charges" that he held life membership in the KKK. Robert L. Vann, who was the Negro editor of the *Pittsburgh Courier*, a special assistant United States attorney general, and also credited with playing the largest role in swinging Pennsylvania Negroes to the Democratic Party, wired Roosevelt to remove Black. "Your friends are on the spot," Vann said. "You must save your friends or you must release them."

Despite this widespread feeling, even Roosevelt's conservative critics in the Senate conceded that nothing could be done if Black decided to stick it out. The President could not oust a Justice, and since he had been lambasted month after month for trying to tamper with the Court, Roosevelt and his supporters surmised that any attempt to coerce Black into resigning would not be well received. People would be led to conclude "that, if the President should request Justice Black's resignation, he might also attempt to drive Justice McReynolds, Sutherland and Butler from the bench." Nor did there appear to be grounds for impeachment. The civil liberties attorney Osmond K.

Fraenkel observed, "I don't believe a judge can be impeached for something that happened before his appointment, but even if that were so, I do not see how he could be impeached for membership in an organization. Membership in the Klan, however politically inadvisable, is not a crime."

The electrifying disclosures exasperated the President. Washington, which so recently had been the self-confident capital of the New Deal, was now jeered at as "Ku-Kluxville-on-the-Potomac." The situation was especially embarrassing to the New Dealers because Roosevelt had taken a firm stand for religious liberty in 1928 while campaigning for Al Smith, a Catholic, and had been severely criticized for having too many Jews in his administration and for giving too many benefits to Negroes. Despite this record the President now bore the onus of having brought the main battle of his second term to a climax by naming a Klansman to the Supreme Court.

In an editorial in the *Emporia Gazette* William Allen White wrote:

> When Franklin Roosevelt is dead and buried and all his bones are rotted, the fact that he played around with Black and appointed to the highest honorable office in American life a man who was a member of the Ku Klux Klan, as Black was charged when Roosevelt named him, well, as we started to say, when Roosevelt is dead and gone he will be remembered in the history of this day and time by the fact that he was not above dishonoring the Supreme Court by putting a Klansman there.
>
> Why could not a man as smart as Franklin Roosevelt, as brave and as benevolent, also be wise in a day of crisis?

IV. "I DID JOIN THE KLAN"

While Roosevelt's prospects were imperiled by the unexpected turn of events, Black's life had become all but unendurable. The clamor followed the new Justice to Europe, where he was still vacationing when the Sprigle series broke. Journalists hounded him, first in Paris, then in London. "A dreadfully worried United States judge hid himself away in a palatial hotel suite in London yesterday while all his fellow countrymen were asking for a straight answer to a straight question," reported the British *Daily Herald*. One newspaperman jumped out of a darkened corridor scaring Black's wife, and another seized his arm as he emerged from a London theater. "I don't see you; I don't know you; I don't answer you," Black told him. The columnist Dorothy Thompson wrote, "In London tonight a Justice of the United States Supreme Court is barricaded behind locked doors. His telephone rings but he does not answer it. Reporters try to interview him but in vain. This man . . . sees only the waiters who bring him food, the maids who tidy his rooms and the traffic of London moving in the streets below. . . . He is front page news in England, where the British are taking revenge for the Simpson case." After letting it be known that he would sail back to America on a large transatlantic liner, on which one of his fellow passengers would have been Mr. Justice McReynolds, Black escaped from his hotel by a service entrance and drove to Southampton where he boarded a small mail steamer, *The City of Norfolk*. He left England, said the *Sun*, "Klandestinely."

No longer would Black be permitted to remain silent. Senator Walsh said that he had to speak out to be fair to the Catholic senators, and to those with Catholic and Jewish constituents, who had voted for his confirmation and who might suffer the consequences in the next election. Democratic Senator Bennett Champ Clark of Missouri commented, "I do not wish to be in the position of concluding as to the authenticity of the charges contained in the newspapers against Justice Black, but it does seem to me that he has had ample opportunity to answer a simple statement of fact." As Black's vessel headed westward across the Atlantic toward Norfolk, a Gallup Poll revealed that 59 percent of those interviewed believed that he should resign if he were proven to have been a member of the Klan. At Felix Frankfurter's suggestion, the young *Nation* editor Max Lerner flew to Norfolk, made his way through throngs of newspapermen, and at breakfast with Black aboard ship argued that he should issue an explanation. That night, Lerner spent four more hours with Black in Alexandria. Under all of this pressure, Black finally decided to accept an invitation to speak over the radio on October 1, but he now had less than two days to draft his speech.

The address, carried over three national networks with three hundred stations, attracted the largest American audience of the decade, except for that tuned in to the abdication of Edward VIII. (The huge audience, however, did lack one prominent listener—Franklin Roosevelt contrived to be in the Pacific Northwest in an automobile without a radio as Black spoke.) The fact of Black's speech was a sensation because of the cardinal rule that Justices do not make statements on public matters, and the dramatic nature of the occasion was enhanced when fiery crosses lit the hillsides in different parts of the country.

In his talk, Black admitted having belonged to the Klan—he could hardly do anything else—but said that he had resigned before entering the Senate and never rejoined. He minimized the grand passport as an "unsolicited card" which he did not view as membership in the Klan, had never used, and had not kept. He also voiced his disdain, without naming the KKK, for "any organization or group which, anywhere or at any time, arrogates to itself the un-American power to interfere in the slightest degree with complete religious freedom."

Black's speech is remembered today as a courageous denunciation of the Klan that foreshadowed his future character as a Justice, but in truth it was not. Black neither explained his past Klan membership nor offered any apology for signing up with the KKK; nor did he account for why he had sat through the Senate discussion of his alleged Klan connections without a word to anyone either in the Senate or, apparently, in the administration. He repudiated none of the atrocities perpetrated by the Klan in Alabama while he was in the secret order. In all, he used only eleven of the thirty minutes allotted to him. The most unfortunate aspect of his talk, however, was not what he failed to say but what he did say. He spent the first third of his remarks cautioning against the possibility of a revival of racial and religious hatred, but he warned that this might be brought about not by groups like the Klan but by those who questioned his right to be on the Supreme Court. He went on to affirm that some of his best friends were Jews and Catholics, told the national audience about his longtime Jewish chum in Birmingham, and mentioned that he numbered among his friends "many members of the colored race.'

Rarely in the twentieth century has any statement by an American public figure brought down such abuse on him in the press as Black's brief address called forth. The *New York Herald Tribune* branded him a humbug and a coward: "The effort of Senator Black to suggest that he is the real protagonist of tolerance and that his enemies are intolerant is perhaps the greatest item of effrontery in a uniquely brazen utterance. Only a man heedless of the truth and a man afraid of his official skin could fall so low." The *Boston Post* called on him to resign, for "one who associates with bigots, bids for their support, takes the bigots' oath and then is so craven that he allows his friends in a crisis to deny it all, can't clear himself by asserting it was all contrary to his real character." About Black's references to Catholic, Jewish, and Negro friends, the *New York Post* said, "We might reply in kind that one of our best liberal friends was a Klansman but we still don't think he ought to be on the Supreme Court." The *Newark Ledger* added that Black had, "resigned from the Klan to maintain an appearance of decency. He should resign from the Supreme Court to attain the substance of decency." Catholic outrage ranged across the political spectrum from the liberal *Commonweal* to periodicals and spokesmen on the right. "Since there was no sign of his being ashamed for himself," wrote the editor of *The Catholic World*, "I was ashamed for him; ashamed too for the Supreme Court, ashamed for the President of the United States."

Roosevelt, however, had no doubt that Black's performance had carried the day. When Jim Farley telephoned him a few days later the President asked, "What d'you think of Hugo's speech of the other night?" "He did the best he could under the circumstances, but I think he should have hit the Klan," Farley answered. "It was a grand job," Roosevelt returned. "It did the trick; you just wait and see."

The President was absolutely right. The address was inevitably applauded, if not altogether convincingly, by Black's supporters in the New Deal. "If you listened to Mr. Justice Black's radio talk," said Senator Green of Rhode Island, "I am sure that you must have felt as I did that he admirably expressed the principles on which Roger Williams founded this State." Elements of Roosevelt's urban coalition also remained loyal. Labor leaders praised Black's speech, and Rabbi Herbert S. Goldstein of Yeshiva College spoke for others in saying, "As a citizen, I do not seek 'the pound of flesh' and as a Jew, I do not seek retaliation." Most important, Black's discourse won the majority of his listeners, albeit not a substantial majority. After the broadcast 56 percent of the people polled by Gallup responded that Black should stay on the bench, which was precisely what he had intended to do all along.

V.   MR. JUSTICE BLACK

On the morning of October 4, three days after Black's radio talk, the
Supreme Court opened its fall term, and huge crowds gathered to see
the former Klansman take his seat. Long lines extended for hundreds
of feet in the corridor, and much of the throng was unable to enter
the courtroom. When the Justices filed in, it was noted pointedly that
Black sat to the "extreme left" of the Chief Justice. For the first time
in public, Black wore the silk robes of a Justice, but the occasion was
not the hour of triumph the man from Clay County, Alabama might
have hoped for. To the dismay of his supporters, two petitions were
filed to challenge his right to be a Justice. For all Black's efforts and
those of Roosevelt, the controversy continued to simmer.

The President quickly remedied the situation. The next day in
Chicago, he delivered his historic "quarantine" address, and by nightfall the country had turned its attention from Black to foreign affairs
and the prospect of a second world war. A distinguished authority on
international law, John Bassett Moore, wrote, "The President never
was more adroit than in his Chicago speech. All the talk about Black,
balancing the budget, the C.I.O., the 'dictatorial drift,' etc. etc., . . .
suddenly ceased when the war cry was raised." Critics charged that
FDR had deliberately seized the headlines in order to distract attention from the Black furor. "The speech would never have been made
if there had been no Black case," Hiram Johnson protested. Actually,
the situation was more complex than such conspiracy notions suggested. From Washington, His Majesty's Chargé D'Affaires sent the
British Foreign Secretary Anthony Eden a more balanced report:

> I have every reason to believe that the speech had long been
> contemplated, but the President was prepared to await the psy-
> chological moment for its delivery. He had returned from his
> Western tour fully convinced that, however lukewarm the feel-
> ing regarding the Supreme Court might be in those parts, the
> electors as a whole had not lost confidence in his personal leader-
> ship. On the other hand the regrettable "Black and Klan" inci-
> dent was still front page news and required something more
> important to remove it to the back page. In fact unkind Wall
> Street wits are talking of "a red herring drawn across the Black
> trail." The President's arrival at Chicago coincided with the

decision at Geneva to refer the Far Eastern crisis to the signatories of the Nine-Power Treaty. Here was a good opportunity for Mr. Roosevelt to make his appeal to the nation to abandon a policy of complete isolation.

Although the quarantine address was followed by reduced attention to Black in the press, lawyers and Washington correspondents continued to scrutinize him closely. Even after the Court summarily dismissed the petitions to deny Black a seat, every eye seemed to be inspecting the new Justice. "I went to the Court last week and had the opportunity to see Mr. Justice Black on the bench," Newton D. Baker wrote to the former Supreme Court Justice John H. Clarke. "He is young enough to make a good judge but he has a wavering expression of the eyes which he will have great trouble in straightening out if he wants to be like the judges on that Court usually are—impervious to all considerations except their view of the public good." The veteran *New York Times* columnist Arthur Krock had a different perspective; he observed:

> Mr. Justice Black's court-room demeanor provided material for interesting study. His face had gained color. His manner had acquired content. He looked benign instead of harried. But now and then, as the Chief Justice read the orders and Mr. Justice Black looked out upon the lawyers and spectators from his impregnable fortress of life tenure, an expression touched his face which is common to certain types of martyrs. It was a mixture of forgiveness and satisfaction, of pity for unreconstructed dissenters and sympathy for himself who had borne so much in comparative silence. Charles Dickens, who gave many passages to the description of Mr. Christopher Catesby, would have recognized it at once.

Black might well have nourished such sentiments in his first year on the bench, for he was permitted to forget neither his Klan past nor his limited judicial background. In his first month, Black drew scathing criticism when the conviction of one of the Scottsboro boys came up on appeal and Black disqualified himself. The treatment accorded him by liberal Justices Louis Brandeis and, more particularly, Harlan Fiske Stone caused greater distress. In strolls through Washington with the newspaperman Marquis Childs, Stone abandoned discretion and vented his distress over Black's inexpertise. Childs later said that Stone was "like an old New England wood-carver, and here they suddenly brought someone in the shop who doesn't know a knife from a hoe. This really upset him very greatly." In an article inspired by his chats with Stone, Childs created a hullabaloo by stating that Black's opinions frequently had to be rewritten by his colleagues in order to bring them up to the standards of the Court and that Black's incompetence had caused the other Justices "acute discomfort and embarrassment."

Yet even in these early days Black won admirers for his courage and skill. Rather than meekly accommodating himself as might be expected of a newcomer tarred by scandal, he boldly advanced iconoclastic notions. "Mr. Justice Black, dissenting" became a familiar phrase; indeed, he was said to have set a record for lone dissents. Walton Hamilton expressed his esteem for Black's cleanly written opinions and the independence of a man who "regards the sacred cows as ordinary heifers." By 1939 Erwin D. Canham was observing that "Mr. Justice Black . . . has climbed out of the pit into which the circumstances of his appointment had hurled him, and is on the way to being regarded as another Brandeis."

The allusion to Brandeis suggested both a craftsmanship that demeaning references to the police court judgeship had not prepared critics for and a solicitude for civil liberties that many people had not expected of an ex-Klansman. In 1940 Black was spokesman for the Court in two notable decisions. In *Chambers v. Florida*, generally thought to be his ablest opinion, he spoke for a unanimous Court in holding that the convictions of four Negroes for murder, obtained by using coerced confessions, violated the due process clause of the fourteenth amendment. In *Smith v. Texas*, he again spoke for all nine Justices in setting aside the rape conviction of a Negro based on an indictment handed down by a grand jury from which Negroes were excluded. Black became best known, however, not as the eloquent voice of a unanimous Court, but as a dissenter urging the Court to break new ground on civil liberties, particularly as an advocate of uninhibited application of the first amendment. Justice William O. Douglas observed in 1956, "I dare say that when the critical account is written, none will be rated higher than Justice Black for consistency in construing the laws and the Constitution so as to protect the civil rights of citizens and aliens, whatever the form of repression may be." A decade later Alexander Bickel wrote of "a Hugo Black majority" on the Court, "for in this second half of Justice Black's third decade of service, the Court was overturning many a precedent that had entered the books over his dissent." When he finally left the bench in 1971, Justice Black, who had once been jeered at for his alleged lack of expertise, was praised for his "extraordinary capacity to clarify and make vivid the issues in a case" through "seemingly impregnable logic," and as one of "the court's intellectual pillars" with a reputation for "judicial integrity, dignity and tight reasoning."

Black's subsequent career made the widespread alarm expressed at his appointment seem badly misdirected and gave Roosevelt a sense of vindication. The President had remained rather touchy about the Black affair. In February, 1938, Raymond Clapper related in his diary an episode that took place in the Gridiron Club, the organization of Washington correspondents: "President Geo Holmes told about visit he and Gould Lincoln made to Rvt on Monday after dinner. Rvt said like dinner except thought one skit in bad taste. Said that was Klan skit on Black. . . . Said Harding had an illegitimate child but Gridiron club never use anything on that. . . . Said matter was dying out skit by being printed in newspapers tended to reopen whole thing keep it agitated. Holmes told us he couldn't see analogy of Rvt's unless he meant that Black was like Nan Britton." When the *Chambers* decision was handed down, Roosevelt seized the opportunity at his press conference the next day to tell reporters, "I would put in a general dig that some of the Press should not only give a little praise but also a modicum of apology for things they have said in the last two years. Is that fair?"

VI.   "A WONDERFULLY GOOD APPOINTMENT"

Black's emergence as a champion of civil liberties has been offered as proof that Roosevelt knew what he was doing all along, that he perceived potential in Black that others did not. Perhaps he did; it is hard to determine, particularly this long after the fact, what one man sensed in another. It is highly improbable, though, that FDR foresaw Black's ultimate accomplishments, even if he may have supposed that Black, like other men, might show new qualities when given the independence of life tenure.

Other commentators have said that Black's post-1937 conduct accorded with his pre-1937 career, for he had come out of a populist tradition in Alabama and had long been an exponent of civil liberties and individualism and a friend of labor and the Negro. This view acknowledges that he had been a Klansman, but contends that the KKK was a populist, prolabor movement that sponsored liberal, humanitarian measures, such as aid for underprivileged children. Some have also claimed that he joined at the urging of a Jewish friend in order to exercise his benign influence within the Klan.

The evidence for these familiar arguments is, at best, ambiguous. It is true that Black appears never to have been associated with Klan violence, that he was an attorney for unions, and that he was responsible for reforms in court procedure in Alabama. Nevertheless, the link of Black to populism has been too easily assumed, quite apart from the difficulty of showing the connection between populism and modern civil libertarianism. Black did have Negro clients, but he was also reproached for making a blatant appeal to race prejudice while defending the accused murderer of a priest. The strongest statement that Daniel M. Berman could make in his informative article in the *Catholic University Law Review* was that "there is no evidence that Judge Black treated Negroes any more harshly than whites." As late as 1932, Black had opposed a government relief bill because it would, in code language, interfere with "social habits and social customs." Correspondent Paul Y. Anderson reported that Black "became hysterical over the prospect of a federal relief plan which might feed Negroes as well as whites, and gave an exhibition which brought a blush to the face of Tom Heflin, lurking in the rear of the chamber." The one thing known for certain about Black's attitude toward the Negro was that, in the very month Roosevelt appointed him to the Supreme Court, Black was planning to speak in the Senate against the antilynching bill.

At a press conference in September Roosevelt responded "No" to the question: "Prior to the appointment of former Senator Black, had you received any information from any source as to his Klan membership?" The President may not have known about "membership," but it is inconceivable that he had no awareness of a Klan connection. It was widely recognized, at the very least, that the Alabama senator had Klan backing when he was first elected to the U.S. Senate. In fact, as a writer in the *Washington Post* noted, "It is difficult to find a sketch

of Senator Black which does not contain some reference to the Ku
Klux Klan." In addition, because of his association with the polio center at Warm Springs, Roosevelt regarded himself as much a son of
Georgia as of New York, and in his many sojourns in Georgia he
would have been likely to have acquired good intelligence about the
politics of neighboring Alabama.

It is more likely that civil liberties considerations did not loom
large in Roosevelt's mind in choosing a nominee. The central issue in
the Court crisis had been the fate of New Deal economic legislation,
and the President was looking for someone to legitimate the growth of
the State. Concentration on such matters, rather than civil liberties
and civil rights, reflected the basic attitudes of 1930s liberalism. It is
true that interest in civil liberties and civil rights grew during the
Depression, fostered by New Deal activities, particularly in the Justice
Department, the inclinations of New Deal administrators like Harold
Ickes, the example set by Eleanor Roosevelt, and the spirit of concern
that the New Deal conveyed. Not until the 1940s, however, did civil
liberties and civil rights come to have a truly prominent place on the
agenda of American liberalism.

For many New Deal supporters, Black's Klan affiliation was distressing, but it was not thought to be central, as it would be today.
Klan membership was regarded as the entry fee Black had to pay for
political advancement in Alabama, nothing more. Senator George
Norris, the most respected of all the progressives and father of the
TVA, who had fought the Klan and been fought by it, called the naming of Black "a wonderfully good appointment." He added, "Even if
he was a member of the Klan, there's no legal objection to that. I've an
idea many members of the House and the Senate belong to the Klan
also but that is their privilege."

Progressives characterized the outcry against Black as a conservative
scheme to discredit the Roosevelt administration and thereby scuttle
the New Deal and prospects for reform. They did not attack what was
said about Black, but rather who said it; when Sprigle's series appeared,
Black's supporters concentrated their fire on his publisher, Paul Block,
and other hostile newspaper titans like William Randolph Hearst.
They offered the defense, in Heywood Broun's words, that "few justices of the Supreme Court swim up to the high bench as immaculate

as Little Eva on the way to Heaven" and contended that the elements opposed to Black would not have shown the same intense concern about the past of a reactionary nominee. The liberal columnist Jay Franklin wrote, "One point only should be made in relation to these charges: If Hugo L. Black had been a labor-baiter, a trust corporation attorney, a man who had amassed a fortune and achieved political prominence as a result of helping the banks, utilities and corporations to loot the State of Alabama and stifle competition by strong-arm monopolies, he could have engaged in devil-worship, he could have practiced polygamy, he could have hunted down run-away share-croppers with blood-hounds, and eaten babies for breakfast, for all that his conservative Northern critics would care."

The New Dealers insisted that Black should be measured by the yardstick of twentieth century social reform and by the imperatives of the Great Depression. *The Progressive*, the organ of the La Follette dynasty in Wisconsin, noting Black's "excellent and long standing record of liberalism," pointed out that Black had fought the big-navy lobby and the power trust. Congressman David Lewis, a Maryland Democrat who had cosponsored the social security bill, asserted, "The real issue is not Black's qualifications, but whether the court is going to keep out of the 'nullification business'—that is quit vetoing acts of Congress." A Providence newspaper observed, "We don't like the idea of a Supreme Court Judge having been at any time or for what-ever purpose associated with the Ku Klux Klan, but the issue is not religion, it is not race or creed; the issue is economics."

In its "Topics of The Times" column, the *New York Times* sati-rized this sentiment in *Alice in Wonderland* style:

> After a while the White Rabbit summed up the debate, no-body dissenting.
> "You see, Alice," he said, "it's all because we have recently discovered that all life is functional. Once upon a time people thought there were definite things like truth, justice, honor, mercy, courage, and so forth. But now we know these things are only functions of the economic system. . . . That is why Lib-erals in the United States feel it does not matter if a member of the Supreme Court used to belong to the KKK. The only im-portant thing is how does he stand on the question of 1½ cents per kilowatt hour f.o.b. Norris Dam."

This preoccupation with economic and social policy had led the President to choose Black, but it was not the only consideration. Roosevelt certainly sought an enthusiastic New Dealer, but he also wanted someone who was young, came from a section that did not have a Supreme Court Justice, and could readily be confirmed. He and Cummings had reduced a list of sixty names to seven, four of whom were federal judges. None of the judges, however, including the highly touted Bratton, had sufficient liberal ardor to suit the President. "Bratton belongs to a judicial school of thought that ought not to be represented on the bench," he later told Farley. So the candidates were reduced to three: Solicitor General Stanley Reed, Black, and Senator Sherman Minton of Indiana.

Reed was crossed off as "middle-of-the-road . . . a good man but without much force or color," and attention focused on the choice of a senator. Roosevelt found that solution particularly beguiling, especially after the Robinson episode in May, in which the Senate in effect made its own nomination of a Justice. If he named a senator, even one regarded as a radical, the Senate would be trapped into going along, a circumstance that appealed to FDR's love of surprise and of turning the tables on his opponents with a clever move. He was initially inclined toward the fiery Shay Minton, but the Hoosier senator recognized that during the recent struggle over the Court bill he had made too many harsh comments about the Justices who would be his colleagues. Moreover, he was needed in the Senate. The President therefore settled on Black, who was young enough at 51, from a large unrepresented circuit in the Deep South, and, most important, a true believer in expanding governmental power.

Far from seeking to placate Congress by picking a moderate like Bratton, Roosevelt wanted to make clear that he was as committed to the New Deal as ever, and his selection of Black was a symbolic and defiant act. FDR's original plan seems to have been motivated by a desire not only to reform the Court, but also to punish the Justices for wronging him in the past. The appointment afforded Roosevelt another opportunity to express his contempt for the illusion that the Court was a body that lived on Mt. Olympus and his conviction that it was essentially a political agency. The Senate was even more of a target for revenge, for it had just humiliated him in the Court-packing battle. Donald Richberg, a prominent New Dealer, confided, as Clapper noted, that "Roosevelt was mad and was determined to give Senate the name which would be most disagreeable to it yet which it could not reject."

The President's faith in Black's liberal proclivities proved well founded. "Although Black's appointment did not mark the precise chronological point from which the Court's philosophy began its deviation from its previous path," Charlotte Williams has written, "it was this event which made it plain beyond all doubt that the Court was about to be reconstituted in the image of the New Deal." Black immediately gave the Administration a 6-3 majority on the Court, and his lone dissents indicated that he favored even more advanced stands than Justices like Brandeis, Cardozo, and Stone. Wallace Mendelson has calculated that in sixty cases involving the Federal Employer's Liability Act from 1938 through 1958, Black sustained workingmen's claims in every case but one, and that in the decade beginning 1949, in nineteen Sherman Act conflicts between business and consumer interests, "only Mr. Justice Black found a violation of the law in every instance."

In nominating Black, the President set the pattern that most of the other selections for "the Roosevelt Court" would follow. To the Supreme Court would go progressives, like Frank Murphy and William O. Douglas, who shared Black's zeal for the New Deal. The typical appointee would, like Black, be several years younger than William Howard Taft's representative choice. Only once would FDR pick a man with prior experience in the federal judiciary; indeed, Black was exceptional in that, except for Wiley Rutledge, the former police court magistrate was the only Roosevelt appointee who had ever served as a judge prior to joining the Court.

Black's appointment turned out to be only the first of many for the President. Roosevelt, who was unable to designate anyone for the Supreme Court in his first term, named eight Justices, including the Chief Justice, in the six years from 1937 to 1943. So rapidly did the composition of the Court change under Roosevelt and Truman that by the late 1940s Black, whose tenure seemed so precarious in 1937, was the senior member. Black remained on the bench through the thirties, forties, fifties, sixties and into the seventies, and would fall only months short of establishing a new record for length of service as a Justice.

The Black controversy is rich in paradox and irony—a former Klansman becoming one of the century's leading exponents of civil liberties,
a Justice chosen for one set of reasons winning fame for accomplishments that had hardly been anticipated, an Alabaman who created
alarm among Negro groups when he was nominated but who lived to
be denounced as a foe of the white South—but not least of the many
ironies is the fact that the President's bitterly fought campaign to re-
juvenate the Court by terminating tenure at the age of seventy would
end in his naming, as his first appointment, a man who would still be
on the bench on his eighty-fifth birthday and whose lengthy and brilliant career would be seen as a testament to Roosevelt's perspicacity.

II

The Detroit Race Riot of 1943

HARVARD SITKOFF

• *Of all the sources of civil disorder in American history, none has been more persistent than race relationships. Whether in the North or South, whether before or after the Civil War, whether in city or small town, this question has been at the root of more physical violence than any other. But because most forms of prejudice were more blatant and more virulent in the South than in the North, blacks sought for generations to cross the Mason-Dixon Line in search of a new land of equality and opportunity. Unfortunately, the big cities of the East and Middle West provided a fresh set of problems, and the continuing migration away from farm tenancy and share-cropping did not immediately improve the quality of Afro-American life. The pattern of the ghetto—residential segregation, underemployment, substandard housing, disrupted family life, inferior education, filth, and disease—was set even before 1920. Neither was violence left behind in the land of the plantation. In the "red summer of 1919," white-black rioting claimed more than one hundred lives and demonstrated again that the most striking feature of black life was not the existence of slum conditions, but the barriers to residential and occupational mobility.*

Following closely upon earlier conflicts in Mobile, Los Angeles, and Beaumont, the Detroit riot of 1943 illustrates the range of racial disorders that broke out sporadically during World War II. The Negro population of the city had risen sharply from 40,000 to 120,000 in the single decade between 1920 and 1930, and had jumped again by 50,000 in the fifteen months before the riot. Sparked by scattered gang fighting on a hot summer day, the riot ended by taking thirty-four lives. It was particularly notable for its ferocity and duration and for the fact that it began on a recreational spot—Belle Isle—that had previously been used by both races. Professor Harvard Sitkoff's article recreates that tragic event and urges us to question whether the United States has moved very far along the path of racial justice in the last third of a century.

For the American Negro, World War II began a quarter of a century of increasing hope and frustration. After a long decade of depression, the war promised a better deal. Negroes confidently expected a crusade against Nazi racism and for the Four Freedoms, a battle requiring the loyalty and manpower of all Americans, to be the turning point for their race. This war would be "Civil War II," a "Double V" campaign. No Negro leader urged his people to suspend grievances until victory was won, as most did during World War I. Rather, the government's need for full cooperation from the total population, the ideological character of the war, the constant preaching to square American practices with the American Creed, and the beginning of the end of the era of white supremacy in the world intensified Negro demands for equality *now*.

Never before in American history had Negroes been so united and militant. Led by the *Baltimore Afro-American, Chicago Defender, Pittsburgh Courier,* and Adam Clayton Powell's *People's Voice* ("The New Paper for the New Negro"), the Negro press urged civil rights leaders to be more aggressive. It publicized protest movements, headlined atrocity stories of lynched and assaulted Negroes, and developed race solidarity. Every major civil rights organization subscribed to the "Double V" campaign, demanding an end to discrimination in industry and the armed forces. The National Association for the Advancement of Colored People, National Urban League, National Negro Congress, A. Philip Randolph's March-on-Washington Movement, and the newly organized Congress of Racial Equality joined with Negro professional and fraternal organizations, labor unions, and church leaders to insist on "Democracy in Our Time!" These groups organized rallies, formed committees, supported letter and telegram mail-ins, began picketing and boycotting, and threatened unruly demonstrations. This as well as collaboration with sympathetic whites helped exert pressure on government officials.

The combined effects of exhortation and organization made the Negro man-in-the-street increasingly militant. After years of futility, there was now bitter hope. As he slowly gained economic and political power, won victories in the courts, heard his aspirations legitimized by

Permission to reprint Harvard Sitkoff, "The Detroit Race Riot of 1943," from *Michigan History* (Fall 1969) was granted by the Michigan History Division, Lansing, Michigan.

respected whites, and identified his cause with the two-thirds of the world's colored people, the Negro became more impatient with any impediment to first-class citizenship and more determined to assert his new status. Each gain increased his expectations; each improvement in the conditions of whites increased his dissatisfaction. Still forced to fight in a segregated army supplied by a Jim Crow industrial force, still denied his basic rights in the South and imprisoned in rat-and-vermin-infested ghettos in the North, he rejected all pleas to "go slow." At the same time many whites renewed their efforts to keep the Negro in an inferior economic and social position regardless of the changes wrought by the war. Frightened by his new militancy and wartime gains, resenting his competition for jobs, housing, and power, whites sought to retain their cherished status and keep "the nigger in his place." The more Negroes demanded their due, the more white resistance stiffened.

American engagement in a world war, as well as the lack of government action to relieve racial anxiety or even enforce "neutral" police control, made it likely that racial antagonism would erupt into violence. President Roosevelt, preoccupied with international diplomacy and military strategy, and still dependent on Southern support in Congress, ignored the deteriorating domestic situation. Participation in the war increased the prestige of violence and its use as an effective way to accomplish specific aims. The psychological effects of war, the new strains and uncertainty, multiplied hatred and insecurity. Many petty irritations—the rationing, shortages, overcrowding, and high prices—engendered short tempers; the fatigue of long work weeks, little opportunity for recreation, the anxious scanning of casualty lists, the new job and strange city, and the need for the noncombatant to prove his masculinity led to heightened tension and the desire to express it violently.

For three years public officials throughout the nation watched the growth of racial strife. Fights between Negroes and whites became a daily occurrence on public vehicles. Nearly every issue of the Negro press reported clashes between Negro soldiers and white military or civilian police. At least seventeen Negroes were lynched between 1940 and 1943. The accumulation of agitation and violence then burst into an epidemic of race riots in June, 1943. Racial gang fights, or "zoot-suit riots," broke out in several non-Southern cities. The worst of these hit Los Angeles. While the city fathers wrung their hands, white sailors and their civilian allies attacked scores of Negroes and Mexican-Americans. The only action taken by the Los Angeles City Council was to declare the wearing of a zoot suit a misdemeanor. In mid-June, a rumor of rape touched off a twenty-hour riot in Beaumont, Texas. White mobs burned and pillaged the Negro ghetto. War production stopped, businesses closed, thousands of dollars of property were damaged, two persons were killed, and more than seventy were injured. In Mobile, the attempt to upgrade some Negro workers as welders in the yards of the Alabama Dry Dock and Shipbuilders Company caused twenty thousand white workers to walk off their jobs and riot for four days. Only the intervention of federal troops stopped the riot. The President's Committee on Fair Employment Practices then backed down and agreed to let segregation continue in the shipyards.

Nowhere was trouble more expected than in Detroit. In the three years after 1940, more than fifty thousand Southern Negroes and half a million Southern whites migrated to the "Arsenal of Democracy" seeking employment. Negroes were forced to crowd into the already teeming thirty-block ghetto of Paradise Valley and some fifty registered "neighborhood improvement associations" and the Detroit Housing Commission kept them confined there. Although ten percent of the population, Negroes comprised less than 1 percent of the city teachers and police. Over half the workers on relief in 1942 were Negro, and most of those with jobs did menial work. Only three percent of the women employed in defense work were Negro, and these were mainly in custodial positions. The Negro demand for adequate housing, jobs, recreation, and transportation facilities, and the white refusal to give anything up, led to violence. Early in 1942, over a thousand whites armed with clubs, knives, and rifles rioted to stop Negroes from moving into the Sojourner Truth Housing Project. Fiery crosses burned throughout the city. More than a thousand state troopers had to escort two hundred Negro families into the project. Federal investigators warned Washington officials of that city's inability to keep racial peace, and the Office of Facts and Figures warned that "unless strong and quick intervention by some high official, preferably the President, is . . . taken at once, hell is going to be let loose." Nothing was done in Detroit or Washington. Throughout that year Negro and white students clashed in the city's high schools, and the number of outbreaks in factories multiplied.

In 1943, racial violence in Detroit increased in frequency and boldness. The forced close mingling of Negroes with Southern whites on buses and trolleys, crowded with nearly forty percent more passengers than at the start of the war, led to fights and stabbings. White soldiers battled Negroes in suburban Inkster. In April, a racial brawl in a city playground involved more than a hundred teenagers. Early in June, twenty-five thousand Packard employees struck in protest against the upgrading of three Negro workers. More than five hundred Negroes and whites fought at parks in different parts of the city. Negro leaders openly predicted greater violence unless something was done quickly to provide jobs and housing. Walter White of the NAACP told a packed rally in Cadillac Square: "Let us drag out into the open what has been whispered throughout Detroit for months—that a race riot may break out here at any time." Detroit newspaper and national magazines described the city as "a keg of powder with a short fuse." But no one in the city, state, or federal government dared to act. Everyone watched and waited. When the riot exploded, Mayor Edward Jeffries told reporters: "I was taken by surprise only by the day it happened."

The riot began, like those in 1919, with direct clashes between groups of Negroes and whites. Over 100,000 Detroiters crowded onto Belle Isle on Sunday, June 20, 1943, to seek relief from the hot, humid city streets. The temperature was over ninety. Long lines of Negroes and whites pushed and jostled to get into the bath house, rent canoes, and buy refreshments. Police continuously received reports of minor fights. Charles (Little Willie) Lyon, who had been attacked a few days earlier for trying to enter the all-white Eastwood Amusement Park, gathered a group of Negro teenagers to "take care of the Hunkies." They broke up picnics, forced whites to leave the park, beat up some boys, and started a melee on the bridge connecting Belle Isle with the city. Brawls broke out at the park's casino, ferry dock, playground, and bus stops. By evening rumors of a race riot swept the island. Sailors from a nearby armory, angered by a Negro assault on two sailors the previous day, hurried to the bridge to join the fray. Shortly after 11:00 P.M. more than five thousand people were fighting on the bridge. By 2:00 A.M. the police had arrested twenty-eight Negroes and nineteen whites, quelling the melee without a single gunshot.

As the thousands of rioters and onlookers returned home, stories of racial violence spread to every section of Detroit. In Paradise Valley, Leo Tipton jumped on the stage of the Forrest Club, grabbed the microphone and shouted: "There's a riot at Belle Isle! The whites have killed a colored lady and her baby. Thrown them over a bridge. Everybody come on! There's free transportation outside!" Hundreds rushed out of the nightclub, only to find the bridge barricaded and all traffic approaches to the Isle blocked. Sullen, the mob returned to the ghetto, stoning passing white motorists, hurling rocks and bottles at the police, and stopping streetcars to beat up unsuspecting whites. The frustrations bottled up by the war burst. Negroes—tired of moving to find the promised land, tired of finding the North too much like the South, tired of being Jim-Crowed, scorned, despised, spat upon, tired of being called "boy"—struck out in blind fury against the white-owned ghetto. Unlike the riots of 1919, Negroes now began to destroy the hated white property and symbols of authority. By early morning every white-owned store window on Hastings Avenue in the ghetto had been smashed. There was little looting at first, but the temptation of an open store soon turned Paradise Valley into an open-air market: liquor bottles, quarters of beef, and whole sides of bacon were freely carried about, sold, and bartered.

As the police hesitatingly struggled to end the rioting in the ghetto, rumors of white women being raped at Belle Isle enraged white crowds forming along Woodward Avenue. Unhampered by the police, the mobs attacked all Negroes caught outside the ghetto. They stopped, overturned, and burned cars driven by Negroes. The mob dragged off and beat Negroes in the all-night movies along the "strip" and those riding trolleys. When a white instructor at Wayne University asked the police to help a Negro caught by a white gang, they taunted him as a "nigger lover." The police would do nothing to help. Throughout the morning fresh rumors kept refueling the frenzy, and rioting grew. The excitement of a car burning in the night, the screeching wail of a police siren, plenty of free liquor, and a feeling of being free to do whatever one wished without fear of police retaliation, all fed the appetite of a riot-ready city.

At 4:00 A.M. Detroit Mayor Edward Jeffries met with the Police

Commissioner, the FBI, State Police, and Colonel August Krech, the highest-ranking Army officer stationed in Detroit. With hysteria growing, and the ability of the police to control violence diminishing, most of the meeting involved a discussion of the procedure to be used to obtain federal troops. They agreed that the Mayor should ask the Governor for troops; the Governor would telephone his request to General Henry Aurand, Commander of the Sixth Service in Chicago; and Aurand would call Krech in Detroit to order the troops into the city. Colonel Krech then alerted the 728th Military Police Battalion at River Rouge, and assured the Mayor that the military police would be patrolling Detroit within forty-nine minutes after receiving their orders. Nothing was done to check the plan for acquiring federal troops, and no mention was made of the need for martial law or a presidential proclamation.

When the meeting ended at 7:00 A.M. the Police Commissioner prematurely declared that the situation was now under control, and federal troops would not be needed. The opposite was true. Negro looting became widespread, and white mobs on Woodward Avenue swelled. Two hours later Negro leaders begged the Mayor to get federal troops to stop the riot. Jeffries refused, promising only to talk with them again at a noon meeting of the Detroit Citizens Committee. The Mayor would discuss neither the grievances of the Negro community nor how Negroes could help contain the destruction in the ghetto. A half hour later Jeffries changed his mind, telling those in his City Hall office that only federal troops could restore peace to Detroit.

Harry F. Kelly, the newly elected Republican Governor of Michigan, was enjoying his first session of the Conference of Governors in Ohio when shortly before 10:00 A.M. he was called to the telephone. Mayor Jeffries described the riot situation to the Governor, asserted that the city was out of control, and insisted that he needed more manpower. Kelly responded by ordering the Michigan state police and state troops on alert. An hour later he telephoned Sixth Service Command Headquarters in Chicago. Believing he had done all that was necessary to get federal troops into the city, Kelly hurriedly left for Detroit. But according to the Sixth Service Command, the Governor's call was only about a *possible* request for troops. Thus, the twelve-hour burlesque of deploying federal troops in Detroit began. The War Department and the White House flatly refused to take the initiative.

Army officials in Chicago and Washington kept passing the buck back and forth. And both Kelly and Jeffries feared doing anything that might indicate to the voters their inability to cope with the disorder.

After Kelly's call to Chicago, Aurand dispatched his director of internal security, Brigadier General William Guthner, to Detroit to command federal troops "in the event" the Governor formally requested them. Military police units surrounding Detroit were put on alert but forbidden to enter the city. In Washington the top brass remained busy with conferences on the use of the Army taking over mines in the threatened coal strike. No advice or instructions were given to Aurand. The Washington generals privately agreed that Aurand could send troops into Detroit without involving the President, or waiting for a formal request by the Governor, by acting on the principle of protecting defense production. But the War Department refused to give any orders to Aurand because it might "furnish him with a first class alibi if things go wrong."

While the generals and politicians fiddled, the riot raged. With most of the Detroit police cordoning off the ghetto, white mobs freely roamed the city attacking Negroes. At noon, three police cars escorted the Mayor into Paradise Valley to attend a Detroit Citizens Committee meeting. The interracial committee roundly denounced the Mayor for doing too little but could not agree on what should be done. Some argued for federal troops and others for Negro auxiliary police. Exasperated, Jeffries finally agreed to appoint two hundred Negro auxiliaries. But with no power and little cooperation from the police, the auxiliaries accomplished nothing. Rioters on the streets continued to do as they pleaded. At 1:30 P.M. high schools were closed, and many students jointed the riot.

Shortly after three, General Guthner arrived in Detroit to tell Kelly and Jeffries that federal martial law, which could only be proclaimed by the President, was necessary before federal troops could be called in. Dumbfounded by this new procedure, the Governor telephoned Aurand for an explanation. Aurand, more determined than ever to escape the responsibility for calling the troops, confirmed Guthner's statement. Despite Jeffries's frantic plea for more men, Kelly refused to ask for martial law: such a request would be taken as an admission of his failure.

Not knowing what else to do, after almost twenty hours of rioting,

Jeffries and Kelly made their first radio appeal to the people of Detroit. The Governor proclaimed a state of emergency, banning the sale of alcoholic beverages, closing amusement places, asking persons not going to or from work to stay home, prohibiting the carrying of weapons, and refusing permission for crowds to assemble. The proclamation cleared the way for the use of state troops but still did not comply with Aurand's prerequisites for the use of federal troops. Mayor Jeffries pleaded for an end to hysteria, arguing that only the Axis benefited from the strife in Detroit.

On the streets neither the proclamation nor the plea had any effect. Negro and white mobs continued their assaults and destruction. The weary police were barely able to restrain whites from entering Paradise Valley or to check the extent of Negro looting. Just as the Mayor finished pleading for sanity, four teen-agers shot an elderly Negro because they "didn't have anything to do." Tired of milling about, they agreed to "go out and kill us a nigger. . . . We didn't know him. He wasn't bothering us. But other people were fighting and killing and we felt like it too." As the city darkened, the violence increased. At 8:00 P.M. Jeffries called for the state troops. The Governor had ordered the force of two thousand mobilized earlier, but now the Mayor learned that only thirty-two men were available. At the same time the Mayor was informed that a direct clash between whites and Negroes was imminent. At Cadillac Square, the police were losing their struggle to hold back a white mob heading for the ghetto. Nineteen different police precincts reported riot activity. Seventy-five percent of the Detroit area was affected. Sixteen transportation lines had to suspend operation. The Detroit Fire Department could no longer control the more than one hundred fires. Detroiters entered Receiving Hospital at the rate of one every other minute.

In Washington, Lieutenant General Brehon Somervell, Commander of all Army Service Forces, directed the Army's Provost Marshal, Major General Allen Guillon, to prepare a Presidential Proclamation. At 8:00 P.M. Guillon and Somervell took the proclamation to the home of Secretary of War Henry Stimson. Sitting in the Secretary's library, the three men laid plans for the use of federal troops; as they discussed the situation they kept in telephone contact with the President at Hyde Park, the Governor in Detroit, and General Aurand in Chicago. Stimson instructed Aurand not to issue the text of the proclamation until the President signed it. Shortly after nine, Kelly telephoned Colonel Krech to request federal troops. At 9:20, the Governor repeated his appeal to General Aurand. Aurand immediately ordered the military police units into Detroit, although federal martial law had not been declared and the President had not signed the proclamation.

As the politicians and generals wrangled over the legality of Aurand's order, three hundred and fifty men of the 701st Military Police Battalion raced into Cadillac Square to disperse a white mob of over ten thousand. In full battle gear, bayonets fixed at high port, the federal troops swept the mob away from Woodward Avenue without firing a shot. The 701st then linked up with the 728th Battalion, which had been on the alert since 4:00 A.M., to clear rioters out of the ghetto. Using tear gas grenades and rifle butts, the military police forced all Negroes and whites off the streets. At 11:30 the riot was over, but the Presidential Proclamation was still to be signed.

After Aurand had transmitted his orders to Guthner, he had called Somervell to get permission to issue the proclamation. Somervell demanded that Aurand follow Stimson's instructions to wait until Governor Kelly contacted the President and Roosevelt signed the official order. Aurand relayed this message to Guthner, but the Governor could not be located until the riot had been quelled. Not until shortly before midnight did Kelly call Hyde Park to request the troops already deployed in the city. President Roosevelt signed the proclamation at 11:55 P.M. The Detroit rioters, now pacified, were commanded "to disperse and retire peaceably to their respective abodes." Twenty-one hours had passed since Army officials in Detroit first planned to use federal troops to end the riot. More than fifteen hours had been wasted since the Mayor first asked for Army manpower. Half a day had been lost between the Governor's first call to Sixth Service Command and Aurand's decision to send the military police into Detroit. General Guthner sat in Detroit for six hours before deploying the troops he had been sent to command. And it was during that time that most of Detroit's riot toll was recorded: thirty-four killed, more than seven hundred injured, over two million dollars in property losses, and a million man-hours lost in war production.

The armed peace in Detroit continued into Tuesday morning. Five thousand soldiers patrolled the streets, and military vehicles escorted buses an trolleys on their usual runs. Although racial tension remained high, firm and impartial action by the federal troops kept the city calm. Following Aurand's recommendations, Guthner instructed his troops to act with extreme restraint. Each field order ended with the admonition: "Under no circumstances will the use of firearms be resorted to unless all other measures fail to control the situation, bearing in mind that the suppression of violence, when accomplished without bloodshed, is a worthy achievement."

Continued hysteria in the city caused most of Guthner's difficulties. Rumors of new violence and repeated instances of police brutality kept the Negro ghetto seething. Most Negroes feared to leave their homes to go to work or buy food. Guthner persistently urged the Commissioner to order the police to ease off in their treatment of Negroes, but Witherspoon refused. Tales of the riot inflamed Negroes in surrounding communities. A group of soldiers at Fort Custer, 140 miles west of Detroit, tried to seize arms and a truck to help their families in the city. In Toledo, police turned back 1,500 Negroes trying to get rail transportation to Detroit. Muskegon, Indiana Harbor, Springfield, East St. Louis, and Chicago reported racial disturbances. Aurand changed his mind about leaving Chicago for Detroit and ordered Sixth Service Command troops in Illinois on the alert.

Unrest and ill-feeling continued throughout the week. The city courts, disregarding the depths of racial hostility in Detroit, employed separate and unequal standards in sentencing Negroes and whites arrested in the riot. With little regard for due process of law, the police carried out systematic raids on Negro rooming houses and apartments. Anxiety increased, isolated racial fights continued, repeated rumors of a new riot on July Fourth poisoned the tense atmosphere. Negroes and whites prepared for "the next one." Workmen in defense plants made knives out of flat files and hacksaw blades. Kelly and Jeffries urged the President to keep the federal troops in Detroit.

While the troops patrolled the streets, the search for answers and scapegoats to give some meaning to the outburst began. Adamant that it really "can't happen here," the same liberals and Negro leaders who had warned that white racism made Detroit ripe for a riot now attributed the violence to Axis agents. Telegrams poured into the White House asking for an FBI investigation of German agents in Detroit who aimed to disrupt war production. When the myth of an organized fifth column behind the riot was quickly shattered, liberals accused domestic reactionaries. The KKK, Gerald L. K. Smith, Father Charles Coughlin, Reverend J. Frank Norris, Southern congressmen, and anti-union demagogues were all singled out for blame. The NAACP aimed its sights at reactionary Poles who led the battle against decent Negro housing. Conservatives were just as anxious to hold liberals and Japanese agents responsible for race conflict. Martin Dies, Chairman of the House Un-American Activities Committee, saw the Japanese-Americans released from internment camps behind the riot. Congressman John Rankin of Mississippi taunted his colleagues in the House who supported the antipoll tax bill by saying "their chickens are coming home to roost" and asserted that the Detroit violence had been caused by the "crazy policies of the so-called fair employment practices committee in attempting to mix the races in all kinds of employment." Many Southerners blamed Negro agitators. Some talked of "Eleanor Clubs" as the source of the riot. "It is blood on your hands, Mrs. Roosevelt," claimed the *Jackson Daily News*. "You have been personally proclaiming and practicing social equality at the White House and wherever you go, Mrs. Roosevelt. In Detroit, a city noted for the growing impudence and insolence of its Negro population, an attempt was made to put your preachments into practice, Mrs. Roosevelt. What followed is now history." A Gallup Poll revealed that most Northerners believed Axis propaganda and sabotage were responsible for the violence, while most Southerners attributed it to lack of segregation in the North. An analysis of two hundred newspapers indicated that Southern editors stressed Negro militancy as the primary cause, while Northern editors accused fifth column subversives and Southern migrants new to city ways.

In Detroit the causes and handling of the riot quickly became the central issue of city politics. The Congress of Industrial Organizations, Negro organizations, and many civil liberties groups formed an alliance to defeat Mayor Edward Jeffries in November, to get rid of Commissioner Witherspoon, and to demand additional housing and jobs for Negroes. Led by United Auto Worker President R. J. Thomas and City Councilman George Edwards, a former UAW organizer, the coalition gained the backing of most CIO locals, the NAACP and Urban League, International Labor Defense, National Lawyers Guild, National Negro Congress, National Federation for Constitutional

Liberties, Catholic Trade Unionists, Socialist Party of Michigan, Inter-Racial Fellowship, Negro Council for Victory and Democracy, Metro-politan Detroit Youth Council, Union for Democratic Action, and March-on-Washington Movement. They were supported editorially by the *Detroit Free Press,* the *Detroit Tribune,* and the Negro *Michigan Chronicle.* Throughout the summer the coalition clamored for a special grand jury to investigate the causes of the riot and the unsolved riot deaths.

Michigan's leading Republicans, the Hearst press, and most real estate and antiunion groups opposed any change in the Negro's status. The Governor, Mayor, and Police Commissioner, abetted by the obliging Common Council, squelched the pleas for better housing and jobs and a grand jury investigation. Unwilling to make any changes in the conditions underlying the riot, the Republicans made meaningless gestures. The Mayor established an interracial committee with no power. After a few sleepy sessions, it adjourned for a long summer vacation. Commissioner Witherspoon refused to allow changes in the regulations to make possible the hiring of more Negro policemen. Instead of a grand jury investigation, the Governor appointed his own Fact-Finding Committee of four Republican law officers involved in the handling of the riot. And the Detroit Council of Churches, nonpartisan but similarly reluctant to face the issue of white racism, called upon the city to observe the following Sunday as a day of humility and penitence.

A week after the riot, Witherspoon appeared before the Common Council to report on his department's actions. He blamed Negroes for starting the riot and Army authorities for prolonging it. The Commissioner pictured white mob violence as only "retaliatory action" and police behavior as a model of "rare courage and efficiency." In fact, Witherspoon concluded, the police had been so fair that "some have accused the Department of having a kid glove policy toward the Negro." No one on the Council bothered to ask the Commissioner why the police failed to give Negroes the adequate protection required by law, or how this policy accounted for seventeen of the twenty-five Negroes killed in the riot having been shot by the police. Two days later, Mayor Jeffries presented his "white paper" to the Common Council. He reiterated the Commissioner's criticism of the Army and praise for the police and added an attack on "those Negro leaders who insist that their people do not and will not trust policemen and the Police Department. After what happened I am certain that some of these leaders are more vocal in their caustic criticism of the Police Department than they are in educating their own people to their responsibilities as citizens." The Common Council heartily approved the two reports. Gus Dorias and William (Billy) Rogell, two Detroit athletic heroes on the Council, advocated a bigger ghetto to solve the racial crisis. Councilman Comstock did not think this or anything should be done. "The racial conflict has been going on in this country since our ancestors made the first mistake of bringing the Negro to the country." The conflict would go on regardless of what was done, added Comstock, so why do anything?

Throughout July the accusations and recriminations intensified. Then, as the city began to tire of the familiar arguments, a fresh controversy erupted. When three Negro leaders asked William Dowling, the Wayne County Prosecutor, to investigate the unsolved riot deaths, Dowling berated them for turning information over to the NAACP that they withheld from him. He charged the NAACP with being "the biggest instigators of the race riot. If a grand jury were called, they would be the first indicted." The NAACP threatened to sue Dowling for libel, and the county prosecutor quickly denied making the charge. "Why, I like Negroes," he said. "I know what it is to be a member of a minority group. I am an Irish Catholic myself." The next day Dowling again charged an "unnamed civil rights group" with causing the riot. Witherspoon endorsed Dowling's allegation, and the battle flared. "It was as if a bomb had been dropped," said one Negro church leader. "The situation is what it was just before June 21."

In the midst of this tense situation, the Governor released the report of his Fact-Finding Committee. Parts I and II, a detailed chronology of the riot and supporting exhibits, placed the blame for the violence squarely on Negroes who had started fights at Belle Isle and spread riot rumors. Content to fix liability on the initial aggressors, the report did not connect the Sunday fights with any of the scores of incidents of violence by whites against Negroes which preceded the fights at Belle Isle. Nor did the report mention any of the elements which permitted some fights to lead to such extensive hysteria and violence, or which allowed rumors to be so instantly efficacious. No whites were accused of contributing to the riot's causes. The sailors responsible for much of the fighting on the bridge, and the nineteen other whites arrested by the police Sunday night, escaped blame. The report emphasized the culpability of the Negro-instigated rumors, especially Leo Tipton's, but let the other rumors remain "lily-white." Although many instances of police brutality were attested and documented, the committee failed to mention them. And while only a court or grand jury in Michigan had the right to classify a homicide as legally "justifiable," the committee, hearing only police testimony, took it upon itself to "justify" all police killings of Negroes.

Part III, an analysis of Detroit's racial problems, completely departed from the committee's aim of avoiding "conclusions of a controversial or conjectural nature." The section on those responsible for racial tensions omitted any mention of the KKK, Black Legion, National Workers League, and the scores of anti-Negro demagogues and organizations openly preaching race hatred in Detroit. Racial tension was totally attributed to Negro agitators who "constantly beat the drums of: 'Racial prejudice, inequality, intolerance, discrimination.' " Repeatedly, the report referred to the Negro's "presumed grievances" and complaints of "alleged Jim Crowism." In the world of the Fact-Finding Committee no real Negro problems existed, or if they did, they were to be endured in silence. Publication of the obviously prejudiced report proved an immediate embarrassment to the Governor. Most newspapers and journals denounced it as a "whitewash," and Kelly's friends wisely buried it. The Common Council then declared the riot a "closed incident."

In Washington, too, politics went on as usual. The administration did nothing to prevent future riots or attempt to solve the American dilemma. The problem of responding to the riots became compounded when the same combination of underlying grievances and war-bred tensions which triggered the Detroit riot led to an orgy of looting and destruction in Harlem. Henry Wallace and Wendell Willkie delivered progressive speeches; leading radio commentators called for a new approach to racial problems; and many prominent Americans signed newspaper advertisements urging the President to condemn segregation and racial violence. But the White House remained silent.

In much the same way it had handled the question of segregation in the armed forces and discrimination in defense production, the Roosevelt administration muddled its way through a summer of violence. The four presidential aides handling race relations problems, all Southerners, determined to go slow, protect the "boss," and keep the shaky Democratic coalition together, fought all proposals for White House action. They politely buried pleas for the President to give a fireside chat on the riots and brushed aside recommendations that would force Roosevelt to acknowledge the gravity of the race problem. The Interior Department's plans for a national race relations commission, and those of Attorney General Francis Biddle for an interdepartmental committee were shelved in favor of Jonathan Daniels' inoffensive suggestion to correlate personally all information on racial problems. Even Marshall Field's proposal to circulate pledges asking people not to spread rumors and to help "win the war at home by combating racial discrimination wherever I meet it," which appealed to Roosevelt, went ignored. The federal government took only two actions: clarification of the procedure by which federal troops could be called, and approval of J. Edgar Hoover's recommendation to defer from the draft members of city police forces. Like the Republicans in Michigan, the Democrats in the capital occupied themselves with the efficient handling of a future riot rather than its prevention.

With a war to win, Detroit and the nation resumed "business as usual." Negroes continued to be brutalized by the police and the "first fired, last hired." In the Senate, the administration killed a proposal to have Congress investigate the riots, and Michigan's Homer Ferguson and Arthur Vandenberg stymied every proposal for Negro housing in Detroit's suburbs. Their constituents continued boasting "the sun never sets on a nigger in Dearborn." Governor Kelly appropriated a million dollars to equip and train special riot troops. Mayor Jeffries, running as a defender of "white supremacy," easily won re-election in 1943 and 1945. The lesson learned from the riot? In the Mayor's words: "We'll know what to do next time." Yet Southern Negroes continued to pour into Detroit looking for the promised land—only to find discrimination, hatred, a world of little opportunity and less dignity. The dream deferred waited to explode. "There ain't no North any more," sighed an old Negro woman. "Everything now is South."

12

Tokyo Rose: Traitor or Scapegoat?

JOHN LEGGETT

• Soon after graduation from UCLA, Iva Ikuko Toguri went to Japan under protest to see her sick aunt. She discovered that she disliked everything about Japan—its customs, its food, and her relatives—but before she could return to the United States, war was declared between the two countries. She became a typist with the Japanese Broadcasting Company and then ultimately a disk jockey who made one fifteen-minute broadcast to American servicemen every day. As such, her voice became famous to millions of young men who fought their way across the Pacific.

John Leggett's article about "Tokyo Rose" points out the ironies in the case—how an intelligent young woman with a degree in zoology spoke for the enemy because the alternative to propaganda broadcasting was work in a munitions factory. As one of many women employed as announcers for the Japanese radio system, she would have seemed an unlikely candidate for controversy. Her war record certainly pales when placed beside that of SS and Gestapo officers who went unpunished. And her broadcasts lacked the fascist political content of another American, Ezra Pound, who performed similar services for Mussolini's Italian government.

But in the patriotic fervor following the victory in World War II, symbolic traitors were needed, and Tokyo Rose was as symbolic as anyone. Not until early in 1977 was she finally pardoned by President Gerald Ford, ending a case that had dragged on for a third of a century. During that time, Iva Toguri switched from being a symbol of bloody aggression to one of martyr to American justice.

For most servicemen, the worst of modern warfare is the boredom of it. On my World War II ship, the U.S.S. Elden, that boredom was as vast as the Pacific itself—day after day, same watches and drills, same food and smells, same heat and shipmates. That is why the Elden's crew, and the rest of the two million young Americans in the Pacific theater during World War II, made so much of the woman they referred to as Tokyo Rose.

Her voice was native-American with a dash of soy sauce, and she played us our songs, the ones we had danced to the summer before (or was it the summer before that?). She was talking to us from Japan, flirting with us, calling forth those romantic illusions from "Terry and the Pirates."

We lost some confidence in her newscasts when she reported us sunk, but that only added to our enjoyment. She knew what was on our minds. She was lighthearted, and sometimes raunchy about it, suggesting that our sweethearts back home were two-timing us, with help from the 4-Fs and fat cats. We didn't take her seriously. There was a tongue-in-cheek quality to the relationship, an understanding between us that is illustrated by the bomber squadron said to have responded to her apology for playing only old records (they were all she had) by addressing her a carton of late releases and parachuting it into the center of Tokyo.

So, for this World War II veteran, it is astonishing and saddening to find what that war brought to an American woman named Iva Toguri. It was her fate to have been one of several women who broadcast from Japan to American troops in the Pacific, and her misfortune to have been the only one convicted of treason and jailed for doing so. Today, at the age of sixty, she lives in Chicago, where her friends know her by her married name, Iva d'Aquino. She is the proprietor of Toguri's, a shop on the North Side, where you can buy parasols, fish kites, books on judo and Zen, incense and, presumably, even the complete teahouse at the back of the big white store.

For many years after her release from prison in 1956, she asked only to be left alone with her work and her circle of friends. She had had enough publicity in the years immediately following the war. But recently, a committee formed in her behalf has brought increasing at-

From *The New York Times*, Dec. 5, 1976 Magazine. © 1976 by The New York Times Company. Reprinted by permission.

tention to her, and last month, Iva sent a letter to President Ford requesting a pardon. At a press conference just before mailing the letter, she said she hoped to get a pardon so that her American citizenship could be restored: "You don't realize the importance or significance of such a thing until you lose it."

On a recent evening I found her at her shop, counting cash in the register and saying good night to her employees as they filed into the street. She has a square, handsome face, clear eyes and a resonant voice that clangs like an iron bell. There is an abruptness to her speech, an all-business tone, but her laughter is sudden, called forth by remembering some preposterous turn of her life, and as American as her frequent "hecks" and the Midwest flatness of her "a's."

Sometimes her responses are immediate, but when she must search back through the decades to recall loneliness and fear in wartime Tokyo, or during her trial, she rattles and wanders as she looks for familiar paths. She is numbed by questions. People have been questioning Iva Toguri d'Aquino for 30 years.

This is how she remembers the first half of her life. She was born in 1916, and grew up in Southern California; she likes to remember that her birthday, July 4th, was always celebrated with fireworks. Her mother and father, being Japanese-born, were denied U.S. citizenship, and they taught her, along with her brother and two sisters, the good fortune of being a native-born American.

The Toguris lived in a typical Los Angeles neighborhood, spoke English at home, and went to the Methodist Church. As a student at Compton Union High School, and later at U.C.L.A., she draws herself as an exuberant bobbysoxer, enjoying friends, sports, her Chrysler and a crush on Jimmy Stewart.

At the time of her college graduation, June 1941, the Toguris had a letter from Iva's uncle in Japan saying that her aunt had fallen seriously ill. Since her mother was also in poor health, Iva was chosen as family emissary. Ship passage was arranged and application made for her passport. The State Department did not issue her a passport, but instead a certificate of identification authorizing a six-month stay.

Iva sailed for Japan in July, arriving in Yokohama on the twenty-fourth, where she was met by her uncle and welcomed to the Hattori house in a ward of Tokyo called Setagaya.

Although the Hattoris treated her as one of their own children, Iva found the diet and language strange and the customs awkward. Most of all, she missed her freedom to come and go and do as she pleased. Wherever she turned there were new restraints. In a letter carried home by an acquaintance, she told of censorship and the destruction of previous letters by postal authorities, of police surveillance, of Government restrictions on everything, of how different her cousins and their friends were in their humor and ideas of a good time. The food was expensive, the clothing shoddy and the people discourteous.

She was grateful for copies of *The Los Angeles Times* that had reached her. "What a joy it is to read English," she wrote, even though it evoked a longing for home. No day went by, she said, without her thinking of her family. She warned them not to return to Japan. "No matter how much you have to take in the way of racial things," she wrote, "better to remain where you are and be thankful you can do as you please."

During the late summer and early fall, while relations between the U.S. and Japan deteriorated, Iva reapplied for her passport at the American consulate, but it was not issued.

On December 1, a week before Pearl Harbor, Iva's father, Jun, cabled her to come home, urging her to book passage on Tatsuta Maru, sailing next day for California. She tried, but was denied clearance by Japanese authorities. It was just as well, for Tatsuta was in mid-Pacific as the war broke out and was ordered back to Japan.

Caught in what was now the enemy fortress, Iva was questioned by the police and pressed to take Japanese citizenship. She explained that she was American, raised an American, unfamiliar with Japanese customs, barely able to speak the language, and refused. Accordingly, she was classified an enemy alien and denied a food-ration card.

If Iva had managed to get home she would not, at this point, have fared much better. The U.S. had rounded up the 110,000 persons of Japanese ancestry on the West Coast, Iva's family included, confining them to relocation centers and imposing a curfew before shipping them to inland detention camps.

Iva had enrolled in the Matsumiya Language School to improve her Japanese, but her clumsiness with the tongue, and, she says, her outspoken loyalty to the U.S. provoked the suspicion of neighbors. Children taunted her, and the police called on her several times a week. The discomfort of her aunt and uncle was such that she moved to a boarding house. With little money left and no ration card, she was in a fair way to starve, so she asked the Japanese authorities to intern her as an American national. Citing the food shortage, they refused.

She looked for and found odd, part-time jobs. One at twenty dollars a month had her monitoring and typing English-language shortwave broadcasts at Domei news agency. Here, in 1942, she met a Portuguese citizen of Japanese ancestry named Felipe d'Aquino. He had been educated by the American order of Maryknoll Fathers and his sympathies also lay with the U.S. Iva liked him, called him "Phil," and they saw each other constantly. Late in the war, in April 1945, they would marry.

In August of 1943, Iva took a new, part-time job as typist in the business office at Radio Tokyo. Here she made friends with some of the 30 prisoners-of-war assigned to the station. When they told of their privations at a POW camp, she brought them fruit, vitamin tablets, and tobacco. Their ranking officer was Maj. Charles Cousens, an Australian captured at Singapore. Another officer was Capt. Wallace Ince, U.S. Army, captured at Corregidor. Both had had radio experience, and they had been put in charge of the English-language "Zero Hour" broadcast.

When Radio Tokyo decided to add a female voice to "Zero Hour," Cousens requested Iva for the job. He would testify later that he and Ince had yielded to Japanese pressure to produce the program after agreeing between themselves to minimize, if not actually sabotage, the intended propaganda. Iva was their candidate for announcer because her voice, which they thought "masculine," would in itself be a thwarting of the Japanese purpose—the female announcers were supposed to sound sexy—and because, they said, she was the only available woman they could trust not to betray their efforts at subversion to Japanese authorities. These, they claimed, consisted mainly of making the "Zero Hour" scripts as bland as possible.

"She was very friendly," Major Cousens said, "so much so that we were very suspicious. But by October we knew that we were on safe ground." When they found Iva reluctant to take part in a propaganda broadcast, Cousens assured her that, "her job would be purely and simply the reading of the script that I had written, which was the introduction of the musical items."

Iva was persuaded, and in November 1943 she began announcing a brief program of recordings. She read the script prepared by Cousens and Ince in the role, suggested by them, of "Orphan Anne," apparently to recall the comic-strip character, Little Orphan Annie.

"And now, gentlemen, the 'Zero Hour' brings you Orphan Anne and her Languideers," Iva began a typical program. "Cheerio once again to all my favorite family of boneheads, the fighting GIs in the blue Pacific. This is Orphan Anne at this end of the situation, hanging her shingle out for a few minutes. What for? To do business of course. . . . Lend an ear to the fighting GI's choice for favorite vocalist singing a well-known melody: 'Two Hearts That Pass in the Night!' "

Another went, "This is Radio Tokyo's special program for listeners in Australia and my boneheads in the South Pacific. Right now I'm lulling their senses before I creep up and annihilate them with my nail file . . . but don't tell anybody! Now here's the next waltz I promised you, Victor Herbert's 'Kiss Me Again.' . . . You heard me!"

The female voice on "Zero Hour" was not always Iva's. She was often replaced by one of the thirteen women who announced Radio Tokyo's many English-language programs. Moreover, similar female disc-jockey programs, beamed at American forces in the Pacific, were originating from nine other stations throughout Asia. None of the women at any of these stations called herself Rose.

But in the loneliness of steamy Quonset huts and lurching forecastles from the Aleutians to New Guinea, American servicemen were building the fantasy of "Tokyo Rose." Hers was so pervasive a myth that for most Americans she was as famous a Japanese as Emperor Hirohito.

At war's end, in the summer of 1945, the first American journalists ashore sought Tokyo Rose's story. When two Hearst reporters, Harry Brundidge of *Cosmopolitan* and Clark Lee of International News Service, were told that her voice was that of many girls, they insisted on meeting one of them. Iva knew of "Tokyo Rose" from foreign news dispatches and an item in Time magazine. Indeed, there was some rivalry among the Radio Tokyo girls over which was the more entitled to the name and notoriety. Iva has said she was aware that in claiming it she would open herself to a charge of treason. At the same time, she felt that she had done nothing wrong, and when she was offered $2,000 for an exclusive interview, she accepted.

On September 3, the day after the formal surrender in Tokyo Bay, Iva went to Lee and Brundidge's room at the Imperial Hotel and, while Lee typed, she explained how the name "Tokyo Rose" was thrust upon her. She told of her life in Tokyo during the war years and of how she and the POWs had had to function under constant Japanese pressure. To illustrate the Japanese surveillance, though not necessarily to illustrate any attempt to subvert the propaganda effort, she described how, after the Battle of Formosa, a Japanese major had directed her to say, "You fellows are all without ships. What are you going to do about getting home now?" and how she had said, "Orphans of the Pacific, you really are orphans now." The quoted words would play an important part in her trial.

Iva did not receive $2,000. Instead she was rewarded by visits from U.S. military police, and eventually taken to Sugamo Prison in Tokyo where General Tojo and other Japanese prisoners accused of war crimes were awaiting trial. Here Iva remained for eleven months, unaware of the charges against her, denied legal counsel, bail, and speedy trial.

Iva's account of these events leaves some bothersome questions. Could she be editing her memoirs to better support her case? The surviving transcripts of her broadcasts document her assertions that their content was innocuous, but could others have been tougher? I can remember, as must thousands of other men, being tantalized by Rose's hints of wild parties in Tokyo, and amused, if not upset, by her suggestions that our wives and sweethearts were being untrue to us back home. And wasn't her report that my own ship had been sunk a piece of specific, if inaccurate, military information? (Of course, the imprecision of memory could be my own as well. I did not, I have to admit, actually hear that report of the Elden's sinking. My shipmates said they had, in the radio shack or over the speaker in the crew's quarters. In other words, it was ship's scuttlebutt, which I had come to regard as fact.)

Furthermore, why had Iva taken the "Zero Hour" job in the first place? She had not been forced to do so. She knew it was propaganda, and however innocuous her role, or however she rationalized it, it was clearly an act of cooperation with the Japanese war effort. One may speculate that consciously or unconsciously she was acting out a grievance against Uncle Sam for his neglect of her, for rewarding her loyalty by forsaking her. On the other hand, if she fully understood the treasonous aspects of the job, why did she give an interview as "Tokyo Rose?"

I am left with a surmise that a young woman, alone in wartime Tokyo and on intimate terms with poverty, hunger and fear, acted out of anxiety and expediency with a goal of day-to-day survival. She had no clear idea, then or now, of so complex a matter as her guilt.

In any event, during the year of her imprisonment by the U.S. Army (the latter half of it for the Department of Justice), she was questioned regularly by both military and Justice Department authorities. She insisted on her loyalty and pointed out that she would not otherwise have clung to her U.S. citizenship.

On April 17, 1946, the Army legal section decided, "There is no evidence that [Iva d'Aquino] ever broadcast greetings to units by name and location, or predicted military movements or attacks, indicating access to secret military information and plans. . . ." It summed up, "There is evidence Mrs. d'Aquino found this work distasteful." The Justice Department took another six months to conclude "that Toguri's activities, particularly in view of the innocuous nature of her broadcasts, are not sufficient to warrant prosecution for treason," and on October 26, 1946, she was released from Sugamo Prison.

To the d'Aquinos, Iva's case appeared closed. They settled in Tokyo and, by 1947, were expecting a child. It was Iva's wish that this child be an American-born U.S. citizen. Moreover, she wanted to see her family again. Her mother had died in 1942, and her father, brother and sisters had moved to Chicago and opened a business there. So Iva applied again at the American Consulate for her passport.

News of Iva's determination to come home was released in the U.S. during the fall of 1947, and it set off new tremors. The State Department could not deny her, for she was a native-born citizen cleared by the Army and Justice Departments. Nevertheless, there were protests from civic and veterans' organizations throughout the nation.

For example, the Kern-Millner American Legion Post of Toledo passed and sent to the Attorney General a resolution, "to protest the re-entry into the United States of one woman of Japanese extraction known during World War II as 'Tokyo Rose.' This woman is un-American by birth and should the laws of this country permit her re-entry, each and every member present stated that she should be tried and convicted for treason. . . ." Walter Winchell, then one of the most influential radio commentators in the country, was particularly indignant. On one broadcast he criticized Attorney General Tom Clark for laxness toward such persons as "Tokyo Rose" and demanded her exclusion. An election year was coming up, and the Republicans were attacking the Truman Administration for softness toward spies and traitors. Loyalty was a critical issue.

In October, Assistant Attorney General T. Vincent Quinn had told the State Department there was no objection to issuing Iva a passport, explaining that, "after a careful analysis of the available evidence, this Department concluded that prosecution of this individual for treason was not warranted." But now in November, Quinn went back to her file and reassessed the wisdom of prosecuting her, reporting in early December that while it was arguable whether she had given "aid and comfort to the enemy," there was no question about the purpose of "Zero Hour": It was to demoralize allied troops, and her acceptance of the job had been voluntary.

Successful prosecution would require two corroborating witnesses to the same treasonous act, to an actual broadcast, not simply to her admission of it. The outcome would depend on procuring such witnesses. Quinn recommended a search of both Japan and the U.S.

Early in 1948, the Justice Department sent Attorney John B. Hogan, along with Harry Brundidge, to Tokyo in hopes of lining up prosecution witnesses and persuading Iva to authenticate the notes of her 1945 interview. Hogan reported that he found most former Radio Tokyo employees reluctant to testify against Iva and U.S. military intelligence there irritatingly uncooperative. However, Iva had come to G.H.Q. to talk with him and Brundidge.

Of this March interview, Iva remembers that she came hoping it would bring her closer to home. Though her expected child had died at birth, her own citizenship was still in question, and she yearned to see her family again, so that, while Hogan warned her of the possibility of further prosecution, she was won over by Brundidge's assurance that her signature on the 1945 interview notes would accelerate her return. Without legal counsel, she signed them.

Back in Washington, Hogan recommended prosecution. Not everyone was optimistic about the Government's chances. Justice Department attorney Tom de Wolfe pointed out that the principal witnesses, the POWs Cousens and Ince, had been cleared of treason charges and would testify that Iva lacked the necessary intent for treason, that her "confession" to Brundidge and Lee would not be admissable and that the Government's case must fail as a matter of law.

Uninfluenced by de Wolfe's caution, the Attorney General gave the order for Iva Toguri's case—"Prosecute it vigorously"—and on August 16 he issued the statement, "The only American girl to whom American troops in the Pacific are believed to have applied the name 'Tokyo Rose' will be brought to this country to face a treason charge."

So on August 26, 1948, Iva was arrested again, charged with treason and brought to San Francisco. Home after seven years, she saw her family at last through the bars of the county jail. Her father told her, "I'm glad you did not change your stripes."

Since the Toguri family was not well-off, there was difficulty in finding a lawyer to represent Iva, but a strong advocate of civil liberties, Wayne Collins, volunteered to represent her without fee. He enlisted the help of fellow-lawyers Theodore Tamba and George Olshausen. For the first time, Iva had access to legal counsel.

In October, a Federal grand jury heard the evidence against Iva. Much of the original material gathered by the Army and Justice Departments during her imprisonment in Japan—on the basis of which both had dismissed charges—had been destroyed. Only six recordings of her broadcasts could be found. Nonetheless, on being assured that other Americans who took part in English-language programs at Radio Tokyo would be similarly charged, the grand jury issued an eight-count indictment of treason against Iva Toguri d'Aquino.

De Wolfe, the prosecutor, reported in to the Department that he had followed instructions, but that "as it was, two of the grand jurors voted against an indictment. It was necessary for me to practically make a Fourth of July speech to get an indictment." Consequently he urged the Attorney General to sent a special agent to Japan for more preparation.

This was done. The FBI located Japanese witnesses to Iva's alleged treasonous acts and nineteen of them were brought to San Francisco at government expense. But when Iva's lawyers petitioned the court to subpoena defense witnesses from Japan, Judge Michael J. Roche denied Iva's constitutional right to summon such witnesses in person, though he did permit her lawyers to take depositions from them.

On her indictment, Iva's counsel had appealed for her release on bail, but Judge Louis B. Goodman had ordered her confined to prison until the beginning of her trial. This did not occur until July of 1949, so that she had served two years in prison before she was brought to trial.

The trial began on July 5, 1949, in San Francisco Federal District Court with Judge Roche presiding. In selecting the jury, the prosecution used peremptory challenges to remove six blacks and two Asian-Americans, and an all-white jury was impaneled.

At her arraignment, Iva had pleaded innocent to all eight counts of treason and the task of the prosecution lawyers, Frank J. Hennesy, John Hogan and James Knapp, was to prove that Iva had committed treason, an act carefully limited by the framers of the Constitution: "Treason against the United States shall consist only in levying war against them, or adhering to their enemies, giving them aid and comfort. No person shall be convicted of treason unless on the testimony of two witnesses in the same overt act."

The prosecution focused on producing two witnesses to the same act of Iva's treason. These were two American-born men who, like Iva, had returned to Japan prior to the war but, unlike her, had renounced their U.S. citizenship.

George Mitsushio, born in San Francisco, educated at the University of California at Berkeley and at Columbia, had left for Japan in 1940 and had been civilian chief of the "Zero Hour" program. Kenkichi Oki, born in Sacramento, educated at St. Mary's College in Moraga, Calif., and New York University, left for Japan in 1939 and became production supervisor at Radio Tokyo. His wife had made English-language broadcasts in the role of "Saturday Night Party Girl."

Both Mitsushio and Oki testified that they had heard Iva's broadcast in October of 1944, following the Battle of Leyte Gulf—the great U.S. Naval victory that had destroyed the remains of the Japanese fleet and left the U.S. in control of Philippine waters—and that she had said, "Orphans of the Pacific, you really are orphans now. How will you get home now that all your ships are sunk?" Similar words had appeared in Iva's 1945 interview.

Then a parade of witnesses, some of whom Iva claims never to have seen before, substantiated Mitsushio and Oki, though there was no evidence in any surviving script or recording that she had ever broadcast these words. Iva says she was stunned by the testimony of Mitsushio and Oki, and she denied that any of it was true.

Her defense was built around the POWs with whom she had worked most closely on "Zero Hour." Major Cousens, cleared of treason charges at home, came from Australia at his own expense to testify for Iva. He told the court that he had recruited her for "Zero Hour," assured her it was to be straight entertainment and urged her to place herself under his orders.

Wallace Ince, cleared of treason charges by the U.S. Army and promoted to Major, confirmed Cousens' testimony. As final defense witness, Iva testified she had had no intent to harm the U.S. and had believed throughout her employment on "Zero Hour" that she was only entertaining her countrymen. She reiterated that she had retained her citizenship and loyalty to the U.S. throughout her ordeal in Japan, despite hardship and pressure from the Japanese.

In his summary for the defense, George Olshausen noted that the Government had to prove the defendant had performed an act that in fact rendered aid and comfort to the enemy and that she performed the act with the intent of betraying the United States. If there was reasonable doubt on either count, she was entitled to acquittal. He went on to point out that Clark Lee's notes had not indicated the "Orphans-of-the-Pacific" broadcast had been made, only that she had been ordered to make it.

Judge Roche, in his instructions to the jurors, took a far stricter view, telling them that they could find Iva guilty if they decided she had committed an act that, if successful, would have advanced the enemy's interest. It was not necessary for the act actually to have been successful. As to the matter of Iva's intent, he explained that it came down to whether she had acted willfully or under duress. As a defense of treason, he said, duress must be a condition that leaves no choice, ". . . one must have acted under the apprehension of immediate and impending death or of serious and immediate bodily harm."

Iva had been a convincing and sympathetic figure on the stand and the press corps in attendance took a straw vote on the outcome. The result was nine to one for acquittal on all counts.

The jury began its deliberations on Monday, September 26. In the early ballots it stood at eight to four for acquittal, but after twenty hours it had swung to nine to three for conviction, where it deadlocked. The foreman, John Mann, told Judge Roche that his jury was unable to reach a verdict.

That evening of the twenty-seventh, Judge Roche called the court into session and told the jury, "This is an important case. The trial has been long and expensive to both prosecution and defense. If you should fail to agree on a verdict, the case is left open and undecided. Like all cases it must be disposed of at some time. There appears no reason to believe that another trial would not be equally long and expensive to both sides nor does there appear any reason to believe the case can be tried better or more exhaustively than it has been tried on each side."

So instructed, in the manner now known as the "Allen," or "dynamite," charge, the jury returned to its deliberations, emerging two days later, on September 29, with a question for the Judge. In his instructions he had told them, "Overt acts of an apparent incriminating nature, when judged in the light of related events, may turn out to be acts which were not of aid and comfort to the enemy." Presumably at odds over the issues of "intent" and "duress," they asked Judge Roche what he had meant by "related events."

The judge declined a direct answer, saying, "The jury is cautioned not to single out any portion, but to give uniform attention to all of the instructions," and he urged them to get to a decision.

Five minutes later they were back with a verdict, finding Iva innocent on seven counts of the indictment, but guilty on one: "That on a day during October 1944, the exact date being to the Grand Jurors unknown, defendant in the offices of the Broadcasting Corporation of Japan did speak into a microphone concerning the loss of ships."

On October 7, 1949, Judge Roche sentenced Iva to ten years in the penitentiary and a fine of $10,000. Thus, at 33 she lost the U.S. citizenship she had tried so hard to preserve—an effort that, in fact, had provoked her trial. Her attorneys moved for a mistrial, for arrest of judgment, for clemency and for bail pending appeal, but Judge Roche denied all the motions.

Felipe d'Aquino had come to San Francisco for the trial and now

Iva said goodbye to him. He was returned to Japan with a warning against re-entering the U.S., and Iva was taken to Alderson Federal Reformatory in West Virginia to serve her sentence.

In the years of Iva's imprisonment, her lawyers made frequent appeals based on her unlawful detention, her lack of access to counsel, her failure to receive a speedy trial, the destruction of favorable evidence, the misconduct of the prosecutors and prejudicial instructions by the judge. All were denied by the appellate courts, and the Supreme Court three times rejected appeals for review. Requests for Presidential pardon, begun under the Eisenhower Presidency, have been ignored.

When Iva was released from Alderson in 1956, her sentence reduced for good behavior, she went to live with her family in Chicago. Her husband could not come to the United States, nor could she leave the country and expect to return. Indeed, the Immigration and Naturalization Service now began proceedings to deport her as an undesirable alien, and relented only with the discovery that she had neither Japanese nor Portuguese citizenship and there was no country to which she could be sent.

But her ordeal was not at an end. At the Toguri's store she was earning only a subsistence, and she had no way to raise the $10,000 fine imposed on her. In 1968 the Justice Department demanded payment. In Chicago District Court Iva was ordered to surrender her only assets, the cash value of two life insurance policies, a total of $4,745. In 1971 the Justice Department again summoned her into court for the balance of $5,255. She was able to satisfy this demand at the death of her father, whose will stipulated that the balance of Iva's fine be paid from his estate.

For all of her troubles, Iva has remained stoic. "Heck, you just have to adjust your life," she says. "I'm very grateful for my friends. They're all aware of my background, but they never bring up the subject. I go to concerts. I have season tickets for the Chicago Lyric Opera. In fact, I have too much to do. I buy from Japan by mail, and that takes time. I've been taking a course in quilting . . . finishing with a nine-patch quilt." Iva has not kept up with Felipe d'Aquino, although she knows he is in Tokyo. She denies any bitterness toward her country, saying, "I'm just disappointed in the way justice is handled sometimes."

Iva does have new grounds for confidence. Subsequent developments have cast the trial procedure in even more dubious light. Principal witnesses have admitted they were coerced into the testimony that brought about her conviction. John Mann, the foreman, has stated it was the judge's pressure for a decision that led his divided jury to convict her. Wayne Collins has asserted that FBI agents interfered with his conduct of the defense, seizing Major Cousens when he arrived at the San Francisco airport from Australia and trying to prevent his testifying for Iva, as well as using its Tokyo agents to put pressure on witnesses from whom Collins was taking testimony.

The backing of the committee to support her—formed by a retired San Francisco pediatrician, Dr. Clifford Uyeda—has broadened to include the 100-chapter, 30,000 member, Japanese-American Citizens League. Aware that Walter Winchellism lives on, the committee had no wish to cause President Ford embarrassment during the election; now that it is over, its hopes are high that he will grant Iva's pardon.

On June 24 of this year [1976], the California Legislature passed a unanimous resolution urging President Ford to grant Iva an unconditional pardon and restore her citizenship. In July, the San Francisco Board of Supervisors followed suit, as did the City of Honolulu. Then, on August 18, the Los Angeles City Council passed a resolution that not only endorsed Iva's pardon and the restoration of her citizenship, but rescinded its own resolution of December 8, 1948, opposing her return.

I see Iva's story as a cautionary tale about naïveté—her own and the nation's—and about the vindictive side of patriotism. It is also a story about the nature of treason, provoking reflection on what the framers of the Constitution intended in their guidelines. Clearly they recognized that ever since those times when Romans found guilty of it were hurled from the Tarpeian Rock, treason has been held a violation of allegiance to the community, the most enormous of human crimes and one that must be punished accordingly.

They were equally aware that since the reign of Caligula, treason law has been abused by those in power. That is why they defined it so strictly and, to forestall conviction by circumstantial evidence, added the Biblical requirement of two witnesses to the same overt act. Iva's experience may show how well-grounded was that concern.

13

The Atomic Bomb and the Origins of the Cold War

MARTIN J. SHERWIN

• In early August, 1945, Japan was prostrate before the economic and military power of the United States. Its once proud Imperial Fleet and great battleships were at the bottom of the Pacific, its best-trained pilots were dead, its Army was decimated by hopeless defenses of isolated islands; its skies were violated with impunity by the bombers of the American Army and Navy, and its population was practically starving. If that were not enough, the Soviet Union was already shifting its armies from Germany and Europe to the Far East, where they would attack Japanese forces on the Asian mainland.

In such circumstances, was the United States justified in dropping atomic bombs on Hiroshima and Nagasaki? Would the Japanese have realized the hopelessness of their position even without the introduction of nuclear weapons? Could the bombs have had an equivalent psychological impact if they had been dropped in rural areas rather than in the midst of crowded cities? Was the atomic bomb the last shot of World War II or the first shot of the Cold War?

Although such questions have inspired a large and diversified literature, perhaps no one has approached the subject with more care and clarity than Martin J. Sherwin of Princeton University. As you read his article, and especially as you reflect upon the statement by University of Chicago scientists in the final paragraph, you might attempt to imagine yourself as the diplomatic representative of another nation—perhaps France or Russia or Japan. What reasons would they have had for assuming that the ultimate weapon was anything more or less than an instrument for advancing American foreign policy? Do you think that the United States was then, or is now, willing to share its military secrets for the benefit of mankind?

During the second World War the atomic bomb was seen and valued as a potential rather than an actual instrument of policy. Responsible officials believed that its impact on diplomacy had to await its development and, perhaps, even a demonstration of its power. As Henry L. Stimson, the secretary of war, observed in his memoirs: "The bomb as a merely probable weapon had seemed a weak reed on which to rely, but the bomb as a colossal reality was very different." That policymakers considered this difference before Hiroshima has been well documented, but whether they based wartime diplomatic policies upon an anticipated successful demonstration of the bomb's power remains a source of controversy. Two questions delineate the issues in this debate. First, did the development of the atomic bomb affect the way American policymakers conducted diplomacy with the Soviet Union? Second, did diplomatic considerations related to the Soviet Union influence the decision to use the atomic bomb against Japan?

These important questions relating the atomic bomb to American diplomacy, and ultimately to the origins of the cold war, have been addressed almost exclusively to the formulation of policy during the early months of the Truman administration. As a result, two anterior questions of equal importance, questions with implications for those already posed, have been overlooked. Did diplomatic considerations related to Soviet postwar behavior influence the formulation of Roosevelt's atomic-energy policies? What effect did the atomic legacy Truman inherited have on the diplomatic and atomic-energy policies of his administration?

To comprehend the nature of the relationship between atomic-energy and diplomatic policies that developed during the war, the bomb must be seen as policymakers saw it before Hiroshima, as a weapon that might be used to control postwar diplomacy. For this task our present view is conceptually inadequate. After more than a quarter century of experience we understand, as wartime policy makers did not, the bomb's limitations as a diplomatic instrument. To appreciate the profound influence of the unchallenged wartime assumption about the bomb's impact on diplomacy we must recognize the postwar purposes for which policymakers and their advisers believed the bomb could be used. In this effort Churchill's expectations must be scruti-

From the *American Historical Review*, 78 (October 1973). Reprinted by permission of the author.

nized as carefully as Roosevelt's, and scientists' ideas must be considered along with those of politicians. Truman's decision to use the atomic bomb against Japan must be evaluated in the light of Roosevelt's atomic legacy, and the problems of impending peace must be considered along with the exigencies of war. To isolate the basic atomic-energy policy alternatives that emerged during the war requires that we first ask whether alternatives were, in fact, recognized.

What emerges most clearly from a close examination of wartime formulation of atomic-energy policy is the conclusion that policy makers never seriously questioned the assumption that the atomic bomb should be used against Germany or Japan. From October 9, 1941, the time of the first meeting to organize the atomic-energy project, Stimson, Roosevelt, and other members of the "top policy group" conceived of the development of the atomic bomb as an essential part of the total war effort. Though the suggestion to build the bomb was initially made by scientists who feared that Germany might develop the weapon first, those with political responsibility for prosecuting the war accepted the circumstances of the bomb's creation as sufficient justification for its use against any enemy.

Having nurtured this point of view during the war, Stimson charged those who later criticized the use of the bomb with two errors. First, these critics asked the wrong question: it was not whether surrender could have been obtained without using the bomb, but whether a different diplomatic and military course from that followed by the Truman administration would have achieved an earlier surrender. Second, the basic assumption of these critics was false: the idea that American policy should have been based primarily on a desire not to employ the bomb seemed as "irresponsible" as a policy controlled by a positive desire to use it. The war, not the bomb, Stimson argued, had been the primary focus of his attention; as secretary of war his responsibilities permitted no alternative.

Stimson's own wartime diary nevertheless indicates that from 1941 on, the problems associated with the atomic bomb moved steadily closer to the center of his own and Roosevelt's concerns. As the war progressed, the implications of the weapon's development became diplomatic as well as military, postwar as well as wartime. Recognizing that a monopoly of the atomic bomb gave the United States a powerful new military advantage, Roosevelt and Stimson became increasingly anxious to convert it to diplomatic advantage. In December 1944 they spoke of using the "secret" of the atomic bomb as a means of obtaining a *quid pro quo* from the Soviet Union. But viewing the bomb as a potential instrument of diplomacy, they were not moved to formulate a concrete plan for carrying out this exchange before the bomb was used. The bomb had "this unique peculiarity," Stimson noted several months later in his diary; "Success is 99% assured, yet only by the first actual war trial of the weapon can the actual certainty be fixed." Whether or not the specter of postwar Soviet ambitions created "a positive desire" to ascertain the bomb's power, until that decision was executed "atomic diplomacy" remained an idea that never crystallized into policy.

Although Roosevelt left no definitive statement assigning a postwar role to the atomic bomb, his expectations for its potential diplomatic value can be recalled from the existing record. An analysis of the policies he chose from among the alternatives he faced suggests that the potential diplomatic value of the bomb began to shape his atomic-energy policies as early as 1943. He may have been cautious about counting on the bomb as a reality during the war, but he nevertheless consistently chose policy alternatives that would promote the postwar diplomatic potential of the bomb if the predictions of scientists proved true. These policies were based on the assumption that the bomb could be used effectively to secure postwar diplomatic aims; and this assumption was carried over from the Roosevelt to the Truman administration.

Despite general agreement that the bomb would be an extraordinarily important diplomatic factor after the war, those closely associated with its development did not agree on how to use it most effectively as an instrument of diplomacy. Convinced that wartime atomic-energy policies would have postwar diplomatic consequences, several scientists advised Roosevelt to adopt policies aimed at achieving a postwar international control system. Churchill, on the other hand, urged the president to maintain the Anglo-American atomic monopoly as a diplomatic counter against the postwar ambitions of other nations—particularly against the Soviet Union. Roosevelt fashioned his atomic-energy policies from the choices he made between these conflicting recommendations. In 1943 he rejected the counsel of his science advisers and began to consider the diplomatic component of atomic-energy policy in consultation with Churchill alone. This decision-making procedure and Roosevelt's untimely death have left his motives ambiguous. Nevertheless it is clear that he pursued policies consistent with Churchill's monopolistic, anti-Soviet views.

The findings of this study thus raise serious questions concerning generalizations historians have commonly made about Roosevelt's diplomacy: that it was consistent with his public reputation for cooperation and conciliation; that he was naive with respect to postwar Soviet behavior; that, like Wilson, he believed in collective security as an effective guarantor of national safety; and that he made every possible effort to assure that the Soviet Union and its allies would continue to function as postwar partners. Although this article does not dispute the view that Roosevelt desired amicable postwar relations with the Soviet Union, or even that he worked hard to achieve them, it does suggest that historians have exaggerated his confidence in (and perhaps his commitment to) such an outcome. His most secret and among his most important long-range decisions—those responsible for prescribing a diplomatic role for the atomic bomb—reflected his lack of confidence. Finally, in light of this study's conclusions, the widely held assumption that Truman's attitude toward the atomic bomb was substantially different from Roosevelt's must also be revised.

Like the grand alliance itself, the Anglo-American atomic-energy partnership was forged by the war and its exigencies. The threat of a German atomic bomb precipitated a hasty marriage of convenience between British research and American resources. When scientists in Britain proposed a theory that explained how an atomic bomb might quickly be built, policy makers had to assume that German scientists were building one. "If such an explosive were made," Vannevar Bush, the director of the Office of Scientific Research and Development, told Roosevelt in July 1941, "it would be thousands of times more powerful than existing explosives, and its use might be determining." Roosevelt assumed nothing less. Even before the atomic-energy project was fully organized he assigned it the highest priority. He wanted the program "pushed not only in regard to development, but also with due regard to time. This is very much of the essence," he told Bush in March 1942. "We both felt painfully the dangers of doing nothing," Churchill recalled, referring to an early wartime discussion with Roosevelt about the bomb.

The high stakes at issue during the war did not prevent officials in Great Britain or the United States from considering the postwar implications of their atomic-energy decisions. As early as 1941, during the debate over whether to join the United States in an atomic-energy partnership, members of the British government's atomic-energy committee argued that the matter "was so important for the future that work should proceed in Britain." Weighing the obvious difficulties of proceeding alone against the possible advantages of working with the United States, Sir John Anderson, then lord president of the council and the minister responsible for atomic-energy research, advocated the partnership. As he explained to Churchill, by working closely with the Americans British scientists would be able "to take up the work again [after the war], not where we left off, but where the combined effort had by then brought it."

As early as October 1942 Roosevelt's science advisers exhibited a similar concern with the potential postwar value of atomic energy. After conducting a full-scale review of the atomic-energy project, James B. Conant, the president of Harvard University and Bush's deputy, recommended discontinuing the Anglo-American partnership "as far as development and manufacture is concerned." Conant had in mind three considerations when he suggested a more limited arrangement with the British: first, the project had been transferred from scientific to military control; second, the United States was doing almost all the developmental work; and third, security dictated "moving in a direction of holding much more closely the information about the development of this program." Under these conditions it was difficult, Conant observed, "to see how a joint British-American project could be sponsored in this country. What prompted Conant's recommendations, however, was his suspicion—soon to be shared by other senior atomic-energy administrators—that the British were rather more concerned with information for postwar industrial purposes than for wartime use. What right did the British have to the fruits of American labor? "We were doing nine-tenths of the work," Stimson told Roosevelt in October. By December 1942 there was general agreement among the president's atomic-energy advisers that the British no longer had a valid claim to all atomic-energy information.

Conant's arguments and suggestions for a more limited partnership were incorporated into a "Report to the President by the Military Policy Committee." Roosevelt approved the recommendations on December 28. Early in January the British were officially informed that the rules governing the Anglo-American atomic-energy partnership had been altered on "orders from the top."

By approving the policy of "restricted interchange" Roosevelt undermined a major incentive for British cooperation. It is not surprising, therefore, that Churchill took up the matter directly with the president and with Harry Hopkins, "Roosevelt's own, personal Foreign Office." The prime minister's initial response to the new policy reflected his determination to have it reversed: "That we should each work separately," he threatened, "would be a sombre decision."

Conant and Bush understood the implications of Churchill's intervention and sought to counter its effect. "It is our duty," Conant wrote Bush, "to see to it that the President of the United States, in writing, is informed of what is involved in these decisions." Their memorandums no longer concentrated on tortuous discussions differentiating between the scientific research and the manufacturing stages of the bomb's development but focused on what to Conant was "the major consideration . . . that of *national security and postwar strategic significance*." Information on manufacturing an atomic bomb, Conant noted, was a "military secret which is in a totally different class from anything the world has ever seen if the potentialities of this project are realized." To provide the British with detailed knowledge about the construction of a bomb "might be the equivalent to joint occupation of a fortress or strategic harbor in perpetuity." Though British and American atomic-energy policies might coincide during the war, Conant and Bush expected them to conflict afterward.

The controversy over the policy of "restricted interchange" of atomic-energy information shifted attention to postwar diplomatic considerations. As Bush wrote to Hopkins, "We can hardly give away the fruits of our developments as a part of postwar planning except on the basis of some overall agreement on that subject, which agreement does not now exist." The central issue was clearly drawn. The atomic-energy policy of the United States was related to the very fabric of Anglo-American postwar relations and, as Churchill would insist, to postwar relations between each of them and the Soviet Union. Just as the possibility of British postwar commercial competition had played a major role in shaping the U.S. policy of restricted interchange, the specter of Soviet postwar military power played a major role in shaping the prime minister's attitude toward atomic-energy policies in 1943.

"We cannot," Sir John Anderson wrote Churchill, "afford after the war to face the future without this weapon and rely entirely on America should Russia or some other power develop it." The prime minister agreed. The atomic bomb was an instrument of postwar diplomacy that Britain had to have. He could cite numerous reasons for his determination to acquire an independent atomic arsenal after the war, but Great Britain's postwar military-diplomatic position with respect to the Soviet Union invariably led the list. When Bush and Stimson visited London in July, Churchill told them quite frankly that he was "vitally interested in the possession of all [atomic-energy] information because this will be necessary for Britain's independence in the future as well as for success during the war." Nor was Churchill evasive about his reasoning: "It would never do to have Germany or Russia win the race for something which might be used for international blackmail," he stated bluntly and then pointed out that "Russia might be in a position to accomplish this result unless we worked together." In Washington, two months earlier, Churchill's science adviser Lord Cherwell had told Bush and Hopkins virtually the same thing. The British government, Cherwell stated, was considering "the whole [atomic-energy] affair on an after-the-war military basis." It intended, he said, "to manufacture and produce the weapon." Prior to the convening of the Quebec Conference, Anderson explained his own and Churchill's view of the bomb to the Canadian prime minister, Mackenzie King. The British knew, Anderson said, "that both Germany and Russia were working on the same thing," which, he noted, "would be a terrific factor in the postwar world as giving an absolute control to whatever country possessed the secret." Convinced that the British attitude toward the bomb would undermine any possibility of postwar cooperation with the Soviet Union, Bush and Conant vigorously continued to oppose any revival of the Anglo-American atomic-energy partnership.

On July 20, however, Roosevelt chose to accept a recommendation from Hopkins to restore full partnership, and he ordered Bush to "renew, in an inclusive manner, the full exchange of infomation with the British." A garbled trans-Atlantic cable to Bush reading "review" rather than "renew" gave him the opportunity to continue his negotiations in London with Churchill and thereby to modify the president's order. But Bush could not alter Roosevelt's intentions. On August 19, at the Quebec Conference, the president and the prime minister agreed that the British would share the atomic bomb. Despite Bush's negotiations with Churchill, the Quebec Agreement revived the principle of an Anglo-American atomic-energy partnership, albeit the British were reinstated as junior rather than equal partners.

The president's decision was not a casual one taken in ignorance. As the official history of the Atomic Energy Commission notes: "Both Roosevelt and Churchill knew that the stake of their diplomacy was a technological breakthrough so revolutionary that it transcended in importance even the bloody work of carrying the war to the heartland of the Nazi foe." The president had been informed of Churchill's position as well as of Bush's and Conant's. But how much closer Roosevelt was to Churchill than to his own advisers at this time is suggested by a report written after the war by General Leslie R. Groves, military director of the atomic-energy project. "It is not known what if any Americans President Roosevelt consulted at Quebec," Groves wrote. "It is doubtful if there were any. All that is known is that the Quebec Agreement was signed by President Roosevelt and that, as finally signed, it agreed practically in toto with the version presented by Sir John Anderson to Dr. Bush in Washington a few weeks earlier."

The debate that preceded the Quebec Agreement is noteworthy for yet another reason: it led to a new relationship between Roosevelt and his atomic-energy advisers. After August 1943 the president did not consult with them about the diplomatic aspects of atomic-energy policy. Though he responded politely when they offered their views, he acted decisively only in consultation with Churchill. Bush and Conant appear to have lost a large measure of their influence because they had used it to oppose Churchill's position. What they did not suspect was the extent to which the president had come to share the prime minister's view.

It can be argued that Roosevelt, the political pragmatist, renewed the wartime atomic-energy partnership to keep relations with the British harmonious rather than disrupt them on the basis of a postwar issue. Indeed it seems logical that the president took this consideration into account. But it must also be recognized that he was perfectly comfortable with the concept Churchill advocated—that military power was a prerequisite to successful postwar diplomacy. As early as August 1941, during the Atlantic Conference, Roosevelt had rejected the idea that an "effective international organization" could be relied upon to keep the peace; an Anglo-American international police force would be far more effective, he told Churchill. By the spring of 1942 the concept had broadened: the two "policemen" became four, and the idea was added that every other nation would be totally disarmed. "The Four Policemen" would have "to build up a reservoir of force so powerful that no aggressor would dare to challenge it," Roosevelt told Arthur Sweetser, an ardent internationalist. Violators first would be quarantined, and, if they persisted in their disruptive activities, bombed at the rate of a city a day until they agreed to behave. The president told Molotov about this idea in May, and in November he repeated it to Clark Eichelberger, who was coordinating the activities of the American internationalists. A year later, at the Teheran Conference, Roosevelt again discussed his idea, this time with Stalin. As Robert A. Divine has noted: "Roosevelt's concept of big power domination remained the central idea in his approach to international organization throughout World War II."

Precisely how Roosevelt expected to integrate the atomic bomb into his plans for keeping the peace in the postwar world is not clear. However, against the background of his atomic-energy policy decisions of 1943 and his peace-keeping concepts, his actions in 1944 suggest that he intended to take full advantage of the bomb's potential as a postwar instrument of Anglo-American diplomacy. If Roosevelt thought the bomb could be used to create a more peaceful world order, he seems to have considered the threat of its power more effective than any opportunities it offered for international cooperation. If Roosevelt was less worried than Churchill about Soviet postwar ambitions, he was no less determined than the prime minister to avoid any commitments to the Soviets for the international control of atomic energy. There could still be four policemen, but only two of them would have the bomb.

The atomic-energy policies Roosevelt pursued during the remainder of his life reinforce this interpretation of his ideas for the postwar period. The following three questions offer a useful framework for analyzing his intentions. Did Roosevelt make any additional agreements with Churchill that would further support the view that he intended to maintain an Anglo-American monopoly after the war? Did Roosevelt demonstrate any interest in the international control of atomic energy? Was Roosevelt aware that an effort to maintain an Anglo-American monopoly of the atomic bomb might lead to a postwar atomic arms race with the Soviet Union?

An examination of the wartime activities of the eminent Danish physicist, Niels Bohr, who arrived in America early in 1944 as a consultant to the atomic-bomb project, will help answer these questions. "Officially and secretly he came to help the technical enterprise," noted J. Robert Oppenheimer, the director of the Los Alamos atomic-bomb laboratory, but "most secretly of all . . . he came to advance his case and his cause." Bohr was convinced that a postwar atomic armaments race with the Soviet Union was inevitable unless Roosevelt and Churchill initiated efforts during the war to establish the international control of atomic energy. Bohr's attempts to promote this idea in the United States were aided by Justice Felix Frankfurter.

Bohr and Frankfurter were old acquaintances. They had first met in 1933 at Oxford and then in 1939 on several occasions in London and the United States. At these meetings Bohr had been impressed by the breadth of Frankfurter's interests and, perhaps, overimpressed with his influence on Roosevelt. In 1944 the Danish minister to the United States brought them together, once again, at his home in Washington. Frankfurter, who appears to have suspected why Bohr had come to America and why this meeting had been arranged, had learned about the atomic-bomb project earlier in the war when, as he told the story, several troubled scientists had sought his advice on a matter of "greatest importance." He therefore invited Bohr to lunch in his chambers and, by dropping hints about his knowledge, encouraged Bohr to discuss the issue.

After listening to Bohr's analysis of the postwar alternatives—an atomic armaments race or some form of international control—Frankfurter saw Roosevelt. Bohr had persuaded him, Frankfurter reported, that disastrous consequences would result if Russia leaned on her own about the atomic-bomb project. Frankfurter suggested that it was a matter of great importance that the president explore the possibility of seeking an effective arrangement with the Soviets for controlling the bomb. He also noted that Bohr, whose knowledge of Soviet science was extensive, believed that the Russians had the capability to build their own atomic weapons. If the international control of atomic energy was not discussed among the Allies during the war, an atomic arms race between the Allies would almost certainly develop after the war. It seemed imperative, therefore, that Roosevelt consider approaching Stalin with a proposal as soon as possible.

Frankfurter discussed these points with the president for an hour and a half, and he left feeling that Roosevelt was "plainly impressed by my account of the matter." When Frankfurter had suggested that the solution of this problem might be more important than all the plans for a world organization, Roosevelt had agreed. Moreover he had authorized Frankfurter to tell Bohr, who was scheduled to return to England, that he might inform "our friends in London that the President was most eager to explore the proper safeguards in relation to X [the atomic bomb]." Roosevelt also told Frankfurter that the problem of the atomic bomb "worried him to death" and that he was very eager for all the help he could have in dealing with it.

The alternatives placed before Roosevelt posed a difficult dilemma. On the one hand, he could continue to exclude the Soviet government from any official information about the development of the bomb, a policy that would probably strengthen America's postwar military-diplomatic position. But such a policy would also encourage Soviet mistrust of Anglo-American intentions and was bound to make postwar cooperation more difficult. On the other hand, Roosevelt could use the atomic-bomb project as an instrument of cooperation by informing Stalin of the American government's intention of cooperating in the development of a plan for the international control of atomic weapons, an objective that might never be achieved.

Either choice involved serious risks. Roosevelt had to balance the diplomatic advantages of being well ahead of the Soviet Union in atomic-energy production after the war against the advantages of initiating wartime negotiations for postwar cooperation. The issue here, it must be emphasized, is not whether the initiative Bohr suggested would have led to successful international control, but rather whether

Roosevelt demonstrated any serious interest in laying the groundwork for such a policy.

Several considerations indicate that Roosevelt was already committed to a course of action that precluded Bohr's internationalist approach. First, Frankfurter appears to have been misled. Though Roosevelt's response had been characteristically agreeable, he did not mention Bohr's ideas to his atomic-energy advisers until September 1944, when he told Bush that he was very disturbed that Frankfurter had learned about the project. Roosevelt knew at this time, moreover, that the Soviets were finding out on their own about the development of the atomic bomb. Security personnel had reported an active Communist cell in the Radiation Laboratory at the University of California. Their reports indicated that at least one scientist at Berkeley was selling information to Russian agents. "They [Soviet agents] are already getting information about vital secrets and sending them to Russia," Stimson told the president on September 9, 1943. If Roosevelt was indeed worried to death about the effect the atomic bomb could have on Soviet-American postwar relations, he took no action to remove the potential danger, nor did he make any effort to explore the possibility of encouraging Soviet postwar cooperation on this problem. The available evidence indicates that he never discussed the merits of the international control of atomic energy with his advisers after this first or any subsequent meeting with Frankfurter.

How is the president's policy, of neither discussing international control nor promoting the idea, to be explained if not by an intention to use the bomb as an instrument of Anglo-American postwar diplomacy? Perhaps his concern for maintaining the tightest possible secrecy against German espionage led him to oppose any discussion about the project. Or he may have concluded, after considering Bohr's analysis, that Soviet suspicion and mistrust would be further aroused if Stalin were informed of the existence of the project without receiving detailed information about the bomb's construction. The possibility also exists that Roosevelt believed that neither Congress nor the American public would approve of a policy giving the Soviet Union any measure of control over the new weapon. Finally Roosevelt might have thought that the spring of 1944 was not the proper moment for such an initiative.

Though it would be unreasonable to state categorically that these considerations did not contribute to his decision, they appear to have been secondary. Roosevelt was clearly, and properly, concerned about secrecy, but the most important secret with respect to Soviet-American relations was that the United States was developing an atomic bomb. And that secret, he was aware, already had been passed on to Moscow. Soviet mistrust of Anglo-American postwar intentions could only be exacerbated by continuing the existing policy. Moreover an attempt to initiate planning for international control of atomic energy would not have required the revelation of technical secrets. Nor is it sufficient to cite Roosevelt's well-known sensitivity to domestic politics as an explanation for his atomic-energy policies. He was willing to take enormous political risks, as he did at Yalta, to support his diplomatic objectives.

Had Roosevelt avoided all postwar atomic-energy commitments, his lack of support for international control could have been interpreted as an attempt to reserve his opinion on the best course to follow. But he had made commitments in 1943 supporting Churchill's monopolistic, anti-Soviet position, and he continued to make others in 1944. On June 13, for example, Roosevelt and Churchill signed an Agreement and Declaration of Trust, specifying that the United States and Great Britain would cooperate in seeking to control available supplies of uranium and thorium ore both during and after the war. This commitment, taken against the background of Roosevelt's peace-keeping ideas and his other commitments, suggests that the president's attitude toward the international control of atomic energy was similar to the prime minister's.

Churchill had dismissed out of hand the concept of international control when Bohr talked with him about it in May 1944. Their meeting was not long under way before Churchill lost interest and became involved in an argument with Lord Cherwell, who was also present. Bohr, left out of the discussion, was frustrated and depressed; he was unable to return the conversation to what he considered the most important diplomatic problem of the war. When the allotted half hour elapsed, Bohr asked if he might send the prime minister a memorandum on the subject. A letter from Niels Bohr, Churchill bitingly replied, was always welcome, but he hoped it would deal with a subject other than politics. As Bohr described their meeting: "We did not even speak the same language."

Churchill rejected the assumption upon which Bohr's views were founded—that international control of atomic energy could be used as a cornerstone for constructing a peaceful world order. An atomic monopoly would be a significant diplomatic advantage in postwar diplomacy, and Churchill did not believe that anything useful could be gained by surrendering this advantage. The argument that a new weapon created a unique opportunity to refashion international affairs ignored every lesson Churchill read into history. "You can be quite sure," he would write in a memorandum less than a year later, "that any power that gets hold of the secret will try to make the article, and this touches the existence of human society. This matter is out of all relation to anything else that exists in the world, and I could not think of participating in any disclosure to third or fourth parties at the present time."

Several months after Bohr met Churchill, Frankfurter arranged a meeting between Bohr and Roosevelt. Their discussion lasted an hour and a half. Roosevelt told Bohr that contact with the Soviet Union along the lines he suggested had to be tried. The president also said he was optimistic that such an initiative would have a "good result." In his opinion Stalin was enough of a realist to understand the revolutionary importance of this development and its consequences. The president also expressed confidence that the prime minister would eventually share these views. They had disagreed in the past, he told Bohr, but they had always succeeded in resolving their differences.

Roosevelt's enthusiasm for Bohr's ideas was more apparent than real. The president did not mention them to anyone until he met with Churchill at Hyde Park on September 18, following the second wartime conference at Quebec. The decisions reached on atomic energy at Hyde Park were summarized and documented in an *aide-mémoire* signed by Roosevelt and Churchill on September 19, 1944. The agreement bears the markings of Churchill's attitude toward the atomic bomb and his poor opinion of Bohr. "Enquiries should be made," the last paragraph reads, "regarding the activities of Professor Bohr and steps taken to ensure that he is responsible for no leakage of information particularly to the Russians." If Bohr's activities prompted Roosevelt to suspect his loyalty, there can be no doubt that Churchill encouraged the president's suspicions. Atomic energy and Britain's future position as a world power had become part of a single equation for the prime minister. Bohr's ideas, like the earlier idea of restricted interchange, threatened the continuation of the Anglo-American atomic-energy partnership. With such great stakes at issue Churchill did not hesitate to discredit Bohr along with his ideas. "It seems to me," Churchill wrote to Cherwell soon after Hyde Park, "Bohr ought to be confined or at any rate made to see that he is very near the edge of mortal crimes."

The *aide-mémoire* also contained an explicit rejection of any war-time efforts toward international control: "The suggestion that the world should be informed regarding tube alloys [the atomic bomb], with a view to an international agreement regarding its control and use, is not accepted. The matter should continue to be regarded as of the utmost secrecy." But Bohr had never suggested that the world be informed about the atomic bomb. He had argued in memorandums and in person that peace was not possible unless the Soviet government—not the world—was officially notified only about the project's existence before the time when any discussion would appear coercive rather than friendly.

It was the second paragraph, however, that revealed the full extent of Roosevelt's agreement with Churchill's point of view. "Full collaboration between the United States and the British Government in developing tube alloys for military and commercial purposes," it noted, "should continue after the defeat of Japan unless and until terminated by joint agreement." Finally the *aide-mémoire* offers some insight into Roosevelt's intentions for the military use of the weapon in the war: "When a bomb is finally available, it might perhaps, after mature consideration, be used against the Japanese, who should be warned that this bombardment will be repeated until they surrender."

Within the context of the complex problem of the origins of the cold war the Hyde Park meeting is far more important than historians of the war generally have recognized. Overshadowed by the Second Quebec Conference on one side and by the drama of Yalta on the other, its significance often has been overlooked. But the agreements reached in September 1944 reflect a set of attitudes, aims, and assumptions that guided the relationship between the atomic bomb and American diplomacy during the Roosevelt administration and, through the transfer of its atomic legacy, during the Truman administration as well. Two alternatives had been recognized long before Roosevelt and

Churchill met in 1944 at Hyde Park: the bomb could have been used to initiate a diplomatic effort to work out a system for its international control, or it could remain isolated during the war from any cooperative initiatives and held in reserve should cooperation fail. Roosevelt consistently favored the latter alternative. An insight into his reasoning is found in a memorandum Bush wrote following a conversation with Roosevelt several days after the Hyde Park meeting: "The President evidently thought he could join with Churchill in bringing about a US-UK postwar agreement on this subject [the atomic bomb] by which it would be held closely and presumably to control the peace of the world." By 1944 Roosevelt's earlier musings about the four policemen had faded into the background. But the idea behind it, the concept of controlling the peace of the world by amassing overwhelming military power, appears to have remained a prominent feature of his postwar plans.

In the seven months between his meeting with Churchill in September and his death the following April Roosevelt did not alter his atomic-energy policies. Nor did he reverse his earlier decision not to take his advisers into his confidence about diplomatic issues related to the new weapon. They were never told about the Hyde Park agreements, nor were they able to discuss with him their ideas for the postwar handling of atomic-energy affairs. Though officially uninformed, Bush suspected that Roosevelt had made a commitment to continue the atomic-energy partnership exclusively with the British after the war, and he, as well as Conant, opposed the idea. They believed such a policy "might well lead to extraordinary efforts on the part of Russia to establish its own position in the field secretly, and might lead to a clash, say 20 years from now." Unable to reach the president directly, they sought to influence his policies through Stimson, whose access to Roosevelt's office (though not to his thoughts on atomic energy) was better than their own.

Summarizing their views on September 30 for the secretary of war, Bush and Conant predicted that an atomic bomb equivalent to from one to ten thousand tons of high explosive could be "demonstrated" before August 1, 1945. They doubted that the present American and British monopoly could be maintained for more than three or four years, and they pointed out that any nation with good technical and scientific resources could catch up; accidents of research, moreover, might even put some other nation ahead. In addition atomic bombs were only the first step along the road of nuclear weapons technology. In the not-too-distant future loomed the awesome prospect of a weapon perhaps a thousand times more destructive—the hydrogen bomb. Every major center of population in the world would then lie at the mercy of a nation that struck first in war. Security therefore could be found neither in secrecy nor even in the control of raw materials, for the supply of heavy hydrogen was practically unlimited.

These predictions by Bush and Conant were more specific than Bohr's, but not dissimilar. They, too, believed that a nuclear arms race could be prevented only through international control. Their efforts were directed, however, toward abrogating existing agreements with the British rather than toward initiating new agreements with the Soviets. Like Bohr they based their hope for Stalin's eventual cooperation on his desire to avoid the circumstances that could lead to a nuclear war. But while Bohr urged Roosevelt to approach Stalin with the carrot of international control before the bomb became a reality, Bush and Conant were inclined to delay such an approach until the bomb was demonstrated, until it was clear that without international control the new weapon could be used as a terribly effective stick.

In their attempt to persuade Roosevelt to their point of view Bush and Conant failed. But their efforts were not in vain. By March 1945 Stimson shared their concerns, and he agreed that peace without international control was a forlorn hope. Postwar problems relating to the atomic bomb "went right down to the bottom facts of human nature, morals and government, and it is by far the most searching and important thing that I have had to do since I have been here in the office of Secretary of War," Stimson wrote on March 5. Ten days later he presented his views on postwar atomic-energy policy to Roosevelt. This was their last meeting. In less than a month a new president took the oath of office.

Harry S. Truman inherited a set of military and diplomatic atomic-energy policies that included partially formulated intentions, several commitments to Churchill, and the assumption that the bomb would be a legitimate weapon to be used against Japan. But no policy was definitely settled. According to the Quebec Agreement the president had the option of deciding the future of the commercial aspects of the atomic-energy partnership according to his own estimate of what was fair. Although the policy of "utmost secrecy" had been confirmed at Hyde Park the previous September, Roosevelt had not informed his atomic-energy advisers about the *aide-mémoire* he and Churchill signed. Although the assumption that the bomb would be used in the war was shared by those privy to its development, assumptions formulated early in the war were not necessarily valid at its conclusion. Yet Truman was bound to the past by his own uncertain position and by the prestige of his predecessor. Since Roosevelt had refused to open negotiations with the Soviet government for the international control of atomic energy, and since he had never expressed any objection to the wartime use of the bomb, it would have required considerable political courage and confidence for Truman to alter those policies. Moreover it would have required the encouragement of his advisers, for under the circumstances the most serious constraint on the new president's choices was his dependence upon advice. So Truman's atomic legacy, while it included several options, did not necessarily entail complete freedom to choose from among all the possible alternatives.

"I think it is very important that I should have a talk with you as soon as possible on a highly secret matter," Stimson wrote to Truman on April 24. It has "such a bearing on our present foreign relations and has such an important effect upon all my thinking in this field that I think you ought to know about it without further delay." Stimson had been preparing to brief Truman on the atomic bomb for almost ten days, but in the preceding twenty-four hours he had been seized by a sense of urgency. Relations with the Soviet Union had declined precipitously during the past week, the result, he thought, of the failure of the State Department to settle the major problems between the Allies before going ahead with the San Francisco Conference on the United Nations Organization. The secretary of state, Edward R. Stettinius, Jr., along with the department's Soviet specialists, now felt "compelled to bull the thing through." To get out of the "mess" they had created, Stimson wrote in his diary, they were urging Truman to get tough with the Russians. He had. Twenty-four hours earlier the president met with the Soviet foreign minister, V. M. Molotov, and "with rather brutal frankness" accused his government of breaking the Yalta Agreement. Molotov was furious. "I have never been talked to like that in my life," he told the president before leaving.

With a memorandum on the "political aspects of the S-1 [atomic bomb's] performance" in hand and General Groves in reserve, Stimson went to the White House on April 25. The document he carried was the distillation of numerous decisions already taken, each one the product of attitudes that developed along with the new weapon. The secretary himself was not entirely aware of how various forces had shaped these decisions: the recommendations of Bush and Conant, the policies Roosevelt had followed, the uncertainties inherent in the wartime alliance, the oppressive concern for secrecy, and his own inclination to consider long-range implications. It was a curious document. Though its language revealed Stimson's sensitivity to the historic significance of the atomic bomb, he did not question the wisdom of using it against Japan. Nor did he suggest any concrete steps for developing a postwar policy. His objective was to inform Truman of the salient problems: the possibility of an atomic arms race, the danger of atomic war, and the necessity for international control if the United Nations Organization was to work. "If the problem of the proper use of this weapon can be solved," he wrote, "we would have the opportunity to bring the world into a pattern in which the peace of the world and our civilizations can be saved." To cope with this difficult challenge Stimson suggested the "establishment of a select committee" to consider the postwar problems inherent in the development of the bomb. If his presentation was the "forceful statement" of the problem that historians of the Atomic Energy Commission have described it as being, its force inhered in the problem itself, not in any bold formulations or initiatives he offered toward a solution. If, as another historian has claimed, this meeting led to a "strategy of delayed showdown," requiring "the delay of all disputes with Russia until the atomic bomb had been demonstrated," there is no evidence in the extant records of the meeting that Stimson had such a strategy in mind or that Truman misunderstood the secretary's views.

What emerges from a careful reading of Stimson's diary, his memorandum of April 25 to Truman, a summary by Groves of the meeting, and Truman's recollections is an argument for overall caution in American diplomatic relations with the Soviet Union: it was an argument against any showdown. Since the atomic bomb was potentially the most dangerous issue facing the postwar world and since the most desirable resolution of the problem was some form of international control, Soviet cooperation had to be secured. It was imprudent, Stimson suggested, to pursue a policy that would preclude the possibility of international cooperation on atomic-energy matters after the war ended. Truman's overall impression of Stimson's argument was that the secretary of war was "at least as much concerned with the role of the atomic bomb in the shaping of history as in its capacity to shorten the war." These were indeed Stimson's dual concerns on April 25, and he could see no conflict between them.

Despite the profound consequences Stimson attributed to the development of the new weapon, he had not suggested that Truman reconsider its use against Japan. Nor had he thought to mention the possibility that chances of securing Soviet postwar cooperation might be diminished if Stalin did not receive a commitment to international control prior to an attack. The question of why these alternatives were overlooked naturally arises. Perhaps what Frankfurter once referred to as Stimson's habit of setting "his mind at one thing like the needle of an old victrola caught in a single groove" may help to explain his not mentioning these possibilities. Yet Bush and Conant never raised them either. Even Niels Bohr had made a clear distinction between the bomb's wartime use and its postwar impact on diplomacy. "What role it [the atomic bomb] may play in the present war," Bohr had written to Roosevelt in July 1944, was a question "quite apart" from the overriding concern: the need to avoid an atomic arms race.

The preoccupation with winning the war obviously helped to create this seeming dichotomy between the wartime use of the bomb and the potential postwar diplomatic problems with the Soviet Union raised by its development. But a closer look at how Bohr and Stimson each defined the nature of the diplomatic problem created by the bomb suggests that for the secretary of war and his advisers (and ultimately for the president they advised) there was no dichotomy at all. Bohr apprehended the meaning of the new weapon even before it was developed, and he had no doubt that scientists in the Soviet Union would also understand its profound implications for the postwar world. He was also certain that they would interpret the meaning of the development to Stalin just as scientists in the United States and Great Britain had explained it to Roosevelt and Churchill. Thus the diplomatic problem, as Bohr analyzed it, was not the need to convince Stalin that the atomic bomb was an unprecedented weapon that threatened the life of the world but the need to assure the Soviet leader that he had nothing to fear from the circumstances of its development. By informing Stalin during the war that the United States intended to cooperate with him in neutralizing the bomb through international control, Bohr reasoned that its wartime use could be considered apart from postwar problems.

Stimson approached the problem rather differently. Although he believed that the bomb "might even mean the doom of civilization or it might mean the perfection of civilization" he was less confident than Bohr that the weapon in an undeveloped state could be used as an effective instrument of diplomacy. Until its "actual certainty [was] fixed," Stimson considered any prior approach to Stalin as premature. But as the uncertainties of impending peace became more apparent and worrisome, Stimson, Truman, and the secretary of state-designate, James F. Byrnes, began to think of the bomb as something of a diplomatic panacea for their postwar problems. Byrnes had told Truman in April that the bomb "might well put us in a position to dictate our own terms at the end of the war." By June, Truman and Stimson were discussing "further *quid pro quos* which should be established in consideration for our taking them [the Soviet Union] into [atomic-energy] partnership." Assuming that the bomb's impact on diplomacy would be immediate and extraordinary, they agreed on no less than "the settlement of the Polish, Rumanian, Yugoslavian, and Manchurian problems." But they also concluded that no revelation would be made "to Russia or anyone else until the first bomb had been successfully laid on Japan." Truman and Stimson based their expectations on how they saw and valued the bomb; its use against Japan, they reasoned, would transfer this view to the Soviet Union.

Was an implicit warning to Moscow, then, the principal reason for deciding to use the atomic bomb against Japan? In light of the ambiguity of the available evidence the question defies an unequivocal answer. What can be said with certainty is that Truman, Stimson, Byrnes, and several others involved in the decision consciously considered two effects of a combat demonstration of the bomb's power: first, the impact of the atomic attack on Japan's leaders, who might be persuaded thereby to end the war; and second, the impact of that attack on the Soviet Union's leaders, who might then prove to be more cooperative. But if the assumption that the bomb might bring the war to a rapid conclusion was the principal motive for using the atomic bomb, the expectation that its use would also inhibit Soviet diplomatic ambitions clearly discouraged any inclination to question that assumption.

Policymakers were not alone in expecting a military demonstration of the bomb to have a salubrious effect on international affairs. James Conant, for example, believed that such a demonstration would further the prospects for international control. "President Conant has written me," Stimson informed the news commentator Raymond Swing in February 1947, "that one of the principal reasons he had for advising me that the bomb must be used was that that was the only way to awaken the world to the necessity of abolishing war altogether." And the director of the atomic-energy laboratory at the University of Chicago made the same point to Stimson in June 1945: "If the bomb were not used in the present war," Arthur Compton noted, "the world would have no adequate warning as to what was to be expected if war should break out again." Even Edward Teller, who has publicly decried the attack on Hiroshima and declared his early opposition to it, adopted a similar position in July 1945. "Our only hope is in getting the facts of our results before the people," he wrote to his colleague, Leo Szilard, who was circulating a petition among scientists opposing the bomb's use. "This might help to convince everybody that the next war would be fatal," Teller noted. "For this purpose actual combat use might even be the best thing."

Thus by the end of the war the most influential and widely accepted attitude toward the bomb was a logical extension of how the weapon was seen and valued earlier—as a potential instrument of diplomacy. Caught between the remnants of war and the uncertainties of peace, scientists as well as policy makers were trapped by the logic of their own unquestioned assumptions. By the summer of 1945 not only the conclusion of the war but the organization of an acceptable peace seemed to depend upon the success of the atomic attacks against Japan. When news of the successful atomic test of July 16 reached the president at the Potsdam Conference, he was visibly elated. Stimson noted that Truman "was tremendously pepped up by it and spoke to me of it again and again when I saw him. He said it gave him an entirely new feeling of confidence." The day after receiving the complete report of the test Truman altered his negotiating style. According to Churchill the president "got to the meeting after having read this report [and] he was a changed man. He told the Russians just where they got on and off and generally bossed the whole meeting." After the plenary session on July 24 Truman "casually mentioned to Stalin" that the United States had "a new weapon of unusual destructive force." Truman took this step in response to a recommendation by the Interim Committee, a group of political and scientific advisers organized by Stimson in May 1945 to advise the president on atomic-energy policy. But it is an unavoidable conclusion that what the president told the premier followed the letter of the recommendation rather than its spirit, which embodied the hope that an overture to Stalin would initiate the process toward international control. In less than three weeks the new weapon's destructive potential would be demonstrated to the world. Stalin would then be forced to reconsider his diplomatic goals. It is no wonder that upon learning of the raid against Hiroshima Truman exclaimed: "This is the greatest thing in history."

As Stimson had expected, as a colossal reality the bomb was very different. But had American diplomacy been altered by it? Those who conducted diplomacy became more confident, more certain that through the accomplishments of American science, technology, and industry the "new world" could be made into one better than the old. But just how the atomic bomb would be used to help accomplish this ideal remained unclear. Three months and one day after Hiroshima was bombed Bush wrote that the whole matter of international relations on atomic energy "is in a thoroughly chaotic condition." The wartime relationship between atomic-energy policy and diplomacy had been based upon the simple assumption that the Soviet government would surrender important geographical, political, and ideological objectives in exchange for the neutralization of the new weapon. As a result of policies based on this assumption American diplomacy and prestige suffered grievously: an opportunity to gauge the Soviet Union's response during the war to the international control of atomic energy was missed, and an atomic-energy policy for dealing with the Soviet government after the war was ignored. Instead of promoting American postwar aims, wartime atomic-energy policies made them more difficult to achieve. As a group of scientists at the University of Chicago's atomic-energy laboratory presciently warned the government in June 1945: "It may be difficult to persuade the world that a nation which was capable of secretly preparing and suddenly releasing a weapon as indiscriminate as the [German] rocket bomb and a million times more destructive, is to be trusted in its proclaimed desire of having such weapons abolished by international agreement." This reasoning, however, flowed from alternative assumptions formulated during the closing months of the war by scientists far removed from the wartime policy-making process. Hiroshima and Nagasaki, the culmination of that process, became the symbols of a new American barbarism, reinforcing charges, with dramatic circumstantial evidence, that the policies of the United States contributed to the origins of the cold war.

14
The Emergence of the Suburbs

KENNETH T. JACKSON

• Henry Ford, who in the 1920s was ranked by college students as the third greatest person of all time—behind Jesus Christ and Napoleon Bonaparte—predicted that "the city is doomed," and that "we shall solve the city problem by leaving the city." There seems to be general agreement that he was an accurate prophet. According to Russell Baker, "The American suburb is as much a product of the automobile as air pollution. Basically, it is storage space for workers in their off hours." Like invading soldiers, mounted on station wagons with bicycles tied to the roofs, millions of Americans have moved to suburbia since World War II. The Republican party recognized the existence of this powerful new constituency in 1968 by selecting Spiro T. Agnew, an administrator in suburban Baltimore County, as its vice presidential candidate.

The following essay by Kenneth T. Jackson treats suburbanization as an historical process rather than a simple phenomenon created by the tin lizzie. Without ignoring the unique contribution of the automobile, he suggests that the suburbs were initially fed by the omnibus, the streetcar, and the steam railroad. He also documents the extent to which the federal government has discriminated against the cities in favor of the suburbs.

As you read "The Emergence of the Suburbs," you might reflect on anthropologist Margaret Mead's prediction that women will never assume their rightful place in America until they stop chauffeuring people around and get out of the suburbs to work. Outlying residential areas, she argues, are devoid of the social and political resources needed to bring women beyond the traditional family and into a larger community.

From THE URBAN EXPERIENCE: THEMES IN AMERICAN HISTORY by Raymond A. Mohl and James F. Richardson. © 1973 by Wadsworth Publishing Company, Inc., Belmont, California 94002. Reprinted by permission of the publisher.

Hundreds and thousands, formerly obliged to live in the crowded streets of cities, now find themselves able to enjoy a country cottage, several miles distant, the old notions of time and space being half annihilated; and these suburban cottages enable the busy citizen to breathe freely, and keep alive his love for nature, till the time shall come when he shall have wrung out of the nervous hand of commerce enough means to enable him to realize his ideal of the "retired life" of an American landed proprietor. (*Andrew Jackson Downing, 1848*)

Relentlessly, almost unconsciously, the United States has become a suburban nation. In 1970, the Census Bureau announced that the suburbs contained 76 million people, or 12 million more than the cities which spawned them. Even the 8 million citizens of New York City found themselves outnumbered by the 9 million outsiders who lived within sixty miles of Times Square. And predictions for the late 1970s uniformly assert that suburbanites will not only remain the largest single element of the American population but they will increase their proportion of the total. By 1980, millions of acres of brush, scrub oak, pine, and prairie will have given way to crabgrass and concrete, and corporate offices, factories, and big-league stadiums will be more commonplace on the urban periphery.

Suburbia, of course, represents different things to different people. The concept is broad and confusing; the word alone is enough to unleash myths. The typical stereotype is one of station wagons, shopping centers, single-family houses, and curvilinear streets, all liberally sprinkled with children on bicycles and young couples giddy from martinis. Uniformity supposedly prevails. In 1967, an Ohio housewife expressed this homogenous view: "Suburbs are small, controlled communities where for the most part everyone has the same living standards, the same weeds, the same number of garbage cans, the same house plan, and the same level in their septic tanks."

Actually, there is no such thing as the "typical" suburb or suburbanite any more than there is a "typical" city or urban resident. Even the most casual investigation will establish that American suburbs come in every conceivable type, shape, and size; from industrial Hoboken to posh Winnetka, from black Robbins to lily-white Cicero; from Polish Hamtramck to Waspish Darien; from colonial Cambridge to innovative Reston. In the face of such a conglomeration, scholars have been unable to agree on the definition of *suburban*. Economists assign suburban status on the basis of the functional relationship between the neighborhood and the larger metropolitan area, ecologists on the basis of residential density, political scientists on the basis of separate legal and corporate identity, and sociologists on the basis of "a way of life." In this essay, I shall regard suburbs as low-density, residential areas (1,500 to 10,000 residents per square mile) at the edge of the built-up portion of large cities.

THE EARLIEST SUBURBS

The term *suburb* (or *burgus, suburbium,* or *faubourg*) has had a versatile two-thousand-year history and has been employed to describe such diverse agglomerations as the estates surrounding the Sumerian city of Ur, the villas ringing Imperial Rome, the housing clusters outside the walls of medieval Toulouse, and the pubs at the Bowery and Astor Place in eighteenth century New York City. John Wycliffe used the word *suburbis* in 1380, and Geoffrey Chaucer introduced the term in a dialogue in *The Canterbury Tales*. By 1500, Fleet Street and the extramural parishes were designated as London suburbs, and by the seventeenth century the adjective *suburban* was being used in England to signify both the place and the resident. On this side of the Atlantic, residential settlements existed outside Philadelphia and New York long before the thirteen English colonies won their independence from King George III. In New Orleans, following the French tradition, communities just outside the legal city were known variously as Faubourg Ste. Marie, Faubourg Marigny, and Faubourg Solet.

Thus in one sense, suburbs are about as old as cities. But *suburbanization,* the systematic and regular growth of fringe areas at a pace more rapid than that of central areas, probably occurred first in the United States, where it can be dated from the second quarter of the nineteenth century. Since that time the process has been heavily influenced by developments in transportation technology, by the institutionalization of the low-interest, long-term, home loan, and by the desire of generations of families to seek their own house on their own piece of land. The historical dimension of the suburban trend is important because the urban structure we have inherited has been largely shaped by the decisions and impulses of a half century and more ago.

In 1825, American cities, like those elsewhere, were essentially "walking cities." Commercial and residential districts were ill defined and overlapping, and the rich and the poor often lived near each other. Despite the availability of inexpensive land on the urban periphery, city inhabitants crowded together. Streets were narrow, lot sizes small, and houses close to the curb. Tiny Elfreth's Alley in Philadelphia survives as an example of the compact nature of urban life two centuries ago. The easiest, cheapest, and most common method of getting about was by foot. Few people could afford the expense or nuisance of maintaining a horse and carriage; thus, there was a significant advantage in living within easy walking distance of the city's stores and businesses. Not surprisingly, the most fashionable and respectable residential addresses were close to the center of town, and neighborhoods generally deteriorated as one moved farther from the core. Indeed, the suburbs of the first quarter of the nineteenth century and before were little better than slums. Building regulations were designed to protect the city, not the periphery; thus, slaughterhouses, tanneries, and brothels were located beyond the city limits, where the air was often rancid from stagnant water, dead animals, and garbage. As late as 1849, one observer noted: "Nine-tenths of those whose rascalities have made Philadelphia so unjustly notorious live in the dens and shanties of the suburbs."

THE EMERGENCE OF THE "NORTH AMERICAN" PATTERN

Between 1825 and 1910, America's large cities underwent a dramatic spatial transformation. In effect, they were turned inside out, as a new pattern of peripheral affluence and central despair emerged. The shift was not sudden, but it was no less profound for its gradual character. In Philadelphia, a dozen suburban areas were consistently outgrowing the central city in population by 1850, as bankers, merchants, and physicians moved out to West Philadelphia or Germantown "for all the beauties of the country, within an easy and cheap communication with the city." In the first decade after the Gold Rush, wealthy San Francisco families exited from the downtown area to the heights of Fern (Nob) and Russian hills or to "steamboat suburbs" such as Oakland and Alameda. In Chicago, the number of suburbs contiguous to the city exceeded fifty even in 1875, and North Shore realtors were busy advertising "qualities of which the city is in a large degree bereft, namely its pure air, peacefulness, quietude, and natural scenery." And in Cincinnati, Sidney D. Maxwell wrote in 1870:

In whichever direction the beholder turns, he sees suburban places. The city is surrounded with hills that are already blossoming like a rose. Beautiful cottages, stately residences, and princely mansions are springing up as by magic. Villages are multiplying along the great thoroughfares. Tasteful suburban homes are each year, in increased number, skirting the waters of the Ohio or peering through the foliage that fringes the summits of the surrounding highlands.

Some of the nation's earliest, most extensive, and most famous suburban areas grew up around New York City. As early as 1823, Hezekiah Pierrepont advertised land in Brooklyn Heights, then undeveloped, as

situated directly opposite the southeast part of the city, and being the nearest country retreat, and easiest of access from the center of business that now remains unoccupied; the distance not exceeding an average fifteen to twenty-five minute walk, including the passage of the river; the ground elevated and perfectly healthy at all seasons; as a place of residence all the advantages of the country with most of the conveniences of the city.

Gentlemen whose business or profession require daily attendance into the city, cannot better, or with less expense, secure the health and comfort of their families than by uniting in such an association.

With its tree-shaded streets, pleasant homes, proximity to Manhattan, and general middle-class ambience, Brooklyn quickly developed many characteristics of the modern suburb. Regular ferry service across the East River to Fulton Street began in 1814; by 1830, Brooklyn's growth rate regularly exceeded that of its giant neighbor, and by 1850, New York newspapers had begun to express concern over "the desertion of the city by its men of wealth." In 1870, work began on the Brooklyn Bridge; thirteen years later the span was completed amid speculation that it was the eighth wonder of the world and the greatest construction achievement in history. Majestic in the sweep of its great cables, the bridge was wide enough for two rail lines, two double carriage lanes, and a footpath. By 1898, when it became one of the five boroughs of New York City, Brooklyn had well over a million residents.

The metropolis was also growing west toward New Jersey and north toward Westchester County. In 1861, a New Jersey booster admitted that "Newark and its vicinity—including the cities of Jersey City, Hoboken, Hudson, and Elizabeth, as well as the villages of Belleville, Orange, and Bloomfield,—has become but a suburb of the great city of New York." On May 6, 1871, a supplement to *Harper's Weekly* included a pictoral map of New York from the vantage point of a balloon. The caption explained:

> On the right, the city of Brooklyn, and the towns lying eastward as far as Jamaica and Hempstead, and northward as far as New Rochelle, with the railroads that make the suburbs of New York, and the islands and headlands of the Sound. On the left he will see Staten Island, with its picturesque villas, Jersey City, Newark and all the pleasant suburban villages and towns of New Jersey as far south as Perth Amboy, westward to West Orange, and northward to Caldwell and Paterson.

Noting such sprawl, the United States Census Bureau announced in 1880 that for certain purposes it would consider New York, Brooklyn, Jersey City, Newark, and Hoboken as "one great metropolitan community."

Suburbanization in New York became especially pronounced after 1860. Although Manhattan Island would not "fill up" until 1910, its decennial growth rate lagged behind its suburbs in every census after 1840. As early as 1825, some parts of the old city were losing population on an absolute as well as on a relative basis; by 1860, as houses and apartments gave way to factories and offices, the area of absolute decline included everything south of Houston Street. A few neighborhoods, notably the Lower East Side and Harlem, were becoming more congested as late as 1900, but the suburban trend for the region was by then unmistakably strong. Even Harlem was thought to be "the country."

The deconcentration process in New York differed in scale but not in substance from that experienced by Boston, Philadelphia, Baltimore, and other large cities. Four mutually reinforcing developments resulted in the physical spreading of the city and the exodus of the middle and upper classes: (1) the growth of the total urban population, especially the urban poor population, on an unprecedented scale; (2) the creation of larger, more impersonal, and more aesthetically obnoxious manufacturing and work organizations, coupled with an increase in urban nuisances; (3) the introduction and expansion of mass transportation systems; and (4) the articulation and popularization of a "suburban ideal."

In part, suburbanization was and is a function of urban growth. In 1840, less than 11 percent of the nation's populace lived in cities; by 1910, the proportion was more than 45 percent. The number of persons in cities of 100,000 or more rose from less than 1 million in 1840 to more than 27 million in 1910; the number of such cities grew from four to forty-four. At the same time, large cities were receiving a disproportionate share of impoverished immigrants from eastern and southern Europe. At a time when less than one-half the national population was urban, more than five-sixths of all first-generation Russian-Americans and Irish-Americans lived in cities. Among immigrants from Italy and Hungary, the proportion was more than three-fourths. This urban concentration was especially marked in the twenty-eight largest cities, which in 1890 contained less than 13 percent of the native-born and more than 33 percent of the foreign-born population of the United States.

But why did the poor newcomers settle at the center rather than at the edges of the city? In large part, the answer is simply that the upper and middle classes came to prefer the suburbs, and they abandoned their old neighborhoods to the less advantaged. And in part, the answer is related to the expansion of the central business district. Greater population concentration led to increasing demand for office and residential space, which caused land prices to rise. The greatest pressure was at the center, but it was difficult to determine just when and in which directions the central business districts (CBD) would expand. Anticipating windfall profits, speculators bought residential properties on the commercial fringe. But years, sometimes decades or longer, intervened between the purchase of these properties and their conversion to business use. Meanwhile, landlords who hoped that their houses or apartments would be demolished to make way for offices had little incentive to keep their holdings in proper repair or to listen to the complaints of tenants. Downtown residential areas, once the most prestigious in the city, deteriorated.

The expansion of central business districts was accompanied by an increase in the average size of factories. In the early years of the nineteenth century, before moving assembly lines or interchangeable parts were commonplace, most urban residents labored individually or in work groups of fewer than a half dozen persons. Typically, they lived and worked in proximity, often next door or in the same building. A journey to work of more than half a mile was unusual. As industrialization proceeded, the average size of factories, stores, and offices increased. In Philadelphia, for example, the number of people working in factories of more than 100 employees increased more than fiftyfold between 1860 and 1930, although the total population increased less than four times. Many of these larger organizations—refineries, machine tool industries, iron and steel mills, and chemical plants—created offensive odors or noises. Nearby neighborhoods lost status, particularly among professional and business people. The close relationship between home and employment weakened, and tendencies toward separation of work and residence increased.

Not every big factory was located in or near the center of the city. Urban congestion, prices, and traffic drove factories as well as individuals to the suburbs. Central area land was scarce and expensive, taxes were high, and municipal regulations were annoying. In 1898, Adna F. Weber noted that "statistical data regarding the location of factories in suburbs are not available, but the strong tendency in that direction is familiar to all Americans." Every city offered examples. Philadelphia's mammoth Baldwin Locomotive Works moved three times in the nineteenth century, each time farther out. In 1880, George M. Pullman began developing a model industrial town eight miles south of Chicago, where he hoped to capitalize on the Windy City's incomparable railroad connections while avoiding its legendary saloons, brothels, and gambling dens. Finally, in 1915, Graham R. Taylor made a study of the industrial suburbs of Chicago, St. Louis, Cincinnati, and Birmingham. "The suburbanite," he wrote, "who leaves business behind at nightfall for the cool green rim of the city would think the world had gone topsy-turvy if at 5:30 he rushed out of a factory set in a landscape of open fields and wooded hillsides, scrambled for a seat in a streetcar or grimy train and clattered back to the region of brick and pavement, of soot and noise and jostle." But, said Taylor, this was the situation being created by the "shifting of factories one by one to the edge of the city." Regardless of location, the increasing size of factories contributed to increasing differentiation of urban neighborhoods. With the passage of every year after about 1850, cities became less "mixed up" and more segregated by function, race, and income.

Advances in transportation technology also led directly to new patterns of urban settlement. In 1825, not even a rudimentary mass transit system existed anywhere in the United States. The first omnibuses (wagons with large wheels) appeared on Broadway in New York in the late 1820s. These crude, twelve-passenger contraptions were uncomfortable, slow, and relatively expensive, but they established the essential conditions for an urban transportation system: operation along a fixed route, according to a regular schedule, for a single fare. Placing the wagons on rails (horsecars) in the late 1850s gave them increased efficiency, comfort, and speed. The popularity of the vehicles rose proportionately; in New York City, the number of transit patrons increased from less than 7 million in 1853 to more than 36 million in 1860.

Meanwhile, ferries, steam railroads, and cable cars provided additional alternatives for the journey to work. Ferries were especially important on the East and Hudson rivers in New York, whereas cable cars found their most extensive use in San Francisco and Chicago. Steam railroads were also important in a number of areas. As early as 1860, for example, the seven railroads serving Boston had introduced season tickets and family rates for commuters and had experimented with free Sunday excursions for persons interested in buying property on the edges of the metropolitan region. The result was that by the time of the Civil War, the Boston railroads had persuaded 10 percent of the city's work force to use the rails and had converted such quiet villages as Dedham, Quincy, Brighton, and Medford into "railroad suburbs." And writing of the relationship between New York and Newark in 1878, an observer asserted:

> When, forty years ago, it took nearly two hours to span the distance between the two cities, the population of Newark was about 20,000. Now, when the distance is reduced to half an hours travel, Newark being joined to New York by no less than 198 trains daily over four lines of railroad, the population is more than six times greater.

But in terms of suburban development, the most important of the nineteenth century transit innovations was the electric streetcar, popularly known as the trolley. In 1888, in a large-scale experiment in Richmond, Frank Sprague demonstrated the feasibility of the new method.

Thereafter, the transition from horse to mechanical power was rapid, and by 1902, more than 96 percent of track mileage had been electrified. Moreover, by raising the speed of the cars to 15 or 18 miles per hour, electrification made practical the extension of tracks into undeveloped areas. Farmland as far as ten miles from the downtown district was subdivided for house lots, often by men with substantial investments in the transit companies. The results were "streetcar suburbs"— like Dorchester and Roxbury in Boston—on the fringes of every major city by 1900. Most of the residents of the new communities were middle-class workers or professional people who could afford ten to twenty cents per day for transit fares and whose jobs allowed them sufficient flexibility to commute for perhaps five to ten hours per week. The lower half of society could afford neither the money nor the time.

Although early mass transportation was relatively expensive, it was not inevitable that the middle and upper classes would gravitate to the urban edges. Many European cities have until recently offered a contrary pattern, as many communities continue to do all over the world. In the Union of South Africa, for example, the privileged white minority occupies the central areas of Johannesburg and Durban, whereas the disadvantaged and oppressed black population must struggle daily with crowded commuter trains. In Calcutta, Santiago, Lima, and Buenos Aires, the most degrading slums are to be found in the miserable quarters on the outskirts, where sanitary facilities, running water, and police and fire protection are practically unknown. In Caracas, the richest city in South America, the magnificent mountains surrounding the metropolis are dotted with the shacks of the very poor; the wealthy live lower in the valley.

In North America, on the other hand, the residents of large cities who could afford to live anywhere had usually decided by 1900 that the good life could best be found on the edges rather than near the centers of cities. This general pattern owes much to the antiurban heritage and agrarian tradition of the United States. Thomas Jefferson, Alexis de Tocqueville, Ignatius Donnelly, and William Jennings Bryan, among others, frequently articulated their distrust of the city and their faith in a people with close ties to the soil. One of the first men to translate the rural ideal into a "suburban ideal" was landscape architect Andrew Jackson Downing. Before the Civil War, he reached a large and predominantly well-to-do audience through a monthly journal of rural art and rural taste known as the *Horticulturist*. The Newburgh, New York, native seldom referred directly to suburbia, but he accepted the romantic concept of the superiority of rural existence over urban life. "In the United States," Downing wrote in 1848, "nature and domestic life are better than society and the manners of towns. Hence all sensible men gladly escape, earlier or later, and partially or wholly, from the turmoil of cities. Downing built secluded estates for the wealthy as concrete examples of the way a satisfying life style could be achieved and also inspired Alexander Jackson Davis's innovative residential community of Llewellyn Park, New Jersey, in the late 1850s.

Another important nineteenth century exponent of suburbia was Frederick Law Olmsted. Best known for his prize-winning design for Central Park in New York in 1857, Olmsted became the nation's most prolific and influential landscape architect in the generation after the Civil War. Unlike Downing, Olmsted saw the suburb not as an escape from the city but as a delicate synthesis of town and wilderness. With his partner, Calvert Vaux, Olmsted laid out suburbs in several American cities, the most famous of which is Riverside, which opened on the west side of Chicago in 1869. Meticulously planned in every detail, Riverside offered generous lots, curved roadways, and a parklike setting. Such communities, Olmsted thought, were "the most attractive, the most refined and the most soundly wholesome forms of domestic life, and the best application of the arts of civilization to which mankind has yet attained." And he made a prediction: "No great town can long exist without great suburbs."

Downing and Olmsted were the forerunners of even more vocal advocates of the naturalness and desirability of suburban living. As the nineteenth century drew to a close, a number of periodicals—*Countryside, House Beautiful, Country Life in America,* and *Suburban Life*— began to cater to the new suburbanites or to those city dwellers who longed to swap their cramped apartments for a house with a garden. As described by Sidney J. Low in 1891, it seemed so healthy and satisfying to be a suburban dweller: "His horizon is not limited by walls of brick and stone. If he does not live in the fields, he may have the fields at his door; he may be able to stretch his limbs by a walk over a breezy common, and get the smoke of the city out of his lungs by a ramble down a country lane."

One way to make the spacious fields and restful shade available to the city resident while adding a few social amenities to suburban life was to organize a "country club." The first of the genus in America was apparently the Country Club of Brookline, which was established in 1882 on a hundred picturesque acres about six miles from the State House in Boston. Within the next dozen years, such venerable institutions as the Westchester Country Club, the Larchmont Yacht Club, the Essex Country Club of New Jersey, and the Philadelphia Country Club had been established. Most found their raison d'être in the encouragement of outdoor sports in the company of social equals, but they soon developed more elaborate activities for women only or for whole families to go along with the golf, polo, tennis, and yachting.

For the wealthy, the country club added important benefits to suburban living that previously had been unattainable. For others, the suburban routine was considerably less exciting. Like their namesakes of the present day, many nineteenth century suburbs were "women's towns" during the week. Writing from Brooklyn before the Civil War, Walt Whitman often commented on the matriarchal and middle-class character of his town. And William Dean Howells, another early suburban resident, in 1870 described a typical weekday morning in his community:

> A sober tranquility reigns upon the dust and nodding weeds of Benicia Street. At that hour (11 a.m.) the organ-grinder and I are the only persons of our sex in the whole suburban population; all other husbands and fathers having eaten their breakfasts at seven o'clock, and stood up in the early horse-cars to Boston, whence they will return, with aching backs and quivering calves, half-pendant by leather straps from the roofs of the same luxurious conveyances, in the evening.

Then, as now, the towns to which the men returned had their share of problems. Soon after his maid quit because of the inconvenience of getting to work, Howells reflected upon the lack of urban services in Charlesbridge:

> We had not before this thought it was a grave disadvantage that our street was unlighted. Our street was not drained nor graded; no municipal cart ever came to carry away our ashes; there was not a water-butt within half a mile to save us from fire, nor more than one thousands part of a policeman to protect us from theft.

But in spite of everything, Howells enjoyed his life in Charlesbridge, and as editor of the *Atlantic Monthly* in 1878, he published an anonymous letter which perhaps paralleled his own sentiments: "In everything except proximity to their business . . . it seems to me the suburban people, in their spacious houses, designed often by the best professional skill, and affording in their interiors light for works of art and room for the varied activities of a refined life, have the best of it." If only the few could afford spacious houses or works of art, almost everyone could enjoy more light and grass in an outlying community.

Through this combination of rapid urban growth, industrial development, transit innovation, and rural ideology, five trends were apparent in all large cities by 1910 and in Philadelphia, New York, and Boston by 1860: (1) at the center of the city, residential density was declining as the area was converted to industrial or commercial use; (2) on the edges of the city, residential density was rising as metropolitan regions tended to spread themselves out; (3) throughout the urbanized areas, the average residential density was declining; in 1850, less than 25 percent of the urban population lived at densities of less than fifty per acre, and by 1890, about 45 percent lived at or below this level of dispersal; (4) throughout the entire metropolitan regions, the density curve representing the variation in density from one ward to the next was leveling—that is, the difference between the most congested districts was becoming smaller; and (5) the wealth of peripheral residents was increasing relative to that of persons in the core. A sixth tendency, that of decreasing residential density with increasing distance from the center, remained operative.

These important trends toward suburbanization in the nineteenth century are not widely recognized because the earliest suburbs did not long remain suburbs. They lost their independence because municipal governments adopted the philosophy that "bigger is better" and expanded their populations and area by moving their boundaries outward to recapture their departing citizens or to insure that new residents would not be part of a separate community. Without exception, such adjustments were the dominant method of population growth in every American city of consequence before 1920, and in the cases of Phoenix, Houston, Memphis, Dallas, and other large communities which continue to register population gains, it remains the most important cause. If annexation (the addition of unincorporated land to the city) or consolidation (the absorption of one municipal government by an adjacent one) had not taken place, there would now be no great cities in the United States in the political sense of the term. Only New York City would have grown as large as 1 million people, and it would have remained confined to the island of Manhattan. Viewed another way, if annexation had not been successful in the nineteenth century, many large cities would have been surrounded by suburbs even before the Civil War. Such cities as St. Louis, Pittsburgh, Cleveland, and Philadelphia contained in 1970 less than one-half the population of their standard metropolitan areas. Their boundaries have not been altered in almost half a century, and they are now extreme examples of older cities being strangled by a ring of suburbs. A St. Louis school administrator recently complained that suburbanites have "erected a wall of separation which towers above the city limits and constitutes a barrier as effective as did those of ancient Jericho or that of the Potsdamer Platz in Berlin." Yet if these cities had been unable to add territory in the nineteenth century, their central areas would have contained a far smaller percentage of the metropolitan population in 1900 than they in fact contained in 1970.

Appropriately, the most significant annexations in the nineteenth century involved the nation's three largest cities—New York, Chicago, and Philadelphia. In 1854, the City of Brotherly Love expanded its area from 2 to 129 square miles by absorbing such formerly independent suburbs as Spring Garden, Southwark, Kensington, and Moyamensing. Chicago's largest consolidation took place in 1889, when 133 square miles and most of what is now the South Side were added. The new city boundaries included pleasant residential villages such as Hyde Park, Kenwood, and Woodlawn as well as such outlying industrial communities as Grand Crossing and Pullman. New York City was the scene of the most important boundary adjustment in American history when in 1898 Brooklyn, Queens, Staten Island, and part of the Bronx were added to Manhattan. The size of the city increased from 40 to 300 square miles; the population jumped by well over 1 million.

Although smaller cities did not match in size the additions of the major metropolises, every large city shared in the expansion boom. St. Louis increased its area from 4.5 to 14 square miles in 1856 and to 17 square miles in 1870. The biggest change came in 1876, when city voters overwhelmed the opposition of rural St. Louis County, raising the municipal area to 61 square miles and creating an independent city. Boston added about 15 square miles by joining with Roxbury in 1868 and Dorchester in 1870, while New Orleans absorbed Carrolton in 1876, which gave the Crescent City most of the area it occupies today. Baltimore more than doubled its size in 1888; Minneapolis, Cleveland, Cincinnati, and Pittsburgh more than tripled through a series of small nineteenth century additions. Thus, suburbs became neighborhoods, and in the official census reports, cities registered startling population increases until well into the twentieth century. In actuality, what was called the growth of Chicago or Philadelphia or Memphis was actually the building up of residential communities on their edges.

THE EMERGENCE OF THE MODERN SUBURB

Between 1900 and 1945, the foundations were laid for the creation of a predominantly suburban nation. In older cities in the East and Midwest, annexation fell into disuse. Among twenty large cities which increased their area by 170 percent between 1870 and 1920, the corresponding figure for the half century between 1920 and 1970 was a minuscule 14 percent. But the outward trend continued and expanded, with the wealthy moving from the inner suburbs to the outer suburbs. By the 1920s, sociologists at the University of Chicago had constructed a concentric zone model to describe the way in which residential neighborhoods improved in quality with increasing distance from the urban core. This "North American pattern" became so dominant that a suburban rabbi recently confessed that when he was growing up in Brooklyn, the Five Towns area of Long Island, even more than Israel, represented the "promised land."

Technological developments such as automobiles, telephones, radios, septic tanks, electric lights, and laundry machines increased the appeal of the twentieth cenutry suburb by bringing the amenities and conveniences of the city to widely scattered subdivisions. But the most basic impulse toward suburbia remained as before: the desire for a home. And where was an individual more likely to find a house than in the developing periphery?

Very few of the new neighborhoods and suburbs were "planned" by experts, a defect which advocates of the garden city and the garden suburb hoped to remedy. The garden city idea was conceived by Ebenezer Howard, a London court stenographer who had lived briefly in Chicago. In 1898, he published *Tomorrow*, a small volume which proposed a new kind of community that would combine the best features of town and country. The garden city would be limited to 32,000 people and would be surrounded by a permanent agricultural belt that would produce food for the community and would prevent suburban sprawl. All land would be owned by the community as a whole, and enough industry would be included to insure self-sufficiency. In 1899, the Garden City Association was formed in England, but the more ambitious plans of the organization were not realized. A quarter of a century later, only two such communities had been built.

Howard's plan had even less success in the United States, where no garden city was ever built. The somewhat similar "garden suburb," a planned residential community on the outskirts of a city, did enjoy a temporary popularity, however. The most important garden suburb was built on Long Island in 1909 by the Russell Sage Foundation. Forest Hills Gardens featured a shopping plaza, a commuter railroad station, curvilinear streets, spacious Tudor-style houses, and a network of small parks. Not far from the Forest Hills project, realtor Alexander Bing built Sunnyside Gardens in Queens fifteen years later. Bing conceived a new town design which eliminated side alleys and used the space saved for small commons in the center. Both of these garden suburbs, however, differed from the garden city concept in that they were not self-sufficient and that they provided homes only for persons of above-average income.

During the 1930s, Ebenezer Howard's ideas threatened to gain an American significance that had previously eluded them when the federal government undertook the greenbelt town program. Designed by Rexford Tugwell, a Columbia University economics professor and member of Roosevelt's brain trust, the plan was to establish, at locations well removed from large cities, new and complete towns that would provide a healthful and safe environment as well as jobs for former residents of urban slums. The greenbelt town program ultimately failed, however; the Roosevelt administration never completed the project, and the three half-finished towns became ordinary suburbs.

Two other government programs had a more lasting influence on the development of metropolitan America. Municipal zoning and the long-term, low-interest mortgage loan were developments of social technology that gave official sanction to the suburban ideal and institutionalized the North American pattern.

Zoning, which is the power to control the use of land and the size of buildings, originated in Germany about 1900. Before that time, many American cities had regulated the construction and height of structures, but New York's comprehensive zoning law of 1916 was the first to limit the general *usage* of land in an important American metropolis. The Gotham ordinance was passed after a group of Fifth Avenue merchants became concerned over "the gathering together of factory operatives at the noon hour on Fifth Avenue." Their objection was that ordinary garment workers were eating lunch from brown paper sacks within sight of the patrons of the nation's most exclusive shops. Their solution was a zoning law that would push the garment district west of Seventh Avenue. In the process, they revolutionized the real estate industry.

In theory, zoning was designed to protect the interests of all citizens by limiting land speculation and congestion. And it was popular. Although it represented an extraordinary growth of municipal power, nearly everyone supported zoning. By 1926, seventy-six cities had adopted ordinances similar to that of New York. By 1936, 1,322 cities (85 percent of the total) had them, and zoning laws were affecting more property than all national laws relating to business.

In actuality, zoning was a device to keep poor people and obnoxious industries out of affluent areas. And in time, it also became a cudgel used by suburban areas to whack the central city. Advocates of land-use restrictions in overwhelming proportion were residents of the fringe. They sought through minimum lot and set-back requirements to insure that only members of acceptable social classes could settle in their privileged sanctuaries. Southern cities even used zoning to enforce racial segregation. And in suburbs everywhere, North and South, zoning was used by the people who already lived within the arbitrary boundaries of a community as a method of keeping everyone else out. Apartments, factories, and "blight," euphemisms for blacks and people of limited means, were rigidly excluded.

While zoning provided a way for suburban areas to become secure enclaves for the well-to-do, it forced the core city to provide economic facilities for the whole area and homes for people the suburbs refused to admit. Simply put, land-use restrictions tended to protect residential interest in the suburbs and commercial interests in the cities, because the residents of the core usually lived on land owned by absentee landlords who were more interested in financial returns than neighborhood preferences. For the man who owned land but did not live on it, the ideal situation was to have his parcel of earth zoned for commercial or industrial use. With more options, the property often gained in value. In Chicago, for example, three times as much land was zoned for commercial use as could ever have been profitably employed for such purposes. This overzoning prevented inner-city residents from receiving the same protection from commercial incursions as was afforded suburbanites. Instead of becoming a useful tool for the rational ordering of land in metropolitan areas, zoning became a way for suburbs to pirate from the city only its desirable functions and residents. Suburban governments became like so many residential hotels, fighting for the upper-income trade while trying to force the deadbeats to go elsewhere.

Federal home loan policies have also been especially beneficial to suburbs. During the 1930s, President Franklin D. Roosevelt and Congress became concerned over the high foreclosure rate as tens of thousands of families proved unable to meet their mortgage payments. Meanwhile, the construction industry was at a virtual standstill. The New Deal responded with federally sponsored mortgage insurance programs and incentives for building. Congressional support for the long-term, monthly payment mortgage with low interest increased even more after World War II, when the government adopted the position that the veteran should own his own home. Through the GI Bill, former servicemen were able to buy homes with as little as one dollar down. By 1972, the federal government had aided more than 10 million families to buy homes, most of them in the suburbs.

Because Congress understood the intensity of the American preference for single-family, detached houses, important provisions in the Federal Housing Administration (FHA) legislation worked to the advantage of new neighborhoods, most of which were in the suburbs. Home improvement loans were difficult to get and were issued only for short periods. New home loans, by contrast, were available under favorable, long-term conditions. Similarly, loans to contractors for building apartments were inhibited through higher rates. Families were thus encouraged by the government to buy new, single-family, detached homes rather than to repair older ones or to move to apartment buildings.

Guidelines not in the legislation but established by the FHA bureaucracy and the real estate industry also stimulated suburban growth. The agency was run as if it were a private business. To protect its investments, the FHA rated neighborhoods according to the estimated safety of housing loans made there. Four categories were established, and each rating was translated into a color, which was then placed on secret maps in FHA offices. Every block in every city had a rating and a color. High ratings were given to homogeneous and new neighborhoods that were well away from the problems of the city. The lowest rating, red, was assigned to communities which contained such "adverse influences," as smoke, odor, or "inharmonious racial and nationality groups." The presence of older properties and slums dramatically lowered the rating of any area and, because of limited funding, practically insured that a neighborhood would be ineligible for federal funds. As urban renewal critic Jane Jacobs has noted, such credit-blacklisting maps were accurate forecasts because they were self-fulfilling prophecies.

A prospective homeowner could increase his chances of acceptance by the FHA by selecting his house in a white, middle-class neighborhood with "enforced zoning, subdivision regulations, and suitable restrictive covenants." With that sort of logic behind federal financing, only 1 percent of the government insured homes constructed between 1945 and 1965 went to blacks. In accordance with its New Deal mission, the FHA was successful in banishing from the land the specter of frequent mortgage foreclosures, and in providing assistance to families that otherwise could not have arranged for adequate loans. In the process, it provided an enormous subsidy to the suburbs.

THE LEGACY OF HENRY FORD

Even more important than zoning and mortgages in determining the shape of the metropolitan landscape have been the road and the car. The gasoline-powered, internal-combustion engine was not invented in the United States; that honor probably goes to Karl Benz and Gottlieb Daimler in Germany in 1885. The first workable American motor vehicle was not built until 1893, when a horseless carriage was fashioned by the Duryea brothers. As late as 1900, when about 8,000 of the curious machines were on American streets, domestic automobile development trailed that of Europe both qualitatively and quantitatively.

Within the space of a single generation, however, Henry Ford turned a novelty of the rich into a necessity of the middle class. Other pioneers such as Ransom E. Olds and Walter Chrysler contributed to the increasing American dominance in automobile production, but it was Ford whose dream of a car for the multitude resulted in the most popular vehicle the world has ever known—the Model T. The tin lizzie was introduced in 1908; when production was halted in 1928 almost sixteen million of them had rolled off the assembly line and every other car on earth was a Ford. Meanwhile, American automobile registrations climbed to 100,000 in 1906, to one million by 1913, and to ten million by 1922. By 1927, when the United States was building about 85 percent of the world's automobiles, there was one motor vehicle for every five Americans. In the 1940s, a Hollywood movie based on John Steinbeck's novel *The Grapes of Wrath* was exhibited throughout the Soviet Union as an example of the distress of capitalism. After less than two months it was removed from the theaters, however, because the Russian people were less impressed by the poverty they saw on the screen than by the fact that everyone seemed to own a car.

With the automobile came the highway. Prior to 1900, there were almost no paved surfaces between cities in the United States, not from a lack of ability to build them but from a lack of demand. For trips of any distance, the railroad was smoother, faster, and more economical than any other form of overland travel. The motor car, and to a lesser degree the bicycle, changed all this. The Federal Road Act of 1916 offered funds to states that organized highway departments; the Federal Road Act of 1921 designated 200,000 miles of road as "primary" and thus eligible for federal funds on a fifty-fifty matching basis. Meanwhile, the adoption of gasoline taxes, beginning with a one cent per gallon levy in Oregon in 1919, provided the necessary state revenues for a massive road-building program. By 1925, the value of highway construction projects exceeded $1 billion for the first time; thereafter, it fell below that figure only during a few years of the Great Depression and World War II. Bridges such as that over the Delaware River between Philadelphia and Camden (1926) and the George Washington Bridge, which connected New York City with northern New Jersey (1931), also spurred suburban growth and increased the demand for feeder highways.

Most of the early road mileage was only one or two lanes in width, but in urban areas wider thoroughfares were soon proposed. The bucolic and meandering Bronx River Parkway, begun in 1906 and completed in 1923, was the nation's first landscaped highway. Running from Bruckner Boulevard in the Bronx alongside the New York Central tracks to White Plains, it stimulated commuting from such Westchester County suburbs as Scarsdale, Mount Vernon, Bronxville, and New Rochelle. Within ten years, the New York area also witnessed the construction of the Hutchinson River Parkway (1928), the Saw Mill River Parkway (1929), and the Cross County Parkway (1931). The Henry Hudson Parkway, the first metropolitan freeway to have limited access, no grade crossings, and service stations of its own, was begun in New York City in 1934, and in 1940, the nation's first long-distance superhighway, the Pennsylvania Turnpike, was opened.

The highway almost created its own raison d'être; many of the factories, shopping centers, and subdivisions of the suburbs were originally attracted by the transportation routes. Its significance in the growth of automobile suburbs can be illustrated by Detroit. Six major arteries radiate from the Motor City toward Pontiac, Toledo, Lansing, Windsor, Ann Arbor, and Port Huron. The road to Pontiac, Woodward Avenue, is Detroit's main street; it begins at the Detroit River and follows the original Saginaw Trail. The twenty-five mile stretch between the city and Pontiac offers several examples of commuter suburbs that sprang up in response to a good transportation facility—the highway itself.

As Woodward Avenue angles away from Detroit, it passes through communities such as Birmingham and Ferndale, which had a long independent history before they became commuter suburbs, as well as villages such as Royal Oak, which have developed more recently. The Woodward Avenue "family" includes Berkley, a poor neighborhood with homes built of whatever materials were available, as well as Bloomfield Hills, one of the wealthiest communities in the United States. All share a dependence on the highway. In 1923, when a Wider Woodward Project was started to provide an eight-lane concrete road all the way to Pontiac, every town along the way joined in enthusiastic support. When the road was finished in the late 1920s, local boosters proclaimed it the nation's best, and developers began to advertise land in terms of its distance from Woodward Avenue. The new facility enabled executives to travel twenty-five miles to their offices in Detroit in less than forty-five minutes.

The decade of the 1920s was the first in which the road and the car had full impact. In the seven years between 1922 and 1929, new houses were begun at the rate of 833,000 per year, a pace more than double that of any previous seven-year period. New suburbs sprouted on the edges of every major city. Of the seventy-one new incorporations in Illinois and Michigan in the 1920s, two-thirds were Chicago, St. Louis, or Detroit suburbs. Statistics for individual communities were startling. Grosse Pointe, near Detroit, grew by 725 percent in the ten years; Elmwood Park, near Chicago, by 717 percent; and Beverly Hills, near Los Angeles, by 2,485 percent. Long Island's Nassau County almost tripled in population. Appropriately, the central character in F. Scott Fitzgerald's novel of the 1920s, *The Great Gatsby*, came east to "make it" in New York and then promptly purchased a suburban estate on Long Island.

The benefits of this suburban boom were not evenly distributed; the biggest gainers were usually real estate promoters who owned land somewhere near the new highways. Every multilane ribbon of concrete was like the touch of Midas, transforming old pastures into precious property. Of course, not all speculators got rich; some even lost money. Particularly in the latter part of the 1920s, overanxious subdividers platted more land than could be occupied, and many were thus driven into bankruptcy. Those who inaugurated their land promotion schemes earlier generally had better luck, and some of their park-like communities—such as Coral Gables, Florida, and Roland Park in Baltimore—retain their charm today. The most successful such developer with J. C. Nichols, who planned Kansas City's Country Club District around 1912. Offering "spacious ground for permanently protected homes, surrounded with ample space for air and sunshine," this six-thousand-acre residential setting became a national model for open spaces, set-back lines, and self-perpetuating deed restrictions, which were the acceptable way of keeping Jews and Negroes out of the preserve.

As a stimulus to the development of suburbs, the automobile had no greater impact than the mass transit innovations of the nineteenth century. In fact, even in the era of the Model T, some of the most spectacular suburban ventures were expressly tied to the fare boxes of streetcar lines. Niles Center, near Chicago; large parts of Queens in New York; and Shaker Heights, southeast of Cleveland, were all designed partially to increase transit revenues. The Ohio community, a several-thousand-acre tract on the site of an old Shaker religious colony, was the work of the Van Sweringen brothers. They developed an upper-middle-class community renowned for its preservation of parklands, its imaginative street plans, and its rigid architectural and construction standards. In 1920, the Van Sweringen electric rapid transit lines reached Shaker Heights; in the next decade, population grew by 1,000 percent, and real estate valuation increased more than fivefold.

However, the automobile did more than simply add additional layers to the streetcar suburbs which already surrounded every city. Unlike the fixed trolley tracks, which almost always led downtown and thus encouraged transit patrons to maintain their economic and social ties with the core, the private car encouraged crosstown or lateral movement and, if anything, discouraged travel to the increasingly traffic-snarled city center. The streetcar was permanent and inflexible; the automobile would go almost anywhere. In the late 1920s, President Herbert Hoover appointed a commission to examine contemporary trends in American life. Published in 1933 as *Recent Trends in the United States*, the report said this about the car:

> In no inconsiderable degree the rapid popular acceptance of the new vehicle centered in the fact that it gave to the owner a control over his movements that the older agencies denied. Close at hand and ready for instant use, it carried its owner from door to destination by routes he himself selected, and on schedules of his own making; baggage inconveniences were minimized and perhaps most important of all, the automobile made possible the movement of an entire family at costs that were relatively small. Convenience augmented utility and accelerated adoption of the vehicle.

The different characteristics of streetcar and automobile can be illustrated by considering the kind of retailing pattern which each encouraged. At the center of every mass transit system was the great department store—John Wanamaker's in Philadelphia; Gimbel's, R. H. Macy's, and A. T. Stewart's in New York; Marshall Field and Carson, Pirie, Scott in Chicago; Hudson's in Detroit; Rich's in Atlanta; Jordan Marsh in Boston. Without exception, these giant downtown stores experienced their greatest growth and relative success between 1870 and 1930, the time of the trolley.

In contrast, the outlying shopping center, whose formula was six square feet of parking for every square foot of selling area, became the symbol of the automobile culture. This new method of retailing was presaged in the 1920s, when Sears, Roebuck and Company embraced the concept of "America on wheels." Executives of this giant Chicago mail-order house decided that their new class A stores would be built in the suburbs. Such locations would offer the advantage of lower rentals, yet because of increasing automobile registrations, they would be within reach of potential customers. The nation's first shopping center, a complex of stores with off-street parking, opened inside Baltimore's city limits in 1907. After Nichols built a magnificent retailing plaza in his Kansas City Country Club District, the former was designated a "neighborhood" center and the latter a "suburban" one. Shortly after World War II, the concept was further expanded by the construction of one-hundred-store "regional" shopping centers remote from downtown. Prototypes such as Northgate, near Seattle; Shopper's World, outside Boston; and Lakewood, outside Los Angeles, were opened by 1950, and within twenty years more than 13,000 such centers had been built in the United States. Meanwhile, downtown areas, especially in older suburbs and smaller cities, became virtual ghost towns of dusty, underused shops.

THE CONTEMPORARY SUBURB

The depression of the 1930s slowed suburban growth as the scarcity of money and jobs encouraged people to stay put. During World War II, armaments production naturally took precedence over the building of homes, although the government did build factories in the suburbs to reduce the danger of enemy air attacks. In Detroit, for example, the Chrysler Tank Arsenal and the Hudson Naval Arsenal were erected beyond the city's boundaries in Warren Township.

The coming of peace in 1945 was followed by a generation of economic prosperity which provided new families with the financial means to act upon their desire for new homes. A vast surge in road construction supplemented the economic boom. Highway expenditures topped

$2 billion in 1949, $3 billion in 1953, and $4 billion in 1955. New housing more than kept pace. Between 1946 and 1955, more than twice as many new houses were built as were constructed in the previous *fifteen* years. The peak year of this record-breaking construction decade was 1950, when over 1 million single-family houses were begun, almost half of them financed by the Federal Housing Administration (FHA) or the Veterans' Administration (VA).

The suburban boom continued into the late 1950s and 1960s on a slightly less dramatic scale. An important stimulus was the passage in 1956 of the Interstate Highway Act, which initiated the largest public works project in history. The 42,500-mile, $60 billion road network has been a special favorite of the highway lobby, one of the broadest-based of all pressure groups. It consists of the oil, rubber, automobile, asphalt, and construction industries; the car dealers and renters; the trucking and bus concerns; the banks and advertising agencies that depend on the companies involved; the American Automobile Association; state and local officials who want the federal government to pay for new highways in their areas; and labor unions. President Dwight D. Eisenhower gave four reasons for advocating the interstate highway program: current highways were unsafe, cars too often became snarled in traffic jams, poor roads saddled business with high costs for transportation, and modern highways were needed because "in case of atomic attack on our key cities, the road net must permit quick evacuation of target areas." Not a single word was said about the impact of highways on cities and suburbs, although the concrete thoroughfares and the thirty-five-ton tractor-trailers which used them encouraged the continued outward movement of industries toward the beltways and expressway interchanges. Moreover, the interstate system, paid for with 90 percent federal funds, helped continue the downward spiral of public transportation and virtually guaranteed that future urban growth would perpetuate a centerless sprawl. Soon after the bill was passed by the Senate, Lewis Mumford wrote sadly: "When the American people, through their Congress, voted a little while ago for a $26 billion highway program, the most charitable thing to assume is that they hadn't the faintest notion of what they were doing."

Large-scale builders knew what they were doing; taking advantage of the various subsidies of the federal government, they developed communities of every size, shape, and income level. Orange County, California, the home of Disneyland, became the nation's fastest growing suburban area, but imposing statistics could be cited for the outer rings of every metropolitan area. Cities varied somewhat in the speed of de-concentration, but not so much as is commonly supposed. New cities in the Southwest, for example, experienced a greater out-migration from the core than older cities in the East. The Census Bureau reported the opposite, however, because the newer communities were annexing vast tracts of new subdivisions, whereas the older cities were trapped within outmoded boundaries.

The move to the suburbs was almost self-generating. As larger numbers of affluent citizens moved out, shopping centers and jobs followed. In turn, this attracted more families, more roads, and more industries. The city was caught in a reverse cycle. As businesses and taxpayers left, property values declined or failed to rise proportionally with inflation, houses became older and more deteriorated, and low-income families moved in. The new residents required as many services from the city government as did the old, but they were less able to pay high property taxes. When municipal authorities had to increase expenditures, they levied higher property taxes, thus encouraging more middle-class homeowners to leave, causing the cycle to repeat. In Newark, currently the most financially impoverished major city in the United States, local real estate taxes are more than twice as high as they are in nearby suburbs, which offer better schools and public services.

The families that moved to Anaheim or Levittown or Park Forest or a thousand lesser-known suburbs after World War II were similar to earlier suburban migrants. Their motivation was simple: they wanted a house, and they wanted that house to be in a clean, healthy neighborhood that promised decent schools for their children. Proximity to work was not as important as a house and a yard. To a lesser extent, the suburbanites sought to separate themselves from the problems of race, crime, narcotics, congestion, and confusion. "Escape to Scarborough Manor," suggested the advertisements. "Escape from cities too big, too polluted, too crowded, too strident to call home."

The new homesites did not always provide the better life that the realtors promised, however. Postwar developers, thinking mostly of profits, crammed as many houses as possible onto a given piece of land. Bulldozers removed every vestige of the original vegetation, so that row upon row of look-alike houses could be built quickly. Along the feeder highways, garish commercial strips blinked neon messages from the entrances of fast-food outlets, gas stations, and motels of every variety. Joseph Wood Krutch dubbed the result a "sloburb" and asserted that if an individual were carried into one blindfolded, he would not even be able to tell what section of the nation he was in. And Russell Baker has bemoaned the fact that either America is a shopping center or that the one shopping center in existence is moving around the country at the speed of light.

According to some observers, the life style of the newest suburbs is as artificial as the physical environment. Fathers, weary from ten hours of commuting every week, are supposedly reduced to the status of weekend visitors in their own homes, and women fare no better in their roles as semiprofessional chauffeurs. In fact, anthropologist Margaret Mead has argued that women will never assume an equal position in American society as long as they are isolated in bedroom communities.

But for all the criticism, it is necessary to remember that the suburbs have grown and doubtless will continue to grow because they satisfy the needs of those who live there better than any currently available alternative. In the late 1950s, Herbert J. Gans lived in and studied Levittown, New Jersey, a community seventeen miles from Philadelphia built entirely by Levitt and Sons. After more than two years of participant-observation in the new subdivision, the Columbia University sociologist concluded that most residents enjoyed their homes and took pleasure in the social contacts available in the largely residential setting. He did not find the boredom and malaise so often attributed to the suburban family, and he did not find that Levittowners were shaped by their environment. Rather, Gans reported that the attitudes of the residents were generally shaped before the move. All in all, Gans concluded, Levittown was a "good place to live."

In every case, the particular appeal to a given suburb or neighborhood is a personal matter. In recent years, however, it appears that the prospect of escape from the problems of the central city has become increasingly important. For example, race has become a particularly explosive issue. Since the end of the Civil War, blacks have increased their representation in American cities, North and South. In the larger metropolises, the shift was especially noticeable after World War I, when Afro-Americans replaced European immigrants as the primary source of cheap labor and as the most conspicuous occupants of the urban slums. Of course, they were effectively kept out of the newer suburban developments by restrictive covenants, "understandings" among realtors, zoning restrictions, and ultimately, violence. Civil rights laws passed since 1957, and particularly the open-housing law, which was passed within a few months of the Reverend Martin Luther King's assassination in 1968, have removed some of the more overt forms of racial discrimination in housing. But in 1970, only 9 of every 200 suburbanites were black, and *suburbia* will likely continue to be a synonym for *white*.

In recent years, some inner suburbs have become acquainted with problems that were once considered peculiar to the central city. During the 1960s, for example, poverty, unemployment, crime, and narcotics addiction all increased faster in the suburbs than in the core cities. Financial distress has followed, as working-class fringe areas have found themselves unable to pay for quality schools without a substantial industrial or commercial tax base. Hamtramck, Michigan, a smoke-smudged, independent suburb surrounded by Detroit, is the only bankrupt community in the nation.

In the long run, the experience of Hamtramck may not prove unusual, partly because the distinctions between city and suburb are largely transitory; they are opposite sides of the same coin. Suburbanization is a continuing, shifting process. As the core of the city expands, the periphery moves farther out. Many contemporary slums, such as Woodlawn in Chicago or Harlem in New York or Bedford in Brooklyn, were once distant suburbs that offered a bucolic atmosphere quite unlike that of the cities which finally engulfed them. Perhaps today's suburbs will lose their privileged status to newer neighborhoods. In any event, contemporary problems, whether they are related to narcotics, disease, or economic depression, do not respect political and suburban boundaries. Increasingly, all metropolitan residents are coming to live in "Spread City," or as one cynic termed it, "Phantom City," because you cannot tell when you enter or when you leave.

Many people make the easy choice. Their solution to contemporary problems is escape to a place yet farther out on the fringe, where they can pretend that they have nothing whatever to do with the distant city. Meanwhile, blight absorbs more and more of the older communities. Cities can thrive only if people accept the proposition that affluent rings around dying cores will ultimately prove disastrous for both the cities and the suburbs. But the prospects are not bright. A century ago Frederick Law Olmsted outlined his hopes for suburbanization:

> The present outward tendency of town population is not so much an ebb as a higher rise of the same flood (of urbanization), the end of which must be, not a sacrifice of urban conveniences, but their combination with the special charms and substantial advantages of rural conditions of life.

Then, as now, however, the promise was only for the well-to-do.

SELECTED BIBLIOGRAPHY

There is no general history of suburbs or suburbanization in America. A brief but provocative essay on the subject is Leo F. Schnore, "The Timing of Metropolitan Decentralization: A Contribution to the Debate," *Journal of the American Institute of Planners*, 25 (November 1959), 200-206. The best study of changing residential patterns in the pre–Civil War city is Allen Pred, *The Spatial Dynamics of Urban Industrial Growth: Interpretive and Theoretical Essays* (Cambridge, Mass., 1966). A methodologically interesting account of intraurban geographical mobility is Peter R. Knights, *The Plain People of Boston, 1830–1860: A Study in City Growth* (New York, 1971). Contemporary reports of suburbanization before 1860 include "The Diary of Sidney George Fisher, 1859–1860," *Pennsylvania Magazine of History and Biography*, 87 (April 1963), 189-225; and George Rogers Taylor, "Philadelphia in Slices; By George G. Foster," *Pennsylvania Magazine of History and Biography*, 93 (January 1969).

On the early development of mass transit in the United States see Charles J. Kennedy, "Commuter Services in the Boston Area, 1835–1860," *Business History Review*, 36 (Summer 1962), 153-70; Glen E. Holt, "The Changing Perception of Urban Pathology: An Essay on the Development of Mass Transit in the United States," in Kenneth T. Jackson and Stanley K. Schultz, editors, *Cities in American History* (New York, 1972), 324-43; and George Rogers Taylor, "The Beginnings of Mass Transportation in Urban America," *Smithsonian Journal of History*, 1 (1966), No. 2, 35-50, No. 3, 31-54. For the development of mass transit in the last part of the century, Sam Bass Warner, Jr., *Streetcar Suburbs: The Process of Growth in Boston, 1870–1900* (Cambridge, Mass., 1962), is indispensable. Students interested in comparative history will want to consult H. J. Dyos's meticulous *Victorian Suburb: A Study of the Growth of Camberwell* (Leicester, 1961) and David Ward, "A Comparative Historical Geography of Streetcar Suburbs in Boston, Massachusetts and Leeds, England: 1850–1920," *Annals of the Association of American Geographers*, 54 (1964), 477-89.

On the development of the suburban ideal, the best study is Peter J. Schmitt, *Back to Nature: The Arcadian Myth in Urban America* (New York, 1969).

Olmsted's ideas may be examined in Albert Fein, editor, *Landscape into City-scape: Frederick Law Olmsted's Plans for a Greater New York City* (Ithaca, N.Y., 1968). The reflections of William Dean Howells on deconcentration are contained in his *Suburban Sketches* (Boston, 1871).

For the early part of the twentieth century, the best book on the move away from urban cores is Harlan Paul Douglass, *The Suburban Trend* (New York, 1925). The author differentiated between urban, suburban, and rural zones and noted that suburbs tended to be nonproductive of goods and critical services. Another important book written during the period is Graham R. Taylor, *Satellite Cities: A Study of Industrial Suburbs* (New York, 1915). Amos H. Hawley, *The Changing Shape of Metropolitan America: Deconcentration since 1920* (Glencoe, Ill., 1956) is dry and unconvincing.

On the history of zoning, the standard works are Richard F. Babcock, *The Zoning Game: Municipal Practices and Policies* (Madison, Wis., 1966); Stanislaw J. Makielski, *The Politics of Zoning: The New York Experience* (New York, 1966); and Seymour I. Toll, *Zoned American* (New York, 1969). There is no satisfactory study of the FHA's impact on urban and suburban spatial patterns.

The only recent overview of the growth of cities through municipal annexation is Kenneth T. Jackson, "Metropolitan Government Versus Suburban Autonomy: Politics on the Crabgrass Frontier," in Jackson and Schultz, editors, *Cities in American History*, 442-62. Earlier studies which remain useful are: Richard Bigger and James D. Kitchen, *How the Cities Grew: A Century of Municipal Independence and Expansion in Metropolitan Los Angeles* (Los Angeles, 1952); Roderick D. McKenzie, *The Metropolitan Community* (New York, 1933); and Paul Studenski, editor, *The Government of Metropolitan Areas in the United States* (New York, 1930).

The literature of the post–World War II suburbs has been vast. Two stimulating essays that should be the starting point for anyone interested in the modern suburb are Herbert J. Gans, "Urbanism and Suburbanism as Ways of Life: A Re-Evaluation of Some Definitions," in Arnold Rose, editor, *Human Behavior and Social Processes* (Boston, 1962), 625-48, and Bennett M. Berger, "Suburbia and the American Dream," *The Public Interest*, 2 (Winter 1966), 80-91. The most famous single work is William H. Whyte's classic study, *The Organization Man* (New York, 1956). An equally distinguished and more recent study of a single community is Herbert J. Gans, *The Levit-towners: Ways of Life and Politics in a New Suburban Community* (New York, 1967). Other important books on the subject include: Bennett M. Berger, *Working Class Suburb: A Study of Auto Workers in Suburbia* (Berkeley, Calif., 1960); Scott Donaldson, *The Suburban Myth* (New York, 1969); William M. Dobriner, editor, *The Suburban Community* (New York, 1958); Robert C. Wood, *Suburbia: Its People and Their Politics* (Boston, 1958); and Benjamin Chinitz, editor, *City and Suburb: The Economics of Metropolitan Growth* (Englewood Cliffs, N.J., 1965).

15

The 1950s: The Era of No Hard Feelings

STEPHEN J. WHITFIELD

• The 1950s present a decade of political conformity remarkable even for the United States. Following President Harry Truman's shift of American foreign policy to the right in the late 1940s, ideological differences became virtually nonexistent at the highest levels of government. Political leaders quarrelled over matters of style, taste, and judgment, as in the case of Senator Joseph McCarthy of Wisconsin, but the basic goal of keeping the nation safe from subversive influences and organized dissent went unchallenged. The preoccupation with the Cold War, with the notion that a ruthless and atheistic Communist Empire lay waiting for American weakness, kept an entire generation silent.

Most historians now regard the 1950s as a nadir in American political history. Within an economy based increasingly on military expenditures and within a society dominated by a siege mentality, little significant debate could or did occur. Because the United States enjoyed a level of prosperity that was then the highest in the world, few persons felt compelled to take the risk of challenging the assumptions that propped up the system.

The pendulum of historical interpretation has recently begun to swing toward a celebration of the 1950s, however. In the relative quiet that has followed the racial and student upheavals of the late 1960s and early 1970s, the Eisenhower decade is being reevaluated. The passive conformity that characterized the period no longer looks so bad or so vacuous. In the article below, Stephen J. Whitfield argues that the absence of "extremes" throughout the decade was the mark of a "humane society." You might ask yourself whether such reflections are as revealing of our own times as they are of the past.

In February 1950 a hand which proved to be quicker than the eye held up a list of 205 Communists in the State Department, though the figure changed to 57, 81, 116, 121, 106, and then ultimately none. In November 1960 a popular margin of approximately 0.1 percent was registered in the Presidential election, after the Democratic candidate decried a "missile gap" which he later discovered did not exist. The Air Force claimed that the Soviet Union had at least 600 ICBMs, the Central Intelligence Agency claimed 450, the Navy claimed 200, and Britain's Institute of Strategic Studies claimed 35. These two mysterious flurries of numbers frame a decade near enough to provoke a shudder and distant enough to invite nostalgia. The period is distinct enough to facilitate the recognition of its end—the Student Nonviolent Coordinating Committee in the South and the National Liberation Front in Vietnam were both founded in 1960—and yet it was so amorphous that even the most feckless of labels, like "gay" or "roaring," do not stick. Resonant generalizations about the 1950s are rare enough to be collectors' items, so that it might not be futile to attempt to capture some fugitive moods, a special idiom and posture, and thus to provide a few notes toward the definition of a decade.

Of course the narratives and the reminiscences have already appeared, and neither the prosecuting nor the defense attorneys have controverted the exhibits introduced as evidence: the hula hoops and coonskin caps, the Bermuda shorts and barbecue pits, the photos of Brando astride a motorcycle and Monroe above the subway grating, the grey flannel suits and bobby sox, the leather jackets inscribed with "Sharks" and "Jets," the Mickey Mouse Club hats and the "I Like Ike" buttons, the scratchy Nichols & May album and the dog-eared paperback of *The Caine Mutiny*. The artifacts are of course endless, and can as easily be summoned to demonstrate the gentle and wholesome texture of life in that period as its banality and irresponsibility.

But perspectives on the 1950s are more difficult to achieve. Not all the chairs of very modern history have been filled; and if this essay is not "revisionist," it is because there is no coherent, inclusive interpretation of the period to revise. It is written in the reluctant recognition that historical truth normally lies a little closer to the unexceptionable

From the *South Atlantic Quuarterly*, 74 (Summer 1975). Copyright 1975 by Duke University Press. Reprinted by permission.

than to the extraordinary. W. H. Auden could get away with summing up the 1930s as a "low dishonest decade," since poets have licenses for which historians cannot qualify. Such licenses are valuable as documents to be filtered by the cultural historian who seeks to determine which truisms tend to be true and to identify the common issues to which contemporary thinkers addressed themselves. The latter task is not especially difficult for the 1950s, since almost all its eggheads put themselves in one basket. The intellectuals and politicians to whom this essay is most attentive thus tended to validate each other's images of America.

The modes of thought of the decade were elusive, indirect, imprecise, sometimes subtle. Political discourse was often as meandering as the transcript of a Presidential press conference. The buck seemed to stop, a liberal cartoonist complained, at "the men around the men around the President." Under the Smith Act leading Communists were imprisoned not for engaging in the physical violence of attempted revolution, not even for advocating such revolution, but rather for conspiring to advocate revolution. Alarmed at the danger to civil liberties, some on the left reacted with "anti-anti-Communism." The Stalinists themselves preferred to be known, understandably enough, as progressives; and the published letters of Julius and Ethel Rosenberg invariably place quotation marks around the word "Communists," as though they were spectral as witches and the hunt for them equally pointless. Even words like "liberal" and "conservative" became so blurred that the sophisticated often uttered them tongue-in-cheek and wrote them between quotation marks as well. What had once been obvious and assumed receded behind a maze of uncertain definitions. Satire and parody, the thinking man's comedies, were deflected, as in the quirky pages of *Mad* magazine, which avoided mockery of the basic institutions of American life and specialized instead in its distorted reflections in advertising and commercialized culture. A funhouse mirror was thus placed against a suburban picture window to expose a family watching a television commercial which had just interrupted a Hollywood rerun.

In such a milieu the substance of rights and beliefs could not be kept in focus. The exercise of liberty and the implementation of ideals were less urgent than the proclamation of their existence. Democracy was defined as process more than substance. "The good society,"

Sidney Hook wrote, "depends not so much on *what* ideals are held as on *how* they are held." Actions spoke no louder than words; even more crucial were motives. Trust was supposed to cement the community, whose members would therefore act in good faith, which is why "phony" became so usable a term of rebuke, especially in the argot of the young. Senator Joseph R. McCarthy, at least in the early days of his fame, was given credit for "sincerity" in ferreting out Communists. Amidst the proliferation of loyalty oaths, the Personnel Security Board of the Atomic Energy Commission asserted the government's right to "search . . . the soul of an individual whose relationship to his Government is in question." To the ubiquitous Congressional committees, confession certified the remission of sin and weighed more heavily than the earlier commission of error or crime. Former Communists who had come to recant and denounce were given very respectful attention and sometimes won unearned credibility. Yet Charles Van Doren, with his beads of sweat and pursed lips, revealed how easily, even when untutored in method acting, "sincerity" might be perpetrated; but he managed to wash away his guilt for fraudulent quiz shows by making a confession just a step ahead of a possible perjury charge.

In the Cold War each side considered the other deceitful. This diminished the obligation to evaluate policies and overtures on their merits. International diplomacy became a heads-I-win, tails-you-lose game in which, from an American viewpoint, the Korean War and the suppression of the Hungarian Revolution underscored Soviet designs upon Western hegemony, while reductions in the budget and manpower of the Red Army and the withdrawal from Austria showed a sinister desire to lull the West to sleep. The architects of American policy assumed its beneficence and, at least in public pronouncements, preferred to emphasize intent more than interest as the standard of international conduct. We asked to be judged by our good will, while the malevolence of our enemies absolved us from looking very hard at our friends. After the German attack on Russia, for example, an unfazed Churchill had pledged support in amoral tems: "If Hitler were to invade Hell, I would at least make a favorable reference to the Devil in the House of Commons." By contrast the anti-Communist despots locked for strategic reasons into the American alliance system were bent beyond recognition into two-fisted fighters for freedom.

In opposition to the assumptions and policies of a Secretary of State who condemned neutralism as "immoral," a school of "realists" arose to warn of the perils of self-righteousness. Its exponents, including George F. Kennan, Hans J. Morgenthau, and Reinhold Niebuhr, proposed a more self-conscious and more consistent use of American power and a repudiation of both legalism and moralism—personified by Woodrow Wilson and his heir, John Foster Dulles—in the conceptualization of national interest. They thus tried to sign death warrants for American innocence, reports of whose demise have so often been exaggerated. The realists spoke for those who no longer sought in politics the regeneration of the human species, who tried to absorb the meaning of the Nazi and Communist experiences. To recoil from innocence was to have ventured, at least vicariously, to the edge of the abyss, to be burdened with images and ideas which were shaped by the perception of inscrutable evil, to know that tragedy was more than a synonym for suffering, to experience traumas threaded with death camps and slave labor camps and incinerated cities. Except from obtuseness, few could feel immune from complicity. "In some sort of crude sense," J. Robert Oppenheimer had told President Truman, "which no vulgarity, no humor, no overstatement can quite extinguish, the physicists have known sin; and this is a knowledge which they cannot lose."

In the 1950s the most disreputable form of political innocence was ignorance of Communism, specifically the premise of the two previous decades that Stalinists inhabited roughly the same moral universe as the liberals and democratic radicals who could also trace their remotest ancestors to the Enlightenment. Innocence was Eleanor Roosevelt, informed that the nice lads heading the American Student Union might be Communists, inviting them into her drawing room to ask them to be candid about their affiliations. Innocence was Henry Wallace touring Siberia in 1944 and, before the undoubtedly astonished wardens of the labor camp at Irkutsk, extolling "men born in wide free spaces." The intellectuals of the 1950s reacted to such gullibility with gritty cynicism and contributed, often with critical discrimination, to the anti-Communist forces of the era. Yet some of these boys in the backroom became, although in a novel guise, what they had most scorned: dupes. For some writers and activists, the power to combat Stalinism in foreign trade unions and in the intellectual arena came not from the barrel of a gun but from a conduit of the CIA. To engage in politics led ineluctably to dirty hands, which were accepted a little too readily as the alternative to amputation.

In an atmosphere fraught with moral ambiguity, a terrible simplifier like McCarthy could flourish. The junior senator from Wisconsin made the political culture of the 1950s distinctive and unmistakable, the -ism attached to his name as special as a signature. More sharply than anyone else, he incorporated the tensions and conflicting impulses which animated his contemporaries, openly representing not only the will to impose conformity and extinguish deviation but—paradoxically—the casual vulgarity, the smirking rebelliousness, the hint of violence which the web of civil society could barely restrain.

The senator's targets, however minor, were generally tracked in the interstices of the most hallowed institutions: the Department of State, the Army, the Eastern colleges, even for a brief moment the Protestant clergy. He got as far as he did largely because reputable Republicans came along for the ride, figuring that only Communists and—more important—Democrats were endangered; and many jumped out upon realization that the reckless driver was crashing into the Republican-controlled armory. As Richard Rovere noted in his shrewd 1959 portrait, McCarthy gloated in his own triumph over gentility, brazenly consuming endless bottles of liquor, pawing women at parties, burping in public, calling President Truman an idiot and a "son of a bitch" who "ought to be impeached." To the delight of his followers, he displayed the arrogance of the roughneck who violates the rules, or rather makes up his own as he goes along. In stalking his prey he lied without compunction, declassified documents on his own, and, when accused of misusing funds, retorted: "I don't answer charges. I *make* them." Ever on the verge of turning politics into a body contact sport, McCarthy once got into an actual brawl with Drew Pearson and, when later asked whether he had kicked the columnist in the groin, is reported to have replied: "Where else?" He was, in the appraisal of a society matron, "such an engaging primitive."

The keenest politicians operate with several sophisticated clocks ticking inside their heads, following the mean time of daily activities while simultaneously abiding by their own alternative long-range schedules. But McCarthy was unencumbered with any sense of the future. He devised the morning press conference to announce nothing beyond an afternoon press conference, assuming that by then he could concoct some new and outrageous accusation to keep himself on page one. McCarthy dropped investigations when the headlines shriveled, not when the subversives were exposed, because he had little comprehension of Communism or deep convictions or program or beliefs any bigger than self-glorification. He once predicted that he would wind up either in the White House or in jail, with his actual preference left dangling; and Rovere therefore concluded that McCarthy was "closer to the hipster than to the Organization Man."

Therein lies one of the most intriguing ironies of the decade. In 1957, the year the junior senator died, Norman Mailer's essay "The White Negro" placed the burden of radical social change upon the shoulders of the hipster, whose fingertips were tingling with modern jazz rhythms and whose lungs were already filled with marihuana smoke. Mailer inflated the hipster into an "existentialist," who in fact looked less like Merleau-Ponty than like Joe McCarthy. Both the senator and the hipster conveyed a latent aggressiveness threatening to disrupt reason and common sense. Both the demagogue and the demimondian pursued instantaneous gratification and adopted a let's-play-it-by-ear approach to ethics. Both combined a rage for disorder and random havoc with a touch of paranoia. Mailer himself was so enchanted with the spontaneous combustion of the hipster's protean personality that, a decade later, he affixed the "existentialist" label to Robert Kennedy, whose loyalty to McCarthy had driven him to Appleton, Wisconsin, to attend McCarthy's interment. The hidden center of the 1950s may well be where two such disparate, engaging primitives as McCarthy and Mailer bump against one another in the dark, in the shadow of the sunny, official complacency.

Two similar incidents may further reveal McCarthy's peculiar significance for the political culture of the decade. Once plunging into the same elevator as the treasonable Acheson, he warmly purred, "Hello, Dean." The response consisted of clenched teeth and a forehead which assumed the coloration McCarthy had ascribed to the secretary's politics. Later, after having accused Edward R. Murrow of participation in the Kremlin's international conspiracy, McCarthy sought him out at a party, wrapped his arm around the liberal commentator's shoulder, and inquired, "No hard feelings, Ed?" Murrow apparently took the question to be rhetorical; he walked stiffly away.

Indifferent to the dignity that some opponents possessed, McCarthy had made an offhand remark illuminating a decade whose every epiphany might be banal. While it was not an era of good feelings, for the mood was too cranky and sour and suspicious for that, it may well be considered an era of no hard feelings.

Admittedly, Murrow himself harbored resentment, and behind the Republican stalwarts behind McCarthy were indeed fanatics. Like some primal horde, they stalked liberal nightmares, their faces gnarled into knots of hostility, flecks of foam about to appear at the sides of their mouths, blood coursing through their nostrils, as they haunted the school board meeting, the library shelves, the UNICEF campaign on Halloween. They were a nuisance especially in all those hometowns, old and new, which tried to maintain those verities corroded by the acids of secularism and the welfare state. But McCarthy himself fit no such character profile; Roy Cohn was not alone in remembering his boss as "a fun guy to be with." McCarthy clearly disagreed with Woodrow Wilson's acetylene belief that "government is too serious . . . to admit of meaningless courtesies," even when that government was infested with subversives. And according to sociologist Edward Shils, only a few hundred thousand Americans composed the rabble which the Senator himself did so little to rouse, either organizationally or orgiastically. Nor could the most careful recent student of his constituency, Michael Paul Rogin, detect any overwhelming popular movement recharging McCarthy's batteries. His successor as junior Senator from Wisconsin was William Proxmire, a liberal Democrat educated in the Ivy League.

For all the fevers of the decade, a large majority of citizens, whether out of ignorance or intelligence, apathy or decency, developed immunity to the bacillus of the far right. Despite the losses incurred in the frustrating stalemate in Korea, despite the incessant peril of the Bomb, most Americans exhibited tranquillity, even at the cost of a bewildering number and variety of tranquilizers. And while candidate Adlai Stevenson's studied "call to greatness" went unheeded, crowds scurried toward a hero who made few of the demands of heroism, whose crusade had been in Europe and in the past, and whose politics, like Galileo's physics, seemed founded upon the principle of inertia. Eisenhower was the most popular masseur of the middle class. He pledged prosperity, which included two recessions his Keynesian critics believed avoidable, and peace, which included a Cuban invasion force and four hundred advisors in Vietnam for his successor to deploy. In keeping with the decade's preference for indirectness rather than, say, overt military intervention, the CIA's department of dirty tricks helped rearrange the governments of Iran, Guatemala, Egypt, and Laos. Governing by remote control, Eisenhower embodied the deactivated mood of the 1950s.

It was a decade more of anxieties than of passions, in which social divergences were kept from flaring into social conflicts. The haves feared the resentment of the have-nots less than their own descent into has-beens. Also affected were those affectless, exotic deviants from square society, the beatniks. If a pad was no longer something to write in, neither was it something to fight in—or from. Indeed a numbed passivity seemed appropriate to the atomic age, when death might be random, anonymous, general, and meaningless, and therefore life might be without either inherent sense or transcendent purpose.

By its ominous presence the Bomb contributed to a constriction of the range of political choice and of the vision of human plenitude. The post-World War I exhaustion with causes, with even the idea of causes, was repeated and amplified. Those who had once hoped to make life perfect decided to settle, with no hard feelings, for making life better. Thundering past the idealists of the 1930s and 1940s came the uncommitted, dominating a society which allowed for few zealots and even fewer heretics, whose stance presupposed an orthodoxy which even the Commission on National Goals, created late in the decade, could not authoritatively construe. A society so muted in the expression of its antinomies, so restricted in the repertory of its publicly debated ideas, so limited in the allocation of its allegiances redefined the word "controversial" to mean, as Jacques Barzun pointed out in 1959, "something (or someone) about which we cannot afford to engage in controversy—virtually the opposite of the former meaning."

The scrutiny of ideas was in disrepute not only because national tradition enshrined "practicality," but also because ideologies had generated such lethal consequences in Europe. If, as one intellectual historian put it, the Nazi invasion of Russia merely renewed the struggle, by other means, between the right-wing Hegelians and the left-wing Hegelians, then perhaps the first premises of the American experiment should be unevaluated. Comity might be achieved most securely with platitudes, without those millennial hopes which needed to be doused in order to reduce social friction. Consensus, in the form of both analysis and advocacy, idea and ideal, was, like the nuclear age itself, disproportionately the achievement of Jewish savants, who were acutely aware of the fate which American citizenship had spared them. And although important differences existed within this group and some intellectuals did not emphasize or even acknowledge consensus at all, the American polity generally earned high praise for its capacity to roll with the punch.

Hovering over the social science of the 1950s was the spirit of the most perceptive and systematically curious of foreign observers, Alexis de Tocqueville. His *Democracy in America* had not been in print for nearly half a century, and its reissue shortly before the decade began helped to quicken the sense of national homogeneity in contrast to Europe, where conflict was assumed to be an independent variable in the social and political equation. Tocqueville had, like a seismographer, recorded the tremors which the predominantly "commercial passions" of an uprooted people had registered. More significantly he grasped the principles of stability and order amidst the flux and the busyness of business; and if he found America a nice place to visit, he would not have wanted to live so precariously under the weight of a mass society and the irresistible force of egalitarianism.

The ambivalence of the aristocrat was shared in varying degrees by his successors, including the cadres of the nascent American Studies movement, whose conservative strategy of eliciting unifying myths and symbols contrasted with the reformism which Charles Beard and James Harvey Robinson had earlier affixed to the New History. In the traditional disciplines, however, the recognition of consensus did not necessarily generate complacency. Daniel Boorstin, whose *Genius of American Politics* (1953) celebrated our historical indifference to speculative ideas, admittedly abandoned the task of criticism for the sake of a learned and sophisticated patriotism. But William Appleman Williams, whose *Tragedy of American Diplomacy* (1959) acknowledged even labor and agricultural enthusiasm for those overseas markets whose pursuit has bedeviled our foreign policy, was hardly charmed by the consensus he detected. As socialists, Daniel Bell and Seymour Martin Lipset sought the incremental political and economic improvements that they also predicted as sociologists. They refused to treat American society as exceptional (as Boorstin did), and instead placed the "end of ideology" within the context of the Western community. In *The Torment of Secrecy* (1956), Edward Shils formulated a theory of "civil politics" by which a populist America compared unfavorably with democratic but deferential England. Without pursuing transatlantic comparisons, but with a mordant subtlety all his own, Richard Hofstadter described an historical consensus which was enmeshed in the calculus of private economic self-interest, which leveled those distinctions and achievements which were not utilitarian, and which compromised and implicated the reformers on its periphery. Louis Hartz demonstrated to almost everyone's satisfaction that *The Liberal Tradition in America* (1955) is virtually the only tradition in America. The absence of a distinct, assertive, class-conscious bourgeoisie meant, in effect, that since no colonial could be a feudal lord, Norman Thomas could not be a President.

Nor, as Hartz's test case of the doomed Southern slavocracy disclosed, have we ever had a fully realized conservatism either. Its champions have been more adept at preserving the gains of the American Revolution than in fabricating a compelling vision of an ascriptive and hierarchical society. Here the 1950s constitutes another test case: for all the talk of a conservative revival, its most self-conscious spokesmen still sounded like marginal dissidents and polemicists rather than votaries at the elbow of the prince. It was somehow appropriate that perhaps the decade's angriest young man was the tory polemicist, William F. Buckley. A literary critic's 1950 generalization was harsh but accurate: "In the United States at this time liberalism is not only the dominant but even the sole intellectual tradition. The conservative impulse and the reactionary impulse do not, with some isolated and some ecclesiastical exceptions, express themselves in ideas but only in action or in irritable mental gestures which seek to resemble ideas." Given the quite mild mental gestures of the regnant liberalism, which scurried for cover behind the legislative achievements of the New Deal and the cultural monuments of Broadway, it was peculiar that Lionel Trilling's remarks introduced a work entitled *The Liberal Imagination*.

The canvas of national experience was no longer comparable to a vast and variegated WPA mural, filled with bulging and fascinating characters. Instead it resembled a still life, abstract in style, scrupulous in composition, limited in its palette. Nowhere was this blandness more evident than in religion. Will Herberg's *Protestant-Catholic-Jew* (1955) described how affiliation with the three leading denominations earned the badge of social legitimacy; to affirm a religious identification was a valid, indeed an obligatory, way to become like everyone else. In the 1950s church membership was probably proportionately higher than ever before; and in 1957, forty-six percent of those polled felt that clergymen were "doing the most good," far more than businessmen and politicians. But in religion as in politics, form outweighed content, and ideals were strangely devoid of substance; the most essential belief was, it was claimed, in belief itself.

This was a religiosity which prophets have historically considered more insidious than apostasy or atheism, for it promoted adherence for dubious reasons. It was a faith to soothe parishioners rather than stir them, in the manner of Norman Vincent Peale's unctuous best-seller, *The Power of Positive Thinking* (1952), which led Adlai Stevenson to call Saint "Paul appealing and Peale appalling." But no wonder a poll showed 14 percent more Americans believing in Heaven than Hell. (This discrepancy, a characteristically American contribution to eschatology, may also account for the failure of Churchill's analogy after the invasion of Russia, cited earlier, to resonate here.) In such a diffident setting, religious bigotry could not flourish, and had never been so rare as in the 1950s; even McCarthy and, to a lesser extent, his epigoni in the John Birch Society appear to have been free of such hatred. Whether watching Bishop Fulton J. Sheen on television or attending a pyrotechnic rally of Billy Graham's or licking political chocolate coating from Dr. Niebuhr's bitter theological pill (without swallowing it) or struggling through Martin Buber's *I and Thou*, Americans shared the latitudinarian spirit of Bertrand Russell's onetime jailer who, when informed that the philosopher in his care was an agnostic, recovered from initial bewilderment to insist that we "all believe in the same God" anyway.

To paraphrase a media message of the period, America had become a family which not only prayed together but stayed together; and while family quarrels are the most poignant, they did not erupt during the 1950s. The labor movement reunited into the AFL-CIO under the presidency of George Meany, who spearheaded a fight against union corruption and was no slacker in the struggle against Communism either. No overall gains in membership were registered. A worker,

Eric Hoffer, in *The True Believer* (1951), was the first to call for an end to ideological passion; and his peers remained anxious to rise from their class rather than with it. They saw no systematic alternatives to capitalism—or rather, in the suave phrase of a president of the New York Stock Exchange, "people's capitalism." In 1956, the last year that the Socialist Party fielded a Presidential candidate, he got fewer votes than the tribune of the Prohibition Party. With the proletariat sidelined, radicals like Mailer used the pages of *Dissent,* an otherwise measured social democratic journal which usually picked targets like mass culture and Communism, to depict the "White Negro" as a potential agent of historical change. Since the quest for the "apocalyptic orgasm" and lesser kicks would inevitably lead to frustration in a highly repressive civilization, an intense hatred might accumulate against the antiseptic political economy itself. For the moment, however, the hipster did not want to change the system but merely to beat it, in a form which Mailer granted was psychopathic. But a manner of assaulting society is not the same as a plausible alternative to it.

Like Sainte-Beuve's French, who remained Catholic after they had given up being Christian, some Americans remained Socialists even after they had ceased to be radicals. To be on the left was a stance rather than an obligation to do anything, except try somehow to infiltrate the national imagination. An exception was Paul Goodman, the anarchist destined to become the most important intellectual of the 1960s; but in the 1950s he kept packing his trunk with unpublished manuscripts. Herbert Marcuse managed to combine utopianism with despair. Assuming the permanence of Western prosperity as freely as any corporation executive, Marcuse could not suggest how to accelerate the locomotive industry, which would no longer require the ingenious services of the capitalist engineer or the stern authority of the capitalist conductor or the toil of the porters. In the future the pleasure-seekers back in the club car could march triumphantly down the aisles and take over in the name of "non-repressive sublimation," the erotic, the aesthetic, the playful. Yet *Eros and Civilization* (1955) was less an exercise in utopian thinking, written in the future perfect tense, than a book extolling the utopian dream itself; and in affirming a principle rather than fulfilling it, Marcuse played a variation upon the decade's familiar theme.

Further radical endorsement of the hermetic character of American society came the following year with the publication of C. Wright Mills' claustrophobic *Power Elite*. Since the Second World War, he charged, politicians in Washington had come to share their power not only with a business elite, as so often in the past, but with generals and admirals as well. Beguiled by the myth of pluralism, Americans were living under an oligarchy without quite knowing it, for the process of decision making was not democratic nor open to genuine debate and public scrutiny. The competition between interest groups for the rewards of wealth and power was rigged, and the chief consequences would not be welfare but warfare to be justified in the name of "crackpot realism." Neither Mills nor Marcuse nor the remaining Socialists keeping themselves warm in the pages of *Dissent* could provide much of an answer to the question which, for radicals, is as ethically self-incriminating as any connected with the Fifth Amendment: What is to be done?

The answer which the decade itself seemed to offer was: Nothing. Its characteristic posture was rigid, as though, in the atmosphere of the Cold War, Americans staked out a claim as God's frozen people. This was not always so. The 1930s convey images of people marching, picketing, struggling, and soon fighting; also evoked are the sense of urgency and excitement, the pride in activism and experimentation. The 1960s were ignited when the Democratic candidate for President vowed to get the country *moving* again; and when this also meant moving deeper into Vietnam, the radicals who arose in opposition called themselves not a party or an organization but a movement. The response to a Stevenson speech, he himself admitted, was appreciation for its eloquence; to a Kennedy speech, an eagerness to be galvanized. Told that a certain campaign position was essential to victory, Stevenson told his 1952 advisors, "But I don't *have* to win." The contrast with the Democratic candidate in 1960 is too obvious to mention.

Immobility was indeed the trademark of the 1950s. Just as the "adult Western" provided more talk and less violence, Dulles blustered but rarely went "to the brink," which was itself the furthest point along a fortified wall of military and political alliances, which Fidel Castro thereupon turned into a Maginot Line. Containment remained a central axiom of foreign policy, even though Kennan, its early theoretician, had second thoughts and suggested disengagement from the European heartland, even though the Viet Cong demonstrated the ineffectuality of SEATO, even though the Baghdad Pact had to shift its headquarters to Ankara and select a new name after a coup d'état in Iraq.

Symbolic of the political posture of the era was the school child crouching under the wooden desk during a mock atomic attack; to protest the descent into shelters during a civil defense drill, pacifists stood immobile in New York City Hall Park. The most inspiring protest of the decade began when a Montgomery seamstress refused to get up from her seat on a segregated bus; and while the 1930s included sit-down strikes and the 1960s their sit-in movements, those decades also projected the sense of motion—forward motion—which the 1950s lacked. At least according to legend, those who attended performances of Clifford Odets' *Waiting for Lefty* in the 1930s rose from their seats to write finis to the play with cries of "Strike! Strike!" Two decades later audiences sat around in Jack Gelber's *The Connection* waiting for Cowboy to bring the actors their dope or, with even greater patience, sat *Waiting for Godot*, which ends when one character tells the other, "Let's go." Yet Samuel Beckett's stage directions are explicitly to the contrary: *"They do not move."*

Eppur si muove. "We are beginning to move again," was how Mills ended his "Letter to the New Left" (1960); it also ended the decade, as here described, though the New Left had then emerged more sharply in Britain than in America. Mills hoped that young intellectuals might connect private malaise with public issues, culture with politics. Already in the 1950s some allegiances were beginning to shift; the reason was race, which in America has generally been more consequential than class. The shift could be detected not only in Mailer's essay but in the fiction of Jack Kerouac, himself a conventional patriot, but also the author of reveries like "At lilac evening I walked with every muscle aching among the lights of 27th and Welton in the Denver colored section, wishing I were a Negro, feeling that the best the white world had offered was not enough ecstasy for me, not enough life, joy, kicks, darkness, music, not enough night. . . ."

In the next decade one white radical would self-consciously seek "the moral equivalent of being black," but the musical equivalent would come first. Identities had not yet sufficiently transferred for an actual black Orpheus to beguile the mass audience; otherwise the successor to somnolent Perry Como, the favorite pop singer of the early 1950s, might have been either the wry, sly Chuck Berry or the frenetic Little Richard. It was left to Elvis Presley to shatter the surface calm of the era, for he was something of a white Negro, and not merely because so definitive a song as "Hound Dog" had first been Willie Mae "Big Mama" Thornton's. During Presley's first Memphis radio interview, the disc jockey made him specify the name of his high school, because "a lot of people listening thought he was colored." The middle-class kids often claimed to like Presley's songs but not his manner, just as their parents often professed to like McCarthy's objectives but not his methods. And yet accusations of vulgarity may reveal the very source of much of their appeal. Both Presley and McCarthy formed the negative print of the decade's self-portrait; and because they projected disreputable but basic drives, they could not be cropped. After initial reluctance, the Ed Sullivan Show granted Presley its imprimatur, although he was televised only from above the pelvis. The rival Steve Allen Show, not to be outdone, thereupon depicted the singer in his entirety, but he was not permitted to move. Prometheus bound. Presley seems to have had no hard feelings.

The race question was rather well avoided in the 1950s, for the oppression of blacks, even when recognized, was not normally something one could *do* anything about. Invisible men and women paid a high price for the smugness entailed in the national indifference to causes. At the beginning of the decade, Malcolm X was working on the Lincoln-Mercury Division assembly lines; at its end, Stokely Carmichael was still attending the Bronx School of Science. Black protest was polite, conciliatory, legalistic—and compelling. The Supreme Court's unanimous ruling in Brown v. Board of Education of Topeka (1954) had no more compassionate eloquence than the Emancipation Proclamation; its effects remain incalculable. Eisenhower later regarded Earl Warren's appointment as Chief Justice as "the biggest damn fool mistake I ever made"; but, perhaps with similar inadvertence, most of his other appointments to the bench were also excellent. A Southern Democrat whom he did not elevate, a Louisiana District Court judge named J. Skelly Wright, once explained his own first realization of the costs of segregation. During one Christmas season, Wright observed a party across the street, in which attendants separated by race those entering the room. It was an institution for the blind. Ex post facto laws are forbidden to legislators, not to historians, who have been known to abuse the privilege of applying retroactive moral judgments; but here surely was a national situation in which white Americans should have known better.

Passivity and neglect fueled much of the mood and context within which the most horrible crimes against blacks, most blatantly in the South, went unpunished. Emmett Till, a fourteen-year-old Chicagoan visiting his grandmother in Mississippi, whistled at a white woman, was kidnapped and later found floating in a river. There were too many other victims, the oblivion shrouding their names perpetuating the injustice already meted out to them. Nevertheless the lynchings which had occurred on an average of twice a week at the dawn of the century declined to statistical, if not moral, insignificance in the 1950s. Since many respectable Southern whites could not stomach the Ku Klux Klan, the White Citizens' Councils were formed after the Supreme Court decision to give racism an extra coat of polish. On the surface at least, many of the blacks who survived continued, in Langston Hughes' phrase, to "swallow pain with a smile."

Invisibility was not unique to blacks, as Michael Harrington later observed in calling for a national program to aid the poor. "The problem that has no name" was what Betty Friedan called women's groping for their own identities. Friedan's study of the two hundred questionnaires addressed to Smith College's class of '42 fifteen years later was eventually to inaugurate whole new climates of opinion and behavior. Not published until the decade was over, *The Feminine Mystique* was in fact the missing half, though not quite the better half, of Paul Goodman's *Growing Up Absurd* (1960), which diagnosed the waste and emptiness and indignity in the lives of young males only. And if the racial and ethnic minorities, the impoverished, and women could not forge authentic identities because their problems were inconspicuous, because nobody knew their name, the young also seem to have matured as "conformists" without generational solidarity. In fact the models of youth were often adults, or in the past; the memorialists, like Renata Adler and Frank Conroy, have recorded their sense, by no means regretfully, of having grown up one at a time.

Civil liberties, on the other hand, was a widely discussed issue, though even its least savvy champions would not have wanted a national referendum on the Bill of Rights. Perhaps only the right to bear arms would have been uninfringed. Under Federal law thirty Communists, whose doctrinaire subservience to Stalinism was a measure of their own freedom of thought, were unjustly imprisoned in violation of their freedom of expression, though no criminal acts had followed from their opinions. The self-image of an open society was badly tarnished; and the careers and lives of non-Communists were smeared in the process, some beyond restoration. Yet because the self-proclaimed enemies of bourgeois legalism were so litigious, civil liberties were safer by the end of the decade. Unlike the earlier shock of the Red Scare, the judiciary consistently demonstrated respect for principles of due process. Mechanisms of repression often became, like formal rights, rusty from disuse: no Communist was successfully prosecuted for failure to register under the McCarran Act, and the six concentration camps authorized under its emergency detention provisions remained unoccupied. Gradually stripped of its powers, the Subversive Activities Control Board managed to survive and receive Congressional funds, though primarily for liturgical purposes. Rights which were threatened in some quarters, such as freedom of association and academic freedom, the judiciary more explicitly protected. In a disgraceful exercise of bureaucratic whimsy, the politically suspect were sometimes not let out to travel in foreign countries. On the other hand, a mere English gamekeeper and his great and good friend, Constance Chatterley, were let in to circulate through the mails.

Mail and travel restrictions nevertheless undermined much of the universality of scientific discourse. No estimation can be attempted of the intellectual and artistic creativity which the atmospheric pressure of the 1950s stifled; a negative proposition cannot be proved. But the suspicion of theoretical or aesthetic distinction, hardly a negligible component of American life, was pervasive, at least until the rockets' red glare of Sputnik illumined some melancholy aspects of the educational enterprise. A Monsanto film of the period, designed to show the appeal of a career in chemistry, reassuringly described the scientists in its laboratories: "No geniuses here; just a bunch of average Americans working together." During the Oppenheimer hearing the testimony of an Air Force general was revealing: "The fact that he is such a brilliant man, the fact that he has such a command of the English

language, has such national prestige, and such power of persuasion
. . . made me nervous." The Oppenheimer affair is further instructive
in that, though the physicist was the most famous American to have
clearly been wronged, he was neither jailed nor, in any substantive
sense, disgraced. The directorship of Princeton's Institute of Advanced
Studies was the equivalent, for the era of no hard feelings, of telling
him to keep his horses for the spring plowing. Oppenheimer himself
continued to express his love of country.

Many other intellectuals also reconciled themselves to their native
land, truly becoming writers and artists in residence instead of firing
salvos from the Left Bank. The history of the artist and society, so
often told as if it were an adversary proceeding, especially in Europe,
was apparently about to have a happy ending. Affection was not fully
requited: suspicion toward the artist lingered, but that was less prevalent than indifference. This was still better than the Soviet Union,
whose government had so recently taken writers seriously enough to
shoot them. But the capital of the art world shifted from Paris to New
York, and no one seemed to mind that it was not the French we were
supposed to be beating. A few writers, preferably those whose best
work was long behind them, were housebroken and transmuted into
celebrities. The ideal of the novelist was Ernest Hemingway—but
Papa, the companionable man's man rather than the craftsman who
had hailed nada full of nada. The ideal of the poet was Robert Frost—
but foxy grandpa, who wrote so pleasantly in first person rural, rather
than one who was acquainted with the night. And yet some books
about ourselves were published which were indeed like Frost's woods—
"lovely, dark and deep"—as books about America should be. A list
that included David Riesman's *The Lonely Crowd*, Ralph Ellison's
Invisible Man, Whittaker Chambers' *Witness*, Vladimir Nabokov's
Lolita, and Leslie Fiedler's *Love and Death in the American Novel*
could readily be expanded. And while her subject matter did not specifically encompass her adopted country, Hannah Arendt's work, beginning with the influential *Origins of Totalitarianism* (1951), can
scarcely be disregarded, not because of the command of political
philosophy at her fingertips, but because those fingertips were as sensitive as a safecracker's.

Compared to the grisly regimentation behind what was then accurately called the Iron Curtain, compared to the gloomy sense of re-

prieve which enveloped much of western Europe, compared to the misery which pervaded what was then tactlessly called the undeveloped world, Americans had warrant, if not for complacency, then surely for some measure of self-appreciation. The dynamic thrusts which this essay has neglected—the spiraling urbanization and industrialization, the increased *embourgeoisement* and technological changes—continued apace and were much celebrated; and the beneficence of this often explosive progress was as unchallenged as the vaunted Protestant ethic itself. If too many Americans exhibited traits of self-absorption and privatism, they at least validated the achievements of the politicized and the embattled who had helped make possible the privilege to be apolitical and uninvolved.

This is not to pay homage to catatonia but to suggest a definition of the good society as that which requires few sacrifices for the sake of its most humane visions, as that which—except when faced with external threat—demands few heroes and martyrs. Such persons may be honored for extending the limits of aspiration, for subverting the assumptions of possibility. They have been honored here. But for all our fascination with power and glory, for all our envy of titans and tycoons, for all the Jay Gatsbys and Charles Foster Kanes whose ambitions can still insinuate themselves into our own, for all our tradition of braggadocio, which is commonly pitched to size and scale, we have usually settled for more moderate and prudent goals. It is in our character, though not peculiarly our own, to avoid extremes, to reduce great distinctions and disparities in cutting a continent down to the size of our own egalitarian ideal. Tocqueville comes in handy here, if evidence is otherwise in short supply, as does Benjamin Franklin, who once explained to prospective immigrants that America had managed to attain "a happy mediocrity."

In this spirit, a riddle first propounded by Zen Buddhists, then frequently and fondly quoted by the end of the 1950s, may open itself to further meaning. For without dissonance or searing internal doubt, the decade itself may well have been making a sound that has not quite ceased to echo, overlapping past and present, the sound of one hand clapping.

16

Growing Up in America

LAURENCE VEYSEY

• *The third of a century which has elapsed since the end of World War II has been characterized by technological change of overwhelming dimension. In 1945, air travel, television, stereophonic sound, and air conditioning were luxuries reserved for the few people who could afford extravagance. There was no such thing as an interstate highway, a microwave oven, a polaroid camera, or a pocket computer; neither could anyone find a Burger King or a McDonald's or a Holiday Inn.*

Laurence Veysey's article, "Growing Up In America," is about those postwar years, but his focus is social rather than technological. He reminds us that not only are we the first generation to have lived under the threat of atomic holocaust, but also the first to experience the limits of growth, the first to confront the meaning of a static society in terms of numbers. Focusing upon four specific institutional areas in American life—the family, education, religion, and community— that are responsible for the transmission of moral values, Professor Veysey demonstrates how each has redefined acceptable behavior. He notes the paradox in our culture that is caused by the veneration of both individualism and equality. As you read this provocative essay, you might reflect upon Veysey's contention that what is most remarkable about the United States is the extent to which it remains a patterned society, the extent to which all of us are molded and shaped by the larger consensus around us.

One of the mistakes we often make as we look around us is to exaggerate the degree of change that has recently occurred in American society. Popular writers on such topics as youth, schooling, the family,

From *American Issues.* Courtesy of American Association for State and Local History.

religion, and community have sometimes been particularly bad of-
fenders in this respect. They have shouted for our attention by striking
the continual note of "crisis." During the past quarter-century we
have been alerted to so many of these crises that we should be pardoned for reacting now with a certain skepticism. A broader historical
perspective teaches us that the trends we are told to worry about are,
at the very least, far more long-term than we commonly think, and
that they may have as much to do with the experience of modern industrialization as with anything that is specifically American. The cautious historian, after all, merely wishes to counsel common sense.
The several rapid zigzags which have occurred in the American social
climate since the 1950s, especially centering on the youth scene,
should have warned all of us against confusing momentary (if dramatic) symptoms with deeper, quieter tides of change that are less
easily defined or blamed upon indiviuals.

An over-frantic pinpointing of our ills led observers first of all, in
the late 1950s, to speak about adolescents as a "vanishing" breed. It
then seemed as though the imitation of an adult style of achievement,
both academically and in such realms as courtship, was spreading
down into ever younger age-levels, making the experience of growing
up in America one of an almost unnatural seriousness. Boys and girls
who dutifully went steady at thirteen were what bothered commentators. On another level, it seemed the danger lay in the docile, unimag-
inative acceptance of a need to prepare oneself for a lifetime career
inside a mammoth, faceless corporation. Middle-class children were
still striving for success, but within a bland, monotonous landscape of
muted expectations. The hunger for adventure had evaporated somewhere in the early twentieth century, leaving only a pathetic craving
for security, intensified by parents' memories of the great depression.

A few years later appraisals of the youth climate had become jar-
ringly opposite. A strident counter-culture, at once pleasure-oriented
and desperately apocalyptic, appeared to leave adults somewhere far
behind. Openly flaunted rebellion produced extreme reaction, as with
the housewife living near Kent State University who told a reporter
after the tragic National Guard shootings that in her view all students
who went barefoot ought to be shot. Youth were suddenly defined as
so alien as to be scarcely human. More wonderingly, it was sometimes
said that we now lived in a child-oriented society, where permissive

upbringings had given the new generation an unlimited sense of freedom to forge its own eccentric customs. Rather than disappearing in a downward extension of adulthood, adolescence was aggressively taking America over. Teenagers had become anarchists, ruthlessly spurning all the slots the established institutions offered, meantime grouping themselves communally to carry on a never-ceasing celebration of unreason. It was predicted, whether joyfully or with alarm, that America would thereafter steadily be transformed by its youth into a permanently unrecognizable locale.

All at once, in the early 1970s, the youth scene shifted once again so rapidly as to make us disbelieve. The sobriety of the 1950s returned, and with it the expectation that training for existing occupations was the only viable course in life. The crisis suddenly no longer centered in the realm of fundamental values, but in that of practical ways and means. Far too many young people aspired to openings in professional specialties which, for reasons both demographic and political, were overcrowded. Less than at any time since the 1930s did the problem seem to lie with youth itself, no matter how they were defined; it was perceived rather as centering on the priorities for expenditure prevalent in the rest of the population. We were no longer a youth-centered society, but an aging one. And we were ignoring legitimate youthful ambitions. We did so, however, not as in the 1950s, by forcing newly arrived adults into soulless large-scale organizations, but by denying them the chance to enter the particular ones they had set their hearts on. The resulting discouragement—that you *couldn't*, for instance, become a professor—made no sense according to the standards of just a few years earlier, when professors were seen as part of an oppressive class.

These rapid shifts have left us breathless. Too seldom do we try to seek out the hidden continuities they may conceal. Such deeper reflection would remind us, for instance, that the hefty shadow of the bureaucratic organization falls across all these varying versions of the youth scene. In the 1950s it swallows up the young; in the 1960s, briefly, they reject it; in the 1970s they attempt to return to it, but not without misgivings. Always in actual fact the large-scale organization remains—whether in its public or its private corporate form, the seemingly unavoidable focal point for existence, first as a school child, then (whether one is working-class or middle-class, rich or poor, in the country or the city) as a wage-earning adult. Scarcely affected by all the noisy outcries against it of the past decade, it remains the arbiter of how one spends a forty-hour chunk of one's weekly waking existence, as well as the provider of sustenance for the whole of one's time on earth. On its educational face, it reaches down to give us the necessary preparation for its own future claims upon us, introducing tiny children to the functional requirements of a standardized, routinized impersonality of treatment at the age of five or six. On its military side, it reminds everyone who nowadays emerges into consciousness that we live in a world whose rhythms may at any time be roughly broken into or obliterated in an instant flash—even if we had better not let our minds become too depressed by this possible scenario. More ordinarily, when not frightening us either as unprepared first-graders or as potential nuclear consumers, large-scale organizations are the quiet shapers of a substantial share of our personalities. These far-reaching institutional structures, in most cases created at some time between the Civil War and World War II, have become our ever-present inheritance, the great common denominators of our potentialities as Americans or as inhabitants of the industrially developed portion of the world. Their role in affecting us is stronger than that of any of the other forces to be examined later—the family, religion, and so on. In a sense, everything else that can be said must be understood as relative to their existence. Alone, they might be enough to guarantee that American society does not suffer crucially from a lack of form or structure.

Their power to pattern a major share of our destiny, to hand us the roles considered necessary and proper for us to learn to play, makes a psychoanalytical perspective on youth as a distinct stage of life seem relatively superficial or beside the point. This Freudian view, popularized by Erik H. Erikson during the years when other commentators were veering more wildly in their diagnoses, has focused on the idea of a standard human "life-cycle" and of a so-called "identity crisis" as an expected feature within it. Paying little heed to exact cultural or sociological circumstance, neo-Freudians pictured youth as a time of almost mystical withdrawal from the real world, a moratorium during which the person unconsciously gathers strength and gains a sense of direction for future engagement. The model here is actually that of the eventual leader or "great man"—Luther, Gandhi, the Harvard student. But even in this day and age, an identity crisis is apt to be a luxury affordable only by the upper-middle class. For the largest number of Americans, as for other peoples, adolescence is far more likely to be shaped by relatively mundane pressures and by dreams and fantasies that are earthier, less transcendental.

Such reflections remind us of how little we can say about growing up in America, beyond the elementary fact of the need to come to terms with big organizations, that will apply to nearly everybody. Indeed, when we pause to consider, we realize that the various trendier accounts of the youth scene in the last quarter-century have all been centered in the middle, perhaps the upper-middle class. The college-bound student, especially the one destined for an Ivy League university, was the model for the prematurely adult "vanishing" adolescent of the 1950s. Again, studies showed that radical drop-out youth of the 1960s came disproportionately from the upper end of the social spectrum. (Polls also revealed, incidentally, that only a small minority— around nine to twelve percent—of the nation's college students identified themselves with the New Left in the peak year of 1969–70.) It is much the same kind of youth, in social terms, who create the picture we have of the anxious professional job-seeker in the 1970s. The proportion of American youth of college age who are enrolled in higher education has indeed risen from fourteen percent in 1940 to forty-one percent in 1971, if junior colleges are included. But this means that even today the majority of the age-group does not share this kind of a growing up experience. (And since 1971, the college-bound proportion has actually declined slightly.) Clearly, when we focus on a single image of the American youth scene, at whatever moments in time, a great deal of unconscious selectivity enters into the process.

Our heightened awareness of the diversity within American society is of course itself largely a by-product of the 1960s. Twenty years ago we were much more confident of the generalizations we could make concerning the national character, and therefore of what it presumably meant to grow up here rather than somewhere else. These inclusive statements, when they rose above the level of ill-defined slogans about "freedom," often centered on the idea of affluence or material abundance. The United States enjoyed the highest living standard in the world. A baby opening its eyes in these surroundings was instantly bombarded by an array of historically novel creature comforts. All through childhood, exposure to material goods continued, fixing expectations for a lifetime of consumerism. The advanced technology that Americans took for granted, and were able to pay for, was the basic force shaping the American character, argued David Potter in his widely read book *People of Plenty*. Much of the social criticism of the 1960s accepted these same facts, making them the basis for a witheringly negative evaluation.

But, beginning as early as 1960, the continued existence of poverty in America began to be startlingly publicized. The great disparity of average income between blacks and whites suddenly seemed an important reminder of conditions we had preferred to ignore in the 1950s, when America was so freely described as one vast success story. Black youths in high numbers were simply unable to get jobs of any kind, even in so-called good times, year after year. The survival of white rural poverty in such areas as Appalachia and among ethnic groups such as the Chicanos in migratory agricultural labor, also received great attention. And a subtler kind of literature began describing the plight of the ordinary blue-collar worker, better off than formerly, but unable to enjoy the security or the full range of amenities in life that were available to the middle class. Meanwhile, the distribution of wealth was not changing. In the comparative sense, the extremes were not diminising, even if in absolute terms poverty engulfed a considerably smaller proportion of the population than in 1900.

In 1965 the most searing book of recent times about a version of youth experience in America, Claude Brown's *Manchild in the Promised Land,* was published. Forcefully it reminded us of the deprivation still possible on the streets of Harlem, and by implication in many other similar neighborhoods across the nation. More than sheer poverty was involved. A heritage of enforced negative self-evaluation, the product of race prejudice, had led to many consequences. Store-front religion offered solace and precious respectability to mothers whose families were collapsing around them. Boys, locked into a street culture that stressed an exaggerated masculinity and prowess, quickly became aware of the short-cuts ot acquiring a status that perodied white middle-class success, though with more emphasis on immediate gratification of desires. Pimping and prostitution were the everyday facts of teenage life. Then upon this scene rose the growing specter of heroin.

Whether drugs be interpreted as a means of desperate internal escape from an insecure and opportunity-less environment, or simply as the physiological consequences of a fad pushed along by cravings for peer group conformity, heroin introduced a new epoch on our urban streets that strangely blended torpor, stealing, and violence. The norms of one conspicuous youth group in America had become very close to suicidal.

Here was a setting, affecting large numbers of people, which clashed with all the generalizations being made about American society by the articulate fathers of the college-bound. In varying forms, its bleak story of exile was being duplicated on Indian reservations, in the forgotten black enclaves along the South Carolina coast, and in the mountains of eastern Kentucky. In still other city districts, working-class Italian-Americans or Irish eked out confined existences, living in much the same housing as their grandparents, taking pride in clannishness, whether family- or gang-oriented, and in a more voluntary way separating themselves from the American mainstream.

Was there in fact such a mainstream in this country, apart from the mosaic of all these particular pockets, neighborhoods, and ethnic groups? Some observers began doubting it, and the very concept of an American character thus fell under increasing question. We have become sensitive to so many glaring exceptions, and in an opposite direction made aware of how many of our values are apparently shared by other industrial peoples, that the self-contained, holistic formulas current in the 1950s, often taking off from the insights of Alexis de Tocqueville, have come to seem glib and far too simple. Or, as some would put the matter more bluntly, a national character was something we had to have—or to invent—in a period of Cold War. The idea formed part of our national arsenal of weapons. Perhaps with the ending of that war, it would no longer be necessary to hold onto it.

For their part, leftwing spokesmen, waxing temporarily in the 1960s, did not always clearly abandon the sense of a special American destiny. The concept of a unique American mission to mankind, inherited from the early Puritans in Massachusetts, still had enough resonance to make radical critics hesitate to abandon it. The national mission might not need scrapping, only redefinition. The "best" tendencies in it, toward equality and justice, could be appealed to—and the memories of Tom Paine and of the abolitionists invoked. To withdraw from faith in America, in this sense, was to lapse into a skepticism sadly ill-suited to any form of political engagement.

But could the unitary conception of an American character, in any version, survive in the wearier, more down-to-earth atmosphere of the 1970s? It appeared that a great watershed in our consciousness had been reached. Before this, supremacy and greatness were the obvious outcomes of American history. We were the shining beacon light. We embodied the strength of unlimited resources and the will to harness them productively. As the columns of so many of our public buildings reminded us, we liked to think of ourselves as the new Rome.

Now, on the other hand, we became aware that world history had not turned out in such a way as to support our self-perceptions. We suddenly discovered that in crucial cases our natural resources had limits on their future supply. To gain oil for our cars, we began to cultivate a strangely deferential relationship with Arab chieftains. We looked across our landscape and discovered how we had casually destroyed much of our own beauty. We lost a protracted war, and one which a large share of our people had defined as immoral in the first place. We discovered various embarrassing flaws of character imbedded in the personalities of our highest elected officials.

Illusions crumbled right and left. We began to realize that after all we were merely a country like any other. Our population was not huge, as compared with China, Russia, or India. Our territory was equalled by several other nations, and in an age of jet travel we were no longer so impressed by its supposedly vast extent. Even our living standard was no longer so uniquely high. Other peoples had cars, divided highways, and colored television. Modern buildings—and the views from the expressway—everywhere looked the same. If our forms and aspirations had been imitated, the result was a growing international uniformity, nonetheless. Comparatively, our industrial productivity statistics no longer looked good beside those of Germany and Japan. Russia had the same space technology and fearful weapons arsenal, and the same degree of hesitation about using it to blow up the world. In social services, America had always lagged behind certain other countries, and the growing demand from the taxpayers was that we worsen our showing. We were suddenly surprised to read that our nation stood far from the top in terms of the reduction of infant mortality.

Still more profoundly, we appeared to be nearing the upward limits in our growth. As technology, in the form of easy contraceptives, greatly lowered the birth rate, the time began to loom when we would have a static society in actual terms of numbers, with vast consequences for everything from the educational system to real estate values. All these facts combined to give us a new sense of flatness as we viewed the world scene and our place in it. It is as if certain blinders had at long last been removed. The result was comforting to nobody of any political persuasion, save a few apocalyptic decentralists.

Of course this new mood might prove to be a transient one. Although some of the symptoms that produced it reflect long-term trends rather than the immediate political and diplomatic climate, it is well to be cautious in assuming that we are incapable of further dizzying zigzags.

However, the present moment is one which allows us to explore the subject of the American character, and of its relations to such key areas of our life as education, religion, the family, and the community, in a spirit of sober realism. We are better able now to stand aside from past rhetorical slogans about our ideals and survey the American social scene in a colder, more searching light that accords well with precepts of historical objectivity. In what many would define as a current national malaise, there lurks at least this one advantage.

THE AMERICAN CHARACTER

The conventional portrait of the American character centers in such concepts as individualism (especially in the economic realm), competitive success-seeking, pursuit of material well-being balanced (or enshrined) by a strident moral idealism, equalitarianism and democracy, mobility and fluidity, optimism, practicality, adaptability, informality (impatience with rules and rituals), and the sort of utilitarianism that prizes efficiency and ingenuity but looks askance at the more pretentious forms of intellectualism. Less flatteringly, observers have pointed to conformism, rootlessness, the lack of respect for fixed standards or institutions, yet rigidity in regard to such areas as divided sex roles, unthinking patriotism, and racial prejudice. Other themes more marginal than these may be added to the list—nostalgia for the frontier and for rural life in general, religiosity at least at a nominal level, and perhaps a fascination with violence, part of an infatuation with exaggerated notions of masculinity.

It has been suggested in a recent book by Michael Kammen that these various traits form contradictions—for instance, between individualism and conformity—and therefore that the peculiarity of Americans is their very paradoxicality. This intriguing idea nonetheless presents a problem. Such an approach noticeably raises the level of abstraction of an already very abstract subject. If ambivalence is the pervasive quality of American life, we are left clutching at nothing very specific. Though far from easy, a greater try at concreteness might be helpful in attempting to winnow fact from fiction. The key traits that have frequently been named ought to be measured against the actual record of tendencies and behavior in the recent past.

It is worthwhile at the outset to see if we cannot simplify our list of character traits. Many of them may be seen to involve a single issue, the relation between the individual and various restraining forces which represent inherited custom and continuity. The positing of a high degree of social atomization in America, the absence of an automatic surrender to the claims of these external agencies or forces, was central to the Tocquevillean concept of the American character so widely put forward years ago. If Americans are individualists, then one may hypothesize that these institutions are relatively weak. Mobility, both social and geographical, no doubt is another corollary of such a conception of individual autonomy and freedom.

A second cluster of values from the same list centers on the idea of equality among people. But it should be recognized from the outset that the notion of equality has usually been embraced only with major qualifications. Legal equality is often distinguished from social equality, and equality of opportunity finds readier support than the goal of a literal equality of condition. Further, equality may be earnestly valued within an in-group which is indifferent toward the similar claims of outsiders. Equality is thus a somewhat weaker theme in the American imagination. In its more thoroughgoing versions, it is a partisan rallying cry for liberals or radicals, whereas nearly everyone identifies with individualism in some sense—economic among conservatives, intellectual and self-expressive among liberals. Nonetheless, since equality enters to some degree into the very idea of democracy, it offers another highly important touchstone for exploration in the present context. Character traits relating to practicality and informality are tied into the idea of equality, for they represent an impatience with custom, form, and ritual ultimately traceable to dislike of irrationally imposed social hierarchies.

The concepts of individualism and equality thus compose two major focal points for testing generalizations about the American character. But discussions about them will benefit from an added degree of concreteness. This is supplied by confining ourselves to four specific institutional areas in American life—the family, education, religion, and community. In each of these areas we shall want to look for symptoms of overall strength or weakness (relevant to our hypothesis about individualism), as well as for internal trends that disclose something about the presence or absence of these key American values.

What these four institutional areas have in common is that they serve as potential agencies of the first import for the transmission of inherited moral values. Together with the large-scale corporate organization, they inform the child who is growing up of a whole range of traditional, customary obligations and expectations deeply connected with the functioning of the society. They tell the child what is considered normal and what eccentric. If they work effectively, they channel youthful energy into safe outlets. They are the engines of social cohesion and continuity.

Of course this defines their role in terms of an ideal model, and one that is conservative in its implications. In actual fact, at no time or place have these four agencies operated at some imagined "full strength" in these terms, in total harness with one another. And great changes have been going on within each of them. At the outset, in the American context, we should remind ourselves of how unevenly they penetrate the lives of the population. This can be seen most simply by reflecting on the amounts of time we typically allocate to each. Just about all of us are involved in family relationships on the day-to-day level for great portions of our existence. For the large majority, this heavy involvement continues straight through, with little interruption, until old age. The family thus claims nearly coequal status with work as one of the two central institutional realms in modern life. By contrast, none of the other three areas is so pervasive in its claims upon our attention. Education most closely approaches it, for schooling again is a universal daily experience during a considerable span of years. But for most people it is over forever by the time one has become an adult. Religion is enormously weaker in terms of the time we habitually spend on it. Less than two-fifths of the population attend church regularly, and, though the experience may be spread across a lifetime, it occupies but a single hour per week. Finally, the steady impact of the community and its rituals and organizations is harder to assess. On its face, such an impact is still less substantial than that of religion for churchgoers, occurring only in brief snatches of newscasts, headline scanning, and on the rare days of elections. Yet there is a sense in which the average person may feel aware of his membership in a community—a neighborhood, town, or city—on a much more constant basis. Partly this is the result of the visual reinforcement of daily making one's way through some of its architectural and asphalt mazes. These effects, however, are elusive compared to those of the family and school, where face-to-face contacts create far more intensity of interaction.

The unevenness of our immersion in these several areas means that, given our present society, the active shapers of the experience of growing up most often include relatives and educational systems (we should also add work prospects and childhood and teenage peer cultures). Religion and, in all likelihood, general community norms, are apt to be notable for their relative absence.

THE AMERICAN FAMILY

Let us begin, then, with the realm that usually involves us for the most hours across the broadest slice of our lives—the family. The belief about the family most widely current is that it is breaking down. Though certain evidence supports this, recent scholarly research suggests a need for careful qualification.

Some hallowed myths about the history of the family are being destroyed. We used to think that before the industrial revolution, extended kin networks spanning several generations commonly lived together under the same roof. The nuclear family—consisting of husband, wife, and children by themselves—was pictured as a distinctly recent creation, itself a major symptom of family breakdown. But now we know that the nuclear family has been the norm throughout American history, from earliest colonial times, and in England as well since at least the sixteenth century. In fact, some scholars question whether extended kin networks have ever normally bedded down together no matter how far back one goes in the record of Western Europe. In this important sense, there has been far less change than one might have imagined. Indeed, some evidence exists—more in England than in America—that the first phase of industrialization brought families closer together, as relatives huddled in closely shared quarters to pool their scant resources. Of course physical crowding does not always make for domestic peace, and such crowding was traditional for most people in both rural and urban surroundings. All in all, it is far from clear that a "golden age" for the family lies anywhere in the past, at least short of the extremes to be found in tribal and peasant societies. In every period, family life has had its drawbacks.

The key change involves attitudes prevailing within the nuclear family. Genuinely new, beginning in the eighteenth century among the aristocracy and spreading gradually across the whole of society, was the rise of the ideal of romantic love. It is astonishing to realize that the expectation of love as a necessary attribute of marriage is so recent. Before then, marriage had been entered into much more matter-of-factly (or for property-oriented advantages among the wealthy). It was a custom to which one automatically submitted, making do with whoever of the correct social level might be locally available. Recently marriage has been made into a far more deliberate (in that sense, voluntary) act. Much higher emotional stakes therefore enter into it. In the present century, for the first time in history, it has come to be considered actually wrong to go on living with someone whom one does not love. This far more demanding expectation about the nature of marriage may lie at the root of the rising divorce rate and also tell us the most about what is distinctive in the meaning and function of the family in our own time. Our impression of the instability or breakdown of the family derives largely from the new kind of burden we have placed on it in these psychological terms.

In this fashion individualism may be said to have penetrated into the heartland of family life. If we as individuals (spouses, children) fail to gain steady emotional satisfaction from the other members of our family, we now feel cheated out of something that is our due. Psychologists, soap opera script writers, and fortune-tellers all keep telling us we have the right to be loved. Thus the standard childrearing practices of earlier centuries, which included much casual brutality, now seem shocking. And it is ever easier to conceive of separating ourselves from even the closest of relatives—wives, husbands, parents—when they fail to live up to this ideal of warmth. Individually to break away, to seek new fortunes elsewhere, becomes the common remedy for what is now regarded as an intolerable situation. But to require affection from the others with whom we are in physical proximity is a distinctly modern outlook. It is an aspect of the revolution of rising expectations. Ultimately, it may be the result of the more luxurious living standard that permits us to spread ourselves thinly within houses (often occupying and cherishing private bedrooms) and routinely to travel across far wider distances, either for new opportunities or for escape from oppressive family relationships. Perhaps the wish for such an escape was always there; new in world history is the ability to act upon it.

For a long time, in the nineteenth century, these changing attitudes were disguised by an upsurge of strident moralism, at once both stern and sentimental, centered in a concept of domestic virtue. Love and devotion were insisted upon in the newly intense way, but they were supposed to endure for a lifetime. Perhaps fortunately in this one respect, a relatively high death rate (especially for women in childbirth) functioned as an alternative to divorce in reducing the length of typical marriage spans. It is also possible that nineteenth century marriages were more often genuinely happier than our own, for the reason that men and women then still accepted the inevitability of living together "till death do us part" and set their sights accordingly. Much restlessness results from the ability to vividly conjure an alternative.

Peculiar to the Victorian age was the idea that both love and permanence were the normal attributes of marriage. Perhaps moralists became so explicit on these themes because of an uneasy apprehension that individualistic attitudes were already threatening to undermine the family as it had been known. At any rate, in the long term theirs was no more than a desperate holding action. For whatever reasons (including the increased longevity of females) the age-old expectation of permanence began to drop out of the formula, and only the modern, surprisingly disintegrative notion of love remained. The facts are blunt: in 1880, only one out of every twenty-one marriages ended in divorce; in 1916, one in nine; today, one in three, and the rate is still rising rapidly.

The technologically created possibilities of modern life are still more directly responsible for another notable change affecting the family, the tendency for its members to spend increased portions of their time apart from one another. In the age of the small farm and the craft-type household industry, husband, wife, and children might intermingle throughout many of their waking hours. Power-driven machinery, which brought into being the factory, suddenly imposed a pattern at an opposite extreme—each family member isolated on a different job for enormously long hours, the group reuniting only for sleeping, hasty meals, and Sunday leisure. Those who remained on farms experienced a similar if somewhat milder change, as the increasing acreage made possible by mechanization forced task-oriented separations no less effective for being confined within the boundaries of one's own property. In the cities, electric streetcars and automobiles made it usual for husbands to distance themselves from their wives across many miles throughout the day. Ultimately, jet aircraft allowed married pairs at the professional level to pursue careers in cities hundreds of miles apart, coming together only for weekends. It might seem difficult to imagine a version of marriage less attuned to physical proximity—until one recalls the highly traditional case of the naval seaman. Both sailors and contemporary co-career professionals of course manifest a highly exceptional extreme. A final, far broader change operating to detach family members from each other is the rise of universal education. Only since the late nineteenth century, for most Americans, have children routinely been kept away from their parents during a major share of every week, nine months or more per year. The family has lost much of its educative function along with its earlier work-centered ethos.

The shorter work week in the twentieth century has allowed families once again to spend more time together. We have never had so much leisure, and in this could lie the opportunity for a strong resurgence of family life. In fact the long weekend and the vacation are now the central occasions for the family as an institution, the high-point in its rhythms. But leisure is a shakier basis than work for family survival. Work could lock families tightly together while they scrimped and saved. Leisure constantly suggests choice, in contrast to the economic necessities that bound the earlier family. And choice is something that every child, no less than the adults, begins to want to exercise on an individual level. There is no utterly compelling urgency about doing one thing rather than another. So each person feels entitled to his or her own predilections, resulting in mutually destructive challenges and tugs-of-war. Today's children, unlike those of earlier centuries, start to express these private demands, as something that is after all expected of them, at an astonishingly early age. Equality is then defined as ice cream cones for everyone, and individualism as the right to insist upon one's own flavor.

The aggressive independence of young children in America was widely noted long before the era of consumerism. The anecdotes of early nineteenth-century British travellers abound with examples of wildly undisciplined, self-assertive offspring regarded with pride by their own parents. ("He's a sturdy republican, sir!" was the frequent fatherly boast after some public outrage.) Here we seem to arrive at the nub of individualism as a value in American society. To strike out boldly on your own (especially if you were a boy), to "make it" with no assistance from the older generation, came more and more to be the approved ideal, recognized by parents and children alike. With such a wide consensus of opinion behind it, it cannot be described as a generational "revolt." In cases where parents or the habitually desperate schoolteachers used the rod freely in an effort to break the child's unruly spirit, sympathy flowed toward the uncowed victim. My great-grandmother, whom I remember as a sweet, gentle woman, suffered from a cruel stepmother in Bangor, Maine, in the 1850s. Her response was to leave home entirely alone at sixteen to join a married sister in San Francisco. Uprooting oneself, moving west, cutting oneself off from the older generation—these were already the applauded social norms, though one was expected thereupon to form a new family of one's own, and the subsequent life was one of endured hardships and sacrifices rather than of leisure. Eventually, when the elderly were relegated to the impersonal care of institutions, the change reflected less a fundamental shift in values than it did the facts of growing longevity, affluence, and the general rise of bureaucratic organizations in American life.

In the nineteenth century, individualism was primarily economic in orientation. During the last few decades, particularly within the middle class, a distinct new stage has been reached. In a time when a high material level of living can be more or less taken for granted, and when psychoanalytic perspectives have largely replaced both the economic and the religious, individualism is by no means abandoned, but becomes redefined more introspectively as self-expression and self-fulfillment. Such desires, no doubt ultimately narcissistic, may have much to do with the recent striking reduction in the number of children that families wish to raise. Once again technology, in the form of the contraceptive pill, makes possible the change. But the pill would matter little if large families were still in vogue. Children are coming to be seen as a distraction and a nuisance, forcibly deflecting attention from one's own pleasures, including the wife's hunger to pursue her own career. Work itself, at this upper-middle level of the society, is looked upon increasingly as an avenue toward self-enrichment rather than as a brute necessity. If followed to its logical end, the ethic of self-development would eventually lower the population to a point requiring no worry over the too rapid consumption of physical resources. Meanwhile, husband and wife often use each other—perhaps unconsciously—as vehicles for their own self-fulfillment. This deeper trend lies of much of the current demand for "women's liberation." In part, the call for equalitarianism in sex roles stems from the drive toward individual self-fulfillment at all costs.

Thus we have begun to use the word "relationships" to describe the connecting links we have with others, even the supposedly most intimate. It is a cold, impersonal word, implying transitoriness and the possibility of manipulation. Such a term would have seemed impossibly artificial as applied to husband and wife, parents and children, in 1900. (One then had "relationships" in one's business.) And a sense of staleness with one's partner, which the man formerly circumvented by resort to prostitutes, now brings forth the idea on both sides of switching, dropping, and experimenting. The blind loyalty that would make years of staleness in a marital relationship seem tolerable, grows ever weaker. The key question is whether the family can survive on its new, more wholly psychological basis—on love, rather than on assumed necessity. It will gradually be answered in the arena of the suburban bedroom.

The emergence of "youth culture," of the conception of adolescence as a distinct stage in life, is a final recent distracting change,

dating from the opening years of the twentieth century. Childhood itself had been given similar status in the popular imagination only a bit
earlier. So long as children customarily worked, whether in and around
the home or outside, they were looked upon as miniature adults. The
shift in their economic function from producers to consumers appears
to have made possible their definition as beings suspended in an artificial oasis, removed from the normal cares of life. Children and youth
are now each assumed to be living inside their own specially defined
cocoons of patterned pleasure-seeking. Ultimately the fate of youth
culture seems less important than what goes on in that crucial meeting-
ground between husband and wife. For these two now have it in their
power to reduce children and youth to far less significant numerical
sectors of the total population.

Is the family doomed? How deeply do all these tendencies penetrate
American society at present? Depending on where you live, geographi-
cally, ethnically, in terms of social level, the situation can seem enormously different. Mid-America offers a reserve of stabler, less innovative values. (Of course its literal influence in the overall mix can be
exaggerated; a few years ago it was surprisingly announced that nearly
half of all Americans now live within fifty miles of either sea coast. Yet
what we call the spirit of mid-America thrives in Glendale, California,
and in Queens.) Certain ethnic groups—one thinks especially of Italian-Americans—cling to an intensely family-centered style of existence.
And the working and lower-middle classes, who still form the bulk of
the population, go on leading lives conditioned by rather blunt, traditional economic pressures. Simply to have the home, the back yard,
the inexpensive vacation, may define the ambition of the largest number of Americans even at this date. The restless quest for psychological
self-fulfillment remains largely a class-delimited preoccupation. But at
the other end of the social scale, chronic unemployment has produced
rising family breakdown from causes entirely unlike those affecting affluent suburbanites. We now know that until recently blacks enjoyed
a remarkably stable family life, given the handicaps. Even under slavery, where marriages were banned, lifelong pairing was the actual
norm. Only in the last decade or two has there been a dramatic rise in
the percentage of female-headed black families, occurring within the
severely deprived, disorganized neighborhoods of the northern cities.

Family life of some sort is still the overwhelming rule in the United

States. Rising divorce statistics may be misleading in two respects. First, they mask the fact that the great bulk of divorced persons remarry. Second, a major share of divorces happen to lower-class couples who married in their teens, apparently too timid to live together out of wedlock. Thus, ironically, a certain conservatism leads to swelling figures of divorce. And, though there has been much publicity about the generally more privileged youth who do cohabit without getting married, so far one discovers no numerical dent in the overall marriage rate. Communal experiments have involved only very small numbers. And even most of these unusual environments have continued to stress the paired couple in their lifestyle. All in all, lifelong companionship may be receding as an ideal, but not the notion of remaining with one other person over a considerable period of time.

Two-thirds of all the marriages in the United States still succeed. So often silent majorities of this kind are too readily forgotten in sensational analyses of the trend toward breakdown. Perhaps the most remarkable fact is that, despite all the pressures to the contrary, marriage along recognizable lines so widely survives. Family routines and occasions—birthdays, anniversaries, middle-class entertainment patterns—continue to occupy a very large share of the energy and attention of great numbers of persons. The thriving greeting-card industry depends on this.

Regardless of all the changes, a distinct vision of the good life in America—only somewhat less potent than its equivalent among the British working-class—centers upon the quiet satisfactions of the enjoyment of domestic comfort, the pleasure of rearing children, and the assumption that the family remains the eternal unit of shared strivings. Divorce, despite its frequency, is typically a wrenching rather than a casual experience for those who go through it. Again, though women may be gaining greater independence and self-esteem, in millions of cases husbands and wives manage to allocate responsibilities, forge reasonable compromises, and remain together more or less as before. (They have had practice. Women have long enjoyed considerably more freedom in America than in any other culture.) The family, at its root, is such a powerful conception that it may be able to endure through all these seemingly profound changes in its function and direction. It is, at any rate, too early to write it off as an institutional force serving as a basic social balance-wheel.

EDUCATION FOR WORK AND LIFE

Education, the second major area for analysis, in a sense stands in a contrapuntal relationship to the first, for the school has often been expected to instill values and habits in pronounced contrast to those of the home. It imposes the discipline of impersonal standards, as against the indulgence (or the less rational discipline) of mothers and fathers. In America, school systems have expanded in the atmosphere of an anticipated tug-of-war with parents. This war has had a class and ethnic aspect to it, as middle-class Protestants have sought to impose their morality upon a frequently unwilling immigrant population, in the name of what was once called "Americanization."

The traditional American commitment to education has been overstated. It centered in the ideal of simple literacy, including the ability to handle elementary arithmetic problems, as practical equipment for living a useful life. No doubt the value of equalitarianism was involved, in the sense that it was believed everyone should be able to compete on the basis of such minimum intellectual resources. The drive for universal schooling took on the aspect of an intense crusade only with the advent of industrialization in the mid-nineteenth century; it was further delayed in the South. On the local level it was often stingily supported. To keep taxes down, teachers were paid extremely low salaries. As late as 1915, many rural schools lacked even outdoor privies; the children were expected simply to use the bushes. Black children in most areas were segregated into parallel schools of their own, where conditions were distinctly worse.

In the emerging big cities, ward politicians held control of school systems for a time in the late nineteenth century. Teachers were often forced to give monetary kickbacks to politicians to keep their jobs. Here too taxpayers were reluctant to assess themselves for adequate school buildings. For decades in Chicago and elsewhere, far fewer desks were actually provided than would accommodate the total number of school-age children in the city, even though there was a compulsory attendance law. In 1900, a teacher was routinely expected to teach sixty or more children in a single class. Teachers were professionals in name only; they were required to have little training and were treated by administrators like marionettes. Textbooks conveyed the basics with a strong flavoring of abstract traditional morality. At the same time, these books were notably anti-intellectual in flavor, preaching a practical utilitarianism suspicious of broader cultural horizons.

The high school remained very much an elite institution, existing largely to prepare the tiny minority bound for college. As late as 1910, less than five percent of the age group went to college. A dozen first-rate universities had been created in the United States in the late nineteenth-century, in partial imitation of the German model, then pre-eminent in the world. Behind them struggled hundreds of other colleges and universities, many of them with standards too low to permit their graduates to go directly on to advanced study.

Objectively, there has thus been a great improvement in American education at all levels during the course of the twentieth century. While teacher salaries have risen faster than the cost of living, class size has gone down to an expected twenty-five to thirty pupils. Teachers have gained somewhat greater autonomy and respect; their training has improved. Compulsory attendance laws have been increasingly well enforced. Between 1890 and 1920, in city after city, school systems were detached from the corrupt political machines and placed under the control of nonpartisan superintendents, to whom local boards of education typically deferred. By mid-century, high school graduation was the norm, not the exception, at least for whites. The colleges boomed, likewise becoming mass institutions, although a great share of their increase flowed into a new network of two-year junior colleges, supported by local communities, which began to spring up in many sections of the country. A more affluent society had clearly begun displaying a new degree of generosity in the range and amount of education it would supply. In large part this stemmed from an awareness that a shift had taken place in the kinds of employment available in the society. Jobs requiring sheer animal muscle were declining, while white-collar jobs, often demanding some degree of technical expertise, expanded. The change accompanied a vast movement of people off farms into cities and suburbs. Too often we forget how relatively recent all these profound alterations have been.

The signs are that this process of transformation is now over. In the last few years the depopulation of rural areas has finally stopped. Taxpayer penury has set in again, partly out of recognition that school bureaucracies were sometimes creating over-bloated empires. A huge jump in the professional sector of the population in the 1960s left an aftermath of overcrowding at that level. Lower-middle class people began to realize that they had been (or would be) over-trained for the routine jobs they could realistically aspire to. As the birth rate went down, schools found themselves with fewer numbers of children to teach. University enrollments also levelled off. There began to be a serious oversupply of teachers. Education appeared to be headed for a period of relative decline.

On another level, expectations had risen faster than objective improvements in the educational system, producing a growing sense of disillusionment and skepticism. The paradox was that in 1900, with sixty students per grammar school classroom, education had been assumed to work. It was regarded as the great molder of the kind of society the middle-class wanted to create, homogeneous, attuned to the needs of industrialism, ambitious within the accepted moral limits. Moreover, despite crowded conditions, immigrants—with only some notable exceptions—took to the American grade schools in a spirit of at least partial willingness. They recognized the need to learn to read and do simple sums. Perhaps immigrant children learned more of their English on the streets than in the classroom, but in these decades their desire to conform and get along inconspicuously in the strange New World setting could be intense. For the masses of blacks who replaced them in the poorer city neighborhoods after World War II, school, even in this basic sense, seemed far more unreal. Centuries of racism had produced the widespread attitude that it was meaningless to try to compete in the white man's world. Meanwhile, schoolteachers were often from the most ambitious white ethnic minorities, projecting an attitude of intolerance for failure. In the 1950s and 1960s, urban schools increasingly became marked by scenes of open violence, erupting out of a background of sullen defiance. Schools came more and more to resemble prisons.

Racial integration of schools slowly gained ground after the Supreme Court ruling of 1954. But as white resistance to full integration manifested itself, black leaders began instead demanding a new, more dignified form of separatism, whereby schools would be adjusted to the realities of black culture, rather than insisting upon homogenized, traditional ideals. A belief in equality of opportunity had been the driving force behind the integrationist campaign. But the new desire for neighborhood and ethnic autonomy was neither equalitarian nor individualist; instead it stressed membership identity in a group smaller than that of the societal whole. Despite the clash of such a conception with some of the most traditional American values, whites often regarded the new black insistence upon cultural autonomy with relief, for it seemed to signal an end to any expectations of forced interracial contact. Pluralism became a mask for the survival of racism, at the cost of the social homogenization that maximizes the role of merit.

Meanwhile, urban upper-middle class whites had likewise been losing confidence in the public school system. But the source of their malaise was different. In part, it sprang from a panicky desire to continue to avoid contact with blacks—the same motive that sometimes produced physical flight into the farther suburbs. Private schools had always been a fixture of elite life, especially on the East Coast; now they became more of a routine expectation in the larger cities, signalling the arrival of something like the British dual system of education along class lines. They spread widely in the South during the 1960s, partly as a means of evading genuine racial integration.

By a smaller faction among the advantaged, the public schools were attacked on more philosophical grounds. Liberal intellectuals deplored their standardizing effect, their inadequate concern for individual growth and expression. School superintendents, successful victors in the earlier war against the political bosses, were perceived as entrenched empire-builders, incredibly self-satisfied and ingrown. With such bureaucrats in charge of them, schools would never foster the free-ranging development of the mind and the emotions. The earlier progressive education movement, which in the 1930s had gained sway in many school systems, trumpeted the slogans of individualism but failed to work enough actual transformation. The rhetoric of educators, whether reformist or stand-pat, appeared to outsiders to float in a cloudland of vagueness that often approached incomprehensibility. One message could be understood, that a hierarchy was determined to go on protecting its own power. A few radical scholars and publicists reacted by questioning the value of compulsory attendance and even of schooling itself as an institution.

Thus from both ends of the society, bottom and top, came accusations that the schools as they existed reflected the plodding (yet doggedly universalistic) values of the lower-middle class. On this every minority could agree, though the affluent whites were divided between the small but vocal element seeking radical individual liberation and the more numerous segment who instead wished conventional academic training, but at a force-fed pace, conducted in surroundings insulated from the distracting influence of the ill-motivated. As a practical matter, blacks concentrated on gaining local control of the segments of the public school systems that served them, while white dissidents more often looked to private schools as an alternative. (So, as always, did Catholics, for their own reasons.)

The result, from all angles, was growing loss of confidence in the public school system as an all-embracing, homogenizing force in the society. By most spokesmen, neither individualism nor equality was so much desired as the freedom to live out one's life dream as a member of a social class or an ethnic group, unhampered by outside interference. The change in attitude appeared to signal a relaxation of the effort toward achieving a better condition for everyone, defined in some single, sweeping fashion, and instead a withdrawal to the comforts (scant or abundant) of a much narrower conception of community.

Higher education had also been the focus of a more universalistic dream, qualified only by a conception of merit. Of course this had once concealed its subservience in social terms to a small minority of the Protestant elite. (Jews were widely excluded from faculty positions, and limited by student quotas, at some of the "best" American universities until the revelations of the Nazis triggered shame.) After 1945 the great rise in attendance obscured the continued predominance of a small number of leading universities. The bulk of the newly admitted enjoyed a style of training, in junior and state colleges, little superior to that of the high school. Attendance at such institutions was often only a socially acceptable holding action, allowing participation in the pleasures of the youth culture and postponing as long as possible the choice among routine, unexciting careers.

At the top level, though, thanks in part to an influx of European refugees, the American university in the 1950s began tardily to fulfill the great expectations of its founders back in the 1890s. The tone of seriousness increased, as a much larger share of students now anticipated going on to graduate school. Fear over Russian achievements in the wake of Sputnik occasioned an uncharacteristic if short-lived national sympathy for basic research, giving higher education an artificial boom from about 1958 to 1966. The scholar and the expert were heralded as the social leaders and planners of the future. It was falsely imagined that politicians would closely listen to their advice. In actual fact, knowledge in hundreds of specialties did enormously expand. The intellectual exhilaration of those days was genuine. But after 1967 student radicalism, constricted budgets, the resurgence of popular anti-intellectualism, and the grim realities of the lowered birthrate dimmed the entire picture. American intellectuals of all political persuasions, so hopeful in the mid-1960s, emerged demoralized in the mid-1970s.

On its face the entire American educational system had grown far stronger and more pervasive in recent decades. But the quantitative outreach masked inner hollowness. Schools were unable to function as an effective moral agency when they fell prey to the dividedness of the population as to what values, what norms, were to be transmitted. Youth of nearly all kinds regarded schools with increasing puzzlement, detachment, and alienated rejection. Yet, in bloated numbers, youth still marched through these institutions, finding in them at least a certain value as centers for social aggregation.

Education, probably more than any other institution, presented the spectacle of an enormous gap between the rhetoric that surrounded it and the realities of its everyday performance. These realities—which could include examples of dedicated teaching—seemed almost impossible to fathom, so blurred were they behind the shrill outcry of all the mutually discordant critics. An apparatus existed. It was not being put to best use. It probably could not be, given the vested stake of the bureaucracy that ran it and the conflicting demands of the various kinds of parents. In this latter respect, the situation mirrored the absence of value consensus in American society on many important levels. If there was a single American ethic, it could no longer confidently imprint itself upon the young in the course of their formal training.

"IN GOD WE TRUST"

When we move from education to religion, we shift from an area of growth (however much we may dispute its meaning) to one of outright decline. The fundamental fact about the long-term history of religion in America is its lessening degree of influence—the secularization of the society.

The process goes back much farther than we used to think. Recent research has revealed seasons of widespread backsliding even in seventeenth-century New England. Periodic revivals would then occur. Rationalism and skepticism were widespread at the time of the American Revolution. We tend to forget this because of the intense new wave of evangelical piety in the opening decades of the nineteenth century. Then, extending roughly from 1850 to 1880, a new and apparently decisive trend toward secularization set in within the urban middle-class. Initially it did not take the form of an abandonment of church attendance, but of a shift in the internal content of religion, away from an other-worldly theology and toward a style of preaching centered in admonitions toward good conduct. Sometimes the new message was complacently conservative, as if specifically designed for businessmen; sometimes, by 1900, it was reformist, urging a changed society. In either case, it now took its tone from the surrounding worldly social context, rather than from the traditional distinctive Christian gospel of individual salvation. Thus, although the percentage of Americans who are church members has actually increased in the twentieth century, the rise reflects the very fact that specific theological beliefs of newcomers are not scrutinized as they once were. And meanwhile church attendance per capita has been slowly but steadily declining ever since Gallup polls were first taken on the subject at the end of the 1930s—with the exception of a temporary upsurge during a few years of the mid-1950s. In all parts of the country today except the West Coast, about forty percent of the population attends church during a typical week. The Far West, with its better climate, finds only about thirty percent attracted.

The United States became more heterogeneous in religious terms after the mid-nineteenth century, as immigrants poured in who were Catholic or Jewish. In general, secularization of beliefs and attitudes spread as rapidly among Jews as it did among Protestants. Catholics remained noticeably more devout; indeed, there is evidence that their religious zeal increased in the New World, the church becoming a symbol of continuity in an unfamiliar environment. Only in the 1960s did American Catholicism begin to show some of the same symptoms of inner atrophy that had long marked Protestantism and Judaism. It seemed likely, in the calmer atmosphere of the 1970s, that religiosity would continue to ebb slowly from the American consciousness, rather than being affected by any abrupt shock waves.

And yet only a tiny percentage of Americans would declare outright that they were atheists. In a nominal sense the idea of a religious commitment seemed to be more widespread than ever, though at the vaguest possible level of belief in "something." The commonest pattern appeared to be that of saying very little about religion, and living one's life as if it did not exist, but stopping short of an open, public break with it. Here was an area where individualism seemingly functioned as a value. It was not good manners to question anyone else's beliefs. Yet this convention may reflect the fact that beliefs had become rather unimportant. Even a generation ago parents would commonly make strenuous objections to the interfaith marriages of their offspring. Now, one Jew out of three marries a Gentile, and the frequency of Protestant-Catholic marriages is also rising. The older generation, so seldom successful in determining the life course of its children, has finally surrendered in this once extremely touchy area. In the 1950s, Will Herberg wrote that Protestantism, Catholicism, and Judaism had become three empty boxes. But part of his point was that each of them was then symbolically being maintained in aloof purity from the others. Now even the last is no longer true, except among small pockets of enthusiasts.

Vitality remains in American religion, but it is at the fringes, in groups such as the Mormons, Jehovah's Witnesses and other Fundamentalist sects, and, for a small sector of the middle-class, in Asian mysticism. These are all religious movements that have continued to require a series of demanding beliefs from their followers. Emphatically they stand out against the mainstream of American life, offering deep psychological rewards to those who are alienated from its pleasure-seeking values. Often, though not always, they are intensely charismatic, attracting converts not just to a doctrine or world-view but, along with that, to an inspired leader or guru. In style, and often in content, these extreme religious groups are not different from those, such as the Anabaptists and Levellers, that appeared during the Reformation, struggling to survive on the fringes of Protestantism. In American terms, they are no sudden phenomenon of the 1960s.

Rather they have had a continuous history. What seemed new about them was a distinct resurgence, based upon an appeal to youth. Previously they had been regarded as survivals in marginal small town or rural locations such as Utah and the Southern states, or in urban centers of the recently transplanted, such as Los Angeles. It was assumed that with growing sophistication they would disappear. Instead they briefly boomed. One hazards the guess, however, that with the return to less obviously unsettling times, we shall again hear less of them, though we have been reminded of their remarkable resiliency.

In general, religion now reflects other outside values and tugs of interest, ranging from women's liberation to ethnicity. It is an arena where these social conflicts are still occasionally fought out, but it fails to pull anything like its nominal weight as an independent force. In most of the present world the nation-state, the political ideology, or the aspiring social group has replaced God as the focus for active, ardent personal commitment. The fact that considerably more Americans than Europeans still go to church tells us little of real importance about the American character. The church, like the high school, is mainly a social meeting-ground.

A SENSE OF BELONGING

Like religion, the more nebulous realm of the community would appear to be a declining factor in American life. (For a contrary interpretation, emphasizing recent neglected examples of civic renewal, see John Fischer's article in *The New York Times*, August 1, 1975, p. 25.) In broad terms such observers as Robert Bellah have pointed to the rituals of civic observance as a modern substitute for religion, involving the transfer of energy and loyalty from an other-worldly focus to the social order. While such an analysis helps explain the phenomenon of mass patriotism, which is itself only about a hundred and fifty years old, on the more local and immediate level it may confuse the wishes of community-minded political scientists with the realities of recent American life.

If we could return to the American town or city of 1900, one of the most striking differences we would immediately notice was the much higher level of participation, in an affirmative, enthusiastic sense, in political activity. This held true both among the evangelically minded reformers seeking to purify municipal government and also, strikingly, among the immigrants who were so frequently tied in to the "boss"-ruled machines. In the latter case, a large share of the attention was practical, linked to the quest for jobs, food, and favors. Yet the result in either event was the same: involved participation. The highest percentages of voter turn-out in our history date from the late nineteenth century, paradoxically a time when the two major parties offered almost no contrast to each other in terms of issues. (The maximum in a presidential race was eighty percent in the contest between Grover Cleveland and Benjamin Harrison in 1888.) Huge crowds at political rallies, torchlight parades, and Fourth of July speeches set the tone. Party loyalties ran very high. The "independent voter," the man who takes pride in making up his own mind at the last minute, was scarcely dreamed of. Politics and civic activism in general went forward in the cheer-the-team atmosphere we now associate with football. The contrast between then and now measures the tendency toward privatization and withdrawal of our commitments from the open, public arena that has occurred during the course of the twentieth century. This is not the result of a change in the caliber of men willing to run for high office. If anything, despite some recent instances to the contrary, a larger number of broad-minded and idealistic candidates run at present than were typical in the 1890s. The earlier automatic intense loyalties existed in a political context which, to our view, appears dull, humdrum, and corrupt. A bit later, within reform circles during the Progressive Era (1901–1917), millions of voters sustained the optimistic belief that through their participation the system could be changed—abuse could be corrected. Though some of that hope survives on the national level today, surfacing in the self-congratulation after the outcome of Watergate, on the state and local civic level there is a far more prevalent attitude of cynicism and powerlessness. It almost seems as though a certain naïveté was required in order to sustain a confident faith in the workings of democratic institutions.

Political scientists, if they are committed to an ideal of universal, harmonious participation in the life of the community, frequently lament this alteration in the American consciousness. Rightly they perceive in cynicism a basic threat to the social order. But the change is in large part a result of the fact that people—ordinary people—have become somewhat more discerning. During the election campaign of 1972, television cameras invaded a Polish-American working-class home on the south side of Milwaukee to record that the husband and wife were leaning in opposite directions, quite sophisticatedly weighing issues and personalities, and sincerely unable to predict how they would vote in advance of election day. How unthinkable this display of cool, measured independence would have been in 1900! Yet the very act of standing back from the fray to make up one's own mind, regarding all slogans and speeches with an inbuilt suspicion, detaches us from the automatic, enthusiastic loyalties that make for an "organic" state of social health. It might seem that when the Poles of Milwaukee behave somewhat like liberal academic intellectuals, the society is in grave danger. Of course the opposite still exists in the old-fashioned style of enthusiasm among the supporters of George Wallace.

It may be that some of this worry is overblown. Privatization, when it amounts to holding aloof from the knee-jerk responses of the crowd, might alternatively be regarded as a further extension of the traditional American value of individualism. It could be offered as evidence that other-directedness, after all, has been retreating rather than advancing, despite the talk we used to hear about rising conformity in the 1950s. It might even be argued that low voter turnout in a race between Nixon and McGovern (given what voters knew about Nixon at the time) recorded a highly understandable mass state of indecision. Who would want to go back to the days of delirious, unquestioning partisanship for the likes of Cleveland and Harrison? Standoffishness toward mediocrity may be a further intrinsic aspect of the revolution of rising expectations, and thus a symptom of enormous progress.

But this leaves us still wondering about the fate of American community-mindedness in the more local sense. Where, concretely, can we locate so much as the memory of it? No doubt the first image that strikes us in this connection is the American small town, especially as it survives in such regions as the Middle West. When we think of community, it is partly of these tree-shaded streets, with their relaxed, slow-moving way of life and shared knowledge of everyone's affairs. Yet historically their collective spirit has often been mixed with prejudice, not as restrictive as pictured in some satirical novels and less so now than in the 1920s, but such towns are seldom havens of diversity or adventure. Small-town Elks clubs have been among the last bastions of outright, blanket discrimination against dark-skinned people in the United States. Within the in-group there is of course much genuine neighborliness and warmth. But in any event, the small town is no longer where most Americans live. Our centralized economic system assures their continuing marginality.

Where else, then, are we to look for symptoms of community spirit in contemporary America? The neighborhoods of big cities sometimes function in this way, though the high rate of in-and-out movement we undergo makes most of them quite impersonal. Moreover, community consciousness in a neighborhood is most apt to leap up defensively against some outside "threat"—once again, typically, a response to a "lower" ethnic group believed to be seeking to worm its way in, or a municipal administration bent on raising taxes. In any event, even such a style of neighborly cohesion is likewise an exception.

A wide tendency of recent years has been the self-conscious attempt to refashion a sense of community on some basis other than geographical. Most importantly, it involves the efforts of ethnic groups to reclaim a sense of their collective identities, after decades or centuries when they had most of all dreamed of being treated like anybody else. Behind the artificiality of many such attempts lay a deeply genuine hunger for belonging and self-pride. The wearing of the *yarmulke* or the *dashiki* recorded a passionate desire to find some basis, in a disillusioned, postindustrial society, for a meaningful group loyalty that could stand independent of self-interested wielders of bureaucratic power. Equally determined, though quite different, were the efforts to recreate community on a small-group basis among radically inclined youth of the white middle or upper class. The commune movement of the early 1970s had the earmarks of a zealous fad. Though inspired by an ethic of thoroughgoing equality, it broke down rapidly because the still stronger drive toward individual self-fulfillment collided with the need for sacrifice, producing constant acts of secession, wandering, and recombination. Membership in an ethnic group was, in one important sense, nonvoluntary; membership in a commune had all the frailty of the totally deliberate act in an age that applauded neverending spontaneity. Historically, the communal spirit has thrived most powerfully when allegiances are inborn, automatic, unthinking, indeed with as little accurate knowledge of "outside" ways of life as possible.

Such a recipe brings home to us the extreme difficulty of reconcocting a binding sense of community at this late point in time. We have eaten of the apple of individualism, relativism, and cosmopolitanism. We know that we can break off relationships, shift roles, move about with ease from one scene to another. We find it hard to imagine a world where there is no choice. Even for blacks inclined toward separatism and an African identity, there is truly no going back home again, for they are too intimately aware of white culture and too deeply entwined with it on at least some levels. Even more effortlessly, many communalists can take a vacation with their parents. The cultural worlds we reject go on subtly influencing us. And the sheer fact of so much intermarriage between groups steadily blurs the dividing lines we willfully seek to keep intact. The very intensity of our hunger for community may reflect how far we have drifted along a course leading away from its possible realization.

The yearning was poignant; but its volume was a yardstick recording failure. Ultimately, mobility in the simplest sense—the fact that a third of all American families move each year—may mean everything. Communities of the more self-conscious types spring to life only haltingly and unevenly because individuals seldom stay put anywhere for very long.

SUMMING UP

After growing up in America, the next thing we do is settle down. Despite all the childhood fantasizing about Wild West gunfighters, the typical young adult marries and tries to buy a house. Mass-produced tastes, in wives and furnishings, predominate. Individualism detaches us from the claims of many of the centrally inherited customs of the longer past. But it leaves us in no sea of open anarchy. Pattern remains. It is still predictable that department store sales will rise each December. The pursuit of pleasurable self-interest is muffled by all sorts of surviving proprieties. The 1960s counterculture did not, in the long run, erase the commonly accepted boundary between behavior considered normal and eccentric. Far from drifting into the liberated utopia a few bold spirits envisioned, we began to hang up signs reasserting the need for a degree of conventional attire in restaurants. The twin realms of work and family go on prescribing that we spend most of our time acting out highly developed roles. The conversations we overhear in public places still nearly always have this patterned quality to them, permitting ready identification of the speaker's role and status. This is as good an indication as any that American society, as we have long known it, is not on the verge of breaking down. Despite its corrosive effects upon a variety of institutions, individualism has never cut that deep. Indeed, it always amounted more nearly to self-assertion in a variety of ways that themselves rapidly became customary and role-defined. The long-term shift has been from the male-oriented individualism of economic aggrandizement to the more universally defined individualism of pleasure and "fulfillment." But pleasure-seeking even now is only exceptionally regarded as a solitary activity, and so it remains attached to the realm of expected social roles and stereotypes. We dream of liberation from some of our roles more freely than we once did; we are more commonly capable of viewing them from a greater distance; but most of the time, most of us go right on playing them.

Equality, the other central theme in estimations of the American character, is perhaps more truly corrosive of social roles than individualism—if the roles continue to be linked to perceptions about social status. In part, equality merely asserts anybody ought to be able to play. But that is its milder definition, centering on opportunity. The deeper vision of the radical equalitarian is not to allow the roles with unusual pretensions to dignity and power (tycoon, politician) to exist. The main focus of the drive toward greater equality in America, which ran its course from the mid-1930s to the mid-1960s in a truly impressive fashion, was toward finally realizing the highly traditional goal of equality of opportunity, buttressed by the most elementary kind of equality of all, that pertaining to the legal sphere. But the harsher, levelling version of equality, involving wealth redistribution and forced ethnic balances in schools, was decisively rejected. And indeed, after about 1968, the demand for any kind of further forward movement suddenly lost steam a tantalizing distance short of the full acceptance of blacks into the casual mainstream of American life. Despite some tokenism, numerous social roles and spheres remained quite precisely identified with prestige—suggesting a given social background, above and beyond considerations of training, expertise, maturity, and merit.

Thus America remained a patterned society, not a chaotic one. To grow up in it was still to spend a lot of one's time learning what and what not to do, even if etiquette was superficially more casual. Indeed, the unmarried sexual affair has its own usual rhythms and expectations of role between the partners. So did the homosexual marriage, and so did the very modern kind of marriage between two career-oriented professionals based on "women's liberation." In all these cases, stability could be achieved, boundaries of acceptable behavior set, and a predictable quality enter into the routines. The changing definition of the family did not lead to copulation in the streets, an outcome that the anarchist Yippie prophet Abbie Hoffman had openly called for in 1968.

Perhaps the remarkable fact is how easy it has been for most Americans to go on living some version of a settled life despite the weakening of some of the central institutions (especially religion and local communities) that had propped up the social order in premodern Europe, despite the widespread failure of the schools to fill the breech, despite the very high rate of physical mobility, and despite the far more venturesome way in which the family itself was being redefined in some circles. America was no late Roman Empire. Instead, it was a postindustrial society. The interesting comparisons are rather with England, France, Germany, Scandinavia, and Japan. To grow up in America was to slide giddily through a faddish oasis of youth culture and then to enter and be conditioned by the two time-honored realms of work and family, often in surprisingly prosaic versions. The value placed upon individualism, equality, and mobility reduced the once awesome aspect of rigid inherited institutions. But, except in certain neighborhoods where life has been disorganized by continuing poverty and prejudice, the result was another kind of social order, not the absence of one. It may be criticized from numerous points of view—as monotonous, inelegant, or too lacking in human feeling. But, with its cleft and subcultures as well as with its wide areas of consensus, it exists. Beneath the level of all the unruly self-assertion, the child growing up is leaning, mainly in informal but highly potent ways outside the classroom, about what it will offer him or her and how one must accommodate oneself to it.

17
The United States and China

BARBARA TUCHMAN

• The 1970s have marked a new era in foreign relations. Emerging nations in Asia, Africa, and Latin America are acting more independently than they have in the past and will continue to move away from formal alliances with the superpowers. The number of nations possessing at least limited nuclear capability has expanded to almost a dozen, and as a result, the United States and the Soviet Union no longer share the only key to world survival.

Perhaps the sharpest shift in international diplomacy came when President Richard M. Nixon made an historic state visit to the People's Republic of China in 1972. It had been twenty-three years since Chiang Kai-shek and his Nationalist Army had been driven from the mainland by Communist forces under Mao Tse-Tung, and the entire period had been marked by intense hostility and distrust between the United States and the new government of the most populous country on earth. But as television cameras flashed pictures of the American President's trip it was as though a heavy curtain was being raised to reveal forbidden sights. A New York department store held a special sale of basketry and other handicrafts from the Chinese mainland, and the store was mobbed by eager purchasers. Shortly thereafter, tall, lean, eye-shadowed models paraded through the pages of high fashion magazines in the latest fad—the straight-cut uniform of the Chinese Peasant. For Americans more accustomed to thinking of the "yellow peril," the rapid shift in their nation's attitude toward China was met with deep-seated suspicion and doubt.

Barbara Tuchman, one of our best known historians, was a young correspondent in China in the 1930s, when the Japanese began to make their first military forays on the mainland. The following speech by Mrs. Tuchman, delivered in 1972 at about the time of President Nixon's trip, provides a harsh but perceptive analysis of American foreign policy in the Far East.

When one proposes to talk about the United States and China, every-one immediately wants to know what one thinks of the President's trip. I will come to that later, but first I think that what a historian can more usefully do is to tell you something of the past that led to the twenty-five years of broken relations and profound mutual hostility through which we have just passed. In 1954—to remind you of the attitude of those years—*Life* magazine described Chou En-lai, Mr. Nixon's recent host, as "a political thug, a ruthless intriguer, a con-cienceless liar, a saber-toothed political assassin." At the same time the Chinese were regularly denouncing us as vicious imperialists and ag-gressors, brutal oppressors, and of course paper tigers. All this name calling was not funny, but a tragic testimony to the failure of our China policy. Considering that the failure led to two wars—in Korea and Vietnam—the damage done, as much morally to this country as physically to Asia, will leave a long-enduring mark.

Our century and a half of relationship with China was broken off in 1949, four years after the end of World War II, with the crash of Chiang Kai-shek's government and his replacement by the Commu-nists. The break marked a wasted effort and the utter defeat of our wartime objective in Asia. That objective was a stable, united demo-cratic China, strong enough to be able to fill the vacuum that would be left by the defeat of Japan, a China that, as the fourth pillar of the United Nations structures, would keep the peace of Asia in the post-war world. This was Roosevelt's constant aim. Stilwell was less de-ceived about possibilities, but both he and FDR, for all that they so miserably misunderstood each other, kept one fundamental goal in mind: that China's vast population, the famous 500 million of that day, between a fifth and a quarter of the world's people, must be on our side in the difficult future. That future is now the present, and the Chinese cannot be said to be on our side in any sense of underlying alliance or common aim. There has been re-opening of dialogue, to be sure, which is certainly welcome and long overdue, but let us not sup-

From *The Colorado Quarterly*, XXI, No. 1 (Summer 1972), The University of Colorado. Reprinted by permission.

pose that it will blossom into friendship overnight or that it is based on anything but a very precariously balanced concept of mutual expediency.

In World War II we had technically won a victory in Asia insofar as we defeated the enemy Japan, but we lost the goal that would have made sense of the victory—a China on our side. The reason for the failure was that we overlooked, or failed to take into consideration, the Chinese revolution. As a result, in the last twenty-two years we have fought two more wars in Asia, one of them the longest, wrongest, least successful belligerent action in our history.

An American foreign policy that brought us to this predicament, dislike abroad and alienation at home, must have something wrong with it. As a historian I believe three main factors can be discerned as responsible: First, the illusion not only that we should, but that we can, shape the destiny of other peoples in conformity with our own; second, the corruption of power, and the greater corruption of becoming a Great Power, which has transformed the United States from a progressive into a reactionary nation in world affairs; third, the persistent failure to form policy on the basis of available knowledge and information.

The first factor is a product of the Christian, especially Protestant, missionary urge to confer our ways, our values, and our methods upon those we choose to regard as heathen, ignoring the fact that they have social and cultural values of their own as valid as ours and older, which may well entitle them to regard *us* as heathen. The Chinese, in fact, have always regarded all foreigners as barbarians and themselves as superior, in token of which no foreigner could approach the Emperor during the last dynasty without performing the kowtow, prostrate on the floor. Their tragedy during their humiliating century of foreign penetration from about 1840 to 1940 was that somehow, inexplicably, superior values could not be made to prevail over barbarian force.

The American missionary impulse that was an essential part of this penetration was based on the twin illusion, as regards Asia, (a) that our ways were applicable, and (b) that they were wanted. The motive is beneficent but the attitude is arrogant, and the beneficence is never unmixed. It was intended to work both ways, as much to the benefit of the donor as the recipient. Originally China's vastness excited the missionary impulse; it appeared as the land of the future whose masses, when converted, offered promise of Christian and even English-speaking dominion of the world. Disregarding the social and ethical structure which the Chinese found suitable, the missionaries wanted them to change to one in which the individual was sacred and the democratic principle dominant, whether or not these concepts were relevant to China's way of life. Inevitably the missionary, witnessing China's decay in the nineteenth century, took this as evidence that China could not rule herself and that her problems could only be solved by foreign help.

Along with this went the alluring prospect of 400 million (as they were then reckoned) customers; if each added a half inch to the length of his shirt-tail and a half ounce of oil to the lamps of China, our commerce would reap grand and illimitable profits. This too proved an illusion, now laid to rest in the textbooks as the "Myth of the China Market."

While that myth was vanishing, another myth was replacing it: that China, following the Revolution of 1911 that overthrew the Manchus, was a developing democracy just like ours. Because Dr. Sun Yat-sen and many of his associates in the new Chinese republic were Christian and westernized, in many cases America-educated, Americans at once assumed that 1911 was China's Bunker Hill and Valley Forge, so to speak. The American public on the whole wanted to believe what the missionaries were always promising, that China of the 400 million was about to transform itself into that desirable and familiar thing, a democracy. When a rebel leader in Hankow, out of Oriental politeness, which believes in telling people what presumably they want to hear, said to reporters that "the object of our revolt is to make the government of China like that of America," nothing could have seemed more natural to American readers. We habitually forget that Thomas Jefferson did not operate in Asia. Americans tend to think of all people in the Near and Far East and Africa as so many young birds waiting with mouths open for democracy to be dropped in. This is a dangerous misconception.

It was crowned by the advent of Chiang Kai-shek. When, as the successor to Sun Yat-sen, he finally established a national government in 1928, the event was hailed by China's well-wishers as the completion of the democratic process. But Chiang Kai-shek's rise to national power was accomplished at the cost of a profound split between right and left within his party, the Kuomintang.

The left, under the controlling influence of the Communists who were then members of the Kuomintang, was dedicated to carrying out the social revolution delayed since the great Taiping Rebellion of the 1850s, China's failed French revolution. In 1927 Mao Tse-tung and his comrades were busy organizing rent strikes and antilandlord demonstrations among the peasants, and Mao was promising that soon, all over China, "several hundred million peasants will rise like a tornado and rush forward along the road to revolution." This was hardly calculated to win the support of landlord and capitalist families, whose adherence Chiang Kai-shek needed. To achieve power he had to have the revenue and loans he could only obtain in alliance with capitalism. The Communists, however, besides organizing the peasants were equally active among the proletariat and labor unions of Shanghai. Chiang was determined that that great metropolis of commerce, banking, and foreign trade should not fall under left-wing control as Hankow already had. Shanghai was where the break had to be made.

On the night of April 12-13, 1927, Chiang's forces carried out a bloody purge of the left, disarming and hunting down all who could be found and killing more than three hundred. The Shanghai purge and the choice it represented was as portentous an event as any in modern history. The Kuomintang Revolution was turned from Red to Right. Chiang's coup was both turning point and point of no return. He was now on the way to unity but he had fixed the terms of an underlying disunity that would become his nemesis.

Foreigners were reassured. The missionaries and educators and advisers, eager to believe that their ideas were taking root, persuaded themselves that the Kuomintang, with its source in the Christian Sun Yat-sen, was the sincerely progressive force that would at last end civil strife and bring good government to China. They, and under their influence the American public, saw in the Chinese a people rightly struggling to be free and assumed that because they were struggling for sovereignty, they were also struggling for democracy.

That the formal unity Chiang had achieved was superficial, that his government rested insecurely on power deals and pay-offs, that for the sake of alliance with landlords and capitalists it had turned against its origins and taken the road of repression and reaction, including a White Terror that claimed an estimated one million victims—all this was given little attention. The more so as Chiang Kai-shek was a Christian, one of the most important and overlooked factors in the American delusion about China.

Chiang was converted to Christianity in order to marry into the wealth, influence, and connections of the Soong family which had been Christian for several generations. His wife was the attractive, sophisticated, thoroughly westernized, American-educated Mei-Ling Soong, a graduate of Wellesley. She was to have immeasurable effect on the image of China that came through to Americans. Once when Stilwell, at the height of his frustration, was trying to analyze what Chiang had working for him vis-a-vis the Americans, he wrote a list of factors and put down as number one, "Mme. Chiang's Wellesley diploma." This was not because Wellesley was anything so special (I speak as a graduate of another place), but because Madame with her American schooling and perfect English made China seem more familiar, more comprehensible to us than in fact it was.

The missionaries and the church groups in America rallied to the Chiangs in self-interested loyalty because the Chiangs' Christianity at the helm of China provided such gratifying proof of the validity of the missionary effort. They overpraised Chiang and once committed to his perfection regarded any suggestion of blemish as inadmissible. "China now has the most enlightened, patriotic, and able rulers in her history," stated the *Missionary Review of the World*. If the leaders of the new China were products of Western influence, surely this indicated that the West could indeed shape the destiny of the East. It was a powerful and flattering idea.

By now were present in force the two chief illusions about China: one that pictured her as our ward, and the second that pictured the Chinese as just like us only a little behind, but coming along nicely toward political democracy and the Bill of Rights. These illusions were given classic expression by two great American presidents, Woodrow Wilson and Franklin Roosevelt. In 1921 in the course of a great famine relief program for China organized in the U.S. under missionary influence, Wilson told the public, "To an unusual degree the Chinese people look to us for counsel and for effective leadership." As an expression of American self-delusion, this has never been surpassed. The Chinese themselves never confused material aid, which was what they looked to America for, with either counsel or leadership.

Roosevelt's statement was made in 1943 in the midst of World War

II. At the time Stilwell was urging that Chiang Kai-shek must be told, not asked for military performance in return for Lend-Lease. In reproof, Roosevelt wrote to General Marshall, his Chief of Staff, to say that the head of a great state could not be treated like that. "Chiang Kai-shek has come up the hard way," he wrote, "to become undisputed leader of 400 million people and to create in a very short time throughout China what it took us a couple of centuries to attain."

Now it is true that the Chinese people had a cultural unity older and stronger than anything in the United States and a tremendous cohesion that enabled them to withstand bad government. But the idea that Chiang's leadership was undisputed or that in only fifteen harassed and embattled years he had obtained the same degree of national consent and representative government as in the U.S. was a fantasy. Nor was it a harmless one, for it allowed America to rest policy on an already collapsing base.

The war, of course, confirmed the image of China as one of us. Since China was resisting Japan, a fascist aggressor, and since fascism was opposed to democracy, China must therefore be a democracy. This syllogism became dogma when we entered the war as China's ally. It was the version presented to the American public and endlessly and effectively proclaimed by China's propagandists from Mme. Chiang down. Yet even before the war it had been clear enough to a sober historian, Whitney Griswold, future president of Yale, that Chiang's regime, as he wrote in 1938, was a "fascist dictatorship." It was exasperatingly clear to every American who worked in China under the conditions of a police state during the war. Stilwell used to mutter in his diary about the strange incompatibility of the American effort to support a government that was just like the government we were fighting in Germany. He called Chiang Kai-shek "Peanut" and referred to his hilltop residence as "Peanut's Berchtesgaden."

Throughout the war our endeavor was to supply, sustain, and support China and so energize her war effort as to enable her to contain and ultimately defeat the Japanese, a huge occupation force of over a million men, on the mainland. This was Stilwell's mission. The purpose was not of course eleemosynary. The object was to utilize Chinese, instead of American, manpower for the war on the mainland. In those unsophisticated days it was a fixed principle of our policy not to fight a war on the mainland of Asia. In the end the attempt to mobilize China was in vain. The Chinese concept of war was not ours; the impulse to reform and energize the army was not China's. The enormous effort that Stilwell commanded, the wealth of arms, supplies, and money poured into China through Lend-Lease, the valiant airlift flown for three years over the Hump through the worst flight conditions in the world, all were wasted. Stilwell himself recognized that to remake an army without remaking the political system from which it sprang was impossible. To reform such a system, he wrote, it must first be torn to pieces.

That unpleasant risk the American government was unwilling to contemplate, although the likelihood of collapse was becoming more and more obvious in China. We had saddled ourselves with support of Chiang and, fearing the alternatives, could not summon the resolution to enlarge our options. Repeatedly our foreign service officers, who made up the best informed foreign service in China, advised against unqualified support of an already outworn regime which in any free election would have been repudiated by 80 percent of the voters. For America to remain tied to such a regime, as one of the Embassy staff wrote, was a policy of "indolent short term expediency."

The terrible dilemma was that the only alternative appeared to be the Communists. If Chiang had long ago stolen their program, and introduced reforms, lowered taxes and land rents, loosened his repressive measures, opened the one-party government to other groups, widened his base of support, or made any real progress toward the original Three Principles of the Revolution, results might have been different. But the Kuomintang had failed its mandate and by now the Communists, entrenched in the north, were the only effectively organized rival.

This was the situation that faced us when the Cold War succeeded World War II, and communism replaced fascism as the menace. To detach ourselves from Chiang under the circumstances now appeared more risky than ever, besides certain to raise domestic outcry. All the evidence showed that his government was a losing proposition—powerless, corrupt, and engaged in a prolonged suicide in which the only sign of life was preparation to fight the Communists. We clung to him, however, partly from old illusions and a lethargic refusal to re-think, partly under the very effective pressure of the China Lobby and the Red-scaremongers at home, but mostly from fear of disturbing the status quo and *because* he was anti-Communist. The attachment would have made sense if our client, which was after all the legal government, had also been an *effective* government rooted in national consent. But there is little virtue in a client being anti-Communist if he is at the same time rotting from within.

Nevertheless we did our best to sustain him. We ferried his troops in their race with the Communists to retain control of North China and Manchuria from the Japanese. We continued to send Chiang Kai-shek arms, money, military advisers, and other forms of support. Since at the same time we were endeavoring to mediate between Nationalists and Communists in the hope of preserving our goal of a firm united China after the war, these measures on behalf of one side in China's civil conflict profoundly antagonized the other side who were soon to be the new rulers of China. It was at this time that our decisions on "the wrong side of history"—to use George Kennan's phrase —were made. As the Communists saw it, our aid to a discredited failing regime was prolonging the civil war in a country desperately weary of wars and misgovernment. America became in their eyes the guardian of reaction, the associate of landlords and aggressors, and the chief representative of all the old evils of foreign penetration. Our position was transformed from friend to enemy.

We had in fact chosen counter-revolution and made ourselves the ally of the *ancien régime*. We were locked into this position by the second factor of our foreign policy, the fact that since reaching world power in the early years of this century we have joined the Bourbons of history. This once brave young republic, the nation Lincoln called the "last best hope of earth," founded in the New World in conscious rejection of the past, had become a status quo power. Our only policy was to preserve the status quo everywhere as a fancied guarantee of safety. Fearful of political change, afraid to move with history, we clutched in desperate attachment to decrepit and outworn regimes which, lacking roots in popular consent, could not stand on their own feet without our support. This was as true of the Nationalist Government under Chiang Kai-shek as of the ally in Saigon in whom we now place our support.

In China in 1949 the Nationalist government finally collapsed and Chiang Kai-shek decamped for Formosa, leaving the mainland to the reign of a new Revolution. Our long support of Chiang was now left

an empty mockery. Worse than wrong, it had been unsuccessful. It
certainly had not succeeded in containing communism.

Meanwhile, Mao had become more doctrinaire, hardened in his
view of the world as divided into two opposing camps—socialism and
capitalist-imperialism—destined by nature for conflict. That, as Mao
insisted, was Marxist law from which there was no escape. The U.S.,
no longer the running dog of the imperialist, but now the arch-
imperialist itself, was the prime source of evil, the kind of figure whom
the Middle Ages (also doctrinaire) would have called Anti-Christ.
As such we could only be regarded by the Chinese as a foe dedicated
to their destruction whose every move must arouse the most profound
suspicion.

The Chinese appeared to us in exactly the same light. Our policy
was in the hands of John Foster Dulles, every bit as doctrinaire as
Mao, who regarded communism as a monstrous octopus whose
grasping tentacles must be instantly chopped off the minute one appeared. He was abetted by the hot air of McCarthyism, whipped up
by a mountebank as cynical as Dulles was priestly, who simply discovered anticommunism to be a good ploy. The American public allowed itself to be gulled, blackmailed, and terrorized into an hysteria
of denunciation and witch-hunts, informing on colleagues and wreck-
ing careers. Communist subversion and Communist plots were made
the convenient answer to all of the vague fears generated by the Bomb.

For total victory had not brought us self-confidence but anxiety. In
the nuclear age Americans felt for the first time what Europeans had
always lived with—the possibility of attack. This was the first great
shock. Then in 1949, the most populous country in the world, the
neighbor of Soviet Russia in Asia, our one-time protégé, our favorite
ally in World War II, was taken over by the Communists. That was
the second shock. Someone had to be blamed; and so followed the
hysteria of McCarthyism in the fifties.

Out of these attitudes on the part of both China and the U.S. came
the Korean War and the Quemoy-Matsu crisis and Dulles brinkman-
ship and the Taiwan treaty committing the U.S., in one of the greatest
absurdities of foreign policy ever self-inflicted by a great power, to the
defense of a discredited, impotent government in exile. And from there,
following the same track, to Vietnam with all its consequences.

I come now to the third factor. We do not choose the Francos and

Greek Colonels and Chiang Kai-sheks and Diems and Kys out of ignorance of their real nature or misjudgment of their strength. Our information is excellent; our foreign service is, or was, knowledgeable and
careful, our intelligence reasonably accurate, at least when the agents
confine themselves to intelligence and stay out of operations. Our
policy-makers could be well-informed if they read and digested the reports and, more important, thought about what they had read. Evidently they do not. Between informants in the field and policy-makers
in the capital lies a gulf whitened by the bones of failed and futile
policies of the past.

The pile accumulates by repetition. After the Russian Revolution
we waited sixteen years before recognizing the Soviet government, a
lapse without discernible benefit to anyone. It certainly did not contain the communism of that time. Learning nothing from the experience, we have now allowed twenty-three years to go by before being
pushed by history—and power politics—to open relations with Communist China. This second lapse, of which the war in Vietnam has
been part, cannot be said to have accomplished anything but damage
to everyone—to the Vietnamese, a people who have never done us any
harm, and to ourselves. Their country has been wrecked and ours
afflicted by a widespread and increasing mistrust of government, all in
the name of anticommunism. Now, suddenly, we have decided to
deal with Chinese communism although it is the same communism
whose potential for expansion we have fought for eight years in Vietnam to arrest. It would appear, then, that the purpose of the war was
invalid, or the danger overrated, which is not much comfort for those
who died. If we can work with Chinese communism today, why not
eight, ten, or twenty years ago?

Fear of communism, which is essentially the fear of the property
owner for the property-taker, has been the key to the trouble in our
foreign policy. If we are so genuinely confident of our own system,
why do we need to fear communism so? Despite Mr. Khrushchev, the
Communists are not going to bury us, nor we them. In the meantime,
why can we not allow a different system to others, whose needs are
different, whose position in history is different? As China's is, for one,
at least in the physical needs of the people. A reporter in Canton recently quoted a Mrs. Wang, now living in the most meager circumstances in two rooms with her family of five, but on *shore* not on a

river boat like generations of her ancestors. "Life in the old days was simply impossible," she said. "My father and older brother died of starvation and so did all of my brother's family."

Surely China had a right to its revolution, as no doubt did Hanoi, which does not mean that it would be right for *us*, but why must we always think of these things in absolute terms, as wrong *per se* if wrong for us? What is unacceptable to us might be necessary for them. If there is anything I have learned through my work, it is that there are few absolutes in history.

I have not personally seen the changes in China since 1949, but I think it is safe to take it from the reports of visitors that the mass of Chinese are better off than they were, in terms of material welfare if not political liberty. For those who for generations have been undernourished, overworked, and overtaxed, enough to eat may well be more important than political liberty and civil rights. Judging from all the documentaries and live news pictures of Chinese life we have seen in recent weeks, there is a regimentation and Big Brother thought control over there which none of us could stand for one week, least of all the Radical Left who are so given to screaming their heads off about oppression in American society. But we have different traditions, different backgrounds, and are accustomed to different liberties than the Chinese, especially in the area of individual rights. We cannot decide for them what values they should live by.

Personally, I think it unlikely that they will succeed in developing a new "Maoist man," in whom personal desires and ambitions have been replaced by dedication to the communal good. Mao may imagine he is doing it, but if he were to come back ten years after he dies, I imagine he would find a few surprises. I doubt that Maoism will prove to be a fixed condition for China. A nation that has undergone in the last decade the "Let a hundred flowers bloom" experiment and then its repression, then the explosion of the Cultural Revolution and then its reversal, cannot be said to be in a state of perfect equilibrium.

I would not venture to predict how China will develop in the next quarter century any more than I would for ourselves. Something is always waiting in the wings to give history a twist in an unexpected direction. I have learned not to predict because human behavior, in states as in individuals, does not follow the signposts of logic.

As for the trend initiated by the Peking visit, I think it is to the good: first, because it is a recognition of realities, which is always better than make-believe; second, because it expands two sets of dual confrontation, the U.S. vs. Russia and China vs. Russia, into a triangle, which makes more room for maneuver.

I am not impressed by all the wailing on the Right about losing the trust of our good friends in Taiwan, Saigon, and Tokyo—I believe they also throw in the Philippines, Thailand, South Korea, and a few others. This is nonsense. The relations of these nations or regimes with us are not based on trust and confidence but on necessity and self-interest. If they do not like our making contact with China, if it has implications that make them nervous, they have very little choice of another protector. But if they are moved toward making deals of their own and toward less dependence on the U.S., that, I think, can only be beneficial to them and to us. The idea that the policy of the U.S. must be tied forever to the tail of Taiwan is hardly sensible. It is an alliance with Rip Van Winkle. Saigon is an alliance with the grave.

Undeniably we are moving away from the spirit of our commitment to Taiwan, but since history is dynamite, not static, that obviously could not last forever—and the Nationalist Chinese would have been foolish if they supposed it could. The treaty has a clause providing for cancellation by either party on one year's notice. Until then it is unlikely that the clause requiring us to defend them militarily will be called upon because I doubt if the mainland Chinese will attempt to retrieve Taiwan by force. That would upset all kinds of apple carts, and they would hardly have invited the president of the U.S. to China if a military adventure—and challenge—of that kind was what they had in mind.

As for our friends in Japan, those worthy people who gave us Pearl Harbor, with whom not so long ago we were locked in a death struggle, the idea that they are necessarily our natural partner, whose tender trust in us we must under no account disturb by recognizing the existence of China, seems to me even more peculiar. The relationship we created with Japan, using them as a kind of advance buffer while they relied on our arms, may have worked so long as we were fixed in a position of rigid hostility to Communist China. But lacking a genuine bond of common roots and language and democratic tradition, as we had for instance with Great Britain, it was opportunist and artificial and could not have remained static. We may as well recognize that the future of Asia will be determined by China as well as, if not more than, by Japan, and it would be the most simple-minded stupidity on our part to choose permanent sides and commit ourselves to either one to the exclusion of the other.

The interesting thing that has been happening lately in international affairs, it seems to me—and I may be imagining it, or sensing something that is not yet at the conscious level, certainly not yet formulated —is a kind of approaching recognition that we are all really in the same boat, in danger of being overturned by environmental disaster; that the enemy is not so much each other as it is the common enemy of all: unrestrained growth and pollution. Perhaps the relaxation in international relations, if there is such, is a kind of subconscious preparation to deal with this state of affairs.

18

The Realities of U.S.–Mexican Relations

RICHARD R. FAGEN

• The United States has always had a peculiar relationship with other nations of the Western Hemisphere. On the one hand, Washington has since 1823 accepted the responsibility of "protecting" weaker countries against foreign dangers. On the other hand, it has failed to take steps to improve social and economic conditions in the region and has usually cooperated with conservative and repressive forces. As a result, "Yankeephobia" has long been a common sentiment in Latin America.

This ambivalent pattern is well illustrated by United States policy toward Mexico. In the 1920s and 1930s, Presidents Calvin Coolidge, Herbert Hoover, and Franklin D. Roosevelt generally withstood right-wing pressure and allowed Mexico to proceed with a number of social and economic reforms. This "Good Neighbor Policy" was designed to prove that the United States would not intervene in the domestic affairs of a sovereign nation even when Washington disapproved of the direction of government policy. Thus it was hoped that the traditional fear of a rich and powerful Uncle Sam would be alleviated.

Unfortunately, the rhetoric of American tolerance sometimes exceeded the reality of actual policy. Recently, when Mexican peasants in the northern parts of that country seized the lands on which they worked, President Luis Echeverría legalized their occupation by supporting genuine land reform. But the resulting shock waves in the American business community that was and is dependent on lucrative winter crops from Mexico were felt in Washington. Partly because of pressure from the United States, Echeverría's successor, López Portillo, backed away from the previously strong governmental support for land seizures by peasants.

As Richard Fagan points out in the article below, the discrepancy between the aspirations of American businessmen

and Mexican laborers will most likely cause increasing conflict unless American policy undergoes substantial change.

When Jimmy Carter toasted José López Portillo on the occasion of
the Mexican President's mid-February [1977] visit to Washington, he
drew a laugh from those assembled in the White House State Dining
Room by saying, "The Mexican people know what Yankee imperialism means, and being from Georgia, I have also heard the same phrase
used." He went on to add:

> There has been a saying of one of President López Portillo's
> predecessors, "*Pobre México. Tan lejos de Dios, tan cerca de los
> Estados Unidos*," which means in English, "Poor Mexico. So
> distant from God, so close to the United States." But I know
> that under President López Portillo's administration the distance
> from God has become much less and the proximity to the
> United States, I hope, will become a blessing and not a curse.

Earlier in the day, when greeting President Carter on the White
House lawn, President López Portillo had remarked:

> To be neighbors means to share everything, the good things and
> the bad things, too. We are absolutely convinced that it would
> not be correct to enhance the bad things that life brings on its
> own. On the other hand, friendship makes it possible for us to
> make progress by deepening and enhancing all good things.
> Therefore, it is advisable for good neighbors to be good friends.

Remarks on official state occasions are notoriously thin threads on
which to hang weighty analyses, but as symbols they are not without
their usefulness. To have Yankee imperialism—hardly a joking matter
to most Mexicans—even mentioned in the White House suggests a
modicum of historical candor. And certainly, whatever the López Portillo administration's relationship with God may turn out to be in
the long run, one can only hope along with both Presidents that there

Reprinted by permission of *Foreign Affairs*, July 1977. Copyright 1977 by
Council on Foreign Relations, Inc.

will be more blessing than curse in Mexico's necessarily close relationship with the United States. But what realities must this hope confront, and what aspects of the total situation can actually be improved upon?

II

When President Carter referred to Yankee imperialism he probably had in mind U.S. military actions, especially the Mexican War of the mid-nineteenth century during which General Winfield Scott occupied Mexico City. In the subsequent treaty, the young republic lost almost half her territory to the United States—invaluable lands comprising what are today the states of Texas, California, Nevada, Utah, and parts of Colorado, New Mexico, and Arizona. If official memory extends into the twentieth century, President Carter might also have been alluding to the U.S. Navy's occupation of the port of Veracruz in April of 1914, an action costing no less than 300 Mexican lives and adding little to Woodrow Wilson's reputation as a man of peace. What the President assuredly was *not* referring to was imperialism in the more modern sense of the extension of financial and corporate control across frontiers in ways that distort the development of the host country, denationalizing and stripping power from ostensibly sovereign elites and peoples. The President, in fact, touched sensitive ground with his toast, for if Yankee imperialism has any dominant meaning in Mexico today, it clearly refers to the U.S. economic presence, not the dusty troops and steaming gunboats of times past.

However evaluated, there is no question but that the U.S. presence in the Mexican economy is enormous. Almost 70 percent of all Mexican exports are directed toward the United States, and better than 60 percent of Mexican imports are of U.S. origin. The United States is the primary source of direct foreign investment (over $3 billion at present—up from $1.2 billion at the start of the 1970s), not to mention the overwhelming U.S. influence on tastes, consumption patterns, and mass media content. By the end of 1976, U.S. private banks were carrying the impressive total of $11.5 billion in outstanding loans and credits to Mexico, an increase of $2.5 billion over the previous year's figure.[1] U.S. tourism and dollar remittances from the millions of Mexicans both legally and illegally in the United States are critical to Mexico's balance of payments; and, until the devaluations of last year, peso parity with the dollar was a keystone of national policy.

The centrality of the United States to the Mexican economy necessarily implies a wide range of influences and pressures on both public and private decision-makers south of the border. Although nationalistic egos continue to be bruised by this reality, it is widely acknowledged in practice. Thus, when López Portillo came to the United States in February, his meetings with representatives of the U.S. banking community followed hard on the heels of his meetings with the President. Although it is difficult to imagine an analogous scenario if Jimmy Carter had gone to Mexico, in this case it was clearly the "logical" and even necessary thing for the Mexican President to do.

The extensive involvement of the United States in the Mexican economy also helps put into perspective the seemingly endless cascade of issues that agitates relations between the two countries. However much newsplay and policy attention they may get at times, issues like the treatment of U.S. prisoners in Mexican jails, the flow of heroin into the United States, Mexican support for the anti-Zionism resolution in the United Nations, Colorado River salinity, the theft of archeological treasures, and even ex-President Echeverría's sponsorship of the controversial Charter of Economic Rights and Duties of States are not the basic and enduring stuff of U.S.-Mexican relations. This is not to say that they are not important, especially to particular groups at particular times; but they do not go down to the bedrock, to the basic structure of interests which links the two economies—albeit at times antagonistically.

With good management, a modicum of good will, and some intelligence these kinds of issues are, in one fashion or another, resolvable.[2] Some, like salinity and prisoners, can actually be removed from the negotiating agenda through treaties, agreements, and cooperative action. Others, like the Zionism flap and Mexico's aggressive advocacy of Third World positions, yield to policy reversals and a bit of well-constructed silence. But when economic bedrock is touched, no such relatively easy resolutions are to be found.

A classic example is Mexico's oft-repeated requests that trade and tariff barriers be lowered to allow Mexico's exports easier access to U.S. markets. This, of course, is not an issue specific to U.S.-Mexican relations, but rather one that can be generally applied to almost all trade relations between the more- and less-developed worlds. As has typically happened in such cases, these requests run into broadly based protectionist counter-pressures from U.S. interests that stand to lose from liberalized trading policies. Thus, since the United States cannot easily respond to the requests, and since Mexico must in its own interest continue to press for freer access, the issue simply will not go away. In fact, the bilateral clash around liberalized trade may, over time, become even more acute as U.S. manufactured and other goods come under accelerated pressure from exporters in both the more- and less-developed countries, thus further narrowing the already restricted room for maneuver that now exists.

Perhaps the thorniest bedrock issue specific to U.S.-Mexican relations involves the millions of undocumented Mexican nationals living and working in the United States. No reliable approximations of the total number of "illegals" in the United States are available, but estimates range from a low of four million to a high of over ten million. Taking the midpoint of this range, and assuming that approximately 60 percent of the total are Mexican nationals, a reasonable guess is that at any given moment there are about four million undocumented Mexicans in the United States.

More exact figures are relatively unimportant, for it is clear that the numbers are very large and the controversies that surround their presence in the United States more than sufficient to fuel debate for years to come. As workers they are located in the lowest paid and least desirable jobs, supplying cheap labor (often at wages well below the established minimums) to industry, agriculture, and the service sector. Resented by organized labor for ostensibly "taking jobs away from American workers," criticized by righteous taxpayers and politicians for allegedly draining off a disproportionate share of welfare services, and often preyed upon by criminal elements before, during, and after their journey north, their lot is by no means a happy one. And yet they continue to come, by the tens of thousands every week.

Their reasons for leaving Mexico are not far to seek. Predominantly younger males from impoverished rural communities, they flee poverty and unemployment in Mexico, drawn by the promise and possibilities of economic opportunities in the north. However miserable these opportunities may seem to northern eyes, they look quite different when viewed from a small town in Sonora. So across the border they come,

sometimes making it on their own, sometimes smuggled across by
coyotes who charge high fees in advance to their human contraband
and then often also collect substantial payments from the employers
to whom they deliver the low-cost labor.

As living testimony to multiple developmental failures, the north-
ward migration is a substantial embarrassment to the Mexican government. But on almost all other counts it is a very positive phenomenon
when viewed from the perspective of Mexican elites. What is perhaps
most important is that the migration annually drains off hundreds of
thousands of persons who would otherwise swell the ranks of the unemployed. In so doing, it undoubtedly slows in some measure the
already cancerous growth of major metropolitan areas by keeping families in the rural areas who might otherwise gravitate to the larger
cities in search of work and other opportunities. Finally, annual remittances back to Mexico from workers employed in the United States
may now total as much as three billion dollars, a sum exceeding Mexican income from all tourist-related activities, and thus a crucial if not
always acknowledged component of Mexico's balance of payments.

In the light of these advantages to Mexico's ruling elite, and the
clearly destabilizing consequences that any major campaign of deportations back to Mexico would have, it is little wonder that both U.S.
and Mexican policymakers usually move cautiously when trying to
deal with this issue. Yet be dealt with it must, at least in the United
States, for multiple pressures exist to render the border less permeable.
Various scenarios and programs have been proposed and are under discussion, ranging from stricter security measures, to various kinds of
identity cards, to fines for employers who knowingly hire undocumented workers. But, at best, all such proposals treat symptoms or
peripheral aspects of the real problem, and many carry with them
serious potential for infringements of civil liberties.

The more basic truth is that the locus of the main structural conditions leading to this immigration is in Mexico, not in the United
States, and it is there that the major remedial actions must be taken.
Very large scale and carefully designed programs of rural development
and job creation are needed to make the north and central plateau
of Mexico at least minimally attractive to the tens of thousands of
new job seekers who come onto the labor market each year. If such
programs are not forthcoming, all the electronic gadgetry, registration

cards, fines to employers, and forced deportations that the United States can muster will not keep Mexicans at home.

This does not imply that there is nothing for the United States to do. On the contrary, if Mexico were to undertake the kinds of programs needed to make a dent on poverty and unemployment, U.S. support in the form of capital, technology, and revised tariff schedules would be essential precisely because of the economic dependence previously mentioned. But to date there are few indications that the resources, organizational models, and political will needed to mount such programs will be forthcoming, and the logic of Mexican politics does not augur well for their appearance until such time as even larger cracks appear in the developmental facade.

The immigration issue thus suggests a basic truth about Mexico, in fact *the* basic truth conditioning U.S.-Mexican relations; despite the impressive growth of the Mexican economy (between six and seven percent during most of the postwar period), the primary benefits of that "miracle" have been distributed only to a minority of the population, although obviously the minority that counts in political and economic terms. As has frequently been pointed out, then, the twin continuing challenges for Mexican political elites are how to maintain rates of growth high enough to support and even extend the current system of rewards and socioeconomic payoffs, and how to ensure that those who do not benefit from the "miracle" do not become excessively troublesome.

III

There is an understandable tendency to divide recent Mexican history—at least since the most tumultuous years of the 1910s and 1920s—into six-year *sexenios* corresponding to presidential terms. But there is also a Mexican reality that cannot be compartmentalized so neatly, that does not correspond to the changing of the guard, that is at the same time both the source of presidential and elite power as well as the albatross hung timelessly around the necks of those who would rule. This is the Mexico of extremes, of boom, of misery, of violence, and of tragedy—the Mexico that sprang from the ashes of the Revolution.

Well over a million persons lost their lives in the years of bloodshed and turmoil that began in 1910 with the revolt against the dictatorship of Porfirio Díaz. Swept away by gunpowder, dynamite and machete were the old Porfirian stability and institutions, and along with them the growth and relative prosperity of the late nineteenth and early twentieth centuries. Also gone—at least temporarily—were the conditions which had resulted in foreigners contributing almost two-thirds of all investment in Mexico during the first ten years of the present century. Brought to life was a set of egalitarian and nationalistic ideas and aspirations, expressed in the Mexican Constitution and a host of other documents that still echo—if sometimes hollowly—in the discourse of top-dogs and underdogs in Mexico today. But also created was a complex and at times contradictory set of centralized political and economic institutions that has resulted in the highest sustained postwar rates of economic growth in Latin America coupled with the maintenance and even intensification of extremes of wealth and poverty—all in the context of a political system that coopts (and when that fails, represses) dissent in a fashion that leaves less successful politicians amazed and even envious.

As multiple commentators have pointed out, this political-economic system, particularly in its post-World War II manifestation, depends heavily on rapid, capital-intensive industrialization, foreign inputs, fiscal stability, and the disproportionate distribution of rewards to foreign investors, certain sectors of local capital, and the expanding middle and professional sectors. Its major engine and goal is aggregate growth, and its major political requirements are working class and peasant quiescence coupled with the active cooperation of the more privileged sectors. "Confidence" in the system is critical: the confidence of foreign investors and creditors that growth and thus profitability and creditworthiness will continue; the confidence of the domestic private sector that the advantageous conditions of the past will continue to prevail; the confidence of the ascendant middle and professional sectors that their children will live at least as well as they do in their recently acquired semi-splendor; and even the confidence of the underdogs that their misery and pain are being attended to, that they also are, in some sense, on the postrevolutionary agenda.

All this, and much more, represents the contradictory legacy of the Mexican Revolution and the ideologies and institutions that took root in its aftermath. No Mexican administration can long operate outside the boundaries set by this legacy, yet it is also by no means clear that the system which has served Mexican elites and their friends so well in the past is equal to the burdens that will be placed upon it in the coming decades. This is both the basic paradox of modern Mexico and the context in which the last several years of Mexican history must be understood.

IV

When Luis Echeverría took office at the end of 1970 as the hand-picked successor of the out-going conservative President Gustavo Díaz Ordaz, his administration inherited not only the full range of contradictions and problems inherent in the postwar Mexican development model but also some particularly pressing political problems as well. As the implementer if not the architect of the pre-Olympics repression of 1968, Echeverría took office with serious personal, political liabilities—at least in leftist and intellectual circles.[3] Furthermore, during Díaz Ordaz's closed and conservative administration, distributional policies had been even more regressive than usual, thus triggering new waves of rural unrest and working-class pressures for a larger share of the benefits of Mexico's impressive aggregate economic growth. Finally, long-standing governmental policies supportive of an "alliance for profits" between foreign and some domestic capitalists had alerted Mexicans in both the public and private sectors to the rate and degree to which the Mexican economy was becoming increasingly denationalized.

Once in office, Echeverría moved on a number of fronts to build political support and arrest the worsening distributive and denationalization tendencies in the Mexican economy. Announcing a policy of "shared development" instead of the "stabilizing development" favored by his predecessors, he established a special advisory committee to study and propose fiscal reforms. Although many of the proposed reforms never left the presidential office—and others proved almost impossible to implement—the specter of a Mexico organized in ways that were not quite so favorable to the owners and managers of capital was sufficient to trigger significant business opposition at home. Equally controversial proposals were promulgated to regulate foreign economic influence. Again, although all three of the laws that were finally passed were much watered down versions of the initial proposals, none was very warmly received by the international business community. Additionally, the Echeverría administration tried to build popular support directly, through costly wage, price, housing, and rural investment programs. Among the most dramatic were the activities of CONASUPO, a decentralized state agency which buys basic foodstuffs at guaranteed prices and then distributes them at correspondingly low prices in poorer areas, thus forcing down retail prices and undercutting the high profits traditionally earned by middlemen. When Echeverría took office, for example, CONASUPO was operating about 1,200 retail outlets; by 1975 the network had expanded to include 6,000 stores. Needless to say, the private sector regarded this as unfair competition.

But even as the Echeverría administration struggled with these and other reform measures—making multiple enemies in the process—the basic dynamics of the Mexican political economy ground inexorably on toward crisis. The macro-statistics tell part of the tale. In 1970, the consumer price index stood at less than eight percentage points over 1968 levels. By the end of 1975, it had risen more than 90 percent. During the same five years, federal expenditures grew from about 3.2 billion dollars to over 12 billion, opening the gap between government income and expenditure from about $500 million in 1970 to $3.3 billion by 1975. The trade, balance-of-payments, and indebtedness statistics were no more encouraging. Mexico's yearly balance-of-trade deficit grew from about one billion dollars in 1970 to over 3.5 billion by 1975. Reflecting this trend, the yearly balance-of-payments deficit rose rather steadily to approximately four billion dollars by 1975, while the accumulated public sector external debt had reached $14.5 billion by the end of the same year.

Other trends and statistics round out the tale. Agricultural production grew so slowly that *per capita* food production continued to drop—as it had since about 1960. With the most dynamic sectors of agriculture oriented toward export markets, massive imports of food were necessary for both nutritional and political reasons. The most optimistic employment statistics suggest that during the first five years of the Echeverría administration employment increased on the average less than three percent a year, while those seeking jobs increased much more rapidly. In round numbers this meant that at least 150,000 to 200,000 persons joined the already swollen ranks of the unemployed and the underemployed each year. In short, a "worst-case" scenario was in the making: reform rhetoric and activities sufficient to raise the expectations of the poorer classes while frightening and angering the private sector both at home and abroad; long-term worsening trends in employment, agriculture, trade, balance of payments, and indebtedness—all of which were exacerbated in the mid-1970s by worldwide recessionary and inflationary pressures.

If the full responsibility for this gathering storm—or even a major part of it—should not be attributed to the Echeverría administration, there is no question but that the President cast himself as the lightning rod for the tempest that followed, thus ensuring his place in history. On August 31, 1976, in a move that caught many by surprise though it had been talked about for many years, the peso was devalued for the first time in 22 years. With the peso floating "like a stone" (according to a phrase often and bitterly repeated in Mexico City and elsewhere), multiple reactions and even panic ensued. While Mexican and foreign dailies headlined "turmoil," "hysteria," and "crisis," as much as $4 billion fled the country seeking safe harbor in Texas banks and elsewhere.[4] Investment slowed down, inflation accelerated, unemployment rose, and the whole complex set of mechanisms by which devaluation and resultant dislocations and hardships are passed disproportionately on to the poorer sectors of society came into play. Twelve days before leaving office, when Echeverría expropriated tens of thousands of acres of prime land in the northern state of Sonora and turned them over as small parcels to peasants, talk of a military coup was heard for the first time in recent memory.[5] Although there was never a consensus on who was supposed to "do" the coup to whom, the predominant version was that Echeverría would use the armed forces to maintain himself in office. It was the crowning touch to a period both absurd and tragic. And when the 1976 statistics were finally in, it appeared that the economy had grown only two percent during the year, that inflation stood at over 30 percent, and that the accumulated public sector debt was close to the $20-billion mark.

López Portillo's inaugural address poured oil on troubled waters, although the literal truth of the metaphor is just now becoming apparent. Proclaimed sober, conciliatory and pragmatic by businessmen, bankers, and most national and international spokesmen, it announced an "alliance for production" between the public and private sectors, a cutback in the growth of government spending, various incentives to stimulate investment, and the necessity of reaching "a well-balanced agreement on profits and salaries." The intended "balance" in this agreement was already apparent by early January when, with substantial support from labor leader Fidel Velázquez and the government-dominated Confederation of Mexican Workers, a ten-percent minimum wage increase guideline was pushed through for 1977—a figure far below expected increases in the cost of living.

Openly advertising his administration as undertaking the long, hard process of recovery from the difficulties of the previous *sexenio*, López Portillo vigorously courted allies at home and abroad. By the end of March, for example, the powerful Monterrey group of industrialists, the sworn enemies of Echeverría, had announced a six-year investment plan totaling 100 billion pesos (almost four billion dollars at current exchange rates). Other plans were under way to woo foreign investment, and conciliatory and cordial noises were heard on a set of bilateral issues between Mexico and the United States, ranging from tourism to prisoners. It was clear that as the first quarter of 1977 ended, the elusive "confidence" so necessary to the recovery of the Mexican economy was in relatively full bloom both north and south of the Rio Grande.

v

For both security and economic reasons, the stakes of the United States in the stability and continued growth of Mexico are immense. Thus, it was not surprising that the U.S. government moved swiftly though quietly in mid-1976 to support the peso when the devaluation and crisis-of-confidence storm was brewing. As early as April, Mexico received $360 million under its short-term lending (swap) agreement with the U.S. Federal Reserve. Other support from the Federal Reserve and the U.S. Treasury followed. These funds backstopped the announcement, on September 20, 1976, that Mexico had arranged a $1.2 billion package of financial support with the International Monetary Fund (IMF)—a package strongly supported by the U.S. government and private interests.

First negotiated under the Echeverría government, and then softened a bit and ratified by the López Portillo administration, the IMF agreement is a classic, fiscally conservative, balance-of-payments oriented document. Projected for a period of three years, it establishes a three billion dollar limit on the net increase of public sector external debt for 1977 and sharply declining ceilings for 1978 and 1979. Through its targets for balance-of-payments, public sector accounts, and savings and investment, it puts substantial pressure on the government to tighten credit, squeeze wages, lower public spending, hold down foreign borrowing, and thus control inflation. At its first unveiling, it was warmly greeted by bankers, industrialists, transnational corporations, and fiscal conservatives of many nationalities. Needless to say, it was less well received by many Mexican politicians and *técnicos*, as well as workers and peasants who, even if they do not read the fine print, are well aware of who finally gets hurt when such austerity programs are followed to their logical consequences.

But in Mexico the resolution—or at least the management—of the contradictions inherent in an IMF-type program is seldom an either/or affair. As López Portillo told all who would listen when he was in Washington, to pump Mexico full of the harshest kind of deflationary and balance-of-payments medicine is not only to risk the health of the patient, but also to run the almost certain risk of what he pointedly called the "South Americanization" of Mexican political life. Although the details of that ominous phrase were never fully elaborated, at a minimum the President meant that if there were not enough resources to provide continued benefits to the more privileged sectors, with at least some consideration given to the basic needs of the majority, massive doses of repression would be needed to hold Mexico together politically. In short, the President said yes to an attack on "inflationary" wage increases and waste in government, yes to cooperation with and incentives to private enterprise, yes to international financial responsibility, yes to a good-neighbor policy toward the United States, but no to those aspects and targets of an austerity program that would bring in their wake unmanageable political problems. He thus called, in his own words, for an increase in supply not a restriction of demand.

To play the delicate game defined by these yeses and noes, additional capital is needed. By definition this can, in the short run, only come from foreign sources. Yet the IMF approach to the restoration of Mexico's health sets sharp limits to the amount of additional indebtedness that can be incurred. It there a way out? The obvious answer is oil.

Mexico may be relatively far from God, but it is providentially close to large amounts of petroleum. No one seems to know with any certainty the quantities involved, but estimates now run from a low of 11 billion barrels to as many as 60 billion. If the 60-billion barrel figure is correct, it would place Mexico second only to Saudi Arabia in reserves. To date, only about 10 percent of Mexico's potential oil-bearing territory has been explored, so the high end of the estimate may well hold. In any event, estimates of Mexican reserves have been changing rapidly, from 3.5 billion barrels at the end of 1974 to the present figures.

Almost immediately after taking power, the López Portillo administration moved to assure interested parties that these reserves would not be as closely held as they had been in the past. It was thus announced that during the 1976–82 *sexenio*, exports of crude and refined products would increase from about 100,000 to 1.1 million barrels a day. Even if no substantial increase in the price of crude is registered during this period, the export earnings generated from such a program would top $22 billion, more than sufficient to turn Mexico's balance-of-payments problems around.

This kind of expansion in Mexican production requires vast sums of investment and operating capital. The budget for PEMEX, the national oil monopoly, is scheduled to increase three-fold under the current administration. From the point of view of Mexico's managers and their friends in the United States, this is obviously money well spent, and thus there is every indication that foreign banks will be more than willing to lend against the promise of oil once they have sufficient indications that the bonanza is as substantial as it appears to be and that Mexico intends to push exports. Whatever tough-minded consensus once existed among the IMF, the U.S. government and the private banks about the debt limits and Mexico's creditworthiness is unlikely to survive this bonanza and its validation. In fact, there is evidence that it is already beginning to crumble. Increasingly dependent on Arab oil with all that that implies politically, alarmed by recent energy scenarios and proposals, the United States would no doubt rather buy petroleum and natural gas from Mexico than from almost any other supplier in the world. The banks will be willing and even eager to lend when Mexican oil is the collateral. And when the moment arrives, the austerity-minded bureaucrats at the IMF will either see the wisdom in a softening of debt limits or will find that an end run has been made around their "sound and sensible" package for levering the Mexican economy back to health.

As providential as this scenario looks, it touches only some of Mexico's problems. Oil may allow Mexico to slip away from the IMF but not from history. Oil exports, the related relaxation of debt limits, and the easing of some aspects of the austerity program give breathing space, another chance for hard-pressed Mexican politicians. But oil by itself cannot respond to peasants' demands for land; nor can it create hundreds of thousands of new jobs each year; nor can it keep millions of Mexicans from crossing the border; nor make rapid inroads on re-dressing a distribution of income that is one of the most unequal in the world; nor reduce public and private corruption; nor deal with the human and social problems generated by a population that doubles in size every 20 years. All that oil can do—and this is not to be scoffed at—is soften and perhaps postpone for some years the sharpening of the contradictions that are inherent in the Mexican development model. It cannot solve them.

VI

What are the policy implications of all this for the United States? What does it mean to be a "good neighbor" to a Mexico laboring under these pressures and with these problems? A first and rather obvious answer is that one should avoid being a truly bad neighbor. This means at a minimum that there must be no massive deporta-tion of undocumented aliens, no yielding to protectionist tendencies of the sort that would further restrict Mexico's access to U.S. markets, no insisting on the full implementation of IMF austerity programs, and no punitive measures against Mexico if it should sometimes take positions in international forums that displease one or another group or interest in the United States.

But the avoidance of bad behavior is only a beginning, and one which prudential statesmen are likely to see as in their immediate self-interest, given the potential importance of Mexican oil. In fact, the latter situation clearly creates multiple pressures for special U.S.

concessions toward Mexico in respect to trade, finance, and the transfer of technology. Less obvious policy concerns derive from a more detailed understanding of the awesome nature of the developmental dilemmas faced by Mexico and the dangers that flow from their mismanagement or the difficulty, if not impossibility, of resolving them within the existing political framework. What is at issue is nothing less than the implications of the "South Americanization" process so ominously suggested by President López Portillo on his visit to Washington.

Given some familiarity with Mexico's history and developmental contradictions, one does not have to be overly imaginative to sketch South Americanization scenarios. Whether the precipitating event is a clash over wages, prices, employment, land, food, or services, all scenarios would have in common the rupturing of the Mexican political consensus, the widespread use of force to suppress dissident groups, and a much larger presence of the military in public life. Viewed from the United States, such scenarios would have very serious ramifications. Border problems would escalate as political migration and pressures were added to the already substantial economic pressures. If the Mexican armed forces and police were turned against their own citizenry at anything like the level of repression existing in Chile and elsewhere, at some point U.S. territory would surely be used as a base for exile attacks back across the border. Private investment and bank lending would suffer and the much vaunted climate of confidence would necessarily crumble. Sooner or later, U.S. citizens would almost certainly be killed if violence were at all widespread or long lasting. The political dynamics unleashed in the United States as families, interests, and established relationships were broken would be unpredictable but surely grave. Additionally, the blow to democratic forces and futures in Latin America would be immense, for the Mexican experience, with all of its shortcomings, still suggests that there are alternatives to brutal dictatorships and massive military intervention in politics.

To sketch such scenarios is not to predict their inevitability. But they are by no means fanciful, and a forward-looking and creative U.S. policy toward Mexico should explore ways in which their probability can be lowered. At one level this means a frank recognition of the "specialness" of the U.S. relationship with Mexico by virtue of the

2,000-mile frontier, the weight of the U.S. presence in the Mexican economy, and the scale and importance of Mexico to the United States. Although the "special relationship" idea is currently out of favor in this age of globalism, there is no other country of the world with which the United States shares so many human beings, so much common geography, and so much history. In the coming years the United States will surely find itself repeatedly discussing a wide range of issues with Mexico in a bilateral context—issues like energy, trade, immigration, capital flows and others that have clear multilateral implications. The challenge will be to respond to Mexico's needs while also maintaining some degree of evenhandedness elsewhere in the hemisphere and the Third and Fourth Worlds.

But an even greater challenge in the long run will be to find ways of supporting those aspects of Mexican development and political practice that promise to increase social justice. The challenge is immense. Not only is there an inherent danger in meddling with domestic issues in another country, but such a policy in respect to Mexico is especially delicate since historically the United States has contributed to tilting Mexican development away from egalitarian goals. Whatever other virtues their friends may attribute to the U.S. banks, corporations and functionaries located in Mexico City, a profound concern with the consequences of their activities for income distribution, employment, peasant agriculture, and deteriorating conditions of life is not among them. What has traditionally been good for the United States in Mexico has not necessarily been good for tens of millions of the latter's citizens.

There may indeed be no way to link U.S. government and U.S. business to the aspirations of the Mexicans who are the cannon fodder rather than the beneficiaries of Mexican development. But to fail to understand that a Mexico in which the fruits of development are not more equitably shared is also a Mexico which cannot indefinitely continue to be a "good neighbor" is to misread history and to ignore geography. The basic test of U.S. policy will thus not be the sophistication with which the oil bonanza is handled. Self-interest may counsel wisdom in this case. Nor will it be the extent to which bad-neighborly actions are avoided. Again, self-interest and diplomatic discipline are likely to curb the worst excesses. Rather, the real test, in Mexico as elsewhere, will be found in the extent to which the

United States discovers ways to support those forces pressing for social justice. Such actions will not be in the interest of those who profit, literally and figuratively, from current arrangements. But in the long run, allying with those who still wish to make real the bread and freedom promised to all Mexicans sixty years ago will surely prove to be in the interest of the majority of citizens, both north and south of the Rio Grande.

NOTES

1. By comparison, all other less-developed countries combined held only $36 billion of U.S. bank loans and credits at the end of 1976. Whether the Mexican share of this total constitutes "overexposure," however, depends not just on the aggregate amount but also on a host of other political and economic factors.

2. In claiming that these issues are resolvable, I do not mean to imply that the *problems* from which they derive can be solved in all cases. The traffic in brown heroin from Mexico is a case in point. Despite close cooperation between the United States and Mexico, and the participation of U.S. specialists and equipment in the destruction of Mexican poppy fields, only a minor dent is being made in the quantity of heroin available in the United States. The very fact of Mexican willingness to cooperate with the United States, however, whatever the outcomes of the program itself, leads to a reduction of the salience of the issue of brown heroin in bilateral relations—and in that sense a resolution.

3. During the Díaz Ordaz government, Echeverría served as Minister of *Gobernación* (State Security). As such, he was directly involved in the pre-Olympic massacre at Tlatelolco during which as many as 300 persons were killed. This was only the most sweeping of many repressive actions carried out during the 1960s against workers, peasants, and students.

4. There is no way to calculate the true figure. This estimate is from *Latin American Economic Report,* Special Report on Mexico, London: March 1977. Nor is it known how much returned.

5. Much to the relief of landowners throughout Mexico, the courts subsequently ruled that the expropriations were improper. The struggle, both in the courts and in the fields, is, however, far from over.